Victorian Poetry,
Europe, and the
Challenge of Cosmopolitanism

Christopher M. Keirstead

The Ohio State University Press / Columbus

Library of Congress Cataloging-in-Publication Data

Keirstead, Christopher M., 1970–
 Victorian poetry, Europe, and the challenge of cosmopolitanism / Christopher M. Keirstead.
    p. cm.
 Includes bibliographical references and index.
 ISBN 978-0-8142-1160-1 (cloth : alk. paper)—ISBN 978-0-8142-9259-4 (cd-rom)
 1. English poetry—19th century—History and criticism. 2. Cosmopolitanism in literature. I. Title.
 PR595.C678K45 2011
 821'.8—dc22

                              2011008729

Cover design by Mia Risberg
Text design by Juliet Williams
Type set in Adobe Garamond Pro
Printed by Thomson-Shore, Inc.

♾ The paper used in this publication meets the minimum requirements of the American National Standard for Information Sciences—Permanence of Paper for Printed Library Materials. ANSI Z39.48-1992.

9   8   7   6   5   4   3   2

For Cathy and Ben

Contents

Illustrations

Acknowledgments

This book would not have been possible without the kind support of many colleagues, friends, and family members. I was fortunate to be able to present portions of my work at a number of collegial and stimulating conferences, including the meeting of the Browning Society on "Our Italians: Anglo-Italian Relationships, 1845–1865," in Vallombrosa, Italy, in 2005; the NAVSA conference at Purdue University in 2006, where I participated in one of two panels on "Victorian Internationalisms"; and the 2007 NVSA conference at Harvard University on the theme of "Victorian Cosmopolitanisms." For their suggestions and thoughts on my work, I would like in particular to thank Lauren Goodlad, Tricia Lootens, Julia Saville, Pamela Neville-Sington, Alison Chapman, Marjorie Stone, Scott Lewis, and Elizabeth Woodworth. Special thanks are due as well to Beverly Taylor for her generous advice and encouragement early on in my study of Barrett Browning. Other friends, colleagues, and mentors who deserve my thanks include Paula Backscheider, Barbara Gates, Michael Cotsell, Terry Meyers, Deborah Morse, and Patrick Collier. I would also like to thank Sandy Crooms, my editor at The Ohio State University Press, for her early interest in the project. And, finally, to my wife Cathy Himmelwright, thank you for your advice, support, and encouragement at every step.

Chapters 3 and 4 represent revised and expanded versions of work that I published earlier as articles in the *Victorians Institute Journal* and *Victorian Poetry* in 2005. I am grateful to the editors and publishers of both journals for permission to include them here. I would also like to thank the Armstrong Browning Library for the use of their archives and for allowing me to reproduce images of the Brownings in their holdings. The image of Clough's letter to his sister Anne in Figure 1 appears courtesy of the Bodleian Libraries, University of Oxford.

My home institution, Auburn University, generously provided me with financial assistance in the form of two Humanities Development grants from the College of Liberal Arts in the summers of 2005 and 2007. The funding for conference travel provided by my department is also much appreciated.

1

Introduction

Arnold, Europe, and the (Future) Destinations of Victorian Poetry

IF ONE WERE to attempt to compose an Atlas of Victorian Poetry— something to chart its destinations locally, nationally, and abroad—no poet would likely pose a greater logistical challenge than Elizabeth Barrett Browning. It was a problem her contemporaries struggled with as well, one compounded by the complex political attachments she felt to the locations of her poetry. After the great success of *Aurora Leigh* (1856), which crossed multiple national and generic borders, *Poems before Congress* (1860) was widely condemned in the British press as the work of a "denationalized fanatic" who could not see past her devotion to France and Italy.[1] The release of Barrett Browning's posthumous *Last Poems* in February 1862, however, provided her supporters with an opportunity to reassess her legacy. To Andrew Wilson writing in *Macmillan's Magazine,* Barrett Browning was simply the latest embodiment of a long-standing tradition of English poets who had traveled to the Continent and featured Italian settings and sources in their poetry, a tradition that went as far back as Chaucer. Nor did he ignore the significance of international politics in her work. In fact, what is most intriguing about his commentary is his rather fanciful account of how Barrett Browning's ideological commitments might live on and continue to inspire a new generation of poets:

Mrs. Browning lived to see Italia all but *unita* and regenerate. We are so close to that event, that we can scarcely as yet appreciate its magnitude, or fully enjoy its poetical aspects. Perhaps it may be that Italy independent, prosperous, and happy, will lose somewhat of its poetic charm; but the realization of its hopes, and its fulfilment [*sic*] of the aspiration of so many great minds should only encourage the poet to wander still farther east, and find other lands, whose ideas are still unfulfilled, that will afford him an external life typifying that of his own soul. He may penetrate to the sublime spectacles of the East, and find repose in the conflict of man with the wild-beast world—in the great tragedies which, even in this age, there assert the existence of unmeasured powers—and in the beneficent sway of social organization over teeming myriads of people.[2]

While Wilson's account of Barrett Browning's interest in nation-building is familiar enough—indeed, it is the focus of much recent discussion of her work—his mixture of safari and colonial administration might strike us as an odd destination to arrive at after reviewing her poetic career. Except for a fleeting wish to visit Egypt and Palestine mentioned occasionally in her letters, the poet expressed little desire to venture outside of Europe. And regardless of her interest in or ability to travel great distances, she was clearly troubled with contemporary trends in British geopolitics, supporting neither the Liberal faith in free markets nor the country's growing acceptance of imperial expansion. "[T]he selfishness & most ignoble narrowness in England sickens me," she wrote to her sister Arabella in 1859, succinctly and forcefully stating an opinion that remained consistent throughout most of her life: "we have always been selfish & cruel in our foreign policy,—always."[3]

Even today, with the benefit of a century and a half of historical hindsight, defining Barrett Browning's engagement with the wider world would be difficult, and I begin with this predicament to illustrate the larger issues that still face us as critical geographers charting the multiple courses of Victorian poetry. Wilson's itinerary is not without a certain logic, in fact, and anticipates the turn that epic would begin to take in the mid-to-late nineteenth century, as Herbert F. Tucker recounts in what is probably the closest work we have as yet to an Atlas of Victorian Poetry, *Epic: Britain's Heroic Muse 1790–1910* (2008). As epic penetrated more deeply into Wilson's ambiguous "East" in the 1860s, it took with it a myth of progress that, Tucker writes, "partially anticipated the ideal condition of modern humanity: categorically Western, presumptively male, emphatically Anglo-Saxon."[4] Although bounded by these imperial and Orientalist frames of reference, such works could nonetheless form the basis of an incipient cosmopolitanism, one genuinely curious about and respectful toward unfamiliar cultures. Edwin Arnold's *The Light of Asia* (1879) was one such work intended to bring East and West into closer dialogue, even if Arnold sends his Buddha on a "westward migration to a safe home among English readers capable of recognizing their own cherished truths in a distant, imported original."[5] This kind of "postnationalist outsourcing," as Tucker reveals, was the culmination of a larger trend that followed the decline of the more patriotic epic efforts of the Napoleonic period. By the 1840s, "emigrant epics" as diverse as Browning's *Sordello* (1840) and Macaulay's *Lays of Ancient Rome* (1842) "reflected the geographic expansion of empire and subjoined to it a bid for the *translatio imperii* from Roman, Greek, and more racially Aryan origins."[6] Epic was a genre that came to the Victorians pre-equipped to travel, in a sense, and it can surprise us with the range of its historical and geographic destinations and the complexity of its ideological commitments.[7]

I would argue still, however, that our Atlas of Victorian Poetry remains incomplete and has not yet adequately mapped the complex geography of Barrett Browning or many of her contemporaries. As my title suggests, this book proposes to strike toward a different heading—not the empire, nor any individual country, but something more abstract, with boundaries that continue to shift and invite controversy. This location is Europe or, more precisely, the ever-impending Europe of the future. It is the Europe that Matthew Arnold describes in "The Function of Criticism at the Present Time" (1864), where he insists that his contemporaries envision "Europe as being, for intellectual and spiritual purposes, one great confederation, bound to a joint action and working to a common result."[8] For Arnold, Europe embodied a cosmopolitan idea of culture with which England must more closely align itself if its global influence was to be at all redeemable or progressive. He would make similar pleas throughout much of his prose and poetry while attempting to sort through the multifaceted political and cultural affiliations that complicate any notion of cosmopolitanism—just as here Arnold interrupts himself, in a sense, and begins qualifying the "purposes" of this new Europe before he actually finishes his thought.

The key purpose missing from Arnold's European confederation, of course, is a *political* one. We can attribute this absence to Arnold's usual coolness toward more radical programs of social change, but his diminished expectations exemplify as well the kind of critical cosmopolitanism—the recognition of the *challenge* of cosmopolitanism—that distinguishes the body of poetry I will examine in this book. This is not to say that these poets saw no role for politics in cosmopolitan thinking: as Barrett Browning's work alone testifies, the rich debate that can erupt between geopolitical and cultural forms of cosmopolitanism gives these poems a vital energy and added relevance to similar debates today. As Arnold reveals, Europe could not be approached with the same sense of cultural proprietorship that characterized more imperial encounters—that right to bestow Wilson's "beneficent sway of social organization" and versify its "unfulfilled" ideas—the same archival, scholastic impulse that stocked the exhibits of Victorian museums. If the nations of Europe could not surpass England in the global marketplace or threaten it militarily, they were nonetheless still *empowered,* the joint custodians of the European ideal Arnold gives voice to. These nations included pre-*unita* Italy, despite the condescension sometimes evident in remarks like Wilson's. And Barrett Browning, we should remember, always stressed that England's cultural indebtedness to Italy was the greater one by comparison.

The Victorian idea of Europe was still Eurocentric in that it did not accord the same political rights to Britain's colonial possessions and thus did not directly challenge imperialist ideology. At the same time, as citizens of the world's only true superpower in the nineteenth century, many Victorians felt history had charged them with the task to be the stewards of a better global future, one free of the "selfishness & most ignoble narrowness" that had rankled Barrett Browning. Whatever "progress" was, it was not something that was uniquely British or Anglo-Saxon, even if another vocal contingent at the time insisted otherwise. This sense of responsibility in turn fueled a strong intellectual and emotional desire among Barrett Browning, Arnold, and many other artists and intellectuals to embrace the challenge of cosmopolitanism. At its core, this challenge consisted of the need to negotiate national identities and aesthetic traditions within a larger European cultural matrix. But there was another dimension to this challenge, one more unique to Victorian poetry and the historical moment it inhabits: an impulse of self-criticism that guarded against the intoxicating rhetoric of cosmopolitanism itself—its confident faith in its own inevitability. A strong awareness of the difficulties of maintaining genuine, transformative contact between cultures permeates the work of the Victorian poets under consideration here. Thus, at the same time Britain's empire expanded globally, the encounter with Europe in verse fostered a sustained scrutiny of British national identity that simultaneously guarded against overinvestment in notions of progress—and overindulgence in poetry's capacity to effect political and cultural change.

In this way, Victorian poetry anticipates how theorists of cosmopolitanism today, including Bruce Robbins and Kwame Anthony Appiah, have sought to temper the concept's former adherence to universalistic modes of thinking and give it new purchase as a guide for individual and national conduct. In his introduction to *Cosmopolitics: Thinking and Feeling beyond the*

Nation (1998), Robbins summarizes the kind of critically oriented cosmopolitanism he sees emerging from the volume as a whole: "the authors of these essays conclude that cosmopolitanism is located and embodied, and they go on to measure such critical, normative power as may remain to it. Exploring a range of diverse cosmopolitanisms, they participate in and comment on the term's scaling down, its pluralizing and particularizing."[9] For Arnold too, as we will see, cosmopolitanism was a flexible but durable ideal that must dwell in verse and prose, in the spirit and the intellect. Appiah, in his contribution to *Cosmopolitics,* speaks of the need to cultivate a "rooted cosmopolitanism" that recognizes the "responsibility to nurture the culture and politics" of one's home while also recognizing that "each local form of human life is the result of long-term and persistent processes of cultural hybridization."[10] To varying extents, the poets I examine here were all self-consciously, even patriotically English and were always well attuned to that intensely Victorian obsession, the Condition of England. At the same time, poets such as Barrett Browning understood the important, even transformative role that poetry could play in reassessing the claims made upon us by local and international attachments, whether in the realms of art, politics, or simple everyday living. Hers was part of an effort that encompassed the whole of the Victorian period and attracted a diverse range of poets. How these poets adapted cosmopolitan thinking to specific European contexts—and how it worked in tandem with their other aesthetic aims—is my overall focus in this book.

In another sense, my aim is to bring poetry into a conversation that has already been underway in Victorian studies more generally, one that has sought to test the applicability of cosmopolitan interpretive frameworks to the period. As Lauren M. E. Goodlad asks in a recent contribution to *PMLA,* turning the question in the other direction, "Can criticism of nineteenth-century literature illuminate our globalizing world in the first decade of the twenty-first century?"[11] This piece follows a recent special edition of *Romanticism and Victorianism on the Net* co-edited by Goodlad and Julia M. Wright which speaks of a turn "away from insular nationalist frameworks and toward the embrace of terms such as *internationalism, transnationalism, cosmopolitanism,* and *geopolitics.*"[12] Amanda Anderson's *The Powers of Distance: Cosmopolitanism and the Cultivation of Detachment* (2001) played an important role in that turn and perhaps remains the best expression of the rich potential yield of cosmopolitan and cross-channel perspectives when brought to bear on Victorian poetry and, more broadly, "any full consideration of Victorian understandings of race, nation, and empire." She adds, "[w]hile cosmopolitanism in certain key instances can be shown to support nationalism and imperialism, and while its own elitist and narrowly European forms must be acknowledged, it still often gives voice, within the Victorian context, to a reflective interrogation of cultural norms."[13] As Anderson advises, the goal of this redirected criticism should be not to dismiss the contradictions within Victorian cosmopolitanism but, quite the contrary, to draw attention to the conflicts of interest that arise when authors attempt to look beyond but also become entangled in other more limiting domestic or imperial commitments.[14] My aim is not simply to offer a happy, revisionist alternative to postcolonial critiques of Victorian literature pioneered, most notably, in the work of the late Edward Said. Indeed, much of my own theoretical and critical vocabulary borrows from authors such as Said, Homi K. Bhabha, and Mary Louise Pratt for the light they shed on notions of travel, border-crossing, and transnational identity. At the very least, as Pratt reminds us, it is important to remember that "Europe was constructed from the outside in as much as from the inside out."[15]

The future of Britain, and of British poetry, was nonetheless, for many, largely to be found *in* Europe—in the notion of a progressive, cosmopolitan cultural and (more elusively) political domain. Returning specifically to Arnold, my study asks what kind of confederation he was seeking and what role poetry—Arnold's primary vehicle for "culture"—must play in it.[16] To pose a question suggested by the title of Benedict Anderson's influential study of nationalism, just what kind of "imagined community" did Europe form for Victorian poets and how did their work attempt to manifest that community? It was a multidimensional contact to be sure, encompassing diverse encounters with European places, peoples, politics, and culture. The poets who make up this study—Arthur Hugh Clough, Elizabeth Barrett Browning, Robert Browning, Algernon Charles Swinburne, William Morris, and Thomas Hardy—have been selected precisely because they engage the breadth of collective European futures—and pasts—and participate in complex acts of translation, border-crossing, and hybridization that transact with theorization of these concepts today. Each poet also examines the uncertain relationship that poetry and literariness share with other manifestations of cross-cultural contact, including trade, whether in goods or ideas; personal encounters through travel and diplomacy; and even war, both as an ironic coming-together between nations and as a possible prelude to a more evolved, united Europe. Closer investigation of their works will enrich our ongoing debates about cosmopolitanism and cross-channel, Anglo-European identity.

Despite this promise, and despite the progress Tucker makes specifically with epic, the study of Victorian poetry in the early twenty-first century remains a mostly nation-centered affair. Current handbooks and critical guides on Victorian literature, for instance, include chapters on poetry and patriotism, poetry and empire, but not poetry and Europe or poetry and cosmopolitanism.[17] This neglect is not without reason, of course. The case for Victorian poetry as a cosmopolitan or widely European genre would seem to be held back by its own constitutive terms "Victorian" and "poetry." To begin first with the problem of genre, it is notable, for instance, that none of the essays included in "Victorian Internationalisms" and, similarly, a special issue on "Global Formations Past and Present" for *Nineteenth-Century Contexts* features Victorian poetry or poets in its analysis.[18] Comparably, the one essay on the Victorian period included in the critical anthology *The Idea of Europe in Literature* (1999) concerns itself with the novel, specifically Charlotte Brontë's *Villette* (1853).[19] Anderson's *The Powers of Distance* likewise focuses almost exclusively on nonfiction prose and the novel, including *Villette*. These biases, again, are not without reason: with its Belgian setting, culturally displaced heroine, and broadly European cast, the cosmopolitan reach of Brontë's novel should be immediately obvious.[20] Anderson also devotes a chapter to George Eliot's *Daniel Deronda* (1876), and once more it would be difficult to name another Victorian intellectual, with the possible exception of Arnold, who was more committed to a full reckoning of trends in continental thought and politics than Eliot (and Arnold never attempted anything as rigorous as translating Strauss's *Das Leben Jesu*). The marginalization of poetry in these discussions may have something to do with the limitations of poetic form and language vis-à-vis the novel. Poetry simply demands more awareness of diction and rhythm—so much so, perhaps, that "no art is more stubbornly national than poetry," as T. S. Eliot once observed.[21] That most ubiquitous of novel champions, Mikhail Bakhtin, finds the epic the epitome of a hegemonic "monoglossia" and poetry in general to be shackled by the demands language places on the form: "Even when speaking of alien things, the poet speaks in his own language. To shed light on an alien world, he never resorts to an alien language, even though it might in fact be more adequate to that world."[22] It would follow that the Victorian novel, less dependent on linguistic subtleties, more multi-vocal, was better suited to imagining cosmopolitan encounters. This observation is true in some contexts: Barrett Browning's decision to write a novel-poem, *Aurora Leigh,* as I will argue, did have a significant impact on how the work dramatizes Anglo-European identity. And however overdetermined Bakhtin's definition of genre may be—Tucker, for instance, demolishes it as effectively as anyone—his arguments can still resonate on an instinctive, practical level.[23] One senses that teachers of world literature today, dealing mostly with monolingual students, tend to opt for novels and short stories in part because more is lost when poetry is translated from one language to another.

What, then, is the case for poetry? Beyond co-opting from the novel, in what ways could it facilitate the kind of complex border-crossing I am attributing to it? It should first be stressed how many Victorian poets—particularly Swinburne and the Brownings—did in fact *translate* elements of foreign language and prosody into their work: diction, structure, and choice of verse form in many cases reflect these poets' deep familiarity with non-English poetic traditions both ancient and modern (and, one might add, their readers' familiarity—something that opens poetic cosmopolitanism to charges of elitism, an issue I deal with more fully in my chapter on Browning). More broadly, poets sought to revivify notions of travel, mobility, and transcendence that had always adhered to classical epic poetry and its descendants while readapting this cultural capital to other subgenres including lyric, epistolary verse, and the dramatic monologue. Similarly, the idea of poetry as an archetypal, universal language, articulated strongly earlier in the century by Shelley and Coleridge, continued to find new advocates. Thomas Carlyle's Hero as Poet, for instance, is also, ideally, a "World-Poet." Drawing an analogy between poetry and Christian ecumenicism that reappears in diverse guises all the way up to Hardy, Carlyle further reflects, "May we not call Shakespeare the still more melodious Priest of a *true* Catholicism, the 'Universal Church' of the Future and of all times?"[24] Arnold would attempt to express something of this transcendent capacity in his Preface to the First Edition of *Poems* (1853), where he challenges "the opinion which many critics of the present day appear to entertain against subjects chosen from distant times and countries" (1:3). Such cosmopolitanism of range is complimented by the poet's prerogative, when armed with the right subject, "to appeal to the great primary human affections: to those elementary feelings which subsist permanently in the race, and which are independent of time" (1:4). Poetry thus charged itself with the mission to cross borders and bring different nations and traditions into dialogue. More practically, continental travel offered a way of ensuring the viability of poetry in the literary marketplace by continuing a successful subgenre of poetic travelogue popularized mainly by Byron earlier in the century.[25] Rather than simply adapting the verse travelogue to new settings and historical developments, however, Victorian poets queried their own authority to travel in an age that increasingly questioned the relevance of the form to the great political issues of the day. At the same time, the Victorian cosmopolitan poet would have to resist the temptation to find refuge in the more patriotic and imperial tradition of the kind Wilson had mapped out for Barrett Browning's successors. In this respect, poetry may have had to work harder than the novel to be cosmopolitan—to do more to escape from narrow nationalistic and self-aggrandizing postures. But if poetry's investment in cosmopolitanism came with greater risk, it was one that could pay higher dividends: the kinds of border-crossing fashioned in these poems resonate with a unique complexity and self-scrutiny.

This complexity points to why I have chosen to stay within the historical bounds of "Victorian" poetry rather than broaden my study to encompass the whole of the nineteenth century and begin, for instance, with Byron or Felicia Hemans. The limitations of "Victorian" poetry still deserve close consideration, however. In a recent *Victorian Poetry* forum devoted to the question of the genre's future, Erik Gray notes that Romanticism, even if its meaning remains the subject of intense debate among scholars, has the advantage of signifying "a European-wide movement in thought and art." *Victorian* poetry, in contrast, "limits the field it names chronologically, generically, and even nationally."[26] In terms of literary history, we would appear to have an imperial epoch book-ended by two more expansive, international movements: the Romantic period looking outward, the Victorian inward, followed again by a more global modernism. Joseph Bristow reveals how as early as the 1890s, critics had begun to set this pattern, weaving an official imperial history of Victorian poetics that boasted of

> a standard of assured maturation, in which the 1830s mark the infancy of modern democracy, agnosticism, and evolutionary theory; meanwhile, the 1890s signal the empire's grown up destiny. . . . [T]he poetic development of the period can be witnessed best through the literary canonization of an exclusive band of poets whose careers advanced in accordance with this escalating chronology.[27]

Barrett Browning, Bristow notes, has been especially ill-served by this national-imperial account of the genre, which leaves no room, for instance, for the study of her ballads. As he bluntly puts it, "as far as I can see, the epithet 'victorian' has no relevance whatsoever to Barrett Browning's critically recovered oeuvre. She could not embody its epoch" (104), while, one might add, a figure such as Tennyson could.

This critical legacy calls upon us, at the very least, to revise and expand our own sense of what "Victorian" poetry can encompass. I am contending here that "Victorian" poetry remains useful in marking a particular kind of poetic engagement with Europe among English poets whose work was published during or right after the reign of Victoria. At the same time, my aim is not to set off the Victorian period as uniquely cosmopolitan: not the least valuable result of a study of Victorian poetry and Europe would be to restore a sense of continuity between the Romantic period, the Victorian era, and the twentieth century. The encounter with Europe in Victorian poetry none-theless reflects specific aesthetic, cultural, and historical factors unique to this time frame, from roughly mid-century to the dawn of the twentieth century. As I hope to demonstrate in the discussion of Matthew Arnold that follows, concepts of a united, cosmopolitan Europe and a Europeanized English verse gained particular momentum in the wake of the revolutions of 1848, pos-ing new challenges and opportunities for poets such as Barrett Browning and Clough. Later in the century, as European geopolitics continued to fluctu-ate, and as new thinking about evolution, race, and ethnicity gained stronger traction in the public sphere, Victorian poetry again met this challenge with complex interventions of its own into the major cultural and political debates of the time.

Arnold's career forms a microcosm of the broader movement I study, and a fuller discussion of his work and its influences will help to illuminate some of the motives that sent these poets to the Continent. Exploring Arnold's early exposure to key German philosophers and writers who sought to artic-ulate a cosmopolitan idea of Europe will also enable me to establish a set of theoretical benchmarks against which to assess various Victorian and Brit-ish modes of internationalism. Some of Arnold's best known poems, includ-ing "Dover Beach" and "Stanzas from the Grande Chartreuse," in which he forges his own poetic engagement with the Continent, provide added insight into the different directions assumed by other contemporary poets in Europe. And even as Arnold turned away from poetry later in his career, his invest-ment in Anglo-European cultural ideals remained strong. Essays and longer studies including "The Function of Criticism at the Present Time," "Hein-rich Heine," and *Culture and Anarchy* in turn aid our understanding of cross-cultural poetics in Browning and Swinburne especially. Similarly, Arnold's attempt to stage the marriage of race and cosmopolitanism in *On the Study of Celtic Literature* (1866) would find an unlikely disciple in William Morris. Arnold also mirrors each of these poets in his struggle to integrate essentially cultural forms of cosmopolitanism with political and economic ones. If he tends to reject the more radically progressive ideas of Europe, most of the dif-ferent aesthetic and ideological directions Europe could take seem to register with Arnold in some way—as he either embraces or discredits them. The lim-its of Arnold's Europeanism, then, are just as telling as its horizons, making him a fitting springboard into a broader consideration of the encounter with Europe in Victorian poetry.[28]

IN ARNOLD we see the convergence of three interrelated ideals—Europe, cosmopolitanism, and poetry—that evolve over the course of his career with the political and cultural upheavals of the time and the influences of a diverse range of European authors. Three German thinkers in particular would have a strong impact on him, just as they would on numerous subsequent commentators in his time and our own: Immanuel Kant, Johann Gottfried von Herder, and Johann Wolfgang von Goethe. Pinpointing which specific texts or passages would reemerge later in Arnold is not my goal so much as to elucidate some of the primary ideas of Europe and cosmopolitanism at work in the nineteenth century. Following this analysis, I take up how these early influences shaped Arnold's reactions to the events of 1848.

It was Arnold's father, Thomas Arnold, who first built up in his son a strong belief in the benefits to be had from travel, multilingualism, and familiarity with a wide range of European authors—a legacy, of course, that he also bestowed on Clough, Arnold's classmate at Rugby. Rugby was unique at the time in insisting on intensive training in French as a full part of the curriculum, later offering German as well.[29] It should thus come as no surprise that Matthew would gravitate so easily toward the works of French Romantic authors such as George Sand, and, though her, Etienne Pivert de Senancour, whose *Obermann* (1804) engraved itself thoroughly upon his consciousness. As Arnold said in "Stanzas in Memory of the Author of 'Obermann,'" though a "sadder sage" than Wordsworth or Goethe, Senancour's "spell" was undeniable: "The hopeless tangle of our age, / Thou too hast scanned it well!" (81–84).[30] Arnold began the poem while visiting Thun in the Swiss Alps in September 1849, a trip undertaken in part as an act of homage to Senancour. In a prefatory note to the same poem, Arnold again touched on the kind of troubled yet hopeful sense of "modernity" that he found in Senancour and was always inseparable from his own encounter with Europe: "The stir of all the main forces, by which modern life is and has been impelled, lives in the letters of *Obermann;* the dissolving agencies of the eighteenth century, the fiery storm of the French Revolution, the first faint promise and dawn of that new world which our own time is but now more fully bringing to light—all these are to be felt, almost to be touched, there" (135–36).

The philosophical prototypes for Arnold's idea of Europe would be found more among the German authors on his bookshelf, although the concept of an idealized "respublica litteraria" of Europe goes back at least as far as Erasmian humanism and was also a defining characteristic of Enlightenment ideals expressed in works by Montesquieu and Voltaire. Writing from a more political perspective, English authors as well had voiced calls for a federal republic of Europe, including William Penn in the *Present and Future Peace of*

Europe (1693) and Jeremy Bentham in his *Plan for an Universal and Perpetual Peace* (1786–89). Kant's "Idea for a Universal History with a Cosmopolitan Intent" (1784) and "Perpetual Peace: A Philosophical Sketch" (1795), however, both of which Arnold may have been familiar with, present the most comprehensive and ambitious conceptual blueprints for a peaceful, cosmopolitan existence for Europe and the world as a whole.[31] Kant looked toward an unprecedented "great political body of the future," the crowning evolutionary achievement of world history:

> Although this political body exists for the present only in the roughest of outlines, it nonetheless seems as if a feeling is beginning to stir in all its members, each of which has an interest in maintaining the whole. And this encourages the hope that, after many revolutions, with all their transforming effects, the highest purpose of nature, a universal *cosmopolitan existence,* will at last be realised as the matrix within which all the original capacities of the human race may develop.[32]

This idea that the future *meant* cosmopolitanism—that the movements of world history were assuredly drawing all nations together—would become a powerful one in the nineteenth century. It was a hope shared not just by Arnold but contemporaries as diverse as Victor Hugo, Prince Albert, and Thomas Hardy, whose Immanent Will, while derived mainly from Schopenhauer, morphs into something very close to Kant's vision by the end of *The Dynasts.* Likewise, many of the challenges posed by Kant's ideas—including the uncertain promise of world trade in achieving a balance of power between nations and the easy slide from universalism to Eurocentrism—find their way into the works examined here and continue to challenge attempts to theorize cosmopolitanism today.[33]

Herder's place in this account of Arnold's cosmopolitanism might seem more uncertain, since he is typically identified with a virulently nationalist, inward-looking *Volksgeist*—a mystical blending of landscape, language, and ethnicity culminating in distinct and pure national units. As James Tully notes, however, Herder's line of reasoning in his *Ideas for the Philosophy of a History of Mankind* (1784–89), even more so than Kant's writing on cosmopolitanism, leads to "the presumption that all cultures are of intrinsic worth and that they have their own histories."[34] Since no particular culture was necessarily superior to or more advanced than another, Herder's concept of nationhood did not by definition rule out a kind of cooperative internationalism. Overall, Herder presented Arnold with an idea of "culture" that was rich, complex, and dynamic, convincing him of the importance of cross-cultural analysis and deep exposure to the languages and literatures of other countries.[35] Hence Arnold's later insistence in "The Function of Criticism" that "every critic should try and possess one great literature, at least, besides his own; and the more unlike his own, the better" (3:284). It was important for the intellectual and artistic elite of each nation, as Goethe would advise as well, to be fully engaged with the cultural output of other nations. The problem with Herder, as we will see, and the kind of "national internationalism" that energized disciples such as Giuseppe Mazzini, was the power it continued to invest in essentialist and easily racialized notions of national identity. In turn, the sense that these intrinsic national identities could not coalesce with other national traditions without becoming "diluted" in the process created suspicion toward more translated, hybridized spaces of culture. As the century progressed, these impressions hardened into an increasingly powerful and dangerous article of faith for some. Arnold found himself arguing against these voices even if, somewhat contradictorily, *Culture and Anarchy* and *On the Study of Celtic Literature* helped to legitimize the belief that race gave individual cultures and literary traditions their essential characteristics and was thus an indispensable interpretive tool for literary criticism.

Goethe, finally, provided Arnold with a model for his mostly belletristic sense of Europe's cosmopolitan future. Goethe shares Arnold's openness to other cultures and the idea that poetry, like Kant's sense of international politics, was moving inevitably toward a broadly inclusive *Weltlitteratur*.[36] Goethe wrote late in life, "I am more and more convinced that poetry is the universal possession of mankind . . . national literature is now rather an unmeaning term; the epoch of world literature is at hand."[37] From Goethe Arnold derived an unswerving faith in the ability of art to restore Europe to a sense of common purpose and rehabilitated spirituality. Arnold included Goethe with Byron and Wordsworth in a triumvirate of great European voices in his "Memorial Verses," written on the occasion of the latter's death in 1850 (and again it is indicative of Arnold's expansive literary sights that he chose to lament Wordsworth's loss as a European event, not just an English one). Goethe had "looked on Europe's dying hour / Of fitful dream and feverish power" (23–24) and concluded, in Arnold's mind, "*The end is everywhere, / Art still has truth, take refuge there!*" (27–28). To some extent, Arnold's wish to Europeanize English poetics was wrapped up in the continual longing that he shared with Carlyle to find the "next" Goethe. He would remark in *On The Study of Celtic Literature* that "when Goethe came, Europe had lost her basis of spiritual life; she had to find it again; Goethe's task was,—the inevitable task for the modern poet henceforth is, . . . to interpret human life afresh, and to supply a new spiritual basis to it" (3:381).

In Arnold and in the poets who make up this study, there always remains this vital if diverse and unevenly articulated spiritual component—the hope that poetry can perform the unifying function once fulfilled by Christianity. Carlyle, as we have seen, had already enlisted poetry in the service of this spiritually recharged and nondenominational World Church. Robert and Elizabeth Barrett Browning, the two poets studied here who most closely identified with Christianity, likewise pushed for a broadly ecumenical, nondogmatic form of Christian cosmopolitanism (and thus one, as they understood it, operating largely outside the auspices of the Catholic Church). It was a religious mission that the arts, of course, had a vital role to play in, as Browning would dramatize in "Fra Lippo Lippi" (1855). In opposition to Church hierarchy, Lippi espouses a freely exercised creativity that invites broad participation and investment by the artist's audience:

> For, don't you mark? we're made so that we love
> First when we see them painted, things we have passed
> Perhaps a hundred times nor cared to see;
> And so they are better, painted—better to us,
> Which is the same thing. Art was given for that;
> God uses us to help each other so,
> Lending our minds out. (300–306)[38]

A world of strangers thus becomes a world of individuals brought together through a divine spirit of recognition: they see God, and themselves, in others. Similarly, the dramatic monologue was a form that created a close if sometimes uncomfortable fellowship between subject, author, and audience. Whether favorable or antagonistic toward the consciousness being portrayed, however, Browning's ultimate message was always the same: "This world's no blot for us," as Lippi puts it, "Nor blank; it means intensely, and it means good: / To find its meaning is my meat and drink" (313–15). For Browning, paying attention to the world around you and getting to know your neighbors, in all of their diversity, were moral, intellectual, and religious imperatives.

Moving from these spiritual and aesthetic varieties of cosmopolitanism to the "People's Spring" of 1848—the moment, in many ways, when the Victorian poem of Europe first begins to take shape—it becomes clear why Europe's great international moment seemed to have arrived. Proclamations of an emerging confederation of Europe reached a crescendo the likes of which would not be heard again until late in the century, and then mainly as a way of countering the militaristic nationalism that would culminate in the First World War. The events of 1848, and their fallout over the next couple of years, would likewise form the political backdrop to Clough's and Barrett Browning's first European poems. Arnold would not return to the Continent until September of that year, but he followed events closely from London, and in a letter to his sister Jane, stressed the wider European significance of the February 1848 revolution that restored republican government to France:

> How plain it is now, though an attention to the comparative literature for the last fifty years might have instructed any one of it, that England is in a certain sense *far behind* the Continent. In conversation, in the newspapers, one is so struck with the fact of the utter insensibility, one may say, of people to the number of ideas and schemes now ventilated on the Continent—not because they have judged them or seen beyond them, but from sheer habitual want of wide reading and thinking . . . I am not sure but I agree in Lamartine's prophecy that 100 years hence the Continent will be a great united Federal Republic, and England, all her colonies gone, in a dull steady decay.[39]

The poet Alphonse de Lamartine was one of the leaders of the provisional government that had replaced France's constitutional monarchy, and the kinds of feelings Arnold attributes to him here, of course, resonated deeply with Arnold himself, steeped as he was in European literature.[40] England failed to take notice of the Continent at its own peril, Arnold proclaims, and his fellow citizens had no right to dress imperialism in the language of "progress" if they were unwilling to engage even their closest European neighbors. In Europe, newspapers such as the *Revue Germanique et Française* and the *Revue des Deux Mondes,* a particular favorite of Arnold and the Brownings, reflected a broad-minded absorption of international trends in science, philosophy, and literature—the building blocks of the civic life of the future.[41] Arnold's comments also reveal his mostly intellectual sense of what "Europe" was: the major concentration of "the best that is known and thought in the world," as he would put it in "The Function of Criticism" (3:283). Poetry that was not fully conversant with European books and ideas simply "did not know enough," an estimation that diminished Byron's achievement in his mind vis-à-vis Goethe's, left Wordsworth, "profound as he is, yet so wanting in completeness and variety" (3:262)—and left Arnold himself, of course, open to charges of gross overstatement. His later battles against "Philistinism," however, were as much about how little Britain's economic capital measured up against a more lasting and vital trans-European intellectual capital—and how little his contemporaries had done to break down borders of the mind as they had on the front of world trade.

The pan-European sentiments expressed in Arnold's letter were echoed widely on the Continent, with many again attempting to establish some kind of correspondence between the increased flow of trade and that of ideas and culture. The following summer of 1849 saw the convening of a "Congress of Peace" in Paris that featured among its proclamations a plan for a "United States of Europe." One of the delegates, Victor Hugo, expressed the heady feelings of the political progressives in attendance: "A day will come when you France, you Russia, you Italy, you England, you Germany—all of you nations of the continent will, without losing your distinctive qualities and your glorious individuality, be blended into a superior unity, and constitute a European fraternity."[42] Hugo, in many respects, was reinvoking the lost dream of a Napoleonic "association européene," but one decidedly less martial and aggressive, a future governed more by merchants and artists than generals. Such sentiments were not entirely unknown in England, despite Arnold's sense of its intellectual isolation: free trade messiah Richard Cobden was an active participant in the Congress—and discussions of a confederated Europe, then as now, often centered on economic issues. In October of the same year, Prince Albert, drumming up support for the Great Exhibition of the Art and Industry of All Nations that would gather two years later at the Crystal Palace in London, offered a vision of a global village united by trade, travel, and advances in science and communication technology:

> Nobody . . . who has paid any attention to the features of our present era, will doubt for a moment that we are living at a period of most wonderful transition which tends rapidly to the accomplishment of that great end to which, indeed, all history points—the realization of the unity of mankind. Not a unity which breaks down the limits and levels the peculiar characteristics of the different nations of the earth, but rather a unity, the result and product of those very national varieties and antagonistic qualities. The distances which separated the different nations and parts of the globe are gradually vanishing before the achievements of modern invention, and we can traverse them with incredible ease; the languages of all nations are known and their acquirements placed within the reach of everybody; thought is communicated with the rapidity and even by the power of lightning.[43]

How Arnold responded to the kinds of sentiments expressed here—particularly the role of culture versus economics in forming this new Europe—provides a barometer against which to measure the attempts of other Victorian poets and intellectuals to formulate their own ideas of Europe. Sustaining a role for poetry alongside these sciences and technologies of cosmopolitanism—telegraphs and railroads, but also books, newspapers and the post—the conveyors of "languages . . . and their acquirements"—becomes a particular preoccupation for mid-century poets such as Clough and the Brownings. Was poetry part of this larger movement or should it define itself against these mostly material forms of fellowship? Was "Europe," in other words, something that should nourish the mind or the body? In what ways could poetry serve as the catalyst for Europe, whatever form it would assume?

As a poet himself, Arnold could not find the immediate answer to these questions, and his own poems of Europe search mostly in vain for the Continent of his dreams. If the more strident internationalism that followed in the direct wake of the 1848 revolutions had faded by the fall of 1851, when Arnold toured France, Switzerland, and Italy on his honeymoon, it was still the year of the Great Exhibition in London, which had opened in May to enormous crowds overwhelmed by the possibility of a world in which all nations would be brought together through peaceful economic exchange. Another international peace conference, again stressing the importance of a future European confederation, was held in Exeter in August. It was, then, a year for reassessing Europe's progress toward unity, an idea that haunts the two most notable poems to emerge from Arnold's tour, "Dover Beach" and "Stanzas from the Grande Chartreuse." Each has important implications for understanding his and the broader Victorian encounter with Europe, and the longing they express maps the direction followed by other poets over the course of the century. Arnold confronts his disillusionment in these poems, to be sure, but we also see the beginnings of the more tempered, critical cosmopolitanism that would continue to evolve in his prose work.

At its core, "Dover Beach" is a poem about failed connections—above all, between humanity and the divine, which the poem tries to compensate for with love between individual human beings. This failure to connect achieves continental proportions as well. The poem begins with England and France in a kind of awkward juxtaposition to each other, both close at hand yet slipping away:

The sea is calm to-night.
The tide is full, the moon lies fair
Upon the straits; on the French coast the light
Gleams and is gone; the cliffs of England stand,
Glimmering and vast, out in the tranquil bay. (1–5)

In this, the first of a series of "self-destructive" metaphors in the poem, as David G. Riede describes them, the two nations appear to recognize each other in fleeting glimmers of light before the more ominous, impenetrable barrier of the cliffs of Dover assumes prominence.[44] These images recall another of Arnold's great poems of separation and longing from several years earlier, "To Marguerite—Continued," where the estrangement of lovers again mirrors a more collective divide.[45] "We mortal millions live *alone*" (4), he declares of an isolation compounded by the feeling that "surely once . . . we were / Parts of a single continent!" (15–16). In "Dover Beach," the ties of faith that once united Europe and held France and England in closer proximity to each other continue to unravel. The continental drift seems only to have worsened, in fact, an effect Arnold registers aurally as well as visually with the sound of the slowly eroding sea shore, one of the many geological references in the poem:

> The Sea of Faith
> Was once, too, at the full, and round earth's shore
> Lay like the folds of a bright girdle furled.
> But now I only hear
> Its melancholy, long, withdrawing roar,
> Retreating, to the breath
> Of the night-wind, down the vast edges drear
> And naked shingles of the world. (21–28)

The poem's littoral setting, one that Browning would use later to great effect from the French side of the Channel in *Red Cotton Night-Cap Country* (1873), stresses the simultaneous presence of boundaries and horizons. The poem resonates with feelings of transcendence but also with impassable distance. England and France, so close geographically, may descend finally into the darkness and rivalry of a continent and civilization self-destructing. While the two nations should be, like Arnold and his lover, "true / To one another" (29–30), the poem's famous closing image leaves the reader "as on a darkling plain / Swept with confused alarms of struggle and flight, / Where ignorant armies clash by night" (35–37). Arnold's simile is broadly applicable to many forms of spiritual or intellectual crisis, but if we recall its specific international context, it also alludes to the fear that the centuries-long military rivalry between England and France will renew itself. These ignorant armies clashing by night embody a Europe of intense energy—of material progress and competition—but missing a deeper, spiritual component to give it a heading and purpose.

"Stanzas from the Grande Chartreuse" continues Arnold's pilgrimage into the heart of Europe and further dramatizes his sense of spiritual loss as he uncertainly "[m]ounts up the stony forest-way" (20) to the mountain home of the eleventh-century Carthusian monastery at Isère. Its inmates and their dogged, stern faith invite the kind of nostalgia for pan-European Christendom that Arnold absorbed from Romantic writers such as Novalis. Arnold's backward spiritual glance, however, was one tempered by an intellectual commitment to the modernity of those "rigorous teachers" who had "seized [his] youth, / And purged its faith" (67–68). Finally arrived at this isolated religious outpost, he asks, "And what am I, that I am here?" (66). Arnold immediately passes from a moment of (literally) high touristic fulfillment—he has traversed a difficult mountain pass and has found what he was looking for largely as he imagined it—to a crisis of travel. This place is indeed a *living tomb*" (72), a performance of an idealized past that is now hollow at its core. Arnold thus endures the failure of the Grand Tour as "heritage tourism"— much as Clough had the year before in Italy, as we will see. Arnold's journey does not strengthen him so much as provide additional grounds for self-indictment. "Wandering between two worlds, one dead, / The other powerless to be born" (85–86), he has discovered little beyond the fact that he is not well situated no matter where he travels in Europe. Indeed, Arnold's oft-repeated expression of the Victorian crisis of faith is a geographical metaphor not just a temporal one: he cannot locate himself in time or space. Caught between past and future, between England and Europe, Arnold looks with foreboding to a still distant modernity that will bring the sort of integrated identity and landscape he seeks.[46]

Arnold's subsequent survey of his Romantic predecessors—Byron, Shelley, and Senancour—further expounds this sense of loss and poetry's unfulfilled task. All had sought out Switzerland and its mountain retreats as the sublime natural center of Europe. Childe Harold, for instance, in a rare moment of peace, floats undisturbed on the waters of Leman, "Which warns me, with its stillness, to forsake / Earth's troubled waters for a purer spring" (3.799–800).[47] Byron's escapism, however, as Arnold sees it, becomes a spiritual dead end, a dramatic display of futility:

What helps it now, that Byron bore,
With haughty scorn which mocked the smart,
Through Europe to the Aetolian shore
The pageant of his bleeding heart?
That thousands counted every groan,
And Europe made his woe her own? (133–38)

These lines mark the cultural divide that opens up between the Europe of Byron and the still unborn Europe of the Victorian poem. While largely critical of Byron, Arnold also pays tribute to the confident poetic authority he embodied and his command of the European landscape, both objects of nostalgia for the Victorian poet who traverses a seemingly more confusing, disintegrated space. As Arnold had put it earlier in "Memorial Verses" with the kind of blanket pronouncement more typical of his prose criticism, Byron "taught us little; but our soul / Had *felt* him like the thunder's roll" (8–9). Like Byron, Arnold himself succeeds only too well at embodying loss. What was needed was a poet who could do more than write Europe's epitaph, someone who possessed "Goethe's sage mind and Byron's force" (61). This new poetry would integrate England with Europe, as Byron had, while restoring a sense of spirituality and purpose that Arnold felt he had not. It would be smarter and more serious—perhaps a "Don Juan without the mockery & impurity"—as Elizabeth Barrett foreshadowed of the epic novel-poem that would become *Aurora Leigh.*[48] Or, not entirely dispensing with mockery and impurity, such a poem might go where Arnold had pointed but feared to tread, where Clough and Swinburne ventured. Whatever form this cultural blockbuster would assume, it would not come from Arnold himself, of course, who largely abandoned poetry after 1851. But from the critical sidelines, Arnold would continue to press poets as he had pressed himself to fashion a more open intellectual engagement with the Continent and to sustain the genre's relevance to other kinds of border-crossing, whether social, economic, or political. How much they listened, and how much they would attempt to fashion their own encounter with Europe *against* Arnold, is the subject of the rest of this book.

EVEN THOUGH she follows Clough in my study, I want to begin my outline of individual chapters by turning first to Barrett Browning and offering some extended analysis of how she responds to the challenges that Arnold saw facing post-Byronic, Anglo-European poetics. She was, as G. K. Chesterton would declare, "by far the most European of all English poets of that age; all of them, even her own much greater husband, look local beside her."[49] Chesterton generalizes broadly here on several levels, but he is correct to identify an influential, long-standing, and multifaceted engagement with Europe in Barrett Browning's work, one that certainly rivaled Arnold's in its depth. They thus make for a revealing juxtaposition. More intensely religious than he, and more boldly political, Barrett Browning would accordingly reformulate Arnold's spiritual and intellectual mission while still retaining his faith that conceiving cosmopolitanism was a task best mastered by poets and artists, not scientists or political theorists.

Arnold would give expression to these dueling claims upon modern identity in a March 1848 letter to Clough, where he charged England as a nation with dwelling in the same historical no-man's-land between past and future that he would find himself in abroad three years later. Simultaneously, he seems to forecast the same way out of this impasse that Barrett Browning would chart more fully in *Casa Guidi Windows* (1851) and later works, including *Aurora Leigh* and *Poems before Congress*—a path that allowed the poet to synthesize powerful spiritual longings with the rationalistic, democratic "spirit" of modern times. Arnold writes, "our weakness [as a nation] is that in an age where all tends to the triumph of the logical absolute reason we neither courageously have thrown ourselves into this movement like the French: nor yet have driven our feet into the solid ground of our individuality, as spiritual, poetic, profound *persons*. Instead of this we have stood *up* hesitating: seeming to refuse the first line on the ground that the second is our *natural* one—yet not taking this."[50] While not necessarily embracing the free-wheeling rationalism Arnold describes here, Barrett Browning did look to France to take the lead in moving Europe forward politically toward universal republicanism. In her work, this political faith merges with the spiritualized, individualistic advocacy Arnold alludes to, which Barrett Browning locates more in a transnational or trans-Herderian sense of the poet's ability to give voice to the "souls" of different nations. She thus just as easily finds Arnold's spiritual "solid ground" in Italy and France as she would in England. In turn, more than any Victorian poet, with the possible exception of Swinburne, she would open herself to charges of repudiating her own nationality.

"Italy and the World," from *Poems before Congress,* does the most to fuse Barrett Browning's religious aims with the more political cause of a united Europe, where "civilisation perfected / Is fully developed Christianity" (51–52).[51] She alludes specifically here to St. Paul's vision of a world united under one church, "No more Jew nor Greek" (46), and thus comes close to advocating what Linda M. Lewis calls "a form of Christian empire," one with antecedents in Dante's *De Monarchia*.[52] Barrett Browning's efforts might be more closely aligned, however, with the kind of religious cosmopolitanism that arose *in conjunction* with Enlightenment rationalism but has since fallen off our historical radar due to the same "Enlightenment metanarrative which proclaims the birth of modernity in the decline of religion," as Srinivas Aravamudan argues.[53] In Barrett Browning, Christianity fully developed becomes indistinguishable from the democratic political rejuvenation she identifies as its catalyst—hence revolutionary, progressive France becomes

Europe's spiritual center rather than the more "Christian" nation, England. Barrett Browning's New Europe, with Italy now at the center of the struggle for freedom, is a spiritual production—God's love rechanneled between individuals, a love that redeems and, with its maternal overtones, as we will see, feminizes the public sphere. New Europe is also just as fundamentally a product of *this* world—a civic body—the rational outgrowth of the natural, political evolution Kant espouses in the "Idea for a Universal History": "The history of the human race as a whole can be regarded as the realisation of a hidden plan of nature to bring about an internally—and for this purpose also externally—perfect political constitution as the only possible state within which all natural capacities of mankind can be developed completely."[54] Once individual states had achieved ideal forms of representative republican government, the larger world fraternity he had dreamed of would follow. Barrett Browning's poem patterns a similar kind of logic. The world would witness, after Italy, "one confederate brotherhood planting / One flag only, to mark the advance, / Onward and upward, of all humanity" (48–50). Later, Barrett Browning would find an unlikely co-prophet of sorts in Swinburne, whose *Songs before Sunrise* (1871) looks as well toward a future European confederation that would germinate in Italy. In "The Eve of Revolution," Swinburne commands his contemporaries to "[b]uild up our one Republic state by state, / England with France, and France with Spain, / And Spain with sovereign Italy strike hands and reign."[55]

The more politicized nature of Barrett Browning's internationalism reveals the limits of how far Arnold was willing to go, outside of the purely literary and intellectual realm, in imagining a confederated Europe. Typically, perhaps, even after Arnold had encouraged Clough in his wish to visit France in 1848 and absorb the flow of new ideas being "ventilated" there, he warned him off politics, reflecting in "To a Republican Friend, 1848," "when I muse on what life is, I seem / Rather to patience prompted, than that proud / Prospect of hope which France proclaims so loud" (15–17). Arnold was also always ambivalent toward the kind of divinely sanctioned national internationalism celebrated by Mazzini and, with greater circumspection, I would argue, by Barrett Browning in "Italy and the World." While supportive of the principle of Italian nationhood, and encouraging England to take a more proactive stance toward achieving that goal, Arnold seems to want to close off all political avenues to that end short of diplomacy. In "England and the Italian Question" (1859) he remarks, "The principle of nationality, if acted upon too early, or if pushed too far, would prevent that natural and beneficial union of conterminous or neighbouring territories into one great state, upon which the grandeur of nations and the progress of civilisation depends"

(1:71). Arnold's belief seems to be that if Europe proceeds boldly with intellectual and spiritual unity, politics will inevitably take care of itself: his wish,
as he detailed later in *Culture and Anarchy*, was for a kind of "smart revolution" from above. Barrett Browning, in contrast, was more willing to sacrifice
political stability to achieve higher ends. To his credit, Arnold does point out
the blind spot in Mazzini's larger vision—the assumption that violence practiced on behalf of the nation would be relatively contained and would cease
once nations achieved their "natural" borders and sovereignty. If history has
proven this belief to have been grossly optimistic, the question remains of
whether Europe should be primarily a cultural idea, a group of trading partners, a political federation, or some combination of all three. Europe's pathway toward Appiah's "rooted cosmopolitanism"—making nationalism and
internationalism work on behalf of each other—was and remains a difficult
road to navigate.

Arnold's pro-Europe comments are never quite so political or religious as
Barrett Browning's, but they do find spiritual common ground with her in
their skepticism toward the belief that the task of uniting Europe should be
entrusted to the same captains of industry who were driving the engines of
Britain's economic progress. For Arnold, the rhetoric of free trade coalesced
all too easily with the aims of a closed-off, profit-seeking middle class that
put monetary concerns ahead of spiritual and intellectual enrichment. Barrett Browning likewise stresses the fatal contradiction behind the notion that
individual profit seeking would somehow invite international cooperation.
Casa Guidi Windows, for instance, mocks the Great Exhibition as a thinly
veiled exercise in economic one-upmanship: "These corals, will you please,"
one nation says to the next, "To match against your oaks?" (2.592–93). Barrett Browning looked toward France to model a more selfless, fraternal kind
of foreign policy: Louis Napoleon's continued failure to live up to that ideal
would be a source of ongoing frustration to her, even if she never lost faith
that France would eventually fulfill the ideals of the revolutions of 1789 and
1848. "Napoleon III in Italy" (1860) thus directly challenges him at the same
time it underscores England's more egregious political failures. France, she
maintains, may yet "[u]nselfishly—shiver a lance / (As the least of her sons
may, in fact) / And not for a cause of finance" (375–77).

Barrett Browning's resistance to marketplace Europe also explains, in part,
her aversion to the nascent forms of communism that were also beginning
to take hold with some intellectuals on the Continent and influencing Char-
tist poets back in England (and, one could add, the later, postconversion
Morris of *The Pilgrims of Hope*). Here she again finds common ground with
Arnold, who likewise appears never to have seriously contemplated the kind

of European union that entailed the radical redistribution of wealth that would also mean the end of national governments, which Marx contended were simply reconstituted forms of class power. The influence of Marx himself had yet to be felt by the time Barrett Browning composed *Aurora Leigh,* but his theoretical precursors—Saint Simonism and Fourierism—come under heavy suspicion in the poem as false political unifiers. Her response to them reveals why communist internationalism could not comfortably coexist with a poetic authority dependent on notions of the spirit and individual creative genius.[56] Aurora, in fact, defines poetry against the collectivist, class-oriented internationalism espoused by her would-be suitor Romney. "Without a poet's individualism / To work your universal," she warns him, his social schemes will fail:

> It takes a soul,
> To move a body: it takes a high-souled man,
> To move the masses, even to a cleaner stye:
> It takes the ideal, to blow a hair's-breadth off
> The dust of the actual.—Ah, your Fouriers failed,
> Because not poets enough to understand
> That life develops from within. (2.479–85)

In the end, the poem decisively, even violently, discredits Romney's theories: the model phalanstery into which he had transformed his estate burns down in a riot started by the very inmates he had intended to help, while he himself is blinded, à la Rochester, when the ancestral Leigh home collapses.[57] Barrett Browning thereby discredits both the liberal faith in free trade and the socialist insistence on the material and economic bases of history and identity: in her mind, both ideologies share the same roots in an anti-spiritual, anti-aesthetic ethos.

Later a reformed Romney reunites with Aurora in Italy, in keeping with the poem's movement toward synthesis of body and soul, individual and collective, and art and politics. If not adopting Romney's more radical political solutions, Aurora does endorse the idea that the poet must become more actively engaged in politics and play a leading role in reinventing Europe. Playing a kind of chorus to Aurora at the end of the poem, Romney pays tribute to the high ideals of her mission:

> The world's old,
> But the old world waits the time to be renewed,
> Toward which, new hearts in individual growth
> Must quicken, and increase to multitude

In new dynasties of the race of men;
Developed whence, shall grow spontaneously
New churches, new economies, new laws
Admitting freedom, new societies
Excluding falsehood: HE shall make all new. (9.941–49)

If not a Marxist vision of the future, Aurora's would still have been recognizable to Herder or Kant in its gravitational movement from smaller to larger units of identity. Churches, like nations, will give way to a more inclusive collective. Similarly, in the manner of Goethe, Barrett Browning unites under one poetic umbrella the aesthetic, spiritual, and the political—the three governing forces of her larger vision of a "new dynasty" of men (and women). These were grand ambitions, as Barrett Browning was well aware, and if they are easy to critique on practical political grounds, we should recall that she was equally concerned with manifesting cosmopolitanism on a more modest, personal scale that was still revolutionary in its own right. In chapter 3, I examine how Barrett Browning's own status as a woman traveler prompted new insight into the ways Aurora and her companion Marian Earle could embody a subaltern "cosmopolitanism from below," one that overturned firmly entrenched assumptions about who held the authority to travel in Victorian society.

Barrett Browning's political and poetic development did not stop with *Aurora Leigh,* however. In later poems discussed in chapter 3, Barrett Browning continues to hammer out possible affiliations between nationalism and cosmopolitanism, with a stronger eye toward the personal sacrifices involved for women in achieving the kind of vision that closes *Aurora Leigh.* "Mother and Poet," for instance, emphasizes the hollow victory of national liberation—and women's political empowerment—if that power comes at the expense of women's maternal identity, broadly defined to include not just child-rearing but empathy across social and cultural borders. Women thus had a unique inroad toward a rooted, even "domesticated" cosmopolitanism that could speak for the "body" and the "soul" of Europe. If Barrett Browning's was a cosmopolitanism that could come only from the marginalized position of a woman poet seeking entry into political discourse, it nonetheless would move to the center of the Victorian poetic encounter with Europe—the one that most broadly encompassed the genre's diverse political, spiritual, and aesthetic ambitions—and the most in tune, in many ways, with attempts to theorize cosmopolitanism today.

My study of individual poets begins not with Barrett Browning, however, but—ironically, perhaps—with Clough: the closest personally to Arnold but the furthest away from him and Barrett Browning in his attempts to bring

Europe into being. Clough made a three-month stay in Paris in the spring of 1848, reporting to Arnold's brother Tom in New Zealand, among other correspondents, on his disappointment at the failure of the revolution to institute substantial reform and enfranchise the peasantry and working class: "there is no doubt that France's prospects are dubious and dismal enough, and one is almost inclined to think that the outbreak was premature."[58] Visiting Rome the following spring, as Mazzini's newly declared Roman Republic struggled to keep itself intact, Clough continued to write letters, but this time in verse as well. In the process, he would create perhaps the most nuanced and highly self-critical investigation of the ideal of poetic border-crossing to be found in Victorian poetry. Clough's *Amours de Voyage* (1849; publ. 1858) immerses itself in emerging European networks of transportation and communication—including the post—of which the poem itself, in some sense, is a product. *Amours de Voyage* aims to test Prince Albert's belief that a more closely knit modern Europe would emerge in the wake of these technologies of cosmopolitanism. In the end, however, even as different European nationalities intermingle with greater ease at the major tourist destinations of Italy, Clough remains a kind of flâneur in crisis. While he criticizes nationalism along with strongly rooted, uncompromising affiliations of any kind, Clough at the same time remains highly attuned to the sorts of class and cultural privilege that inform the seemingly free-floating, uncommitted nature of the traveler as flâneur. A cosmopolitan Europe—one that exists apart from the cash nexus of tourism and aggressive strains of nationalism and imperialism—remains a distant, unrealized prospect for Clough. He instead embraces travel-in-verse as a necessary exercise in destabilizing one's own cultural and ideological attachments—a cosmopolitanism of negation, perhaps—but one that provided him with a powerful critical tool for exploding false affinities.

With Robert Browning and Swinburne, my study moves toward less directly political interventions in Europe and instead analyzes the poets' efforts to fashion poetry into an idealized cultural "space-in-between," to adapt Homi K. Bhabha's concept, one that balances the idea of travel as personal enrichment with the demands of a more engaged ideal of world citizenship. Bhabha describes this space as an "an interstitial temporality, . . . an endlessly fragmented subject in 'process,'" an engagement that is essentially "translational" rather than "concentric."[59] As a postcolonial subject, Bhabha, of course, is forced into this kind of translation, one he seeks to take charge of and transform into a new identity, neither rooted in a more "authentic" and illusory ethnic ideal nor dictated by the lingering intellectual apparatus of colonialism. Browning is a translational subject by choice, but in some sense, he faces the same dilemma as Bhabha. He experiences the rich rewards offered the well-traveled, well-read intellectual, and values his multiple national affiliations—Italian, French, even Greek and German—while never losing his deep attachment to those "home-thoughts" celebrated (from abroad) in the title of his most famous short lyric. But Browning must also cope with the potential of this ideal to descend into a self-absorbed, privileged cultural elitism. Aijaz Ahmad, for instance, cautions us that "speaking with virtually mindless pleasure of transnational cultural hybridity . . . amounts, in effect, to endorsing the cultural claims of transnational capital itself."[60] This is a challenge at the heart of cosmopolitanism as Appiah sees it as well, which has always alternated, he suggests, between a sense of ethical "obligations to others that stretch beyond those to whom we are related by ties of kith or kind" and the celebration—and consumption—of what distances us, "which means taking an interest in the practices and beliefs that lend them significance" and "learn[ing] from our differences."[61]

Browning's whole career, one could argue, was an ongoing process of engaging, dramatizing, and learning from those differences. With his earliest short dramatic monologues in *Bells and Pomegranates* (1842), Browning sought to enter into the varieties of European national consciousness, as he mapped out in his section titles—"Italy" for "My Last Duchess," "France" for "Count Gismond," and "Cloister (Spanish)" for "Soliloquy of the Spanish Cloister." These poems, along with *Sordello, Pippa Passes* (1841) and, of course, *The Ring and the Book* (1868–69) all offer suitable case studies for probing Browning's border-crossing, but I argue that it was in a relatively late poem, one set in modern France, that Browning delved most deeply into the ways travel replicates the same tensions that define his signature form, the dramatic monologue. *Red Cotton Night-Cap Country* is a poem consumed with borders and the urge to transcend them—borders of lyric and drama, England and Europe, culture and politics, and, not least of all, men and women. Browning stages a debate between himself and the poem's interlocutor, Anne Thackeray, over what it means to travel in Europe and to reinscribe that experience: where does one establish the border between self and other, between home-thoughts and those that can come only from dwelling abroad? Finding himself on both sides of cultural and political divides that begin to open up in the 1860s, Browning likewise forms a borderline or transitional figure in my book as whole. On the one hand, Browning must defend himself from critics such as Charles Kingsley, who berated him for abandoning England in favor of an attenuated cosmopolitanism—and, at that, one fixated on Italy and France rather than on what Kingsley (and Carlyle, among others) increasingly regarded as England's true racial and cultural peer, Germany.[62] In Kingsley's mind, Browning failed to turn "all his rugged genial force into the questions and the struggles of that mother-country to whom and not to Italy at all, he owes all his most valuable characteristics."[63] On the other hand, *Red Cotton Night-Cap Country,* even as it champions Anglo-French cultural exchange in the face of such criticism, still reveals Browning's determination to distance himself from more radically destabilizing kinds of internationalism: politically, the threat posed by class revolution—symbolized in the poem by the Paris Commune of 1870—and, culturally, the sensual "effeminacy" he associates with aestheticism. Browning's ideal of cosmopolitan engagement with Europe, as we will see, co-evolves with his attempts to sort through the complications of Victorian gender and cultural politics—to create an open, responsive, yet still apparently masculine and heterosexual kind of border-crossing.

Indeed, Swinburne, that most notorious of poetic aesthetes, takes the spiritual and intellectual confederation envisioned by Arnold into radical new territory, recharging the notion of a culturally receptive, cosmopolitan England and in the process revealing that crossing national boundaries involves the testing of other cultural boundaries, including those grounded in sexuality and gender. In another sense, *Poems and Ballads* (1866) simply executes the more radical if muted of Arnold's aims in *Culture and Anarchy,* as Robert J. C. Young describes them: "For Arnold the public functions for culture are all rigorously stabilizing, harmonizing, and reducing all conflict or dissent. But at the same time, culture's role is also, paradoxically, to destabilize."[64] Europe was not a destination for Swinburne so much as an object of translation—a discursive entity—which partly explains the paradox of why Victorian England's most "French" poet spent so little time there, as he revealed to E. C. Stedman in 1875: "I was never in France or Italy for more than a few weeks together, and that not more than three or four times in my life."[65] Swinburne's is thus a France of the imagination, a place not as "real" or contemporary as Browning's, and yet, in another sense, *Poems and Ballads* seems more deeply immersed in the matter of France—or more thoroughly and troublingly *outside* England. As one of Swinburne's fiercest critics, Robert Buchanan, would observe, "no one accuses the author of [*Pippa Passes*] and of the "Ring and the Book," of neglecting the body; and yet I do daily homage to the genius of Robert Browning."[66] Similarly, John Morley, who praised *The Ring and the Book* for jarring a complacent British public with "a rude inburst of air from the outside welter of human realities," had unloaded on Swinburne several years before, whom he deemed "all aflame with the feverish carnality of a schoolboy over the dirtiest passages in Lemprière."[67]

Clearly the frank sexual desire of poems such as "Love and Sleep" was guaranteed to affront many critics, but I argue in chapter 5 that their reactions betray that something more than "good taste" was at stake in the cultural crisis precipitated by the publication of *Poems and Ballads*. To these critics, Swinburne becomes the icon of a dangerously "continental" strain of poetry obsessed with the aesthetic surfaces of the body and language, one that threatens to undermine a stronger, more authentic English verse. Even allies such as William Morris felt a certain unease with Swinburne, complaining once that he "never could really sympathize with Swinburne's work; it always seemed . . . to be founded on literature, not on nature."[68] This sense of alienation from oneself and nature in fact reveals how vital *literariness*—as a specific kind of cultural translation—is to cosmopolitanism. For Swinburne, aestheticism becomes a twin process of negotiating culture *and* negotiating desire. The marriage of England and the Continent mirrors the overriding question in *Poems and Ballads* of what it means for two people to come together and desire each other—with all of the complex feelings of longing, uncertainty, and discomfort that ensue. A literary/cosmopolitan body emerges from the volume whose essence is its very difficulty to translate—to locate in England or France, in the present or in the many historical spaces that the poems occupy. Swinburne's verse resides at the crossroads of the "natural" and the "literary," destabilizing both entities in the process and anticipating the radical cross-cultural "poisoning" associated later in the century with Decadence.

The controversy over aestheticism and the fluidity of England's cultural borders points as well to the greater role that race would play in Victorian discussions of national and European identity. Arnold was again a leading voice in the debate, arguing on behalf of inquiry into the racial history of different European populations while still insisting on the essentially unifying, cosmopolitan fruits of such an investigation.[69] The "English mind," for instance, as he maintained in *On the Study of Celtic Literature*, embodied a mixture of European racial tendencies that should make it flexible and receptive to the products of many cultures. It was a gift, however, that needed to be understood to be deployed effectively: "so long as we are blindly and ignorantly rolled about by the forces of our nature, their contradiction baffles us and lames us; so soon as we have clearly discerned what they are, and begun to apply to them a law of measure, control, and guidance, they may be made to work for our good and carry us forward" (3:383).[70] Of the poets I study here, William Morris follows Arnold most closely in making the case, through poetry, that to know race is to know England and to know Europe. Assuming a different compass heading than Arnold, Morris turns to the "Northland of old and the undying glory of dreams" (9:125), as he remarked in "Iceland First Seen," composed during the first of two trips to

Europe's farthest Atlantic margin.[71] Choosing a geographically and historically remote setting, Morris nonetheless insisted that he had found a lost cultural center, "the first grey dawning of our race" (7:286), as he wrote in the verse prologue to his translation of the Volsunga Saga, which he would rerender shortly after in an epic poem of his own.

And yet, given this kind of claim, Morris's epic poetry of the North turns out to be remarkably racially *un*charged. Morris aims to redraw the map of European culture, but he never seems to invest as heavily as Arnold in the fruition of poetic racial recovery—that it will somehow "carry us forward." It is enough that it carries us back. To adapt another of Arnold's phrases from *On the Study of Celtic Literature,* Morris writes the poetry of the "science of origins," one that seeks to meet Norse culture on its own terms, achieving a kind of objective, distanced reverence. "The Lovers of Gudrun," the longest of the tales from *The Earthly Paradise* (1868–70), and *Sigurd the Volsung* (1876) portray the struggles of Europe's most mobile, sea-oriented culture as it engages with other regions of Europe. Sigurd, with his gestures toward a pan-European community governed by ideals of justice and fairness, embodies Morris's efforts to balance ideals of rootedness and travel. In the end, it is difficult to cull a clear political or ideological message from Morris concerning race and European identity: what he delivers is a sort of poetic-racial aestheticism. Race for Morris is a powerful component of language and the literary production that grows out of it, but it does not seem to hold much more beyond that for him; race is a given, but one that needs to be understood critically, not glorified. Through Morris, Victorian poetry engages in a cosmopolitan, counterracial discourse even if, at times, it validates the contemporary tendency to view cultural traits as being somehow racially imbedded. Overall, despite his orientation toward Icelandic and Nordic landscapes and literature, Morris is just as prepared to celebrate wider notions of travel, hybridity, and cross-European migration.

Morris is the only poet in these chapters who beats a path away from the central destinations of the Grand Tour, which perhaps raises a question: beyond Italy, France, ancient Greece, and Scandinavia, one could inquire, where is the *rest* of Europe in this study? I should stress first that my aim is not to provide an encyclopedic overview of Anglo-European poetics, but even so, I admit that there are important destinations that have been passed over. Eliot's *The Spanish Gypsy* (1869), for instance, situated at Europe's westernmost border with the Islamic world, would provide another opportunity for reflection on race and European identity.[72] Elsewhere, the ongoing movements for Greek and Polish independence attracted attention from poets including Barrett Browning but also Walter Savage Landor.[73] This book nonetheless stays within the main geographical boundaries of Victorian "Europe"—the powerful and emergent countries of the western half of the continent—and also the North, so important to specifically *Anglo*-European notions of identity.[74] My study thus perpetuates a certain Western European geographical bias, but one reflective of the historical moment it concentrates on and one that does not invalidate what was still in many ways a dynamic and multifaceted engagement with Europe in Victorian poetry.

One missing destination in particular, however, merits more explanation in light of its important role in the history and culture of Europe in the nineteenth century. With such a strong philosophical presence in European cosmopolitan thinking and in Victorian intellectual life at large, why was Germany largely "off the map" for poets? One explanation is simply cultural habit: for centuries, Italy and France had always held stronger attraction for literary artists and travelers. Germany, nonetheless, would come to play a significant role in Victorian travel poetry *because* of its absence—an absence that speaks volumes about how poetic authority had been defined by Arnold, for instance, and re-echoed in the Brownings. Germany could signify any number of things to different Victorian writers and artists, but Arnold's *On the Study of Celtic Literature* gives perhaps the best indication of why Germany—Goethe's efforts aside—was perceived as being antithetical to poetry's "spiritual" mission. Germany was to be praised for its "industry, well-doing, the patient and steady elaboration of things, the idea of science governing all departments of human activity." Its culture, however, tended toward a "lack of beauty and distinction in form and feature," reflected as well in "the slowness and clumsiness of the language" (3:342). Germany was a set of contradictions for Arnold, although never enough so to undermine his faith in the accuracy of these stereotypes in the first place: Germany was spiritual, yet hostile to faith; intelligent, but ploddingly so.[75] *Aurora Leigh* conveys much the same idea in its presentation of Aurora's brief encounter with an anti-religious English student studying in Germany, a prototype of sorts for Eliot's Will Ladislaw in *Middlemarch* (1871–72). Aurora listens silently at a dinner party as the student condemns Romney's Christian socialism, boasting, "You're slow in England. In a month I learnt / At Göttingen enough philosophy / To stock your English schools for fifty years" (5.755–57). Later in the poem, however, she delivers a rebuke meant to capture what's missing from German intellectual life. Barrett Browning's specific target is Friedrich Augustus Wolf, who, with his assertion that Homer was an editorial invention, had done to him what the Higher Criticism was now attempting to do to Christianity: "Wolf's an atheist; / And if the Iliad fell out, as he says, / By mere fortuitous concourse of old songs, / Conclude as much too for the universe" (5.1254–57). Aurora instead turns towards Italy and France, where she will fashion a more faith-based republicanism that shuns materialist and dryly historicist accounts of cultural identity. Germany becomes the source of an anti-spiritual modernity for her, no longer the benign, largely pastoral home of Goethe and Carlyle's Romantic idealism. It also did not help that Germany was so closely associated with Austria, the primary obstacle toward the realization of Italy's freedom. In Part II of *Casa Guidi Windows*, Austria comes off as a militaristic, spiritually wanting culture, "wearing a smooth olive-leaf / On her brute forehead, while her hoofs outpress / the life from these Italian souls" (2.418–20).

Robert Browning's stance toward Germany also helps illustrate why the country did not assume a greater, more positive presence in Victorian poetry. He shared Elizabeth's distrust of the Higher Criticism and attacked Strauss in *Christmas-Eve and Easter-Day* (1850), where he appears in the guise of an off-putting and vain lecturer who once again hails from "Göttingen,— most likely" and addresses an audience on the "Myth of Christ" (794; 859). Contemporary German intellectual life had little to offer the Victorian poet trying to rehabilitate Christianity and reunify Europe along more spiritual lines. France, of course, had its own set of committed secularists and over-fondness for theory—"[t]oo absolute and earnest, with them all / The idea of a knife cuts real flesh," as Aurora Leigh opined (6.22–23)—but these forces were counterbalanced by another: a greater dedication to democratic and egalitarian principles and to the arts as a means of advancing them. Browning's wrath quickened only when these impulses fell out of balance with each other and became extreme, as they had in the case of Léonce Miranda, whom he profiles in *Red Cotton Night-Cap Country*. Thus Browning's sometime hostility toward France should not be confused with the kind of High German cheerleading one sees in Carlyle. "That noble, patient, deep, pious, and solid Germany," Carlyle wrote to *The Times* at the outbreak of the Franco-Prussian War, "should at length be welded into a Nation, and become Queen of the Continent, instead of vapouring, vainglorious, gesticulating, quarrelsome, restless and oversensitive France seems to me the hopefullest public fact that has occurred in my time."[76] These were adjectives Browning might apply to Louis Napoleon, whom he caricatures in *Prince Hohenstiel-Schwangau, Saviour of Society* (1871), but not to France as a nation. For Browning, the year 1870 did not signal the triumph of Germanic over French culture and principles but was, rather, "folly's year in France" (3233), when it failed to live up to its own best national standards. Overall, then, in Victorian poetry, Germany fails to resonate as an actual destination but it does provide a vital source of friction and debate. Even Morris, as we will see, with his preference for the more northern reaches of Europe, was careful to distance the type of cultural work performed by his translations and adaptations of Icelandic sagas from the "Teutonism" on display in Carlyle and, as we saw earlier, Kingsley.

As it moves from Morris to Hardy at the turn of the century, my study also passes over some late-century poets who could conceivably find a viable place in a study of Victorian Anglo-European poetics. I plead the usual limits of time and space, but would also observe that during this era, Victorian poetry, when set abroad, did in some respects take the mostly imperial turn that Wilson anticipated upon the death of Barrett Browning. One thinks, for instance, of Rudyard Kipling's *Barrack-Room Ballads* (1892) or Robert Louis Stevenson's "Travel" from *A Child's Garden of Verses* (1885), where he famously "should like to rise and go / Where the golden apples grow; / Where below another sky / Parrot islands anchored lie" (1–4).[77] By and large, what is missing from Victorian poetry following Morris are what one might term the "big" poems of Europe—whether epic or of epic ambitions or length—that continue the kind of project undertaken by mid-century poets to map Anglo-European space and dramatize its multilayered encounters.[78] (I would include Swinburne's *Poems and Ballads* among these major efforts even if it is not one continuous narrative or travelogue.) That said, the kinds of cultural translation pioneered in *Poems and Ballads* would indeed continue to flourish and evolve but in different directions after Swinburne— a promising subject for a study concerned with more specifically aesthetic or fin-de-siècle encounters with Europe.[79] Arthur Symons' *London Nights* (1896), for instance, brings France over to England in ways not ventured by Swinburne, who, despite his admiration for Baudelaire, did not attempt to recreate the specifically urban, contemporary cosmopolitanism of the flâneur, who becomes a much more visible figure in British Decadent verse. Such a study could also explore the ways "Michael Field" (Katherine Bradley and Edith Cooper) combined elements of travel and aesthetic appreciation in *Sight and Song* (1895), which carefully notes the museum "setting" of each of these ekphrastic poems. Like Swinburne's "Hermaphroditus," which he situates "*Au Musée de Louvre, Mars* 1863," Bradley and Cooper reconfigure the encounter with art in European galleries less as distanced appreciation and more as active interrogation of the cultural and gender borders art puts on display.

The Victorian long poem of Europe would dramatically reassert itself, however, with Thomas Hardy's *The Dynasts: An Epic-Drama of the War with Napoleon* (1904–8), the capstone to my investigation and to the Victorian effort to give poetic shape and spirit to Europe. As an author who first encountered Europe through the more local lens of the Wessex novels, Hardy likewise provides an occasion for reexamining basic questions of genre: indeed, in comparison to his historical novel of the same period, *The Trumpet-Major* (1880), *The Dynasts* dramatically revises what happens to local identity in the context of a European-wide conflict. The poem's complex structure and multiple perspectives work to destabilize forms of national and local allegiance while still paying tribute—as Morris had—to the powerful grip they hold over individuals. Hardy's closest affinity in this study, however, is with Barrett Browning, for he returns in many ways to the same question that confronted her at mid-century: how the quasi-religious devotion that defines the imagined community of the nation could evolve into the intellectual and spiritual confederation of Europe that Arnold had anticipated. Comments from the preliminary notes to *The Dynasts* echo Barrett Browning's call in the preface to *Poems before Congress,* as we will see, to balance patriotic feeling against wider interests: "Patriotism," he wrote, "if aggressive and at the expense of other countries, is a vice; if in sympathy with them, a virtue."[80]

For Barrett Browning, poetry becomes the essence of a new spirituality that would expand and promote larger public goals. If Hardy, in contrast, could not re-tailor Christianity into the spiritual fabric that would reunite Europe, the poem is still deeply spiritual in its own way, suggesting there was an essence beyond material reality, a larger web of energy or Will that, though unconscious of itself, weaves its way collectively through each individual mind. As it manifests itself in *The Dynasts,* the "Immanent Will" bears some affinity to the national will that Barrett Browning wishes to see ignited in *Casa Guidi Windows* and "Italy and the World." By the turn of the twentieth century, however, the imperial ambitions of Germany made it much more difficult for Hardy to celebrate emergent European nationalisms. With the benefit of this historical hindsight, Hardy portrays the greatest military conflict of the nineteenth century as a "Clash of Peoples" (4:5) animated by powerful but blind national feeling. During the Battle of Borodino, the "Spirit of the Years" observes,

> *Thus do the mindless minions of the spell*
> *In mechanized enchantment sway and show*
> *A Will that wills above the will of each,*
> *Yet but the will of all conjunctively;*

A fabric of excitement, web of rage,
That permeates as one stuff the weltering whole. (III.1.5.4–9)[81]

When individuals act on behalf of national identity, or think they do, they merely carry out the indifferent energy of the Will. The concept of the Will also notably diminishes the importance of race in calculations of national and European identity: such distinctions seem merely arbitrary and destructive. Only when humans perceive the working of the Will, and the two work in tandem—*"Consciousness the Will informing, till It fashion all things fair"*— will such collective cosmic energy become the spirit that goes international (III. After Scene.110). In terms of crafting a cohesive spirit of Europe, and, eventually, the entire world, one could say that Hardy and Barrett Browning both finally arrive via different paths at the doors of the same World Church—one centered on the faith that there is some kind of constructive, immaterial force that can bind nations and peoples together. To some degree, they both follow Kant in the belief that war, whether the great European conflict at the beginning of the nineteenth century or later wars for national independence, might finally steer humanity toward a cosmopolitan future: "All wars are accordingly so many attempts (not indeed by the intention of men, but by the intention of nature) to bring about new relations between states, and, by the destruction or at least the dismemberment of old entities, to create new ones."[82] As *The Dynasts* conveys through its form and content, cosmopolitanism was all about gaining the right critical vantage point on oneself and on the world at large.

Together, the chapters that follow seek to rechart Victorian poetics, establishing the importance of the encounter with Europe to poets across the period, from Arnold to Hardy. Each author affirms that poetry must cross borders and conceive cosmopolitanism in ways not being realized in the political realm or in the culture at large. *"Europe wants to be one,"* Friedrich Nietzsche would insist in *Beyond Good and Evil* (1886): "The mysterious labour in the souls of all the more profound and far-reaching people of this century has actually been focused on preparing the path to this new *synthesis* and on experimentally anticipating the Europeans of the future."[83] For many Victorian poets, as for Nietzsche, Europe was always about the future, something that would emerge out of this mysterious soul work in which poetry must play a vital role. From our own perspective in the early twenty-first century, as readers of these poets, Europe served them just as crucially as the testing ground for debating questions not just of international politics, but of religion, economics, sexuality, and gender that still confront us. By examining their efforts, I hope to reveal the important position Victorian poetry holds in understanding the ongoing British effort to define its place in Europe and in the wider world. At the same time, I hope to revise our understanding of poetry itself, showing its flexibility and adaptiveness to international contexts—its promise as a discourse of critical cosmopolitanism.

2

Letter from Europe

The Epistolary Interventions of Clough's
Amours de Voyage

My dear Stanley

Ichabod, Ichabod, the glory is departed. Liberty, Equality, and Fraternity, driven back by shopkeeping bayonet, hides her red cap in dingiest St. Antoine.

—*Clough to Arthur Penrhyn Stanley, Paris, May 19, 1848 (1:207)*

Paris is tranquil and dull: the bourgeoisie, which had at first awkwardly shuffled on the blouse, is gradually taking heart to slip on its fine clothes again and perhaps ere long will unbutton the breeches pocket.

—*Clough to Richard William Church. Paris, May 30, 1848 (1:212–13)*

St. Peters disappoints me: the stone of which it is made is a poor plastery material. And indeed Rome in general might be called a *rubbishy* place; the Roman antiquities *in general* seem to me only interesting as antiquities—not for any beauty. The Arch of Titus (sculptured on which you see the triumphal procession of Titus with the golden candlestick from Jerusalem—this, the guidebook informs me, being the original from which all representations of that said candlestick are taken) is I could almost say the only one really beautiful relic, that I have yet seen.

—*Clough to his mother, Ann Perfect Clough. Rome, April 18, 1849 (1:252)*

My dear Annie

Perhaps it will amuse you hereafter to have a letter commenced while guns are firing and, I suppose, men falling, dead and wounded. Such is the case on the other side the Tiber while I peacefully write in my distant chamber with only the sound in my ears.

—*Clough to his sister, Anne Clough. Rome, April 30, 1849 (1:253)*

I found a crowd assembled about 9 p m at the north-east corner of the Piazza Colonna, watching these pretty fireworks—Ecco un altro!—One first saw the 'lightning'—over the Post Office, then came the missive itself, describing its tranquil parabola, then the distant report of the mortar, and finally the near explosion, which occasionally took place in the air. This went on all night.

—*Clough to Francis Turner Palgrave. Rome, June 28, 1849 (1:262–63)*[1]

CLOUGH'S ENCOUNTER with Europe was as much an encounter with the post office, and I begin with these passages to convey a broad sense of the kind of Anglo-European space he was crafting for himself—and the role he was performing for recipients back home. Between May 1848 and August 1849, he would spend a total of seven months on the Continent: first in postrevolutionary Paris and then in Italy, as Mazzini's short-lived Roman Republic confronted troops sent by the new French government on behalf of the Papal States. This second journey begat another, more singular kind of postal performance: the "Epistolary Comi-Tragedy" (2:540) Clough called *Amours de Voyage*.[2] Epistolary poetry had its precedents, of course, but these were not epistles in the manner of Horace or Alexander Pope. The poem consists primarily of letters sent from Clough's alter-ego Claude to his friend Eustace in London.[3] Claude reflects at length on politics, religion, and culture while also weighing his possible attraction to another British tourist, Mary Trevellyn, whose own letters, along with those of her sister Georgina, make up the rest of the poem. Apart from the hexameter form it shares with Horace, *Amours de Voyage* was altogether new and "thoroughly contemporary," as one critic later described it.[4] With numerous interjections, asides, abbreviations, and even P.S.es, Clough took the already informal nature of the epistolary poem to a new level, making it almost comically "unpoetical." All that was missing to complete the illusion of reality were address flaps and postmarks, and a number of passages in the poem do in fact echo comments from Clough's own letters to his family and friends. Claude and Clough both find Rome "*rubbishy*" (1.20), for instance.[5]

With *Amours de Voyage,* Clough thus ventures into the broader cultural and ideological implications of what would seem to be a rather routine and uninteresting fact of daily existence, especially for the traveler—posting a letter.[6] But to be on the spot in Europe was to engage in a kind of postal intervention: to establish lines of communication back home, to discourse on events seen firsthand, and, as often seems the case, to take issue with other travel texts, whether guidebooks—the ubiquitous Murray—or the reports of foreign correspondents in newspapers. The traveling, cosmopolitan self comes into existence only after entry into this postal nexus—after being inscribed and repackaged for perusal back home. As an epistolary, posted poem, *Amours de Voyage* both embodies and resists nineteenth-century distance-closing technologies and the great "coming together" that were supposed to ensue in their wake. At the same time, the poem foregrounds some basic questions about cosmopolitanism, asking what it means to connect to others as friends, lovers, members of churches, citizens of nations, and citizens of modern Europe. Two of the poem's key words, as we will see, are *affinity*—Claude's difficult ideal of genuine togetherness—and *juxtaposition,* the merely being side by side that characterizes the random associations of modern mass culture, which brings people together through the speed and efficiency of its postal and transportation networks. *Amours de Voyage* thus espouses what could be called a cosmopolitanism of negation: one that deconstructs false or specious connections—but one that also endeavors to craft modes of affinity *out of* juxtaposition. By means of this new and "thoroughly contemporary" kind of poetic discourse, Clough would attempt to deliver, finally, what the highly touted post of his day could not.

FOR PRINCE ALBERT, as we saw in chapter 1, this exciting new ability to communicate ideas with the "power of lightning" was one of the key factors contributing in his age to the coming "unity of mankind." While he no doubt had the telegraph primarily in mind, the European-wide reform and modernization of the postal service was just as often invoked in reflections on progress.[7] Thirty years after Albert, for example, Nietzsche speculated that a new race entirely, "European man," would soon emerge thanks in part to commerce and industry but also, next in importance, to "the post and the book-trade."[8] Such sentiments were even more common in Great Britain in the decade that followed the implementation of penny postage in January 1839, along with other standardizations that created the postal system as we recognize it today—with self-adhesive stamps, regular addresses, and set times of delivery. The mail indeed now seemed to move with something like the power of lighting, as Elizabeth Barrett remarked in an 1843 letter chastising her American correspondent, Cornelius Mathews, for his country's failure to adopt the same cost-saving reforms:

> Why will you not as a nation, embrace our great Penny Postage scheme & hold our envelopes in all acceptation? You do not know—cannot guess what a wonderful liberty our Rowland Hill has given to British spirits,—& how we "flash a thought" instead of 'wafting' it from our extreme south to our extreme north, paying "a penny for our thought" & for the electricity included—I recommend you our Penny Postage as the most successful revolution since the "glorious three days" of Paris.[9]

Barrett's analogy to a revolution-in-waiting alludes, partly tongue-in-cheek, to the kind of wide-eyed progressivism that surrounded postal reform at the time.[10] Only partly, however. To mail a letter overseas was, in some sense, to participate in a new kind of global, democratic citizenship. Hill's *Post Office Reform: Its Importance and Practicability* (1837) had promised that the penny post would "benefit all sects in politics and religion; and all classes, from the highest to the lowest," who would now be given "the means of communication with their distant friends and relatives, from which they are at present debarred."[11] After surveying the success of these reforms in 1850, *Fraser's Magazine* concluded that there was no better indicator of the "progress of our civilization" than the "great metropolitan heart of communication with the whole world," the central London Post Office.[12] As if to make this point on a smaller if still vaguely revolutionary scale, Clough notes in one letter that the Chartists' petition had been forwarded to him in Paris about a month after their ill-fated march on London—although he seemed deflated at having to pay 3 francs postage due (1:211).[13]

France, in fact, would adopt prepaid postage several months after Clough received the petition—at the behest, fittingly, of the new liberal-minded French government that had otherwise largely disappointed him. Well before then, however, the European postal service—through which Clough's (and Claude's) letters would have passed—was still highly regarded, especially in France. In fact, one of the arguments advanced on behalf of penny postage, as postal historian Howard Robinson reveals, was that it would prevent the British postal service from falling behind its more innovative French counterpart.[14] Although typically singled out by British travelers for lacking modern efficiencies, Italy was still part of this larger system. Murray's *Handbook for Travellers in Central Italy* (1843), for instance, gives no indication that unusual precautions needed to be taken when sending and receiving mail from Rome or to expect long delays.[15] Even during the period of social unrest covered by the poem and Clough's visit, there is little sense of serious threat to the stream of postal correspondence. Those delays that did occur were due more to Clough's own uncertain movements from one destination to another rather than a breakdown in the system. At one point, he complains of a "stupid banker" who neglected to forward letters to him in Florence (1:270). He also mentions a letter "sent by private hand" to his sister that may have miscarried: "However it was very short and no great loss" (1:257).[16]

If Clough personally never indulged in the more millennial postal rhetoric of some of his contemporaries, he was still fundamentally a creature of the post: someone like him—upper middle class, highly literate, often traveling whether in Britain or in Europe—would be one of its primary beneficiaries. In *Amours de Voyage,* Claude can't do without the post, and this feeling feeds directly into many of the poem's other self-questionings, cautionings, and afterthoughts, its scrutiny of what tended to be dismissed as simply being among the "normal" givens in life. As the poem unfolds and its letters begin to accumulate, the effects of the post on notions of individuality and citizenship become increasingly evident. Identity itself, in essence, becomes "a function of delivery," as cultural theorist Bernard Siegert outlines in *Relays: Literature as an Epoch of the Postal System* (1999).[17] Siegert does much to illuminate why an epistolary poem would have suggested itself to Clough at this particular historical moment. In many ways, it was the perfect literary vehicle for rendering the current state of Europe in all of its political and cultural turmoil—along with his own ambivalent position in its burgeoning networks of communication and mobility. With its promises of democratic empowerment, the mail offered reassurance to people at the same time it served as a way of managing discourse: "The danger emanating from the noise of the people was dispelled as soon as it was intercepted by a network that controlled, redirected, sorted, and calculated it, thus ensuring that its waves were not emitted at unanticipated speeds or in unanticipated directions."[18] Not coincidentally, Siegert's description sounds a lot like the failure of the Chartists' march on London: the threat of violence averted, their demands were nonetheless "delivered" to Parliament (and Clough, postage due, in France). The idea that people "were capable of determining their own affairs postally" became entrenched in a way that benefitted the seats of political and economic power.[19] Postal reform was thus as counterrevolutionary as it was egalitarian—a suspicion *Amours de Voyage* shares and dramatizes through Claude's efforts to establish ironic distance from the conventions of letter writing—to fashion some space of control and textual authority. Like Clough's own personal letters, the poem asks, if cosmopolitanism is based on "conversation" facilitated by a global postal network, what kind of conversation is taking place? Who was speaking and to what ends?

Consider again one of the passages quoted at the opening of this chapter—Clough's speculation on whether his sister Anne will find it "amusing" to receive a letter (reproduced in figure 1) composed in the safety of his hotel while a battle rages just outside the city. On one level, his is a rather routine personal letter meant to reassure a family member that he is safe. However, Clough can't help commenting on how the political struggle going on around him casts this routine correspondence in a new light: he realizes there's something odd about what he's doing. What he discovers, and what *Amours de Voyage* would scrutinize more closely, is how the protection afforded him as a British subject with the means to travel overlaps with his role as correspondent. The letter, as Siegert states, had become fetishized as the "private space of bourgeois freedom," and Clough inadvertently participates in a celebration of that freedom.[20] The postal system promised a kind of mystical fellowship between safe and fully self-actuated individuals. *Fraser's* captures something of this feeling when it marvels that "the thoughts of lawyers, lovers, and merchants . . . lie side by side, enjoying inviolable secrecy" at the London Post Office.[21] The letter provides the illusion of dialogue across distances, between England and Italy, and across classes. The post could even do its part to close the gender gap—or so it seemed—delivering Anne the sense of proxy citizenship Victorian culture afforded women as sympathetic listeners to the men of their domestic circle (a citizenship, incidentally, she would lay claim to more directly later in life, when she became actively involved in the cause of women's rights and higher education). *Amours de Voyage,* as we will see, also captures how the letter determines and diffuses political action by dispatching it into a postal network. By composing an epistolary *poem,* Clough put the post in a new context, turning it into a literary performance that allowed it to be seen, in some sense, for the first time.

More broadly, Clough strategically positions *Amours de Voyage* within Victorian networks of communication and social mobility—forms of what social scientist David Singh Grewal describes, in fact, as "network power" in his recent account of the history of globalization and how it manifests itself in everyday experience. By network power, Grewal does not just mean online networks or other international systems of commerce or communication, but, for instance, the English language and other "languages, points of reference, customs, rules, laws and regulations—that must follow the compression of space for the creation of a global society."[22] As Grewal emphasizes—and as students of nineteenth-century culture already well know—it is incorrect to assume that these forms of power only began to take shape in the twentieth

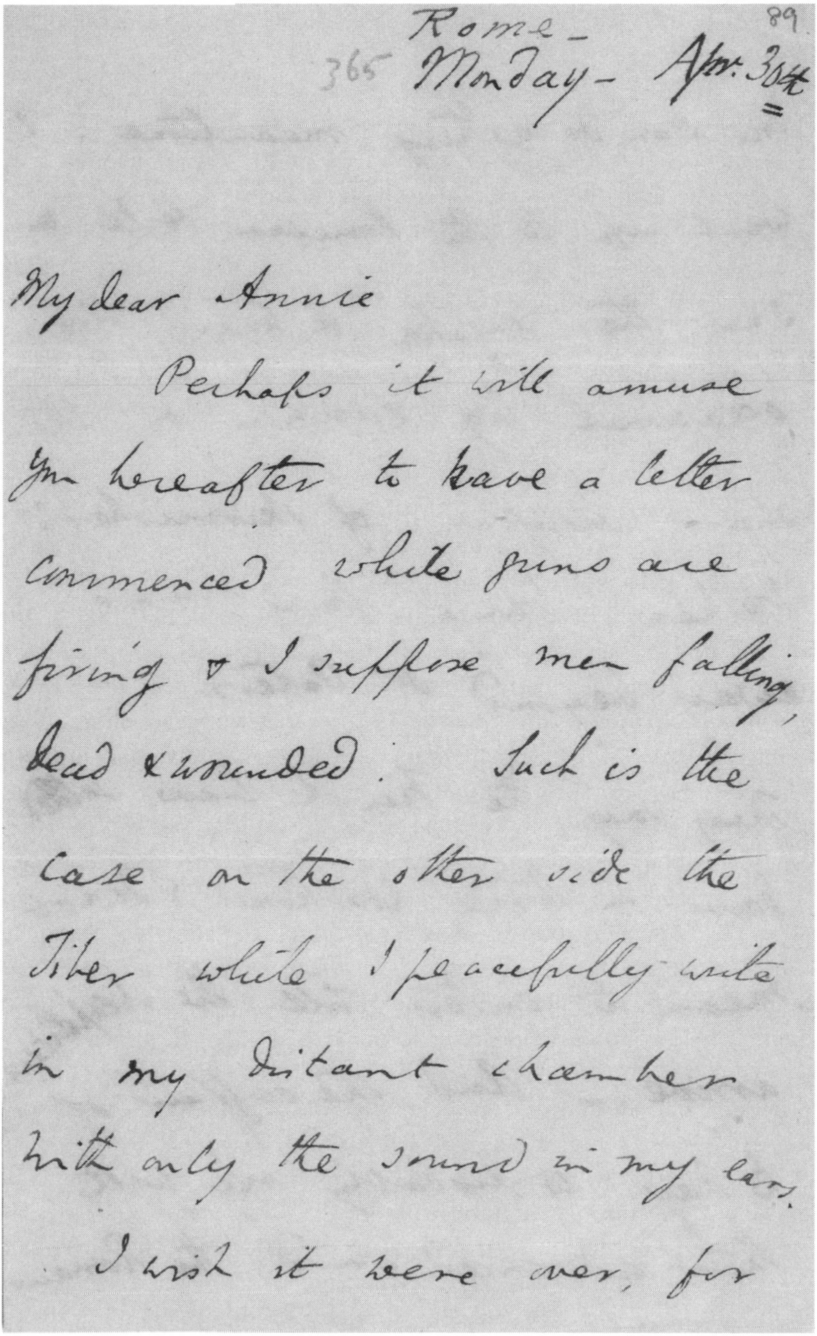

Rome –
365 Monday – Apr. 30th

89.

My dear Annie

Perhaps it will amuse
you hereafter to have a letter
commenced while guns are
firing & I suppose men falling,
dead & wounded. Such is the
case on the other side the
Tiber while I peacefully write
in my distant chamber
with only the sound in my ears.
I wish it were over, for

Figure 1 Letter from Clough to his sister Anne, Rome, April 30, 1849 (courtesy The Bodleian Libraries, University of Oxford [MS. Eng. Lett. D. 176, fol. 89r]).

century.[23] Thomas Babington Macaulay, for instance, boasts in *The History of England* (1848),

> Of all inventions, the alphabet and the printing press alone excepted, those inventions which abridge distance have done most for the civilisation of our species. Every improvement of the means of locomotion benefits mankind morally and intellectually as well as materially, and not only facilitates the interchange of the various productions of nature and art, but tends to remove national and provincial antipathies, and to bind together all the branches of the great human family. In the seventeenth century the inhabitants of London were, for almost every practical purpose, farther from Reading than they now are from Edinburgh, and farther from Edinburgh than they now are from Vienna.[24]

Amours de Voyage concerns itself with what Macaulay misses here—the exercise of cultural *power*—when he presents these changes as an essentially apolitical, natural advance promoting familial bonds of friendship and understanding. As a means of communicating and bridging gaps, the postal system provided the same kind of quasi-revolutionary progress claimed on behalf of transportation technologies. In Clough's epistolary travel poem, the post and other means of cultural "mobility" begin to overlap with each other, doing as much to restrict as to facilitate border-crossing and individual autonomy and expression. Claude seems to ask continuously, how much control can I really exercise with respect to my movements, my associations, and my affinities? How willing am I to enter into these networks, speak their languages, and play by their norms? These are the familiar questions raised by globalization in the twenty-first century as well, as Grewal explains: "we clamor for connection to one another using standards that are offered up for universal use. Yet, while we may all come to share these new global standards—to the extent, at least, that we desire access to the activities that they mediate—we may not all have much influence over their establishment in the first place."[25] Likewise, Victorian network power of the kind Macaulay describes works mostly to advance those nations and classes already positioned to take advantage of it: their ideas, their goods, and themselves—as passengers, as tourists—flow freely through its infrastructure and interfaces. Claude's Grand Tour of Europe becomes one of ambivalent entree into globalizing forms of network power and the affiliations they demand.

This dilemma is enacted socially through Claude's encounter with the middle-class Trevellyns, who seem fully integrated into the technologies and discourses of network power. The postal network of the poem, in some sense, belongs to them, associated as it is with liberal notions of progress and the facilitation of trade, as do the biased English newspapers Claude detests: hence the Trevellyns' antipathy toward "this dreadful Mazzini" (2.230) and fear of "republican terrors" (2.318). Their letters, such as those sent by Mary's sister Georgina, are the most "letterly" and display the ease with which they adapt to the norms of the genre:

> Dearest Louisa,—Inquire, if you please, about Mr. Claude—.
> He has been once at R., and remembers meeting the H.'s.
> Harriet L., perhaps, may be able to tell you about him.
> It is an awkward youth, but still with very good manners;
> Not without prospects, we hear; and, George says, highly connected.
> Georgy declares it absurd, but Mamma is alarmed and insists he has
> Taken up strange opinions and may be turning a Papist. (1.253–59)

Whereas Claude's letters, as we will see, show some self-reflexive creativity, becoming meta-letters of a sort, the Trevellyns' remain more systematic and predictable. The way the salutation in this passage fits neatly into the dactylic rhythm of the line comically underscores this rigidity, as would similar phrases later in the poem, like "Dearest Miss Roper" (3.98) or "here is your letter arrived this moment" (3.247). The extensive use of postscripts— as many as four per letter at one point—is another hyper-postal feature of their correspondence and one of the few jokes Clough's friend Thomas Shairp seemed to enjoy in a poem that otherwise disappointed him: "Post. No. 2. You see I have caught infection from Mary Trevellyan's P.S.S." (1:276).[26]

The Trevellyns' adherence to these letterly conventions seems of a piece with their strict observation of the other social forms expected of them. Claude notes at one point how the mother "[q]uotes, which I hate, Childe Harold" (1.209), a subtle reference to Byron's ubiquitous and mostly sanitized presence in Murray's guidebook.[27] As Georgina's remarks above reveal, travel merely extends the social networks they left behind in England and within which they attempt to place Claude. She sizes him up as a potential mate for Mary, assessing how well he conforms to set patterns of Protestant, middle-class, masculine English identity. As far as the Trevellyns are concerned, Claude is on the margins of good society—polite but awkward, with good connections, but indifferent to those connections. Claude sends the Trevellyns mixed signals about his interest in Mary, conveying, as I will argue, some confusion and denial about his own national and class identity. "What can the man be intending?" (2.232), Georgina asks at one point. Claude wants to be able to "opt out" of these class-bound social and discursive networks but also recognizes the power and protection they afford him—as, for instance—when he realizes that the otherwise embarrassing Murray keeps him safe from angry mobs who might mistake him for a priest: "I was in black myself, and didn't know what mightn't happen" (2.193). As for Clough in real life, to opt out of these secure networks involved risk; he was to forego reliable means of professional and economic advancement. The Thirty-Nine Articles of Anglican faith, which Clough refused to swear to in order to keep his fellowship at Oriel College, were not just a system of belief but something that granted one access to power. From this regard, Claude's snobbery toward the Trevellyns—"bankers very likely, not wholly / Pure of the taint of the shop" (1.125–26)—is as much a kind of defense mechanism as anything else. He is right to view them with suspicion, for they embody an unsettling expansion of British cultural and commercial power. The question then becomes how closely he will identify himself with the Trevellyns— and whether he has any real choice in the matter. Later in the poem, Claude must decide whether he will join their party and follow them—as a traveling companion and as a potential husband for Mary, who, we will see, shows her own signs of wanting to break free of the networks that restrict her.

AMOURS DE VOYAGE opens not with Claude's first letter, but with the first of ten elegiacs that begin and close each of the poem's five cantos. The "author" of these more melodious, classically intoned parts of the poem is never clearly specified, although it seems Clough may have intended us to imagine that these were Claude's own attempts at a more traditional kind of Grand Tour poetry, or moments when Clough's voice and "Claude's" merge to take on a wider, more omniscient point of view. If distinct along these lines from the poem's letters, the elegiacs nonetheless engage them in ways that are key to understanding what makes the poem as a whole so revolutionary from a formal angle. The elegiacs are the poem's "envelope" in a sense, posing questions about Claude's direction and purpose, as at the beginning of Canto IV: "*Eastward, or Northward, or West?*" (4.1). Similarly, the opening elegiac for the last canto asks, "*are we to turn to / England, which may after all be for its children the best?*" (5.7–8). In the following passage taken from the beginning of the poem, Clough lays out some broader conceptual and spatial possibilities for Claude:

> *Come, let us go; though withal a voice whisper, 'The world that we live in,*
> *Whithersoever we turn, still is the same narrow crib;*
> *'Tis but to prove limitation, and measure a cord, that we travel;*

Let who would 'scape and be free go to his chamber and think;
 'Tis but to change idle fancies for memories wilfully falser;
  'Tis but to go and have been.'—Come, little bark, let us go! (1.5–10)

Culturally, what is at stake in *Amours de Voyage* could not be stated more directly: Clough queries whether cosmopolitanism can be conceived at all through travel and rerendering the experience in poetry. At the beginning of Canto 2, the poem asks more directly what connections exist between pilgrim, place, and history: *"Is it illusion? Or does there a spirit from perfecter ages, / Here, even yet, amid loss, change, and corruption, abide?"* (2.1–2). Clough could not raise this question without invoking Romantic precedents such as Samuel Rogers or Byron, whose presence was never very far away thanks to quotations in Murray's Italian travel guides. The elegiacs *sound* like Rogers or Murray's sanitized Byron, but they pose a different, more persistent set of questions than these forbears, leaving the impression of a modern poet trying vainly to assume a more antiquated point of view. At one point, for instance, this modern voice breaks through, with Claude chastising himself for perhaps being just another *"dullard and dunce"* come south *"to pry and to stare"* (2.10). Visually, the elegiacs' italic type-setting, along with the second line indentation, help to create a more cosmetically "poetic" kind of stanza: they are Italy as *italics,* a fanciful idea of Italy, as if Clough were quoting some voice otherwise foreign to the language of the poem. The elegiacs thus map one kind of Europe, the letters another—a more confusing, accelerated Europe of steamers, trains, newspapers, and posts.

With its opening salutation, "Dear Eustacio," Claude gives some indication of how he will answer the questions posed in the elegiac opening about his overall purpose in Italy. He writes mainly to be *"en rapport"*—that is—to have an audience (1.11–12). Like the quasi-Italian persona he creates for his receiver, Clough will perform a highly self-conscious parody of the Englishman abroad and the travel letter as a genre. He complains, for instance, about "the weather, which truly is horrid," but notes thankfully that Rome "is other than London" and allows one to be "rid, at least for a time of / All one's friends and relations." Then, three lines later, he admits, "Yet, in despite of all, we turn like fools to the English" (1.15; 27; 28–29; 32). Claude thrives in his epistolary guise and is full of sharp, critical observations often directed at himself. Even the mostly critical Arnold, as we will see, conceded that there was a high degree of "vigour and abundance" in Claude.[28] Like the salutation quoted above, the closings and signatures to Claude's letters provide him with additional opportunities for self-parody. Later, sharing with Eustace his doubts about whether he has the courage to "lay down [his] life for the

British female" (2.66), he closes with the remark, "And is all this, my friend, but a weak and ignoble refining, / Wholly unworthy the head or the heart of Your Own Correspondent?" (2.93–94).

Claude's letters also reveal how the poem's dactylic hexameters, counted by stress rather than by syllable, work in tandem with its epistolarity. Clough confines Claude metrically but gives him the freedom to play within the form—the line quoted above being a good example—where Claude slips into a more uniform dactylic rhythm to underscore the restraint he is under as a mere "correspondent." As Erik Gray contends, the English hexameter by its very nature is an awkward hybrid of the colloquial and the highly artificial: "The reader is conscious of a sophisticated but anachronistic rhythm overlaid upon the idiomatic vernacular of Clough's modern-day travelers."[29] Shairp complained that, as a result, the poem "has always a feeling of parody" (1:277), although this seems precisely the tone Clough aims for. *Amours de Voyage* is ironic where it *should* be assertive. One does not so much "get somewhere" as fulfill the need to finish the "unnaturally" long line for English verse: "As for Hope,—to-morrow I hope to be starting for Naples" (5.203). The persistent interjections and "oaths" also add to this impression, as if Claude can't help interrupting himself rather than progress smoothly toward a conclusion.[30] Claude seems constantly on guard against his own observations and unsure of his footing. The poem's epistolarity and hexameter rhythm underscore just how much his discursive movements, like his physical ones, seem regimented and subject to some unseen but persistent control—networks that guide and direct the "individuals" within them but also invite resistance and agitation.

Claude conveys some of this resistance through his satirical treatment of the conventional, sunny travel letters of the period that cast Rome as the fountainhead of an orderly, progressive European civilization. "Rome is a wonderful place" (1.56), Georgina Trevellyn concludes, while Claude proceeds more to dismantle what he sees before him. Rome's ruins and its cathedrals, for instance, speak to how religion serves mostly as a vehicle for roughly asserting the most aggressive of national tendencies. Rome has been the site of one theological Gothic invasion after another: "No, the Christian faith, as I, at least, understood it, / Is not here, O Rome, in any of these thy churches" (1.70–71), Claude remarks, later citing the "infinite gauds and gewgaws" forced on churches by "the barbarian will of the rigid and ignorant Spaniard" (1.79, 82). While his comments are typical, perhaps, of offended Protestantism, Claude is just as quick to question his own preprogrammed, cultural default positions. Having set the contemporary reader up for the inevitable praise of Northern European progress and wisdom, he instead undercuts this assumption in the next letter: "Luther, they say, was unwise; like a half-taught German, he could not / See that old follies were passing most tranquilly out of remembrance; / Leo the Tenth was employing all efforts to clear out abuses" (1.87–89). Luther "must forsooth make a fuss and distend his huge Wittenburg lungs, and / Bring back Theology once yet again in a flood upon Europe" (1.93–94). Protestantism, then, was not a great advance but at best a disruption of more measured reforms, although Claude's somewhat breezy claims on behalf of Leo X seem deliberately overstated. His point, however, is that the whole debate finally falls back upon one's religious and national prejudices. Theology becomes a source of humor as much as anything else in the poem, and the most one can accomplish by revisiting its controversies as a traveler and correspondent is to play along. After taking on Luther, Claude returns to the Spanish in an attack loaded with his signature "oaths," conveying a mock outrage that again subtly suggests the whole debate is simply a kind of discursive performance for him:

> Luther was foolish,—but, O great God! What call you Ignatius?
> O my tolerant soul, be still! But you talk of barbarians,
> Alaric, Attila, Genseric;—why they came, they killed, they
> Ravaged, and went on their way; but these vile tyrannous Spaniards,
> These are here still,—how long, O ye Heavens, in the country of Dante?
> These, that fanaticized Europe, which now can forget them, release not
> This, their choicest of prey, this Italy. (1.102–8)

Different nationalities assert their authority over Italy in a system of alternating hegemonies. At present, "Europe" is a longing, an absence only. "Utter, O some one, the word that shall reconcile Ancient and Modern!" (1.200), Claude declares, but, in the meantime, he can offer only a hardened, irreverent sort of critical scrutiny that questions affiliations religious, national, and international.

Unable to reconcile ancient and modern, Claude, at Eustace's request, next dwells on the current state of Roman politics: "What do the people say, and what does the government do?—you / Ask" (2.13–14). Claude answers that Rome's struggle is shaped by the same complex, competing national interests that have always played themselves out in Italy: how else could one account for Republican France's support for the Pope? And while Eustace grants him a certain authority for being there on the spot, Claude proceeds to undercut that authority, emphasizing how his need to keep himself safe compromises his perception. Overlooking a battle off in the distance, a group of tourists, like their countries of origin, merely stand side by side, their conversation characterized as much by the weather as politics: at "Twelve o'clock, on the Pincian Hill, with lots of English, / Germans, Americans, French,— the Frenchmen, too, are protected,— / So we stand in the sun, but afraid of a probable shower" (2.113–15). Claude also makes a subtle class commentary, noting that even as the French are besieging Rome, its citizens with the means to travel are granted immunity, as if the battle is not really theirs. The lack of anything like interaction or fellow-feeling among tourists mirrors the political restraint of their nations of origin. Not sparing himself, Claude, in his account of what he does after the battle, draws attention to the ways national and class affiliations seem to override all other considerations:

> Down I go, and pass through the quiet streets with the knots of
> National Guards patrolling, and flags hanging out at the windows,
> English, American, Danish,—and, after offering to help an
> Irish family moving *en masse* to the Maison Serny,
> After endeavoring idly to minister balm to the trembling
> Quinquagenarian fears of two lone British spinsters,
> Go to make sure of my dinner before the enemy enter.
> But by this there are signs of stragglers returning; and voices
> Talk, though you don't believe it, of guns and prisoners taken;
> And on the walls you read the first bulletin of the morning.—
> This is all that I saw, and all I know of the battle. (2.134–44)

Like these other travelers, Claude flies his flag of neutrality and self-sovereignty, all the while enjoying the protection British citizenship affords him and reserving the right to distance himself from the actions—or nonactions— of his government.[31] His earlier criticism of England for not intervening more actively on Italy's behalf now rings hollow: "my stupid old England,— / You, who a twelvemonth ago said nations must choose for themselves, you / Could not, of course, interfere,—you now, when a nation has chosen" (2.23– 25). Like the British Foreign Office, Claude reveals that as an English citizen he just watches, intervening only to assist fellow British citizens when necessary, whose fears he dismisses as exaggerated. All along, Claude's contact with actual Italians has been minimal and revolves mostly around food: whether making dinner arrangements or asking for milk in his coffee only to be told, "*Non c'è latte*" due to the siege (2.100).

Claude thus seeks refuge in a kind of discursive, postal existence, one he knows offers self-insight but is impotent as a means of engagement outside of that system. His most important aim, it seems, is to reveal just how impotent he is, as during the scene when he comes the closest to actually participating in the Roman conflict. Claude excitedly writes, "So I have seen a man killed!," although he immediately begins to diminish his own reliability, "a man was killed, I am told, in a place where I saw / Something; a man was killed, I am told, and I saw something. / I was returning home from St. Peter's; Murray, as usual, / Under my arm" (2.162; 165–68). In truth, Claude mocks his own desperate search for some relevant role to play beyond his consumption of art at St. Peter's, the reference to Murray reinforcing the idea that the murder for him is simply another "sight" to be seen. He tells Eustace, "You are the first, do you know, to whom I have mentioned the matter. / Whom should I tell it to, else?—these girls?—the Heavens forbid it!— / Quidnuncs at Monaldini's?—idlers upon the Pincian?" (2.198–200). Claude raises the problem of whom to address his comments to outside of other English tourists hanging out on the streets of Rome or in reading-rooms. He has no reason to speak to the Roman authorities, for Murray has provided all the protection he needs. Overall, the scene brilliantly illustrates the illusion of engaged citizenship offered by the post. By the end of the letter, Claude returns entirely to guide-book speak, noting how Murray directs his movements for the remainder of the day: "So by the narrow streets to the Ponte Rotto, and onwards / Thence, by the Temple of Vesta, away to the great Coliseum, / Which at the full of the moon is an object worthy a visit" (2.214–16). The letter thus fittingly ends with the mechanical reproduction of travel discourse. Claude has been fully situated and contained by textual systems—guidebooks, newspapers, and the post. Writing letters merely offers the frustrating simulation of participation and dialogue with authority, like his attempts to correct the misimpressions left by newspapers: "I / Gnash my teeth when I look in your French or your English papers, / What is the good of that?" (3.61–63).[32]

Despite Claude's realization of the limits of cosmopolitan engagement and his disavowal of the fruits of political activism, he remains troubled by the isolation that presents itself as the only alternative. Claude continues to seek affinities and continues to post letters. Earlier, he had wondered whether human beings are essentially solitary creatures, like so many limpets cling-ing to rocks: "we open our shells to imbibe our / Nourishment, close them again, and are safe, fulfilling the purpose / Nature intended" (2.43–45). This is an entirely plausible conclusion to reach after Claude has tested and found wanting nearly every circle of community branching out from the self, including his religion, nationality, and internationality—his potential investment in Italy's struggle. Right to the end of the poem, he emphatically declares, "Politics farewell, however! For what could I do? with inquiring, / Talking, collating the journals, go fever my brain about things o'er / Which I can have no control" (5.188–90). These repeated disavowals, however, as

Stephanie Kuduk Weiner suggests, point as much to Claude's disillusioned republicanism, and how much the failure of his ideals truly stings him.[33] This continued longing to connect meaningfully to others is what fuels the amours in *Amours de Voyage.*

John Goode's 1971 essay "1848 and the Strange Disease of Modern Love" perhaps remains the most insightful inquiry into how love and politics intersect for Clough, beginning with *The Bothie of Tober-na-Voulich* (1848). For Clough and other disillusioned radicals in his circle like Tom Arnold, "Love is the life of life because it is what brings us to the unity of the universe. In a society based on division, love is cursed, distorted into the dualistic laws of the world. Love and revolution are thus brought together—their fates are bound up."[34] Goode argues that *The Bothie* corrects for these divisions of class (and nation) with the successful love affair of a Scottish peasant girl and an Oxford undergraduate who meet each other while the latter is on vacation: "The poem celebrates the possibility of love, and defines its relationship to the contemporary social structure. Precisely because it is such an affirmative poem about love, and love cannot merely be seen as a relief or escape from the social structure, it necessarily becomes a radical critique of society and a vision of the possibilities of historical change."[35] In some sense, Clough raises the stakes in *Amours de Voyage:* the setting is a good deal less pastoral and familiar culturally than *The Bothie,* and Clough resists the too-easy revolutionary symbolism that would come with Claude falling in love with, say, an Italian peasant girl—which is not as farfetched a possibility as it might seem. Browning in effect does as much in *Pippa Passes*—marrying his own hopes of a cosmopolitan, politically charged poetics to the moral symbolic authority he invests in Pippa. *Amours de Voyage* asks if love can survive the voyage between members of the same culture and roughly the same class and still be *love*—transcendent and revolutionary in its denial of its own apparent self-interest, whether economic or sexual—a love that is "its own inspiration" (2.278). There is something that draws people together, and Clough wants to understand what this force is with the same acuity he applies to his investigation of what keeps people, and nations, apart.

Early in the poem, Claude reveals to Eustace that he finds himself attracted to Mary for reasons that he hopes are not delusional or "factitious," his preferred term for affinities based not on truth but on "[s]ome malpractice of heart and illegitimate process" (2.271–72). He wants to distill his attraction to her, if possible, from physical beauty alone and from mere chance or convenience of location. "I am in love, you declare," he writes to Eustace. "I think not so; yet I grant you / It is a pleasure, indeed, to converse with this girl. Oh, rare gift, / Rare felicity, this! she can talk in a rational way, can / Speak upon subjects that really are matters of mind and of thinking, / Yet in perfection retain her simplicity" (2.252–56). Claude's assessment here is obviously sexist in its insistence that Mary show learning beyond most Victorian women yet that she still be safely "feminine." His sexism, in fact, was even stronger in earlier versions of the poem. For the final version, Clough chose to omit the lines, "Never, however you tempt her, however you urge it, consents to / Unsex herself, and come out as a Lady Macbeth of letters."[36] This could, however, be a case where Clough's and Claude's opinions part ways. Later Clough raises the possibility that Claude may be underestimating the very intelligence and independence of thought he values in Mary merely because she is a woman. Her letters indicate she is more willing than he realizes to break free from convention and attach herself to the uncertain social commodity he represents. Chauvinistic as they are, Claude's comments nonetheless reveal a genuine feeling that he and Mary can communicate beyond the kinds of "small talk" expected of young people at the time. There is a complex flirtation going on between them even as their movements and conversation seem closely monitored by others traveling with Mary. In some small way, they have managed to break free of the pattern of imposed discourse that characterizes so much of the poem.

The uncertain way they both describe their interest in each other also argues against its factitiousness. From the beginning they seem willing to honestly confront their reservations about each other. Mary, for instance, says tepidly of Claude after first meeting him, "I do not like him much, though I do not dislike being with him" (1.268). Later, she says, "he rather repels me. / There! I think him agreeable, but also a little repulsive" (2.329–30). Mary also seems well attuned to Claude's confused attitudes toward women—that they be intelligent but not threateningly so—and that he expects people in general to meet him *more* than half way. She understands that the high value he places on genuine affinity will perhaps keep him from fully embracing any kind of relationship:

Was it to you I made use of the word? or who was it told you?
Yes, repulsive; observe, it is but when he talks of ideas,
That he is quite unaffected, and free, and expansive, and easy;
I could pronounce him simply a cold intellectual being.—
When does he make advances?—He thinks that women should woo him;
Yet, if a girl should do so, would be but alarmed and disgusted.
She that should love him must look for small love in return . . . (3.31–37)

As Mary confesses here, there's clearly something striking about Claude that promises to expand her own intellectual and social horizons. She juxtaposes him, for instance, with Georgina's more conventional suitor, George Vernon, whom she says "has a very fair right to be jealous" of Claude (1.267). Mary's letters always convey a sense of just how restrictive that social world can be—how her attraction to Claude must be preaddressed through the people she is with, in a sense. Later, after interference by her sister and George, Mary can reach Claude only by asking her correspondent Miss Roper to act on her behalf. What Mary and Claude need to be able to do, ideally, is address each other outside of the social structures that shape the poem. Until that point, their interactions will always be characterized by uncertainty and miscommunication. Claude is never able to shake the feeling that he does not see her and his attraction to her for what it *really* is, whatever that truth may be.

Claude's romantic and political dilemmas come down to a fundamental question of human relations that he debates with Eustace, whose opinions he reconveys second-hand to the reader. Put simply, Claude's fear is that nobody really knows anybody else. It is a reflection in some ways of what Raymond Williams termed the "crisis of the knowable community": the sense of individual alienation growing out of the social displacement caused by nineteenth-century industrial capitalism and urban expansion.[37] Clough, in fact, had a long-standing suspicion of the extravagant promises made on behalf of border-crossing free trade, one expressed as early as 1840 in an essay composed while he was a student at Balliol. "The claims of Commerce have been triumphantly established, as one great and principal glory of European Civilisation," Clough conceded. However, anticipating Marx and Engels to some extent in the *Communist Manifesto,* he worried that commerce "carries away with it gradually every vestige of local attachments."[38] *Amours de Voyage* would make the same connection between the conditions of modern mass culture—with its trains and steamers—and the sense that one daily has more contact with people but remains, paradoxically, even more isolated. The modern world is one of masses of people *juxtaposed* with one another, with nothing drawing them together other than chance:

> Juxtaposition, in fine; and what is juxtaposition?
> Look you, we travel along in the railway-carriage, or steamer,
> And, *pour passer le temps,* till the tedious journey be ended,
> Lay aside paper or book, to talk with the girl that is next one;
> And, *pour passer le temps,* with the terminus all but in prospect,
> Talk of eternal ties and marriages made in heaven. (3.107–12)

All connections, Claude suggests, are a kind of invention, a pattern imposed on what is essentially a random redistribution. Is modern love no better, a factitious effort to "make sense of it all," like the book or newspaper he puts aside? Eustace apparently objects to Claude's characterization of modern life as a series of juxtapositions: "Juxtaposition is great,—but, you tell me, affinity greater" (3.151). Affinity, Claude counters, is often simply "familiarity," what seems natural after so much repetition—a connection made "greater and lesser, / Stronger and weaker . . . by the favour of juxtaposition / Potent, efficient, in force,—for a time" (3.152–54).

Claude recognizes a powerful critical purchase to the notion of juxtaposition that Eustace misses, something that underpins Claude's cosmopolitanism of negation. If the modern world has lost a sense of local rootedness, it might yet develop a more open, expansive paradigm in its place.[39] Understanding juxtaposition can lessen the grip of those misleading, sometimes destructive affinities that take the form of rigid certainties—calcified notions of what is "natural" or "normal." If the nationality, class, and religion one is born into are the products of chance, it follows that the high investment one places in these is also ungrounded. Admittedly, this is the kind of cosmopolitanism that critics such as Gertrude Himmelfarb disparage as being lifeless and coldly intellectual: "What cosmopolitanism obscures, even denies, are the givens of life: parents, ancestors, family, race, religion, heritage, history, culture, tradition, community—and nationality. These are not 'accidental' attributes of the individual. They are essential attributes."[40] Himmelfarb's point rings true to the extent that we all recognize the nurturing role of these factors in our lives: to deny them, at the very least, just seems ungrateful. Her criticism nonetheless overlooks the insight that comes when one attempts to suspend those affiliations and view them critically.

Clough seems especially wary of the understanding that religion should form one of those essential givens. "Allah is great, no doubt, and Juxtaposition his prophet" (3.137), Claude remarks, transposing his earlier phrase and hinting at how the will of God can be used to justify the state of relations that chance has brought into effect. For Clough, Christianity was no better than Islam in this respect, a belief he refused to back down from for the sake of his professional advancement. Writing to Edward Hawkins, the Provost of Oriel College and the man to whom Clough would have to submit his resignation later that year, he wondered, "Is Xtianity really so much better than Mohometanism, Buddhism (a more extensive faith) or the old heathen philosophy? Are those virtues and graces, which are our moral and religious tradition, really altogether Christian?" (1:249).[41] The kind of ecumenicism Clough preaches here comes into being only when one questions "the givens of life." Religiously speaking, his questioning may have taken him farther away from those givens than any other poet studied here. While the Brownings, for instance, would agree that religion must serve cosmopolitan ends and not contract itself over questions of dogma, their world church still mostly assumes a Christian outline.

Clough continued to expand on these kinds of ideas in an essay drafted in his 1852–53 Notebook. Making what would prove to be his most explicit connection between cosmopolitan thinking and religious openness, Clough writes, "we cannot refuse to know when we are told it on good authority that there are many more Buddhists in the world than there are Christians.—And it appears to me that it is much more the apparent dispensation of things that we should gradually widen than that we should narrow and individualize our creeds. Why are we daily coming more and more into communication with each other if it be not that we learn each other's knowledge, and combine all into one."[42] What made Christianity special for Hawkins, Clough implies, was not that it was nearer the truth but that it was familiar and, in its Anglican form, safely English. Clough's remarks also serve as a revealing comment on empire: Britain's global expansion is of little progressive use if its goal is simply to spread English ways of thinking or create what would later be christened "Greater Britain" by Charles Dilke. England needed to be equally open to transformation and modulation from the outside. The challenge for the critical cosmopolitan then becomes how to build new affinities or reaffirm old ones that survive this test of exposure and juxtaposition. As Martha Nussbaum has said, cosmopolitanism, "is often a lonely business," one that "offers only reason and the love of humanity."[43] Claude has plenty of the former, but remains uncertain as to where and how to cultivate the latter. It could be, as Himmelfarb insists, that one cannot thrive without resting finally on givens such as nation or race, which history has shown to be stubbornly complex and persistent modes of identification. Fundamentalist brands of religion, likewise, continue to prosper worldwide, often by targeting more ecumenical mainstream sects. Claude wants affinities that aren't factitious, but the risk he takes is that no affinity is "quite sure to be final and perfect" (3.156). The poem provides no easy answer to his dilemma.

Aligning Claude with Mary seems one way out, but Clough finally denies him this possibility. What to make of this denial is the poem's ultimate interpretive problem, one that Clough, in some sense, simply drops into the reader's lap. As I have already argued, the poem provides enough evidence to suggest that they share some kind of affinity, and nothing really happens between them in the poem to undermine this conclusion.[44] The circumstances of how their affair comes to unravel, however, suggest that

Clough's main objective might be to underscore just how difficult it can be to overcome or resist that network power through which personal affinities must be channeled. In some sense, Clough never gives us or his protagonists the chance to find out if they are "meant" (by him) for each other. They are undone by a confusing combination of interference from others, misdirected or misunderstood letters, and the sudden, rapid nature of their movement between various Italian cities.

Social complications begin to intervene in the form of Mary's sister Georgina, who asks George to "say something" to Claude (2.337), we discover, in a letter she writes to their sister Louisa. George carries out her wish, and thus begins a series of interferences and attempts at recovery that finally seem to sap the will of both Claude and Mary. As she writes, "It seems, George Vernon, before we left Rome, said / Something to Mr. Claude about what they call his attentions" (3.240–41). Claude in turn is "astounded" and "horrified," but "obtaining just then, as it happened, an offer / (No common favour) of seeing the great Ludovisi collection," he begs off of going with them to Florence: "How could I go? Great Heaven! to conduct a permitted flirtation / Under those vulgar eyes, the observed of such observers" (3.274–76; 278–79). Beneath Claude's snobbery resides a genuine sense of imposition on himself and Mary; they are being forced prematurely to turn from the language of ideas to that of social obligation. Mary shares Claude's vexation at George's interference and indicates her own wish to escape from such restrictions. "It is *so* disagreeable and *so* annoying to think of! / If it could only be known, though we never may meet him again, that / It was all George's doing and we were entirely unconscious, / It would extremely relieve—Your ever affectionate Mary" (3.243–46). In a postscript, she asks the recipient of the letter, her friend Miss Roper, to meet with Claude: "Say whatever is right and needful for ending the matter. / Only don't tell Mr. Claude, what I tell you as a secret, / That I should like very well to show him myself I forget it" (3.256–58). Mary hereby reveals the difficulty that her own inability to speak with Claude leaves her in. Like him, she wishes to return to their earlier state of affairs, but the demand that she keep moving—ironically, so that her family can make preparations for her sister's wedding—prevents any chance, it seems, of a personal encounter. As the poem pushes towards the close, her letters become briefer and more written to the moment, testifying to the fact that, unlike Claude, she is not in control of her movements: "We shall be off, I believe, in a hurry, and travel to Milan, / There to meet friends of Papa's, I am told, at the Croce di Malta" (3.265–66). This she reveals in another postscript, again underscoring the unsettled state she has been thrown into, swept up in the social network of the British middle class abroad.

Claude almost immediately second-guesses his decision not to accompany them, realizing that he may have been making an excuse of George's interference to absolve himself from fully examining the true nature of his attraction to Mary. He adopts a middle course of sorts, following a day or two behind the Trevellyns. As a result, letters and notes begin to multiply and miss their destinations, with Claude himself becoming a kind of letter without a clear address: "Gone to Como, they said; and I have posted to Como. / There was a letter left, but the *cameriere* had lost it. / Could it have been for me?" (4.19–21). Mary likewise gets caught up in a kind of postal frenzy: "I wrote him a note" (4.65), she tells Miss Roper, referring to the one Claude never received, which was in fact meant to clarify the misimpression left by another note in a hotel register about their movements. Mary had hoped to connect with Claude at Bellaggio, "but this was suddenly altered" (4.60)— why or by whom is not made clear—and as a result her note ends up misdirecting him. In his account to Eustace, Claude writes, "I have returned and found their names in the book at Como. / Certain it is I was right, and yet I am also in error. / Added in feminine hand, I read, *By the Boat to Bellaggio.—*" (4.39–41). Describing her subsequent letter, one intended to redirect Claude but never delivered, Mary writes, "I wrote three lines to / Say I had heard he was coming, desirous of joining our party;— / If so, then I said, we had started for Como, and meant to / Cross the St. Gothard, and stay, we believed, at Lucerne, for the summer. / Was it wrong? And why, if it was, has it failed to bring him?" (4.68–72). She also wonders, "Or may it, perhaps, have miscarried? / Any way, now, I repent, and am heartily vexed that I wrote it" (4.74–75). How to address each other seems a hopelessly complicated and entangled affair, full of misimpressions and misdirections. On some level, Claude and Mary seem verbally matched—conveyed subtly by Claude's excitement at seeing her handwriting—but their words and their movements never emerge in tact from this matrix of postal and transportation networks.

It gradually becomes clear that the most important letter in *Amours de Voyage* is the one between Claude and Mary that was never written. That brief note she leaves in a hotel register indicating their next move is their only direct written communication. The tragedy of this "epistolary tragi-comedy or comi-tragedy" (2:546) is thus that they *might* have connected had they been able to address themselves to each other more freely.[45] One could also find fault with Claude for insisting that Mary measure up to an idealized and perhaps impossible affinity. But even if he had resolved to think otherwise, it seems that events move too quickly for their relationship to have any chance to recover. Mary, in fact, writes the last letter of the poem, and while, like

Claude, she resolves to put their affair behind her, she confesses, "Ah, well, more than once I have broken my purpose, and sometimes, / Only too often, have looked for the little lake-steamer to bring him" (5.207–8). This is in many ways a brilliant metaphor for all of the missed connections of *Amours de Voyage,* one that recalls Claude's earlier shipboard reflection on juxtaposition. The modernized lake-steamer reminds one as well of Macaulay's insistence that better technologies of transportation were all people needed to bring themselves together. The end of Clough's poem, in contrast, is one of rapid-fire letters and movements to and fro where everyone seems to be hurrying up to arrive at no particular destination. Fittingly, the Trevellyns return to England, and Claude, listlessly, heads "Eastward, then, I suppose, with the coming of winter, to Egypt" (5.205).

AS MARY moves out of reach, Claude confronts the possibility of a life of isolation and wandering in ways that have strong implications for Clough's own social and ideological aims as a poet. Most of Canto V is a test of Claude's resolve as he tries to build something worthwhile from the ruins of his failure to connect: "I will not cling to her falsely," he states, invoking limpets once more, "Nothing factitious or forced shall impair the old happy relation." He resolves to "hit the open road," as we would say now, in a typically male celebration of traveling free-agency: "I will let myself go, forget, not try to remember; / I will walk on my way, accept the chances that meet me, / Freely encounter the world, imbibe these alien airs" (5.51–55). But Claude's grand plans quickly turn more inward and sterile, as Clough implies with a metaphor that appears to suggest something more than limpets: "I, who refused to ensfasten the roots of my floating existence / In the rich earth, cling now to the hard, naked rock that is left me" (5.66–67). Clough then extends the parallel a little further when he reveals that Claude, in fact, does not intend to post this particular letter: "Yes, it relieves me to write, though I do not send" (5.70).[46] But has Claude, in some sense, been writing only to himself all along? Clough's decision to excise drafts of two letters written by Eustace from the final edition of the poem would appear to support this impression.[47] Recall as well that from the beginning Claude stated his primary objective in writing was simply to be *en rapport,* and now he fears the loss of even this tenuous affinity: "So in your image I turn to an *ens rationis* of friendship. / Even so write in your name I know not to whom nor in what wise" (5.75–76). This suspicion that letters never address a person so much as an absent presence, a ghost or invention of one's own imagination, has haunted the poem all along.[48] Tennyson, in fact, confronts much the same anxiety in *In Memoriam* (1850) before finally insisting on the trans-substantive power of letters. Faced with the possibility that Hallam's physical presence has been totally lost to him, or that, even worse, he never really knew him to begin with, he famously resolves his doubt in Section 95 of the poem by rereading a letter in Hallam's hand: "So word by word, and line by line, / The dead man touched me from the past, / And all at once it seemed at last / The living soul was flashed on mine" (95.33–36).[49] Claude, however, no longer allows himself this kind of comfort. With the total collapse of the ideal of the personal letter, Claude must accept the possibility that he has merely engaged in a kind of verbal masturbation all along.

Without a clear compass heading or sense of audience, Clough enters the mode of the Flâneur in Crisis—the traveling version, if you will, of the "Radical in Crisis," as Isobel Armstrong has described him.[50] Clough shuttles between two opposing artistic identities. The first disdains convention and longs to walk freely, if only along the margins of society. The other identity still clings to Carlyle's more publicly engaged Hero as Poet, someone seeking a more affirmative connection to modern European culture, one characterized by the higher (and more uncertain) intellectual and spiritual essence of Arnold's proposed confederation. Clough is not ready to concede that his exile from the seats of political and cultural power is irrevocable and that he must become something more akin to Baudelaire's painter of modern life.[51] Rather, Clough wants the freedom to offend his audience, to plumb spiritual and moral depths—as he would do even more unreservedly in *Dipsychus*—and still be reclaimable by that audience. This may explain Clough's need to test the poem against the opinion of his perceptive if more conventionally minded friend Shairp, who, as we have seen, seemed genuinely disturbed by it on Clough's behalf: "On the whole I regard 'Les Amours' as your nature ridding itself of long-gathered bile. Once cleared off I hope you have done with bile. Don't publish it—or if it must be published—not in a book—but in some periodical" (1:275). Clough responded to Shairp's pointed objections with good humor, beginning one reply, "Good Heaven! don't be afraid.—You are a very gentle beast and of a good conscience and roar me like any sucking dove" (1:276). Clough did not back off entirely, however, asking, "But do you not, in the conception, find any final Strength of Mind in the unfortunate fool of a hero?" (1:278).[52]

One scene in particular near the close of *Amours de Voyage* brilliantly dramatizes Clough's internal culture war. For one moment, Claude's anxieties appear rather suddenly to have resolved themselves:

> Comfort has come to me here in the dreary streets of the city,
> Comfort—how do you think?—with a barrel-organ to bring it.

Moping along the streets, and cursing my day, as I wandered,
All of a sudden my ear met the sound of an English psalm tune.
Comfort me it did, till indeed I was very near crying.
Ah there is some great truth, partial very likely, but needful,
Lodged, I am strangely sure, in the tones of the English psalm tune.
Comfort it was at least; and I must take without question
Comfort however it come in the dreary streets of the city. (5.86–94)

Claude, as we know by now, is *incapable* of taking it without question. The repetition of the soothing "comfort" becomes a verbal drug of sorts, helping Claude, like the lines in this passage, slide into a reassuring and rhythmic dactylic order, the same kind of pleasure he got earlier from repeating the alliterative *"Mild monastic faces in quiet collegiate cloisters"* (3.182 and 189). Claude briefly resides in the kind of religious certainty he associates with home and an earlier, more rooted existence. But he recognizes this is a "partial" epiphany at best, a quasi-mystical experience that smacks of factitiousness. What he experienced was merely juxtaposition, being in the right place at the right time:

Almost I could believe I had gained a religious assurance,
Found in my own poor soul a great moral basis to rest on.
Ah, but indeed I see, I feel it factitious entirely;
I refuse, reject, and put it utterly from me;
I will look straight out, see things, not try to evade them:
Fact shall be fact for me; and the Truth the Truth as ever,
Flexible, changeable, vague, and multiform, and doubtful—
Off, and depart to the void, thou subtle fanatical tempter! (5.96–103)

Dismissing false comfort, Claude recaptures his "Strength of Mind" and affirms of himself, as he had at the outset of the poem, "I can be nothing at all, if it is not critical wholly" (1.144). Shairp too conceded this point, albeit somewhat grudgingly: "everything crumbles to dust beneath a ceaseless self-introspection and criticism which is throughout the only inspiration" (1:275). Even so, he still insisted, "one has supped one's fill of negations and now would prefer a draught of something stronger" (1:277). Clough, as we know, would not take the leap of faith that would have allowed him to bring Claude and Mary together. If they were meant for each other, their union could take place only in some dim and distant future, in a space not yet invented. In the meantime, there would be no closure, no teleology. Such was the uncertain promise—and power—of Clough's cosmopolitanism of negation.

In an earlier letter advising Clough on his religious doubts, Shairp held out the hope that "Christianity may live and put forth a new power of life amid forms of life yet undreamt of," thus continuing to provide the spiritual and cultural basis of European civilization: "Sometimes I console myself with hoping that all this confusion and perplexity and suffering comes from its passing into its newer forms—while we like the men in Thucyd[ides'] night battle know not friend from foe" (1:218).[53] One senses that Clough looked hard for these new forms in the Europe of his day, but simply could not locate them, as he had written in "Easter Day. Naples, 1849":

> Through the great sinful streets of Naples as I past,
> With fiercer heat than flamed above my head
> My heart was hot within me; till at last
> My brain was lightened, when my tongue had said
>   Christ is not risen! (1–5)[54]

As a result, Clough remains dogged by the sense that he was not doing his part to breathe new spirit and energy into poetry—that he was merely recycling a debased Byronism for an audience that had already supped its full of negations. In this respect, Clough's closest companion among the other poets I discuss in this book might be Swinburne, who would find ways to affirm Clough's cosmopolitanism of negation, remapping the Anglo-European contact zone as one of necessary disruption and alienation. Swinburne, in other words, would recognize the important role of offending people in order to communicate with them.[55] Working before the emergence of Swinburne's post-crisis-of-faith intellectual and spiritual confederation, however, Clough, like Claude, cannot as yet figure out whom to address his poem to.

Amours de Voyage concludes, in fact, with a problem of address: the "L'Envoi," as Clough labeled the poem's final elegiac stanza in his first draft of the poem, serves, as it were, as the poem's shipping instructions:

> *So go forth to the world, to the good report and the evil!*
>   *Go, little book! thy tale, is it not evil and good?*
> *Go, and if strangers revile, pass quietly by without answer.*
> *Go, and if curious friends ask of thy rearing and age,*
>   *Say,* I am flitting around from brain unto brain of
> Feeble and restless youths born to inglorious days;
>   But, *so finish the word,* I was writ in a Roman chamber,
> When from Janiculan heights thundered the cannon of France. (5.217–24)

Clough's poem travels by fits and starts, like himself: still in motion but para-doxically fixed in his chamber. Likewise, with the italics and Roman print now closely interwoven, the elegiacs and letters of the poem finally come together in this passage and speak to each other—conceptually and visually. Poetry reports what it sees but will not engage in a factitious arrangement of cause and effect or attempt to reinvent the Europe of the past. It will not fashion connections where there are none, and thus Clough refuses to make the Roman Republic part of a larger historical narrative. The cannon make a lot of noise, but for no apparent objective: he can give their location only. Clough had created a new kind of cosmopolitan verse, but as yet he could address it only to the future.[56]

P.S. Arnold and *Amours de Voyage*

Arnold, for certain, would not be that audience, even though Clough had reason to believe he might recognize attitudes they shared as committed but somewhat disillusioned Anglo-Europeans.[57] But whereas Shairp at least had some specific criticism to offer, Arnold tersely concluded, "as to the Italian poem, if I forbore to comment it was that I had nothing special to say— what is to be said when a thing does not suit you—suiting and not suiting is a subjective affair and only time determines, by the colour a thing takes with years, whether it *ought* to have suited or no."[58] After two more years had passed, Arnold was able to offer some muted praise vis-à-vis Tennyson's *Maud:* "From the extracts I have seen from Maud, he seems in his old age to be coming to your manner in the Bothie and the Roman poem. That manner, as you know, I do not like: but certainly, if it is to be used, you use it with far more freedom vigour and abundance than he does—Altogether I think this volume a lamentable production, and like so much of our lit-erature thoroughly and intensely *provincial,* not European."[59] The "Roman poem" was incisive and full of energy, but it was a misdirected energy, not settled on more constructive poetic ends, as Arnold saw them. Clough's was not the Europe of Arnold's dreams and no doubt seemed merely to amplify the sense of lost connection that closes "Dover Beach": both poems, in fact, end with the sounds of a doomed and pointless military engagement echo-ing in the reader's ears. Could Clough at least infer that Arnold detected a broader absorption of contemporary European intellectual trends in *Amours de Voyage?* Or was he to infer the opposite—that, like Tennyson, he too was being provincial? Arnold's point was unclear, much like the overall status of their friendship, which had already begun to taper off before Clough left for the United States in October 1852. Now conducted via transatlantic post and aimed mainly at correcting perceived misunderstandings, theirs had become, as Claude might have put it, an *ens rationis* of friendship.[60]

Arnold offered another piece of advice to Clough the following February that, although meant to be critical, might finally serve as the most apt expression of Clough's unique strengths as a poet and as a commentator on the possibility of cosmopolitanism. For Arnold, all Clough's problems could be summed up in one tendency—the failure to find his *assiette*—his seat or position—and stick to it:

> You ask me in what I think or have thought you going wrong: in this: that you would never take your assiette as something determined final and unchangeable for you and proceed to work away on the basis of that: but were always poking and patching and cobbling at the assiette itself—could never finally, as it seemed—"resolve to be thyself"—but were looking for this and that experience, and doubting whether you ought not to adopt this or that mode of being of persons qui ne vous valaient pas because it might possibly be nearer the truth than your own.[61]

By the measure of Arnold's ideal of a unified intellectual and spiritual confederation of Europe, Clough's journey was a failure. He could not invent that higher, more orderly essence that poetry *ought* to embody in order to "inspirit and rejoice the reader" (1:2), as Arnold demanded of the form later that year in his Preface to *Poems* (1853). To be fair, then, Arnold was subjecting Clough on a more psychological level to the same scrutiny that would soon cast his own *Empedocles on Aetna* (1852) into critical exile. Here was another poet failing to connect, caught up in "the dialogue of the mind with itself" (1:1). While this suggestion might have been good personal advice to Clough, one finds it harder to forgive Arnold—as a literary critic—for failing to recognize that this shifting, unsettled ground *was* Clough's assiette: challenging the givens, ranging freely among ideas, and—in more Arnoldian terms—poking, patching, and cobbling at the best that is known and thought. Arnold was certainly not alone among Clough's friends in finding fault with *Amours de Voyage*. Still, one thinks, it *ought* to have suited him more.

3

Barrett Browning and the Spaces of Cosmofeminism

From *Casa Guidi Windows* to "Mother and Poet"

IF EUROPEAN TRAVEL was a necessary though exasperating means of self-discovery for Clough, Barrett Browning clearly thrived abroad. Writing to Mary Russell Mitford, who, as the author of such homebound volumes as *Our Village* (1824–32) and *Country Stories* (1837), served her as a kind of domestic foil, Barrett Browning revealed a sense of having joined a new and vibrant community of women writers abroad:

> Ah, you, with your terrors of travelling—how you amuse me! Why the constant change of air . . . made me better & better instead of worse! It did me infinite good! Mrs.- Jameson says, she "wont call me *improved,* but *transformed* rather." I like the new sights & the movement, ... my spirits rise: I live—I can adapt myself. If you really tried it & got as far as Paris, you would be drawn on, I fancy, & on . . . on to the East perhaps with H[arriet] Martineau.[1]

Harriet Martineau was traveling in Egypt in 1846, a journey that would culminate in *Eastern Life, Present and Past* (1848). Anna Jameson had developed a substantial friendship with the Brownings and was accompanying the newly married couple through France to Italy. At the time, Jameson was just beginning her career as a critic of Italian Renaissance art; she was better known to Barrett Browning as the author of *Winter Studies and Summer Rambles in Canada* (1838) and *Social Life in Germany* (1840). Jameson's first published work, *Diary of an Ennuye* (1826), mixes fiction with guidebook-like descriptions of Italy in the manner of Madame de Staël's *Corinne*—another strong influence on Barrett Browning, who declared it an "immortal" book worthy of being read "three score & ten times" (*BC* 3:25).[2] Felicia Hemans and Letitia Landon (L.E.L.) had set the European stage more poetically for Barrett Browning: the latter's "Improvisatrice" also bears a strong debt to Staël's vision of Italy as a country that nurtured female creativity.[3] For Barrett Browning, travel was empowering. To record that experience in writing was a rare opportunity for authoritative self-expression for women.

In other respects, Europe was a more foreboding landscape for a woman author. About a year or so before her elopement, Barrett Browning had been reading Mary Shelley's *Rambles in Germany and Italy in 1840, 1842, and 1843* (1844), which had come under attack in *The Observer* for straying too closely into political subjects: "With her, as with all women, politics is a matter of the heart, and not as with the more robust nature of man, of the head; and consequently, her arguments take the tone of passion, and her convictions the tone of personal feeling. It is an idle and unprofitable theme for a woman."[4] Soon enough, Barrett Browning would have to deal with similar critical harassment herself—whether in the press or even, at times, from family members. Her brother George Barrett would take her to task in February 1852 for continuing to support Louis Napoleon even after he had staged a *coup d'état,* the first step in his eventual proclamation as emperor. "I'm a bad patriot, I believe," she confessed to George, "I care more for the world & humanity every year, & less for local & national interests."[5] In the long run, however, Barrett Browning would not back down from such criticism and boasted in a later letter to George, "May not, after all, these 'political mistakes' of Ba's . . . be nearer the truth than we fancy? May she not know the real colour of things better in Tuscany & Rome than Mr. So & So who sees them at Brompton?"[6]

Being on the spot provided one kind of authority, but by simply being a *poet,* and one of England's most well-established and well-respected at that, Barrett Browning espoused another kind of authority—a distinctly powerful, transcendent form of discourse that she and many of her contemporaries felt had direct political relevance. With this authoritative vision, Barrett Browning could claim to see into the conscience of a nation in a way that a political economist or a prose travel writer such as Shelley could not. As she would remark in *Casa Guidi Windows,* "My words are guiltless of the bigot's sense. / My soul has fire to mingle with the fire / Of all these souls, within or out of doors / Of Rome's church or another" (1.942–45). It was not a power that Barrett Browning took lightly, and as we saw in chapter 1 with poems such as *Aurora Leigh* and "Italy and the World," she continued to insist that the poet could indeed point the way toward "another" church, one more truly catholic and global. For Barrett Browning, poetry always remained something that must cross borders and move souls, hearts, *and* minds in the process.

In many ways, this chapter is about how Barrett Browning put that kind of power to work. Hers is a complex cosmopolitanism that evolved over the course of a long career and emerged in many ways out of the forms of nationalistic devotion on display in her works.[7] *Casa Guidi Windows,* for instance, embraces Herder's ethnically and spiritually charged *Volksgeist,* which offered a particularly enticing form of cultural authority to a woman expatriate poet such as herself. The result is an incompletely realized national internationalism: the hope that a united, cooperative Europe would emerge *sui generis* out of the fulfillment of individual nationalist struggles. Her next major poem, *Aurora Leigh,* experiments with more of a person-to-person encounter with Europe—or an "actually existing cosmopolitanism" that centers on the unique dynamics of women's travel, and not just that of the upper and middle-class travelers who had been the focus of so much previous women's travel writing.[8] Aurora forges an Anglo-European citizenship grounded not in nationalities but in travel itself: the ability to move between borders and to actively identify with specific others, much as Barrett Browning had in her own experience. One of her last poems, "Mother and Poet" (1861), unites the public and private viewpoints of these earlier works by exploring how the concept of motherhood, which Barrett Browning had closely aligned with the nation in *Casa Guidi Windows,* could instead become the basis of a more expansive, "cosmofeminine" sense of civic belonging. This concept, as articulated by Carol A. Breckenridge, embodies "a new understanding of the domestic, which would no longer be confined spatially or socially to the private sphere." The domestic would instead be understood as a "vital interlocutor and not just an interloper in law, politics, and public ethics."[9] Ultimately, what characterizes Barrett Browning's work is this struggle to push beyond boundaries of self, family, and nation and to make cosmopolitanism something that is lived, not just contemplated or debated.

BEFORE MOVING ON to a closer analysis of Barrett Browning's poetry, I want first to offer a fuller definition of cosmopolitanism as it evolves over the course of her work and begins to anticipate theories of cosmopolitanism in our own time. Barrett Browning herself appears to have rarely used the word *cosmopolitan,* although she does write in her letters of the value of being a "citizen of the world"—the term's literal meaning in the original Greek— especially in reference to her son's education, as I touch on later.[10] Her choice of terminology is significant, for the concept of world citizenship adheres closely to the more politically aware, multi-layered cosmopolitanism defined, for instance, by Steven Vertovec and Robin Cohen in *Conceiving Cosmopolitanism* (2002):

> Cosmopolitanism suggests something that simultaneously: (a) transcends the seemingly exhausted nation-state model; (b) is able to mediate actions and ideals oriented both to the universal and the particular, the global and the local; (c) is culturally anti-essentialist; and (d) is capable of representing variously complex repertoires of allegiance, identity, and interest. In these ways, cosmopolitanism seems to offer a mode of managing cultural and political multiplicities.[11]

I want to suggest here that this understanding of cosmopolitanism exists in more embryonic forms in Barrett Browning. Both then and now, whether one was a cosmopolitan or a citizen of the world, these terms encompass something more than an educated familiarity with other cultures and languages. I am thus less concerned in this chapter with the influence of specific continental authors and literary forms on Barrett Browning's work than with cosmopolitanism in this broader sense—being immersed in Europe—politically, intellectually, even physically. Familiarity with the language and literatures of other nations represents a necessary precursor of cosmopolitanism but not its ultimate essence, which is more ideological.[12] Benjamin Disraeli, for one, would make this abundantly clear in an address to Conservative Party loyalists gathered at the Crystal Palace in 1872, where he warned of the triumph of "the philosophy and politics of the Continent" over a healthier interest in expanding and maintaining England's overseas holdings. "The time is at hand," he insisted, "when England will have to decide between national and cosmopolitan principles."[13]

The notion of the poet as cosmopolitan traveler, identified as such in the poem, entails a crucial awareness of the civic aspirations of the people—men *and* women—among whom the traveler lives and moves; the poet must resist slipping into easy patterns of cultural colonization. Barrett Browning thus strives to integrate the roles of world citizen and cultural consumer and, in a broader sense, the aims of internationalism and cosmopolitanism—terms that are similar but not synonymous, it should be stressed. If internationalism suggests more of a diplomatic and political ideal, cosmopolitanism points to something that begins on a personal level and is defined more by how one interacts with specific individuals, locations, and cultural forms. This slippage from one term to the next highlights a conflict between public and private identity that informs many aspects of Barrett Browning's poetry—as it had Clough's too and would Robert Browning's as well. Initially, her work gravitates more toward internationalism: *Casa Guidi Windows* commits poetry to the political objective of Italian nationalism and privileges the poet's access to an idealized language of the nation, albeit with the implicit goal of paving the way toward a more peaceful and cooperative world. Nonetheless, the nation comes before the individual and remains the focal point of personal and poetic identity, with sometimes destructive consequences for the private sphere. While continuing to give voice to this inter(nationalist) ideal, later poems would take women's uncertain public and political identity as the starting point for imagining forms of cosmopolitanism that look beyond the nation and do more to close the gap between the personal and the political and between the private and the public. In Barrett Browning, cosmopolitanism is a continuous effort to realize the universal in the particular while not erasing the particular.

Casa Guidi Windows

Barrett Browning's first major poem set on the Continent, *Casa Guidi Windows,* embraces the dream of a new Europe of distinct yet cooperative nationalities at the same time it becomes entangled within some of the more strident rhetoric that adhered to the creation and justification of the modern nation-state. What Barrett Browning actually witnessed from the windows of Casa Guidi in Florence was the celebration that ensued when Duke Leopold II of Tuscany announced the formation of a civic guard, the first of several liberal reforms. Part I of *Casa Guidi Windows* recounts the initial hope inspired by this event, while Part II expresses the poet's disappointment with the Duke's eventual betrayal and the failure of the Italian people to capitalize on their earlier gains. By its very structure, then, the poem replicates just how unstable the nation can be, especially while still in its formative stages. Italy appears in moments of vision that political events alternately confirm and deny. Barrett Browning draws attention to these issues of sight and authority in the poem's preface or "Advertisement":

> This poem contains the impressions of the writer upon events in Tuscany of
> which she was a witness. 'From a window,' the critic may demur. She bows

to the objection in the very title of her work. No continuous narrative nor exposition of political philosophy is attempted by her. It is a simple story of personal impressions, whose only value is in the intensity with which they were received, as proving her warm affection for a beautiful and unfortunate country, and the sincerity with which they are related, as indicating her own good faith and freedom from partisanship. (xli)

Recent commentators on the poem have been concerned less with Barrett Browning's somewhat obligatory disavowal of political objectives (witness Shelley) than with the need to refute her potentially more damaging admission that the poem's fenestral point of view may misrepresent political reality.[14] Leigh Coral Harris, for one, chooses to stress the potential strengths of the window as a mediative device: "the framed space from which Barrett Browning views the scene allows her to produce a more vivid and extreme representation, since her real and imaginary purview is greater than if her discussion were bound by actual involvement: the sight of real events prompts the poet to contemplate the past. Her account is neither totally subjective nor totally objective; it occupies representational space between the two."[15] By situating herself at the border between past and present and between public and private, Barrett Browning achieves a unique perspective into political events as they unfold. Echoing the praise of other recent commentators, Harris proposes that the poem "constitutes a shift in the representation of Italy in the British imagination from *mythos* . . . to nationalized *logos* as a unified, independent, and political reality."[16]

In light of this and similar claims, it may seem almost regressive to argue that a problem of authority remains in the poem, one that emerges when the poet attempts to make a transition from witness to a more direct kind of agency. In several places, *Casa Guidi Windows* calls on Italians to be prepared to sacrifice the individual life on behalf of the nation, even echoing the Marseillaise at one point by contending that "dead heroic faces will start out / On all these gates, if foes should take the field, / And blend sublimely, at the earliest shout, / With living heroes" (1.1071–74). This aspect of the poem seems to have always disturbed readers, and as I discuss in more detail below, even the most sophisticated efforts to diffuse such rhetoric by placing it in historical and generic context have only partially succeeded. In other words, even after accounting for changes in historical perspective, readers should still find such passages troubling for reasons that do not stem from any blindness specific to Barrett Browning but from a blindness characteristic of nationalism itself.[17] With her assumption of the poetic authority to call upon Italians to commit their lives to the nationalist cause, a conflict between nationalism and cosmopolitanism erupts, one that hinges upon the seamless way in which religious language is invoked to articulate and justify the formation of nations. This tendency to cast individuals not as living bodies but as "souls" taking part in a grander theological design undermines the kind of empathy on which Barrett Browning's cosmopolitanism in later poems will depend.

In his classic study *Imagined Communities,* Benedict Anderson argues that nationalism and religion became mutually reinforcing discourses in the nineteenth century that legitimated the kinds of personal sacrifices that made and continue to make violence on behalf of the nation possible. The result of this commingling was "a secular transformation of fatality into continuity, contingency into meaning. . . . If nation-states are widely conceded to be 'new' and 'historical,' the nations to which they give political expression always loom out of an immemorial past, and . . . glide into a limitless future."[18] The specific connection between Christianity and early-nineteenth-century nationalism has received more direct attention in Marianne Perkins's *Nation and Word 1770–1850* (1999). Perkins suggests that nationalism offered the poet a discourse "which went beyond particular political and social remedies to develop the moral and spiritual quality of the prophetic voice. The nation was invested with a primarily spiritual, rather than political, destiny and mission."[19] This understanding was shared by some of the most recognized supporters of the Risorgimento, including Giuseppe Mazzini, whose *The Duties of Man* (1861) positions the nation as the "fulcrum" of personal and cultural identity. While one's first duty is to God and His law, followed by humanity, country, family, and oneself, it is country—the nation—that forms the center of this grouping and bridges the distance between God and the individual: "And may the constant thought of your soul be for Italy, may all the acts of your life be worthy of her, and may the standard beneath which you range yourselves to work for Humanity be Italy's. Do not say *I;* say *we.* Be every one of you an incarnation of your Country."[20] Not surprisingly, Mazzini tended to congratulate those English poets who celebrated these values in their work and, as we saw, expostulate with those who had not, such as Swinburne. One of the former was Sydney Dobell, whose *The Roman* (1850) follows the career of an Italian revolutionary bearing a close resemblance to Mazzini himself and closes with a revolutionary uprising and chants of "Down with the Austrians! Arms! Blood! Charge! Death—death to tyrants. Victory! Freedom!"[21] After the success of *The Roman,* Mazzini wrote to him, "You have written about Rome as I would, had I been a poet. And what you did write flows from the soul, the all-loving, the all-embracing, the prophet-soul."[22] As a deeply devout Christian and Italian nationalist, Barrett Browning likewise tended to see the fulfillment of both of these ideals in each other. How to get from there to the more peaceful, ecumenical vision of a democratic World Church—the dream of "Italy and the World"—was a challenge that defined her career in many ways.

Evangelical nationalism held another kind of appeal for Barrett Browning by giving her a way of expressing a connection to Italy that could be at once political but also safely feminine. While a more demystified, contractual paradigm of nationhood and citizenship would, in theory, allow for greater border-crossing between nationalities—as Jürgen Habermas contends—oddly enough, such a concept does not authorize the woman poet, even one foreign born, with the same force as the more ethnically restricted *Volksgeist*.[23] Contractual citizenship, one should recall, is based on the franchise, a form of power to which women were not granted access (a realization that sheds additional light on Barrett Browning's continuing faith in Louis Napoleon, whose lack of respect for constitutional law was what so upset her brother and other English observers). This linguistic component to nationalism additionally provided a kind of diplomatic pass to Barrett Browning. Poetry becomes a *lingua franca,* one that allows her to locate forbears in Dante and Milton alike, whose ghostly forms seem to inhabit the Florence in which she now resides. At one point, she speaks of visiting Vallombrosa in the hills outside Florence, where Milton had been thought to reside: "Therefore is / The place divine to English man and child, / And pilgrims leave their souls here in a kiss" (1.1162–64). If Barrett Browning could not be Italian in body, she could fashion a poetic connection grounded more in location (being on the spot) and in the soul.

The traditional identification of Italy with women in the nineteenth century further empowered writers such as Barrett Browning, although within "a language closely associated with their perceived feminine values and positions," as Maura O'Connor stipulates in *The Romance of Italy and the English Political Imagination* (1998).[24] One sees this language at work in the preface, where Barrett Browning defines her interest in Italy as one of compassion, a "warm affection." In the poem itself, Barrett Browning exploits the possibilities of this connection right from the beginning: "I heard last night a little child go singing / 'Neath Casa Guidi windows, by the church, / O bella libertà, O bella!" (1.1–3). She concludes, "the heart of Italy must beat, / While such a voice had leave to rise serene / 'Twixt church and palace of a Florence street!" (1.8–10). The child symbolizes the hope of a new Italy and the idea of the Risorgimento as a rebirth; the child/mother/poet dynamic also allows Barrett Browning to deliver a political message in language that simultaneously disarms the critic ready to charge her with abandoning the domestic sphere. In a sense, her poem merely translates the voice of this child, the voice of this new Italy, into poetry: the nation becomes an emotive essence conveyed via the language of feeling to which the poet is especially attuned.

This spiritualized sense of nationhood is what allows the poem to move so easily from the idea of Italy as a mostly benign cultural entity to one for which individual Italians should be willing to sacrifice their lives. In the poem's most forthright celebration of this endeavor,

> Rows of shot corpses, waiting for the end
> Of burial, seem to smile up straight and pale
> Into the azure air and apprehend
> That final gun-flash from Palermo's coast
> Which lightens their apocalypse of death.
> So let them die! (1.1205–10)

These are bold but troubling lines, and in his study of Victorian poetry and nation-building, Matthew Reynolds offers a careful reading of the poem that foregrounds questions of genre. This is not journalism, he reminds us: "the poem has assumed the prophet's task: to identify and to hymn an Ideal."[25] Reynolds adds that as prophecy, the poem should be understood to refer less to specific political events or agents and more to the nation in an abstract, timeless sense. One could add that this prophetic, apocalyptic mode would have been readily familiar to Barrett Browning's contemporaries from popular evangelical epics such as Robert Pollok's *The Course of Time* (1827). Placed in this context, her work seems all the more daring with its challenge to readers to think of sin and redemption in more geopolitical terms. At the same time, it is precisely the prophetic tone of the poem, and the couching of nationalism in millennial language, that makes this image of Italy's dead so difficult to pass over. The Italians themselves, in some sense, do not exist in the passage, at least not in the reality of the present, making it difficult to see their deaths as part of an actual political and historical process. One must be careful, of course, not to indulge in an easy moral hindsight that fails to recognize that doing nothing at this time would have been akin to tolerating injustice, precisely as Barrett Browning herself warns: "I love no peace which is not fellowship, / And which includes not mercy. I would have / Rather, the raking of the guns across / The world, and shrieks against Heaven's architrave" (2.399–402). Simon Avery, for instance, draws an analogy between the Risorgimento and nationalist uprisings against colonial authority in Africa, adding that "[w]hile Barrett Browning is clearly against brute force . . . she certainly recognises that violence against the oppressive coloniser is necessary for liberation and purification to take place."[26] Even so, the difference between "brute force" and the more liberating and purifying kind of violence is mostly one of semantics: bodies (individuals) are destroyed in an effort to purify the soul (the nation). Ultimately, the poem leaves the reader with two uninviting options: acceptance of colonial oppression or language that mystifies violence on behalf of nationalism.

The idea of the nation as *Volksgeist* is what leaves the poem at this impasse, for it requires that Barrett Browning cast Italians as souls rather than as bodies, with the result that only those who are Italian in body can actively participate in the creation of the nation; only they can sacrifice the body that will release the soul. As a foreign-born poet, Barrett Browning, in some sense, has come upon a border she cannot cross. At first, what I am suggesting here might seem to run counter to the cosmopolitan ideal articulated at the outset of this chapter: that one must feel empowered to cross borders and mix national identities. What happens in *Casa Guidi Windows*, however, is that this attempt ends up erasing individual Italians, in the sense that they do not exist until their bodies have been animated by the spirit of the nation. Until then, the Italians are not "heroes" who will be counted among the nation's liberators, but "oil-eaters with large live mobile mouths / Agape for macaroni" (1.200–201). The body politic of Italy does not begin to live until born again in the spirit of the *Volksgeist,* when a dynamic figure will emerge and "strike fire into the masses" (1.837), and "make of Italy a nation" (1.840).

The division between the spiritual and the material informs the second part of the poem as well, when the fate of Italy on the international diplomatic stage becomes more of a concern for Barrett Browning after the general failure of the uprisings of 1847–49. Part of her critique in Part II is reserved for those European nations who failed to come to Italy's aid and now gather together at the Great Exhibition of 1851. Once ensconced in the magical Crystal Palace,

> Every nation,
> To every other nation strange of yore,
> Gives face to face the civic salutation,
>   And holds up in a proud right hand before
> That congress, the best work which she can fashion
>   By her best means. 'These corals, will you please
> To match against your oaks?' (2.587–93)

For Barrett Browning, the self-interest that defines Britain's foreign policy overshadows any gesture toward internationalism and world peace. She continues to mock the mostly economic and material understanding of international relations embodied in the Exhibition, which positions nations as rivals rather than as neighbors. The passage thus masterfully exposes the limitations of the Victorian faith in progress via free trade and technological advancement. By the same token, however, the passage exposes the poem's own conceptual boundaries with regard to national identity. As a potential nation, Italy appears to exist apart from any economic or military attributes of its own, and this omission, ultimately, is what divides nineteenth-century ideals of nationalism from internationalism. As Pheng Cheah explains, "before the nation finds its state, before the tightening of the hyphen between nation and state that official nationalism consummates, the ideals of cosmopolitanism and European nationalism in its early stirrings are almost indistinguishable."[27] *Casa Guidi Windows* draws attention to this tightening, the pressure point where the more hopeful sounding rhetoric of nationalism begins to buckle. The poem struggles to find that W/word that will bring the higher, spiritual essence of poetry and nationhood into accord with the realities of the political present, to find a cosmopolitanism that can operate among states as well as nations.

What, then, does the poem finally achieve in terms of cosmopolitanism? Barrett Browning did craft a powerful voice that insisted on the primacy of poetic vision in an attempt to subvert the disengaged, "idle" persona that mid-century Victorian culture demanded of the woman traveler.[28] The *Eclectic Review,* for instance, implicitly acknowledged this transformation, calling the poem "the natural product of the contemplation of the events which have passed in Italy since the great European outbreak of 1848, . . . by a mind of deep observation and high and generous feeling."[29] *The Athenaeum* proclaimed that the voice of *Casa Guidi* emerged "out of the graves of the patriots," granting the poem considerable cultural authority, but also capturing its ideological debts.[30] The poem takes a necessary first step toward reimagining means of forging connections between citizens of different countries, even if the rhetoric of nationalism provided an enticing kind of poetic power that Barrett Browning, like many contemporary poets, found difficult to resist. Returning to the preface of the poem, we can see now that Barrett Browning, even if she had overstated the poem's blindnesses, was acknowledging some genuine uncertainty about the nature of the bridge she had constructed between herself and Italy—just how far that warm sympathy had extended and what it entailed. Her striving for a connection that would transcend boundaries of many sorts, including national ones, is a project that she continues in *Aurora Leigh,* in which the languages of soul, body, and politics come together and inform each other in new ways.

Aurora Leigh

In *Casa Guidi Windows,* Barrett Browning writes as herself, an expatriate delivering a first-hand travel account. *Aurora Leigh* goes a step further: it *naturalizes* the poet's presence abroad, making the poet cosmopolitan in flesh as well as spirit. Aurora is born in Italy, matures and becomes a poet in England, travels extensively in France, and then finally settles back in Italy.[31] As the daughter of a Florentine with "rare blue eyes" (1.30) and an "austere Englishman" (1.65) who had come abroad to study architecture, Aurora mixes national heritages in a way that gives her an added authority to inhabit and inscribe other nations. This kind of hybridization, however, is not ultimately what defines cosmopolitanism in the poem. More so than *Casa Guidi Windows, Aurora Leigh* concerns itself with embodying and practicing cosmopolitanism in the form of the poet herself, who evolves as she travels and models ways of encountering modern Europe for the reader. The nationalist agenda that energizes *Casa Guidi Windows* is less of a force in *Aurora Leigh,* except toward the close with Aurora's arrival in Italy: as a result, cosmopolitanism does not emerge as a by-product of nationalism but more from an impulse to fashion a livable, everyday sense of human connection. A self-styled "novel-poem," *Aurora Leigh* narrativizes cosmopolitanism by placing Aurora amongst fellow travelers with whom she is compared and contrasted. The change in genre thus creates a change in perspective: *Aurora Leigh* sees and encounters Europe in a manner different from the more oracular vantage point of *Casa Guidi Windows.*[32] *Aurora Leigh* continues Barrett Browning's dialogue of England and Europe, public and private, and individual and collective, all of which become subsumed under the poem's broader goal of synthesizing opposites through the union of Aurora with Marian and, later, with Romney.

The first book of the poem locates Aurora in a peculiar position between Italy and England. After the death of her parents, the young Aurora travels to England for the first time to be raised by her aunt, who seems determined to contain Aurora's identity within strict codes of nationality and gender. She insists that Aurora adopt more reserve in her personal appearance and purge her speech of any traces of foreignness:

> I broke the copious curls upon my head
> In braids, because she liked smooth-ordered hair.
> I left off saying my sweet Tuscan words
> Which still at any stirring of the heart
> Came up to float across the English phrase

As lilies, (*Bene* or *Che che,*) because
She liked my father's child to speak his tongue. (1.385–91)

The sort of Italianized English taught to her by her father, she learns, is not the language of her aunt; it nonetheless remains with Aurora as a kind of instinctive language of the heart for Aurora that later resurfaces in her poetry.[33] As someone who "had lived / A sort of cage-bird life, born in a cage, / Accounting that to leap from perch to perch / Was act and joy enough for any bird" (1.304–7), Aurora's aunt forms a distinct counterpoint to Aurora's cosmopolitan origins and tendencies.

Her aunt's role in the poem mirrors that of several other characters who either do not travel or, when they do, seem to *mis*travel and cultivate a kind of false cosmopolitanism—one that Aurora herself must also resist at key moments in the poem. In this regard, the poem to some extent adopts the familiar dialectic of earnest traveler/idle tourist that James Buzard and others have argued is central to so many texts of the period, when "anti-tourism evolved into a symbolic economy in which travelers and writers displayed marks of originality and 'authenticity' in an attempt to win credit for acculturation; and visited places were perceived as parts of a market-place of cultural goods."[34] Looking more deeply, however, one sees that there is more at stake in Barrett Browning's portrait of a traveler like Lady Waldemar than the kind of striving for cultural capital alluded to by Buzard. She tells Aurora, "I took a master in the German tongue, / I gamed a little, went to Paris twice" (3.448–49), in order to escape her passion for Romney. She seems to learn German simply as a mark of fashion and goes to France to gamble, a distinctively upper-class, vaguely disreputable form of travel as amusement. Aurora labels Lady Waldemar a "woman of the world" and a "centre to herself, / Who has wheeled on her own pivot half a life / In isolated self-love and self-will" (4.513–16). By calling Lady Waldemar a "woman" of the world and not, by contrast, a "citizen" of the world, Barrett Browning makes a simple but key distinction. Older, more passive models of travel and travel writing encouraged for women, and symbolized in the poem by Lady Waldemar, leave no room for a political commitment that looks beyond the self: the broader ideal of Anglo-European citizenship that Barrett Browning pursues through Aurora. Furthermore, as the poem makes clear with her arrival in France, Aurora's cosmopolitanism must continue to grow and become an active, responsible way of living, not just an outlook or disposition.

While not so deplorable a character as Lady Waldemar, Lord Howe offers another kind of contrast to Aurora as someone who makes gestures toward radical pan-European politics and ideas but who ultimately backs off of any

investment that threatens his own class status. Aurora calls him "A born aris-
tocrat, bred radical, / And educated socialist, who still / Goes floating, on
traditions of his kind, / Across the theoretic flood from France" (4.710–13).
Lord Howe stands as a relic of an earlier generation of Grand Tourists who
traveled Europe with the aim of self-improvement and making social connections with other aristocrats. "He never could be anything complete, /
Except a loyal, upright gentleman, / A liberal landlord, graceful diner-out"
(4.723–25). It is also telling that later in the poem Lord Howe brokers an
offer of marriage from a "John Eglinton, of Eglinton in Kent" (5.864) that
partly prompts Aurora's decision to leave England. Aurora suspects that the
desired union emerges not from respect for her poetry but from a connois-
seurship of female artists: "I will not read it [the proposal]: it is stereotyped; /
The same he wrote to,—anybody's name, / Anne Blythe the actress, when she
died so true / A duchess fainted in a private box" (5.898–901). Lord Howe
suggests that Aurora might be willing to use this opportunity to provide her
the income to write:

> In this uneven, unfostering England here,
> Where ledger-strokes and sword-strokes count indeed,
> But soul-strokes merely tell upon the flesh
> They strike from,—it is hard to stand for art,
> Unless some golden tripod from the sea
> Be fished up, by Apollo's divine chance,
> To throne such feet as yours, my prophetess,
> At Delphi. (5.936–43)

By this time, Aurora has already undergone the crisis of poetic faith in Book
5 that commits her to modern subjects. Howe's patronizing tone and couching of artistic achievement in ancient terms is a signal that she would be con-
strained to write "pastorals"—the "counterfeiting epics" alluded to earlier in
the poem (1.990). She would no more be a kept artist, however, than a kept
woman. After the incident, Aurora concludes, "We are sepulchered alive in
this close world, / And want more room" (5.1040–41). England is cast as
provincial in its attitude toward art and female creative achievement: to write
her modern epic she must escape to the continent. France, where "[a]rt walks
forward, and knows where to walk" (6.103), is her first destination. Once
there, Aurora must remap the continent for a new class of traveler—one, in
fact, *not* restricted by class affiliation.

What Aurora discovers in France is not a particular place, but a person,
Marian, who in some sense alters the face of Europe for Aurora, transform-

ing her mostly personal artistic venture into one of larger social and political significance.[35] Earlier, Marian had virtually disappeared from the poem after her refusal to marry Romney as part of his larger scheme to promote class solidarity. Aurora finds out, however, that Lady Waldemar had arranged for her to emigrate to Australia in what was actually an elaborate kidnapping plot: Marian is taken off the ship after it stops first in France and is then drugged, raped, and abandoned. Aurora happens upon Marian by chance among the many faces that pass by her in Paris, disrupting what had up until that moment been a mostly ambulatory and passive encounter with the city. Aurora, for instance, strolls "through the Market-place of Flowers / (The prettiest haunt in Paris)" (6.424–25)—putting the comment in parentheses, as if she recognizes it is not quite to the purpose. Up to now, she had no greater objective for her Paris sojourn than "wandering, musing, with the artist's eye" (4.427). Under Marian's redirection, France ceases to be a spectacle Aurora observes from a safe distance. Marian leads her away from the "peopled streets" (6.507) to a ravaged countryside: "All the place / Seemed less a cultivation than a waste. / Men work here, only,—scarce begin to live: / All's sad, the country struggling with the town" (6.518–21). After her rape and pregnancy, Marian moves from one occupation to another within this part of France, finally earning a living as a seamstress. In a sense quite different from the way cosmopolitanism is generally understood, Marian has become French.

By introducing Marian into the poem and into Aurora's journey through Europe, Barrett Browning expands what it means to travel in the same way that cultural studies today, following James Clifford, stresses that "many different kinds of people travel, acquiring complex knowledges, stories, political and intercultural understandings, without producing 'travel writing.'"[36] Marian's whole life has been one of displacement, as she had told Aurora in Book 3, but on a different social scale from hers: in childhood, her family's poverty kept them constantly on the move—thus making it all the easier for Lady Waldemar to convince her that her best option in life is to *keep moving* and emigrate to Australia. Marian thus underscores Clifford's observation that "travelers move about under strong cultural, political, and economic compulsions and that certain travelers are materially privileged, others oppressed."[37] Through Marian, the poem politicizes cosmopolitanism, showing its debt to class discrepancies that are, in a symbolic way, bridged by her and Aurora's decision to travel together to Italy. This is, of course, ultimately a limited, personal gesture on Aurora's part, but it in a crucial way emphasizes the point that cosmopolitan identity and citizenship cannot be divorced from individual encounters such as theirs. Marian relocates Aurora within the social spectrum of Europe, expanding and enriching Aurora's poetic objectives.

Aurora's journey with Marian to Italy takes place via railway, as if to make them icons of a new, forward-looking Europe, a sign as well of Aurora's growing interest in merging material and spiritual forms of connectedness. In contrast to the more technophobic Clough, Barrett Browning makes a place for poetry on board the train by endeavoring to subsume the latter within the higher, more transcendent discourse of poetry. At the same time, she offers one of the most vivid descriptions of train travel to come out of the nineteenth century, one worth quoting at length:

> So we passed
> The liberal open country and the close,
> And shot through tunnels, like a lightning-wedge
> By great Thor-hammers driven through the rock,
> Which, quivering through the intestine blackness, splits,
> And lets it in at once: the train swept in
> Athrob with effort, trembling with resolve,
> The fierce denouncing whistle wailing on
> And dying off smothered in the shuddering dark,
> While we, self-awed, drew troubled breath, oppressed
> As other Titans, underneath the pile
> And nightmare of the mountains. Out, at last,
> To catch the dawn afloat upon the land!
> —Hills, slung forth broadly and gauntly everywhere,
> [. . .]
> While, down their straining sides, streamed manifest
> A soil as red as Charlemagne's knightly blood,
> To consecrate the verdure. Some one said,
> 'Marseilles!' And lo, the city of Marseilles. (7.429–42; 446–49)

Their tunnel passage becomes a kind of sexual consummation, one reinforced by the phallic description of the train and its orgasmic cry—topped off by the "consecrating" blood that stains the soil as they emerge from the tunnel. It is a symbolic union on a number of levels: male and female, material and spiritual, the Europe of the present with that of Charlemagne, who made the first great efforts to reunify Europe after the fall of the Roman Empire. Noting Barrett Browning's merger of epic and modern transportation technology, the *Literary Gazette* remarked, "Mrs. Browning lights up with the radiance of her genius the things which to most people are least suggestive of the poetical."[38] This, of course, is what Barrett Browning (through Aurora) had argued poets should do all along: "Their sole work is to represent the age, / Their age, not Charlemagne's,—this live, throbbing age" (5.202–3). The same review offers *Aurora Leigh* as a counterexample to those poets who would waste "their fire on galvanizing the *simulacra* of the past."[39]

Such celebrations aside, my attempt to center Marian in Aurora's personal and poetic development might seem headed for the same obstacle that derailed earlier efforts to read *Aurora Leigh* as a prototype of Victorian feminist epic: Aurora's marriage to Romney and Marian's subsequent displacement, which would also seem to compromise the uniquely feminine cosmopolitanism she and Aurora had achieved.[40] One way out of this impasse, as Reynolds proposes, is to recognize the political symbolism of Aurora's marriage itself and her creation of a household that still includes Marian and her child. Political identity in the poem, he argues, comes to reside not in the state alone, "but in individuals, each of whom collaborates freely with others to form a community."[41] Their household consists of disparate individuals all of whom were compelled to travel in order to find community and recover a sense of political purpose. If Romney had imagined Aurora in childhood as his "fairy bride from Italy" (9.766), this fairy tale disappears in a celebration of work. That work, he reveals, in one of the poem's few explicit references to the Risorgimento, is specifically political: "You'll make a work-day of your holiday / And turn it to our Tuscan people's use" (8.98–99). Together, Romney and Aurora realize that they cannot simply return to the idealized Italy of their childhood; nor is simply *being* half-Italian, as Aurora is by birth, enough. They must reforge their connection to the nation. Cosmopolitanism, likewise, is not an identity that is readily provided in the form of a national or ethnic inheritance, but one that must be cultivated and practiced.

The Brownings' own marriage, of course, in some ways mirrors the poem's ideal that cosmopolitanism should be something reflected in one's work and one's daily life. For all of its romantic overtones, their elopement to the continent was also a career move, as Barrett Browning explained to Mitford: "We go to live a quiet, simple, rational life—to do work . . . to write poems & read books, & try to live not in vain & not for vanities" (September 18, 1846; *BC* 14:5). As with *Aurora Leigh,* part of that work was to craft a hybrid Anglo-European identity, and her poetry becomes a site of continuous renewal of that identity. Public and private are never very far apart in Barrett Browning's life and work, so it is fitting that she would try to make her son Robert Wiedeman Browning—"Penini" or "Pen" for short—a kind of case study in cosmopolitanism (his nickname, appropriately enough, was derived from the child's Italianate mispronunciation of Wiedeman).[42] From a young age, Pen began to speak Italian, French, and even some German. In letters to her sisters, Barrett Browning commented on the progress of her son's education and boasted of his identification with Italians and the Italian cause: "he shall be a 'citizen of the world' after my own heart & ready for the millenium [sic]."[43] Unlike Aurora, Pen would not be compelled to straighten his copious curls, nor would he have to shed the somewhat fancy clothing that made him look more Italian than English to some observers (see figure 2). Indeed, one senses that lurking behind the mother/son interactions of poems such as "A Tale of Villafranca" and, most important, I will argue, "Mother and Poet," is the more personal question of how to develop her own son's sense of civic identity and responsibility: what languages can and should the citizen of the world speak?

Poems before Congress and "Mother and Poet"

Barrett Browning's next major work after *Aurora Leigh* was *Poems before Congress,* which opens in the preface with what would be her most direct and public appeal to a cosmopolitan ethics: "if patriotism be a virtue indeed, it cannot mean an exclusive devotion to our country's interests,—for that is only another form of devotion to personal interests, family interests, or provincial interests, all of which, if not driven past themselves, are vulgar and immoral objects" (4:553).[44] Barrett Browning longs for a day when an English statesman will have "a heart too large for England" (4:554)—echoing Aurora's boast in France that "a poet's heart / Can swell to a pair of nationalities" (6.50–51). Overall, as Elizabeth Woodworth puts it in a recent study, *Poems before Congress* is a "small but loud-voiced volume . . . one thick with criticism (and praise), brash condemnation, and brave hope"—one that in complex ways furthers Barrett Browning's aim of crafting a space for women in political "congresses" of many sorts.[45] In some sense, Barrett Browning makes the politician's mission the poet's, who must point the way toward a more cosmopolitan future. "Italy and the World," as discussed in chapter 1, calls for the cultivation of a language divorced from "cheap vernacular patriotisms" (39) and characterized instead by the expansive voice of poetry. Literally, it seems, the poet's voice is one that crosses borders and ranges across the whole of Europe, as when Barrett Browning proclaims, "I cry aloud in my poet-passion, / Viewing my England o'er Alp and sea" (96–97). The poet describes her ideal world as one of expanding concentric circles, a figurative way of representing cosmopolitanism that can be traced back to the Stoics. She declares that "certain virtues have dropped to zero" (121), and in their place, she proposes,

Figure 2   Elizabeth Barrett Browning and son Pen Browning, 1860 (photographer Fratellis D'Alessandri; courtesy Armstrong Browning Library).

National voices, distinct yet dependant,
Ensphering each other, as swallow does swallow,
With circles still widening and ever ascendant,
In multiform life to united progression. (127–30)

Under this vision, each nation, in essence, remains distinct but cannot exist by itself. Julia Kristeva employs a similar image to describe what she calls a global *esprit général,* a phrase she appropriates from Montesquieu to contrast with the more inward-looking *Volksgeist.* The *esprit général* "respects the particular if and only if, it is integrated into another particular, of greater magnitude, but that at the same time guarantees the existence of the previous one and lifts it up to respecting new differences that it might tend to censor if it were not for that logic."[46] Similarly, Barrett Browning does not advocate the obliteration of national identities but rather proposes that they be crossed more freely.

With the exception of "A Tale of Villafranca," which closes with the fatalistic observation, "In this low world, where great Deeds die, / What matter if we live?" (83–84), other poems included in *Poems before Congress* present just these kinds of ideals in practice—largely hopeful images of international cooperation instigated in many cases by women. "A Court Lady," for example, features a Milanese noblewoman who consoles a dying French soldier with the words, "Each of the heroes around us has fought for his land and line, / But thou has fought for a stranger, in hate of a wrong not thine" (37–38). With a riposte no doubt intended for England, she adds, "Happy are all free peoples, too strong to be dispossessed. / But blessed are those among nations who dare to be strong for the rest!" (39–40). Despite Barrett Browning's disappointment with the terms of the Villafranca treaty, which left Venice and other parts of Italy still in Austrian hands, she celebrates the example set by France in aiding Italy, one she hopes will prove prophetic for the future of European geopolitics. "The Dance" again offers thanks to the "liberating nation" France (23), as it imagines Italians and French soldiers mingling together in their camp before an Italian noblewoman calls for a dance to begin. Again, it is a woman who facilitates the next, higher stage of diplomacy, one that serves as an example to men:

Then the sons of France bareheaded, lowly bowing,
    Led the ladies back where kinsmen of the south
Stood, received them; till, with burst of overflowing
    Feeling—husbands, brothers, Florence's male youth,
    Turned, and kissed the martial strangers mouth to mouth. (46–50)

The spontaneous, even passionate, overtones of international fellowship here reflect Barrett Browning's belief that such impulses are, in effect, *natural* and cross gender boundaries. They are earthly manifestations of the "Oneness of God," as she proposed in an earlier letter: "the unity of God preserves a unity in men—that is, a perpetual sympathy between man & man" (*BC* 3:219)— one too often held in check by the kinds of national self-interests that finally won out at Villafranca.[47] She concludes "The Dance," however, with a final gesture toward that divine cosmopolitan consummation: "God had spoken somewhere since the morning, / That men were somehow brothers, by no platitude,— / Cried exultant in great wonder and free gratitude" (58–60).

If *Poems before Congress* largely expresses the dream or ideal of internationalism via Italian nationalism, "Mother and Poet" explores the difficulty and personal cost of truly realizing that vision. In many ways, the poem is Barrett Browning's final and most complex reflection on the prospects for a new kind of postnationalist European citizenship. The poem was first published in May of 1861 in *The Independent* and then posthumously in her *Last Poems* (1862) edited by Robert Browning. In inquiring, provocative ways, the poem synthesizes the more personal vision of cosmopolitanism given expression in *Aurora Leigh* with the larger political ambitions of *Casa Guidi Windows* and *Poems before Congress*. In terms of its subject matter, the poem accomplishes this merger by focusing on the plight of an individual Italian: the Turinese poet Laura Savio, who lost two sons in the 1861 uprising that liberated most of northern Italy from Austria. The poem's dramatic monologue form—deployed without ironic distancing—helps to convey a sense of empathy between author and speaker, as Barrett Browning imagines herself intensely into Savio's state of mind.

"Mother and Poet" draws immediate attention to the crucial role that language plays in the formation of national identity and the maternal source of that linguistic inheritance: "*I* made them indeed / Speak plain the word *country. I* taught them, no doubt, / That a country's a thing men should die for at need" (21–23). As Anderson suggests in *Imagined Communities,* "What the eye is to the lover—that particular, ordinary eye he or she is born with—language—whatever language history has made his or her mother tongue—is to the patriot. Through that language, encountered at mother's knee and parted with only at the grave, pasts are restored, fellowships are imagined, and futures dreamed."[48] To forsake this powerful language was difficult, even traumatic for Barrett Browning—and that sense of trauma pervades the poem. The progress of the conflict gradually begins to undermine the authority of that maternal language: "At first, happy news came, in gay letters moiled / With my kisses" (31–32), and then after the first son's death, "letters still came, shorter, sadder, more strong, / Writ now but in one hand" (45–46). Finally the last communication she receives comes via telegraph:

> On which, without pause, up the telegraph line
>   Swept smoothly the next news from Gaeta:—*Shot.*
> *Tell his mother.* Ah, ah, "his," "their" mother,—not "mine,"
>   No voice says "*My* mother" again to me. (56–59)

The telegraph resonates in several ways here, being at once sublime, with its mysterious speed, and brutal in its impact: in four quick lines lie foreshadowed all the mechanical indifference to life and death that would characterize the great European war of the next century. What should be a human voice (and a poetic one) has been replaced by the stunted, impersonal announcement of a government bureaucracy. As discourses of war, poetry and the telegraph contest with each other, and the telegraph triumphs in this instance, just as it had over the personal letter. Indeed, even the kind of quasi-personal contact Claude achieves in *Amours de Voyage* via the post seems lost here. In this one powerful passage, Barrett Browning reflects sharply on the broken promises of Victorian technological cosmopolitanism, an ideal that had taken many for a ride—herself included, perhaps, as during her highly energized description of Aurora Leigh and Marian traveling by train to Italy. She instead here foreshadows a different, grimmer coming together: the important role that the telegram would play in bringing death on the battlefield back to parents on the home front. The telegraph also belies the comforting image of Italy as a largely pastoral, aesthetic entity that, if united, posed no serious threat to international stability. Italy was becoming a modern nation, one with telegraphs and railroads, one capable of waging war and marshaling the latest technology in that effort.

"Mother and Poet" underscores the difficulty poetry faces as it attempts to bridge the nation in its material and more idealistic guises and, similarly, its inability to conjoin individual and collective identity under the banner of nationhood. The mother's personal grief overshadows any sense of a more transcendent national identity: while Italy cheers, "*this* woman, *this,* who is agonised here" cannot join in (8). Barrett Browning thus challenges the confidence with which Mazzini could proclaim that the individual must "not say *I;* say *we.*" As in the telegraph passage above, "Italy" becomes a pronoun without an antecedent, an abstraction only. The poem's attempt to assuage grief by looking toward rebirth in spirit form–both for the individual and for the nation—rings hollow. God, in some sense, disappears from the poem when the spirit of Guido, the first dead son, fails to intervene to protect his brother, as he had hoped: "he was safe, and aware / Of a presence that turned off the balls,—was imprest / It was Guido himself" (51–53). Likewise, the dream of reunion with her sons in a heavenly "country" in Stanza 18 seems to provide small consolation. The poem is finally overrun with grief, ending with an echo of the same "Dead" stanza that opened the poem. The contrast to the more millennial vision of *Casa Guidi Windows* could not be starker. For a poet always ready to see the hand of God behind political events and whose work embodies what Linda Lewis aptly calls an "internalization of the doctrine of Apocalypse" and its "injunction to renovate and resurrect this present world," God's absence here speaks volumes.[49]

One should still be careful not to read the poem as a complete disavowal of nationalism. Even in the midst of her profound grief, the mother still seems able to place her loss within a wider political context: "the birth-pangs of nations will wring us at length / Into wail such as this—and we sit on forlorn / When the man-child is born" (93–95). This passage, as Tricia Lootens argues, reveals that the mother "still speaks with a patriotic voice: her cry does not condemn the natural unavoidable process that has given birth to her (masculine) nation, even as it killed her sons."[50] At the very least, however, if the poem does not outrightly condemn nationalism, it does offer a serious reappraisal of where the nationalistic struggle was eventually leading Europe, and, specifically, the women of Europe. Alison Chapman argues that "Mother and Poet," like other works in *Last Poems,* attempts to overturn conventions of what women's poetry—indelibly linked in the minds of contemporary readers with sensibility—might accomplish politically: "Barrett Browning's creation of a poem out of Savio's refusal to write in the cause of the Risorgimento performs the withdrawal of the woman poet's personal emotions from political poetics. Poetry is divorced from the body of the woman poet."[51] I would contend only that it is Savio's recognition of the inescapably political status of her body—as a poet and as a mother—that causes her to reassess the public impact of her poetry. In some sense, what Savio had been doing all along was attempting to divorce the body from politics, overlooking its material reality in pursuit of an idealistic notion of a higher, more spiritual nation and poetics—the same uncertain aim, of course, that defines *Casa Guidi Windows.* The achievement of "Mother and Poet" is that, even in the midst of the nationalist fervor that had overtaken much of the continent, Barrett Browning was already looking ahead to its aftermath and the nature of a postnationalist Europe. Cosmopolitanism likewise takes on a new spiritual essence, one characterized less by prophecies and grand designs and more by individuals attempting to manifest that divine "sympathy between man & man" on closer, more intimate levels.

The poem asks, "What art can a woman be good at?" (11), or, in other words, what language will the mother teach the child if not the language of the nation? The last line of "Mother and Poet" points to a possible answer—a more cautionary, civilizing role for the mother and poet—a role that contains the destructive tendencies of nationalism and attempts to reimagine affiliations of family, community, nation, and world. Defiantly, the poem closes, "If in keeping the feast / You want a great song for your Italy free, / Let none look at *me!*" (98–100). In doing so, the mother invokes the same ideal that Barrett Browning expressed in the preface to *Poems before Congress:* the love of the mother for the child, like that of the citizen for the nation, is ultimately unavailing, even destructive, if it stops at those borders. In her writings on nationalism and women today in Europe, Kristeva makes a similar kind of plea:

> [I]t is not impossible that in strengthening this bond [between mother and child], in becoming aware of its risks and its depth, women will transfer it from private intimacy or esthetics, to which tradition has confined it, and adapt their speech in the civic sphere to its measure. This would not be their least contribution to a politics that remains to be constructed, as a regime not of authority and domination bur harmonization of differences—which is precisely the goal of modern democracies.[52]

Kristeva's point should not be misinterpreted to mean that the proper role of someone like Barrett Browning, a woman seeking a greater voice in questions of international politics, is to retreat from the public sphere into a heterosexist ideal of nurturing maternity. Rather, it is the public sphere that must be reconstituted. "Mother and Poet" begins to fashion the kind of cosmopolitan or cosmofeminine outlook that Kristeva describes, one that attempted to bridge public and private and to legitimate the perspective of the mother in international political debate.

At the end of her career, Barrett Browning was trying to find a way out of the extremes of international politics—a way of replacing sacrifice with survival and of balancing prophecy with pragmatism. Likewise, by 1861, the Risorgimento also seemed to be entering a new phase, one where diplomatic initiatives such as those fashioned by Cavour offered as much promise as victory on the battlefield. After Cavour's sudden and unexpected death that same year, Barrett Browning surmised, "A legion of Garibaldis would not make such a man."[53] Her comment is not so much a repudiation of the Risorgimento's most famous military figure as it is an acknowledgment of the need for a transition to a new, more progressive way of thinking about international relations. "Perhaps the nationalism/internationalism argument would look different," Bruce Robbins writes in *Feeling Global: Internationalism in Distress* (1999), "if the examples had more to do with ordinary forms of life, such as love and child care, that are repeated everywhere every day than with extraordinary, one-shot choices of life or death. Perhaps the more pertinent [question is] not what you would die for but what you live for."[54] It was in this hopeful direction—a poetics of negotiation and diplomacy—that Barrett Browning had begun to turn shortly before her own death, several weeks after Cavour's, on June 29, 1861.

4

Browning at the Border

Red Cotton Night-Cap Country

ROBERT BROWNING'S periods of residence and travel on the Continent coincided with some of the great political upheavals of the time, but the closest the poet may have ever come to being in any personal danger due to such unrest was in the late summer of 1870, during the Franco-Prussian War. At the time, Browning and his sister Sarianna were enjoying a seaside holiday at St. Aubin-sur-Mer on the Normandy coast. His good friend Joseph Milsand lived in a cottage only "two steps off," Browning wrote to Isa Blagden, while they stayed in "another of the most primitive kind on the sea-shore—which shore is a good sandy stretch for miles and miles on either side."[1] During previous summers in Brittany, Browning had developed an enthusiasm for swimming which he now indulged almost daily, although he confessed that the "sadness of the war & its consequences go far to paralyse all our pleasure" (342). If convinced that France was being justly punished for its misplaced faith in Napoleon III, Browning still felt a vague attachment to the struggling nation that compelled him to remain on the scene: "I am glad to be in France rather than elsewhere just now" (344). His sympathy was also quickened, no doubt, by witnessing Milsand's difficult efforts to secure his home and belongings in Paris.

But even as German armies began a steady advance toward the capital after capturing the emperor himself, Browning remained confident that they could make it back to the safety of England without difficulty: "we can reach Havre from Caen in a few hours—& thence get to Southampton when we please," he wrote to Blagden in mid-September, "so I think we have decided to remain till the end of the month" (345). Within a week of penning these reassuring words, however, Browning began a frantic departure from France. Milsand was concerned that the poet might have already been mistaken for a German spy by restless villagers. State authorities were also on the lookout for French nationals trying to leave the country, which had been forbidden by government order. As a result, the boat to Havre, along with most trains and coaches, was no longer in service. Only through Milsand's last-minute efforts were the Brownings able to secure passage out of the country, at midnight, on a cattle boat bound for Southampton.[2]

How near Browning truly came to being detained or arrested is not entirely clear, but, at the very least, the shock to the psyche of this suddenly accidental tourist must have been profound. The incident is telling in other ways as well, and reveals something of what inspired *Red Cotton Night-Cap Country,* perhaps Browning's most ambitious attempt to inscribe contemporary French culture and his own presence within it. Recounting a more placid vacation two summers later in St. Aubin, the poem takes the form of a dramatic monologue spoken by Browning to a fellow traveler, Anne Thackeray, in which he rhapsodizes over the peacefulness of the landscape before introducing a darker, hidden truth. Not far from where they were staying, Antoine Mellerio (1827–70), the wealthy son of a Parisian jeweler, had committed suicide by leaping from a tower on his estate. As the poem explains, Mellerio seems to have been motivated by a desperate religious faith that compounded his guilt over an extra-marital affair (in an earlier effort to atone for his sins, Mellerio had destroyed his love letters—and his hands—by holding them over a fire). With the help of Milsand, who had first told Browning of the incident, the poet examined press reports and court records associated with the case, and eventually decided that he had hit upon "a capital brand-new subject" for a poem, one that would untangle Mellerio's complex web of personal and spiritual obsessions.[3] With names and places changed to prevent the possibility of libel suits (Mellerio, for example, became Léonce Miranda, and St. Aubin became St. Rambert), Browning's poem hit the press less than a year after Mellerio's contested estate had been settled by the court at Caen.

Mixing seaside strolls and sightseeing with the tale of a gruesome suicide, the poem is another vacation interrupted by reality—a comforting, inviting surface that hides more troubling forces at work. But in many ways, these kinds of intrusions were nothing new for Browning, whether in France or Italy. They were indispensable to him, in fact: his authority as a travel poet hinged upon the tension between the expected and the unexpected, the comforting and the threatening. Weaker travel discourse, to him, merely recycled what was reassuringly familiar. To make this point to Elizabeth, he singled out Mary Shelley's *Rambles in Italy and Germany*, which, as we saw earlier, she had read and loaned to him in September 1845:

> why don't you tell us that at Rome they eat roasted chestnuts, and put the shells into their aprons, the women do, and calmly empty the whole on the heads of the passengers in the street below; and that at Padua when a man drives his waggon up to a house and stops, all the mouse-coloured oxen that pull it from a beam against their foreheads sit down in a heap and rest. But once she travelled the country with Shelley on arm; now she plods it, Rogers in hand. (*BC* 9:70)

In some sense, Browning pays tribute here to the kinds of obscure but telling markers of Italy he had unearthed in his own verse. In *Pippa Passes* (1841), for instance, a peasant girl may not eat roasted chestnuts and dump the shells on tourists, but she does recount how an old man feeds her "on his knees with fig-peckers, / Lampreys and red Breganze-wine" (3.236–37). In "The Englishman in Italy" (1845), Browning's distinctively Italian culinary delights almost begin to overwhelm the speaker, who imagines "grape-gleaners (two dozen, / Three over one plate) / With lasagne so tempting to swallow / In slippery ropes" (95–98).

If such fine details were enough to distinguish Browning from Samuel Rogers and the other "tourists in rhyme" who had succeeded him, to rest alone on this kind of consumption of the exotic and unfamiliar was still in many ways to miss what he considered most important to the poet as traveler.[4] What apparently drew Barrett Browning to Shelley's book—its tentative intervention in the political sphere—even if it misses Robert's notice here, was still a vital part of seeing and assimilating Europe. Like the unobtrusive but ever-vigilant poet of "How It Strikes a Contemporary" (1855), where Browning again imagines himself into the mind of a European, "He took such cognizance of men and things, / If any beat a horse, you felt he saw; / If any cursed a woman, he took note; / Yet stared at nobody" (30–33). The need to be relevant, earnest, and, at times, contemporary and political never left him and still authorized his presence abroad in more clandestine ways. It would keep interrupting him, as it had in *Sordello* (1840), when a "sad, dishevelled ghost / That pluck at me and point" (3.696–97) compels him to break off from his historical poem of the thirteenth century and reflect on his own crisis of poetic and political purpose: "There is such niggard stock of happiness / To share, that, do one's uttermost, dear wretch, / One labours ineffectually to stretch / It o'er you" (3.706–9). The girl would return again in the guise of Pippa, urging the rest of the poem's cast into various forms of repentance with her song. She returns still later in *The Ring and the Book* (1868–69) as Pompilia: Browning "discovers" her in a marketplace in Florence, where he again seems to be idling his time like any casual traveler. The "Old Yellow Book," a legal relic from the early eighteenth century describing her murder and the trial of her estranged husband Guido Franceschini, sits inconspicuously enough among other "odds and ends of ravage" (1.53) before it calls to Browning and insists upon the epic transformation it would receive at his hands.[5]

Now in modern France, Browning had returned in many ways to the same fundamental question: when visiting a location for reasons of personal or artistic enrichment, how does one avoid ignoring the political and social realities of the people who call it home? Cosmopolitanism, as Amanda Anderson reminds us, is an ideal that depends in large part upon "a mobility that is the luxury of social, economic, or cultural privilege." How does one, in turn, negotiate the "complex tension between elitism and egalitarianism" that accompanies the effort to cross into another culture?[6] In *Red Cotton Night-Cap Country*, as during that summer in 1870, Browning was not entirely successful at fashioning this idealized in-between space, one that balances the idea of travel as vacation—an escape from the pressures of urban mass culture—with the demands of a more engaged kind of Anglo-European citizenship and identity. What *Red Cotton Night-Cap Country* attempts, in essence, is to play in earnest. It invokes the pleasure of the beach but insists on the presence of danger, becoming like Normandy itself: a pristine borderland seemingly isolated from the urban centers of Paris and London, but also, according to Browning, peculiarly at the heart of political and cultural conflict in Europe. The poem strives to cope with the contradictory impressions that his lifelong encounter with Europe created in him—impressions that blended identification with distance and sympathy with judgment. These are, of course, the same tensions that define Browning's signature form, the dramatic monologue, as Robert Langbaum first proposed in *The Poetry of Experience* (1957). And as I will argue in this chapter, more so than any other Browning monologue, *Red Cotton Night-Cap Country* underscores the intricate ways in which the dramatic monologue form reproduces the dynamics of travel itself, revealing how the one practice continued to fuel the other even at this relatively late stage of his career. Browning's poetry exists at borders, in numerous senses, as has long been recognized by commentators on his work: between poetry and prose, lyric and drama, England and Europe, culture and politics, men and women. Each of these sets of borders comes into play in *Red Cotton Night-Cap Country*, and in attempting to dwell at the border, the poem finally reveals just how difficult, and necessary, it is to occupy this liminal space.[7] In particular, Browning's encounter with Europe seems always to come back to women—as figures in his poetry, as we have already seen—and as authors themselves—his wife Elizabeth included. Women would occupy both roles simultaneously in *Red Cotton Night-Cap Country*, offering added insight into why Europe, and the cosmopolitan, were such gendered spaces for Browning.

BROWNING'S AMBIVALENCE toward France reflects the attitude of many British liberals at the time. As Clare A. Simmons reveals in *Eyes across the Channel* (2000), these mixed feelings were especially evident in the alternating enthusiasm and dread for plans to build a channel tunnel between the two countries—plans which were briefly put into effect in 1882 and which, it should be noted, Browning opposed.[8] His wish to leave Britain's natural borders intact, however, was not necessarily due to the kind of Francophobia one sometimes sees in Browning's compatriots. And while his overall enthusiasm for French culture may not have rivaled Barrett Browning's, I am still suggesting that *Red Cotton Night-Cap Country* embodies a stronger connection than is conveyed, for instance, by insisting that he inhabits France with a sense of detachment akin to naturalism or that he always remains an "outsider" in the poem, as different readings of it have proposed.[9] His life and work, rather, reveal an intense if indeterminate sense of belonging to France.

In several senses—personally, professionally, and, of course, geographically—France was closer to Browning than the other nations of Europe—closer even than Italy in some key respects. One telling contrast is that France by and large exists in the present for Browning: two earlier long poems, *Prince Hohenstiel-Schwangau, Saviour of Society* (1871) and *Fifine at the Fair* (1872), likewise deal with contemporary French people and subjects. In a way that Italy had not yet achieved, France was a part of modern Europe for Browning, a nation with a more immediate impact on the course of art, politics, and the sciences. With a long exposure to French language and literature, like Arnold, and frequent visits to Paris and the coasts of Brittany and Normandy, Browning no doubt felt that he could inhabit the minds of contemporary French people, whether Miranda or Napoleon III, with the same authenticity that he could with other subjects of his dramatic monologues. *Prince Hohenstiel-Schwangau*, he claimed, revealed "just what I imagine the man might, if he pleased, say for himself."[10]

To adapt Mary Louise Pratt's familiar term, it could be said that Browning inhabits a different kind of contact zone in France as opposed to Italy, which a brief comparison to *The Ring and the Book* demonstrates.[11] There Browning remains distanced from the protagonists of his poem not just historically but structurally, in a sense, by speaking *in propria persona* only at the margins of the poem, as if peering over into his subject.[12] In *Red Cotton Night-Cap Country*, rather than creating the illusion that Italy unfolds itself before the reader's eyes, Browning mingles with his subject and its location throughout the course of the poem. This effect is characteristic of what Donald S. Hair terms Browning's later "parleying" poems. As Browning converses with Thackeray, "the two voices begin to sound like a complex argument comprehended by a single consciousness and advanced by a single voice, especially when one speaker proposes or conjectures positions for the other."[13] Browning's overall encounter with France becomes a kind of parleying or negotiation between the author and those who inhabit France with him, including his fellow travelers. The kind of authorial distancing one is used to with Browning's more historicized dramatic monologues in part disappears here.

This sense of greater closeness to French people and culture had very real origins in the bonds that Browning developed with individual French citizens: key among these associates, of course, was Milsand, who in 1851 published one of the earliest and most appreciative critical surveys of Browning's poetry.[14] It may be no exaggeration to say that, second to Elizabeth, Milsand was the closest person Browning had to a kind of soul mate, one who shared his wife's willingness to comment carefully on his work, a duty which Milsand took over after her death in 1861. Theirs typifies the devoted and openly affectionate male friendships of the time. Milsand's daughter Marie Blanc-Milsand later recalled that during those summers in St. Aubin, "Every day the two men could be seen on the beach, the arm of Browning always round Milsand's shoulders."[15] An illustration accompanying her article recreates a photograph of the two men in a similar pose as they soak in a painting by Browning's son (see figure 3). The illustration conveys something of the intellectual and aesthetic symbiosis of their friendship, a prototype of the broader ideal of cross-cultural fertilization that Browning endorses in *Red Cotton Night-Cap Country*—one characterized, as we will see, by a specifically masculine kind of bonding. Milsand, in fact, is the only person referred to by name in the poem, that "Milsand, who makest warm my wintry world, / And wise my heaven" (2945–46). That Browning felt the need to express such public gratitude to his friend—making him, in essence, a part of the poem—is not surprising, for without him there might not have been a poem

Figure 3 Robert Browning and Joseph Milsand looking at a painting by Browning's son, 1882 (photographer William H. Grove; courtesy Armstrong Browning Library).

at all. It was Milsand who guided Browning to landmarks associated with the Miranda story and who gained him access to court records that might otherwise have been restricted to foreigners. In the poem and in Browning's real life, Milsand, more than any other single individual, was the mediator through whom Browning interpreted France.

This personal connection between England and France—a mutual desire to know and understand each other—broadens and takes on a geographical dimension in the poem. The first part of the poem underscores the proximity of Normandy to England as well as its equidistance between Paris and London, the metropolitan centers of Europe. Normandy, of course, was also the origin of the 1066 invasion that briefly united France and England under one monarch. Miranda's distinctive "*Parc Anglais*" (704) is one of several reminders of this cross-cultural pollination: the very English-sounding French phrase, like others in the poem, subtly reinforces the linguistic overlap between the two cultures. Similarly, Browning's need to alter the names of the people and places in the poem provided him with the opportunity to turn the village of Douvres into "Londres":

> Take the left: yonder town is—what say you
> If I say 'Londres'? Ay, the mother-mouse
> (Reversing fable, as truth can and will)
> Which gave our mountain of a London birth!
> This is the Conqueror's country, bear in mind,
> And Londres-district blooms with London-pride. (421–26)

Londres stands now as a symbol of peaceful coexistence between France and England, although the reference to "the Conqueror" reminds the reader that Browning and Thackeray are walking a landscape crisscrossed by invading armies and defined by cultural clashes: where French, Norse, and English all sought at one time or another to reclaim land they thought was theirs or to maintain a foothold in continental Europe (an idea, we know now, that would prove prophetic in ways Browning could not have imagined). Although now mostly a retreat for holiday makers, the shoreline resonates with a grander historical legacy and significance. Rhetorically as well, it was a land worth fighting over.

Browning's objective is indeed to lay claim to this landscape, and his contest takes the form of a verbal battle with Thackeray, whose active presence in the poem, as Hair describes, belies that of the typical auditor of the dramatic monologue. The staging of the poem as a conversation between two British travelers with contrasting views of the region is partly based on reality: during his 1872 vacation, Browning visited Thackeray at nearby Lion with the aim of healing a rift that had opened up between them after he became convinced that she had spread rumors he planned to remarry.[16] With their friendship restored, the poem begins cordially enough: "And so, here happily we meet, fair friend! / Again once more, as if the years rolled back / And this our meeting-place were just that Rome / Out in the champaign" (1–4). While all may be well between them on the surface (Browning even dedicates the poem to her), what the reader gradually begins to see unfold is a knock-down contest for textual authority—for ownership of the seaside they both lay claim to as travelers and authors. Browning later admits as much with an appropriately pugilistic metaphor to describe their conversation: "British maid / And British man, suppose we have it out / Here in the fields, decide the question so?" (381–83).

The spoils of their contest is St. Aubin itself, this "[m]eek, hitherto un-Murrayed bathing place, / Best loved of sea-coast-nook-ful Normandy!" (20–21)—a place where one could still experience authentic solitude, although this would not last long, as the ambivalent "hitherto" reveals. With this backhanded tribute to the same Murray who had accompanied Clough, Browning engages his poem in the battle for cultural capital that had been raging throughout the nineteenth century between a mass-culture "tourism" and a more selective anti-tourism or "travel." Browning thus fits the pattern of other self-fashioned travelers who, in James Buzard's words, "lay claim to an aristocracy of inner feeling, the projection of an ideology of originality and difference."[17] In terms of genre, such distancing served to reinforce the idea that poetry—particularly long, challenging poems in the style of *Red Cotton Night-Cap Country*—was a special genre reserved for more selective readers. Such poems might lack popular appeal, but they remained, like the mountain retreat where Browning would later set *La Saisiaz* (1878), "[y]et untroubled by the tourist, touched on by no travel-book" (60). Before retreating to the mountains, however, he was more preoccupied with preserving St. Aubin's "unpretending beach" (17), a goal that had gained renewed momentum in 1871 with the passage of the Bank Holiday Act, which created leisure time for a new generation of tourists eager to experience the joys of the seaside both at home and abroad.[18] The seaside serves as the reader's entry point into France and into the country of the poem: to know one, it seems, is to know the other. Browning acknowledges that he and Thackeray are both attempting to relocate France and cosmopolitan identity away from metropolitan centers such as Paris. At the same time, however, Browning insists that the seaside must remain poetic turf.

The authority of Browning's claim would rest in large part on an already well-established British tradition of littoral verse, one that appears to have crested around the time of his visits to France, a span which witnessed the publication of Swinburne's "The Triumph of Time" (1866), Dante Gabriel Rossetti's "The Sea-Limits" (1870), and, of course, Arnold's "Dover Beach" (1867). Earlier in the century, Romantic poets, Byron especially, had helped to transform the beach, in the words of cultural historians Lena Lenček and Gideon Bosker, from, at best, a medical necessity into "an outpost for reflection and self-discovery, a place where nature, in her infinite dynamism and enigma, presents a subtle script through which the human spirit cryptically reveals itself."[19] Browning had already paid tribute to sea-bathing as physically and spiritually rejuvenating in the "Amphibian" prologue to *Fifine at the Fair,* which features Browning enjoying a swim off of the Breton coast as he draws a series of connections between swimming, flight, and the will to transcend different elements and modes of existence. With the aid of the poet, the beach becomes a border between the here and the hereafter: "Unable to fly, one swims" (48) and, in a similar act of transference, "[w]e substitute, in a fashion, / For heaven—poetry" (55–56). Swimming even creates in him a foretaste of a celestial reunion with Elizabeth: "Does she look, pity, wonder / At one who mimics flight, / Swims—heaven above, sea under, / Yet always earth in sight?" (73–76). The beach affords the closest thing there is to communion with heaven while simultaneously teaching one to accept the limits of earth and time: it is a lesson, we will discover, that the impetuous Miranda would have benefitted from.

Browning swims in *Red Cotton Night-Cap Country* too, inspiring a burst of alliteration as a wave "flecks [his] foot with froth, nor tempts in vain" (40), but for the most part he stays out of the water, dwelling instead on the value of how all of the different natural elements of the seaside come together to form one uniquely gratifying environment. The poem becomes an ode of sorts to beachfront property, even if one possesses it only as lessee. Browning is like many who rent property near the shore in search of repose and a good view: "That, just behind you, is mine own hired house: / With right of pathway through the field in front" (22–23). This particular beach, he notes, holds another natural enticement:

Be sure I keep the path that hugs the wall,
Of mornings, as I pad from door to gate!
Yon yellow—what if not wild-mustard flower?—
Of that, my naked sole makes lawful prize,

Bruising the acrid aromatics out,
Till, what they preface, good salt savours sting
From, first, the sifted sands, then sands in slab,
Smooth save for pipy wreath-work of the worm:
(Granite and mussel-shell are ground alike
To glittering paste,—the live worm troubles yet.) (26–35)

Lying in Browning's pathway, the mustard flower (like the Miranda narrative he later discovers), belongs to him by "lawful" right. Indeed, the image of the wild-mustard flower crushed open to reveal an acrid odor serves as a metaphor for the poem itself: the reader moves from an invitingly pleasant landscape to more hidden trouble. Placing oneself on the beach means both getting away from it all and getting to the heart of the matter.

Browning then proceeds to draw a contrast between his own view of the region and that of Thackeray, who seems more drawn to its peaceful aspects and proposes to pay tribute to St. Aubin in a work of her own— either a kind of travel guide or picturesque novel—with, as Browning puts it, a "[s]ubsiding-into-slumber sort of name, / Symbolic of the place and people too, / 'White Cotton Night-cap Country'" (144–46). Hers is just the sort of book that might have broad appeal to other British travelers in France who were likewise in search of destinations away from the major seaside developments of Dieppe, Dunkirk, and Trouville. Initially, Browning greets the idea with good-natured humor, but his words gradually take on a more concerned tone, one that borders on sarcasm:

Oh, better, very best of all the news—
You mean to catch and cage the wingèd word,
And make it breed and multiply at home
Till Norman idlesse stock our England too?
Normandy shown minute yet magnified
In one of those small books, the truly great,
We never know enough, yet know so well?
How I foresee the cursive diamond-dints,—
Composite pen that plays the pencil too,—
As, touch the page and up the glamour goes,
And filmily o'er grain-crop, meadow-ground,
O'er orchard in the pasture, farm a-field
And hamlet on the road-edge, floats and forms
And falls, at lazy last of all, the Cap
That crowns the country! (157–71)

Browning's attention to bibliographical features—the inclusion of sketches, the cursive typeface—suggests a finished product that is more commodity than text, something that will be bought for its packaging. The content of Thackeray's hypothetical book is also a kind of package: a glossy surface, replete with farms, pastures, and peasants—a preconceived notion of pastoral France. In effect, Browning restates poetically what he said earlier of Mary Shelley's *Rambles in Italy* to Elizabeth. *White Cotton Night-cap Country,* he implies, is strangely domestic for a travel book; this "small book" does not travel at all or reveal the true color of the region. Thackeray thus becomes, in essence, the anti-poem within the poem: a travel text in her own right, but one that misdirects readers.

In part to legitimate his own act of textual production, Browning of necessity must problematize the very escapism his poem otherwise validates, and it is Thackeray's presence as auditor that makes this possible. Throughout their discussion, he has been subtly undermining the pleasantness of the countryside, arguing that the metropolis and modernity intervene there in ways only dimly apparent—ways that had, of course, taken himself by surprise two summers earlier. Amid the "sweet rusticities" (114) of a land seemingly removed from the fluctuations of history, Browning notes that a bill posted on a barn, "still placards the Emperor / His confidence in war he means to wage, / God aiding and the rural populace" (134–36). Paris, the center of France and of politics, and its leader, appear as trace memories on the countryside, scars that seem to hide deeper wounds. The region becomes a borderland isolated from the city but always subject to its political power. Browning, in turn, attempts to fashion a poetic space between city and country, a pretty flower with an acrid odor. His rhetorical strategy amounts to a kind of *otium cum dignitate:* a working vacation—a mix of the recreational and the serious, the tourist and the traveler. One encounters the whole of France, in all its pleasure and danger, not at its center, Paris, but at its periphery. Browning-sur-mer and citizen Browning thus inhabit the poem together, striving to wed the pleasure of travel with a sense of responsibility for the region's political and cultural identity.

The poem's main narrative continues to expound on Browning's impression of true versus false kinds of cosmopolitanism. Like Thackeray, Miranda is portrayed as a *mis*traveler, someone unable to cultivate that liminal space between the recreational and the serious. Physically he may have moved himself to the border region inhabited by Browning, but, intellectually, he has not. He insists instead on dwelling in extremes: on the one hand, an empiricism grounded in the Enlightenment, and, on the other, a lingering spirituality that manifests itself in the popular craze for miracles, such as the famous sighting of the Virgin Mary at Lourdes, and more specific to Miranda's case, her sighting at La Délivrande, which he makes a particular object of his munificence and devotion. Rather than canceling out his religious faith, Miranda's insistence on facts demands that the existence of God be confirmed by miracles: it is this vain hope that compels him, in Browning's judgment, to leap from his tower with the expectation that an angel will intercede to save him and carry him to La Délivrande.

The poem offers what at first seems like a rather simple explanation for Miranda's failure to negotiate these extremes—an explanation, however, that would appear to undercut any endorsement of cosmopolitanism or border-crossing that the poem might otherwise espouse. Miranda, the son of a French mother and Spanish father, might be genetically predisposed to fall victim to contradictory impulses within French culture:

> Monsieur Léonce Miranda, at his birth,
> Mixed the Castilian passionate blind blood
> With answerable gush, his mother's gift,
> Of spirit, French and critical and cold.
> Such mixture makes a battle in the brain,
> Ending as faith or doubt gets uppermost;
> Then will has way a moment, but no more:
> So nicely-balanced are the adverse strengths,
> That victory entails reverse next time. (1151–59)

Such a diagnosis recalls Browning's old distrust of "all hybrid & ambiguous natures & nationalities," the same impulse that made him quit Florence for London soon after Barrett Browning's death to ensure that Pen would be educated at English schools.[20] While Browning does play rather casually here with cultural stereotypes, the passage, I would suggest, has a more precise aim than to be a blanket condemnation of cultural cross-pollination. His point is not that Miranda would have been better off growing up in one national climate or the other. Rather, the problem is that France and Spain, from Browning's point of view, are too much alike: they do not edify and enhance each other so much as reinforce what is already there (as opposed to France and England, an implication that I analyze more closely later.) Miranda's dual ethnic inheritance is thus not the cause of his downfall but magnifies the larger flaw in his character: he is uniquely positioned to reap the intellectual benefits of dwelling at the border and of traveling between nationalities, but for all of his pretensions toward cosmopolitanism, he limits his cultural contacts, and stays locked within a stagnant series of influences. Browning's point of view here is not far from Matthew Arnold's in "The Function of Criticism at the Present Time," where he advises critics to "try and possess one great literature, at least, besides his own; and the more unlike his own, the better" (3:284). Along similar lines in "Heinrich Heine," Arnold held up his subject as an example of a beneficial mixing of cultures and races: "Heine's poetry . . . perpetually blends the impression of French modernism and clearness, with that of German sentiment and fulness; and to give this blended impression is, as I have said, Heine's great characteristic" (3:124). Miranda resists such mixing and seems disinclined to probe too deeply into his own or anyone else's ideas. He instead plays the part of the dandy and adopts a dilettantish, false worldliness.

With wealth and access to education and the arts, the possibility of cultivating a more balanced intellectual disposition presented itself to Miranda, but he does not take advantage of this opportunity. The intellectual forces doing battle within Miranda, as he fluctuates back and forth between the demands of the body and the spirit, are all French, Browning stresses, and work toward the same end: "Fat Rabelais chuckled, where faith lay in wait / For lean Voltaire's grimace—French, either foe" (1234–35). Again, being French in itself is not what renders these forces damaging; it is their failure to be counterbalanced by other intellectual traditions, which gives the former uncontested sway over Miranda's mindset:

> the world lay strewn
> With ravage of opinions in his path,
> And neither he, nor any friendly wit,
> Knew and could teach him which was firm, which frail,
> In his adventure to walk straight through life
> The partial-ruin,—in such enterprise,
> He straggled into rubbish, struggled on. (1103–9)

Miranda's intelligence lacks the depth that comes from concentrated, extended exposure to different ideas—the sort of rigorous mental exercise that lays the building blocks of critical thinking. Instead, his thoughts never leave the surface realm of "opinion," where each idea seems interchangeable with the next. His way of reasoning forms the epistemological equivalent of Thackeray's proposed travel book: all surface in content as well as form, and based on a too-easy superimposition of one culture or idea onto the next.

After Miranda transfers himself to the Normandy countryside, the wits he surrounds himself with, while part of a celebrity-packed cultural elite, do not aid him in forming a well-rounded perspective on the political and spiritual dilemmas of modern Europe. Instead, they serve mostly to keep him entertained: "half-hour playings at life's toil, / Diversified by billiards, riding, sport— / With now and then a visitor—Dumas, / Hertford—to check no aspiration's flight" (2134–37). The poem does not dwell on what the by then aged Alexandre Dumas or the Marquess of Hertford might have contributed to Miranda's intellectual development—and that, in fact, is Browning's point: they are just names to Miranda, signifiers of art and ideas. Similarly, the alterations he makes to his estate, including a priory that dates back to the middle ages, reveal his preference for mingling ideas together rather than endeavoring to evaluate them critically: he wishes both to restore the priory to its original state and to have all of the extras that current tastes in architecture demand. The end result, according to Browning, is a study in incongruity: "a sense that something is amiss, / Something is out of sorts in the display, / Affects us, past denial, everywhere" (710–12). Miranda's mother, apparently, concurs and sees in this unholy mix of ancient and modern shadows of a falsely restored religious faith, one that attempts to deny the contradictions at its heart: "'Clairvaux Restored': what means this Belvedere? / This Tower, stuck like a fool's-cap on the roof— / Do you intend to soar to heaven from thence? (2228–30). Her words, of course, prove all too prophetic. The grounds of his estate offer no retreat from the aesthetic onslaught. His park "*à l'Anglaise,* as they compliment! / Grass like green velvet, gravel-walks like gold" (657–58), as Browning's exaggerated description implies, is a "[m]odish adornment" (704) that draws attention to itself as a mark of style, not substance. Rather than being a monument to Miranda's familiarity with English culture, the park testifies to his lack of true appreciation for it—his failure to look beyond his own nation and cultural milieu. Altogether, his home and the life he makes for himself in the countryside are simply "Paris expounded thus to Normandy" (745).

That true "friendly wit" who might have better educated Miranda, we discover, is none other than Browning's friend Joseph Milsand. Instead of looking toward La Délivrande for a miracle, Miranda might have directed his gaze toward St. Aubin, where he would have seen something else entirely:

> There he stands, reads an English newspaper,
> Stock-still, and now, again upon the move,
> Paces the beach to taste the Spring, like you,
> Since both are human beings in God's eye.
> He will have understood you, I engage. (2913–17)

From this description, it is easy to mistake Milsand for Browning, the only other person in the poem, one would imagine, who might read an English newspaper while walking the beach, and they are, in some sense, cultural doubles.[21] Milsand traverses that same borderland of spiritual peace and rejuvenation, the beach, and thus stands as a model of Anglo-French cross-dwelling. Milsand's genius, Browning claims, is also essentially cosmopolitan—a capacity for sorting out competing ideas and offering in return a tolerant, humane understanding:

> He will have recognized, ere breath be spent
> And speech at end, how much that's good in man,
> And generous, and self-devoting, makes
> Monsieur Léonce Miranda worth his help;
> While sounding to the bottom ignorance
> Historical and philosophical
> And moral and religious, all one couch
> Of crassitude, a portent of its kind.
> Then, just as he would pityingly teach
> Your body to repair maltreatment, give
> Advice that you should make those stumps to stir
> With artificial hands of caoutchouc,
> So would he soon supply your crippled soul
> With crutches, from his own intelligence,
> Able to help you onward in the path
> Of rectitude whereto your face is set. (2921–36)

Milsand embodies faith with depth, a practical intelligence—one perhaps quintessentially French, as Arnold too had opined—that integrates the ideas and insights of today, such as advances in artificial limbs, with the wish to provide spiritual comfort. Milsand reminds one as well of another cosmopolitan figure in Browning, the Arab physician Karshish—someone French in spirit if not in person and born of a culture that in Biblical times signified the highest achievement in medical science, as France did in modern Europe. And if not Christian, neither is Karshish dismissive of the intellectual challenge Lazarus's account of Jesus poses for him; he approaches the question rigorously and openly. Similarly, it was Milsand, Browning notes in the tribute quoted earlier, who "made wise his heaven." Both men had gone through crises of faith—Milsand, in fact, had converted to Protestantism after his—and shared a desire for a spirituality that did not retreat from modernity but allowed them the space to dwell comfortably as intellectuals and as believers. Theirs would be a "fresh distillery of faith" (3033), to borrow a phrase from the poem.

Without such guidance, Miranda ends up crossing borders he should not and falls victim to the contradictory impulses of modernity. His looking for angels and miracles—not unlike spiritualism, another modish foe of Browning's—was a symptom of the times, a need to verify faith in the afterlife along quasi-scientific lines. Miranda flings himself from the tower, imagining that an angel will intervene to save him, thus performing a miracle that would at once restore faith throughout Europe: "The news will run / Like wild-fire. 'Thousands saw Miranda's flight!' / 'Tis telegraphed to Paris in a trice" (3539–41). The irony of the telegraph carrying news of the miracle is lost on him, however: the telegraph itself is the miracle, against which Miranda's nostalgia for reality-defying demonstrations of God's presence appears a sort of intellectual relic. Rather than reconciling modern times with the faith of the past, Miranda jumbles the two together to create what is at essence a vainglorious, reactionary gesture:

> Regenerated France makes all things new!
> My house no longer stands on Quai Rousseau
> But Quai rechristened Alacoque: a quai
> Where Renan burns his book, and Veuillot burns
> Renan beside. (3553–57)

This book-burning fantasy mirrors Miranda's own fruitless efforts to burn away the desires of the flesh by holding his mistress's love letters over an open flame. France will again be ruled by the Bourbons, he imagines, and the streets will be renamed after the likes of the seventeenth-century saint Alacoque or Miranda's contemporary Louis Veuillot, editor of the conservative Catholic journal *The Universe* and a relentless critic of Renan. Browning's point, however, is that modern France must not dwell in either extreme: a religious conservatism that preys upon a popular desire for miracles, or a soulless rationalism that finds its logical outcome in the Paris Commune. Browning makes his case against the latter by stressing that Miranda's anticlerical physician, Beaumont, although he blames "those priests" (2611) for his patient's disturbed state of mind, would soon become the indiscriminate victim of radicals like himself: "for the Commune ruled / Next year, and ere they shot his priests, shot him" (2673–74).

Milsand, in contrast, models the new Anglo-French cosmopolitanism Browning endorses—spiritually oriented and cultivated at the border between the two countries—the Enlightenment tempered by faith. It was an intellectual and spiritual confederation after Matthew Arnold's own heart, and in an odd way, *Red Cotton Night-Cap Country* does read as a sequel of sorts to "Dover Beach": it invites those embroiled in the Victorian crisis of faith to cross over to a different shore and cultivate a truer, more enduring spiritual fellowship. If the agnostic Voltaire's Paris was the embodiment of cosmopolitan Europe in the eighteenth century, then in Browning's poem, Milsand's un-Murrayed bathing place becomes that locus. With the help of Milsand, Browning reinvents France, or more precisely, that traveler's landscape between France and England: Browning's Norman invasion reclaims the area for both countries and thus bears something of his own English image. Miranda's troublesome Spanish/French constitution now takes on a new dimension: it underscores the more successful international exchange that Browning endorses through himself and Milsand. Together, France and England form the ideal partnership of European nationalities for coping with modernity. Miranda, however, never truly left Paris, never partook of what St. Aubin had to offer: friendship with Milsand, the spiritual rejuvenation of the beach, and a closer proximity to England. Thus the form that successful border-crossing assumes in the poem is not without a tinge of anti-Catholicism (although it should be made clear that the poem does not identify Milsand as Protestant or make any explicit anti-Catholic references). To contemporary readers not inclined to identify with the Catholic Church, however, Miranda's downfall could have easily been interpreted as the outgrowth of problems that Protestantism, so the thinking went, had striven to correct. Catholicism remained a religion too concerned with surfaces—performing rituals, doing good works—rather than with ministering to the real condition of the soul underneath.

BROWNING'S FRENCH connection is thus not without restrictions, and I want to explore more fully some of the religious, political, and gendered exclusions that adhere to it. The turn toward Milsand briefly acknowledges what is a mostly hidden source of authority in the poem, one that reveals how privileged Browning's position is vis-à-vis Miranda's and Thackeray's. While she, for example, remains culturally isolated in the poem, experiencing the country at the level of visual surfaces alone, Browning is able to revel in the strong masculine friendship that lends him greater access to France. Writing against Thackeray allows Browning to establish his own more intimate and knowing relationship with this complex landscape. Cosmopolitanism, in turn, becomes an identity open only to those invited into its circle: a Cosmopolitan Club, in effect, not unlike the London society of the same name to which Browning belonged.[22] The cosmopolitan club of the poem likewise depends ultimately on personal connections and friendships between men like the one Browning shares with Milsand, which draws attention to another point where the critique of Thackeray and Miranda intersect. Miranda, one recalls, also lacks earnest male companionship: he is alternately dictated to and undone by his mother, his mistress, and, finally, by the Virgin Mary.

Looking ahead to Swinburne, one wonders as well if a more indirect target of Browning's in this poem is the "florid impotence" he associated with him and aestheticism in general, which was variously attacked by critics for its preoccupation with the body, Catholic iconography, and with the France of *l'art pour l'art*. Browning made the remark about Swinburne in a March 1870 letter to Blagden, adding that his verse suggested to him "the *minimum* of thought and idea in the *maximum* of words and phraseology" (333). In a later letter he linked Swinburne with Rossetti, whom he also charged with a lack of depth: his works were "*scented* with poetry, as it were," and displayed the characteristic "effeminacy of his school,—the men that dress up like women" (336). Virginia Blain has also drawn attention recently to these comments, with the aim of highlighting what she sees as "some of the fascinating intersections between gay and straight even in the heartland of high Victorianism, well before the fin de siècle: Tennyson/Browning/Arnold country."[23] Indeed, *Red Cotton Night-Cap Country* is precisely this kind of country, where gay/straight forms yet another complex border area at work in this poem. Browning attempts to validate homosocial bonding as key to cosmopolitan understanding, so long as it does not cross over into a more threatening kind of physical indulgence. Miranda's failure to control his bodily desires, his obsession with saints and miracles, his false worldliness, are all finally of a piece.

In its effort to cross national boundaries, *Red Cotton Night-Cap Country* thus in turn reinscribes another complex set of gender and genre boundaries. In a curious way, however, the poem finds itself at its close attempting to undo these same boundaries, an effort forced upon Browning by Thackeray's lingering presence in the poem. The need to welcome her into the poem at its outset and then, in effect, exclude her from it later creates the problem of how to re-invite her, and the vacation poem *Red Cotton Night-Cap Country* started out as, back into its overall purpose. Now returned to London, Browning recalls how they "paced the sands before [his] house" (4234), and wonders whether "what Saint-Rambert [St. Aubin] flashed [him] in a thought, / Good gloomy London [will] make a poem of" (4239–40). To put his vacation toward this more sober poetic purpose, Browning again invokes the ideal of *otium,* a border discourse between work and leisure. His purpose in addressing Thackeray was to

> Play ruddy herald-star to your white blaze
> About to bring us day. How fail imbibe
> Some foretaste of effulgence? Sun shall wax,
> And star shall wane: what matter, so star tell
> The drowsy world to start awake, rub eyes,
> And stand all ready for morn's joy a-blush? (4242–47)

Poetry here becomes what wakes one up to reality, leaving one edified and refreshed to begin life again. The ending thus strives to put back together what the poem had separated—red and white, the Miranda narrative and the travelogue. And, in this way, *Red Cotton Night-Cap Country* concludes much as Browning's abortive vacation of 1870 had, in the safety of London after a momentary brush with danger. The political danger of the Franco-Prussian war and its aftermath in the Paris Commune enter *Red Cotton Night-Cap Country* only to remain at its margin. The poem pays tribute to the political reality (and anxiety) of France—the red cap of revolution—and insists on its relevance to a complete picture of the country. At the same time, the poem is equally determined to escape from the threat radical politics poses to its own ideological security. If Browning insists nonetheless on remaining connected, it must be accomplished discursively. For him, writing the poem accomplishes this end, as interpreting it, he suggests, does for the reader/traveler: "through the place he sees, / A place is signified he never saw, / But, if he lack not soul, may learn to know" (62–64). Normandy here remains a working vacation, a rich cultural text dotted with signs speaking to those with the ability to interpret them. Such is the luxury of the border to which Anderson earlier alluded—a state of being that depends in part for its existence on the gender and class privilege of the traveler. The poem, in effect, wants to have its signs and decode them too—to dwell both with the signifier of the region and its comforting surface, and with the truer "soul" beneath, to which the poem provides special access.

I would thus challenge some earlier readings of the poem which champion Browning for undermining his own textual authority in the manner of post-structuralism. Walter M. Kendrick, for example, in what remains a brilliant, almost prototypical model of deconstructive analysis, suggests that "[i]n place of Miss Thackeray's language, which limits the associations of words according to an intention which is 'meant' by them, the narrator has employed a language which moves freely within itself." Kendrick adds, "His character does not govern the meaning of what he says, nor is his language the expression of something about him. He is a location on the surface of discourse."[24] By the very act of displacing Thackeray's language, however, Browning assumes a power that indeed lies outside the play of language within the poem, originating instead in cultural assumptions about gender and genre. Brendan Kenny also inadvertently reveals how much the argument for a poem without a center ultimately depends upon the presence of Thackeray as rhetorical Other: "Browning rejects the notion of a neutral observer if this means expressing admiration for an alien and archaic cultural system which one has no intention of participating in oneself—the position of Miss Thackeray. Browning's obtrusive narrative voice makes it evident that he is making an evaluative judgment on French culture and that he expects a critical assessment of his own role by the reader."[25] I would suggest rather that the poem does not so much "expect" this critical assessment as force the reader into making one in its absence. Tellingly, while Kenny's analysis of the poem has much that is insightful to say about Browning's criticism of Thackeray and of French culture, at no point does it indicate on what specific grounds a "critical assessment" of Browning himself might be formulated.

To bring the poem more in line with recent work on Browning and the dramatic monologue, one could position it—with qualifications—as a kind of "double poem" after Isobel Armstrong's definition in *Victorian Poetry: Poetry, Poetics and Politics*. For Armstrong, the double poem is "literally two things at once, lyric and drama concurrently. . . . each poem within the poem, lyric and drama, has a dangerous edge of ambiguity and instability, so that the interface is never clear—it is never quite clear where lyric is displaced into drama, or where drama is dissolved in lyric feeling."[26] By placing himself at the center of the poem as its speaker, however, Browning takes some of the edge off of that ambiguity, revealing instead the kind of "yearning after the condition of lyric" that Herbert F. Tucker detects in Browning's other, more clearly dramatic speakers—voices not ready to concede their own authority.[27] As noted earlier by comparison to *The Ring and the Book,* Browning's authorial self-positioning in *Red Cotton Night-Cap Country* mirrors that of his own location within France, one more deeply imbedded in the country that is the subject of the poem. The reader, in turn, does not appear to stand outside of the poem with the author critically judging the truth claims of its speakers, as is the case with Browning's epic of Italy. It is for this reason, in part, that *The Ring and the Book* seems more conclusively to undermine the possibility of a centered, authoritative voice within poetic discourse.[28]

Armstrong's concept of the double poem nonetheless helps one to articulate the dilemma at the heart of Browning's cosmopolitanism: there always remains an irresolvable tension between the self-oriented mode of lyric—travel as self-enrichment—and the dual aim of constructing that self through its dramatic engagement with the outside world. In this respect, *Red Cotton Night-Cap Country*, like Browning's travels in France, was one more effort to get a handle on those "unstable entities of self and world," which Armstrong traces back to Browning's earliest attempts at the dramatic monologue form.[29] In the process of this struggle, Browning lays bare the sort of stumbling blocks that may impede any effort to inscribe cosmopolitanism, even as it has been reconstituted in our own time in the wake of postcolonial criticism and cultural studies: that is, a cosmopolitanism that commits itself, in essence, to removing the "club" mentality from efforts to forge a global vision. Vinay Dharwadker captures this impulse in his introduction to *Cosmopolitan Geographies* (2001) when he asks hopefully for a cosmopolitanism that will "dissociate itself from class, hierarchy, and affluence, so that it might transform itself someday into a 'true cosmopolitanism from below'"—something, for instance, very like what Barrett Browning strove for over the course of her career, as I argued in the previous chapter.[30] In this guise, cosmopolitanism is less a personal identity or achievement than an ideology: a movement not of "cosmopolites" but of individuals who value the aims of cultural diversity and wish to see a more equitable distribution of wealth and power throughout the world. What *Red Cotton Night-Cap Country* reveals, however, is the difficulty of squaring the progressive political aims of cosmopolitanism, whether in the nineteenth century or in ours, with its essence as a form of cultural authority and privilege. The poem questions whether the ability to know and empathize with another nation first demands that one be able to familiarize oneself closely with its history, literature, and culture—the kind of knowing that comes from education but perhaps, just as crucially, from the friendships that travel and residence abroad cultivate. In other words, it is less likely that someone would adopt the progressive internationalism Dharwadker calls for without having first had access to the class advantages that tainted earlier manifestations of cosmopolitanism. Those taking a more suspect view of the new cosmopolitanism, such as Robert Pinsky, make much the same claim, calling it an identity open only to "people like ourselves: happily situated members of large, powerful nations, prosperous and mobile individuals."[31]

Challenging Pinsky, however, I would not therefore conclude that cosmopolitanism is an illusion, but rather that its political ambitions cannot be comfortably integrated with its origins in forms of class and gender privilege.

This is one explanation for why neither citizen Browning nor Browning-sur-mer ever emerges with satisfying cohesiveness out of *Red Cotton Night-Cap Country*. Their conflict underscores the difficulty of attempting to dwell at the border: it is an identity always open to the charge that it is mostly a self-gratifying pose—a quest for personal enrichment—not a program of political activity. And at least one critic of Browning, Robert Viscusi, paints precisely such a picture of the poet's engagement with Italy, seeing in his apparent endorsement of free trade at the close of "The Englishman in Italy" a template for a kind of aesthetic colonization, one that reduces Italy to a "simple object of desire."[32] However valid this claim may be in certain contexts, it also presupposes the existence of an alternative, ideologically safe form of cultural exchange that does not involve the exercise of cultural power. It is little wonder then that, thinking much along the same lines, the former poet-laureate Pinsky advises the more achievable goal of cultivating one's own garden. In contrast, Browning leaves us stranded at the border, but in a way that might finally be for our own good: he insists upon the imaginative effort needed to inhabit other minds, nations, and historical moments, even if such dwelling at times makes us uncomfortable. Achieving this broader aim demands a much more serious and difficult engagement that travel only begins to put in motion: a true cosmopolitan citizenship requires deep immersion within the language, landscape, and culture of the country one seeks to know. Browning's response to the crisis of Anglo-European identity, then, was not unlike his response to the crisis of religious faith: to land finally on something like solid ground, it would take serious, concentrated intellectual labor of the kind Miranda fled from. "How very hard it is to be / A Christian!" (1–2), Browning would remark at the outset of *Easter-Day*, foreshadowing the intellectual challenge that awaited readers of the poem and that would continue to engage him over the course of his long career.

Red Cotton Night-Cap Country similarly schools us in the challenge of cosmopolitanism, accomplishing this in two ways: through its problematic exposure of Thackeray and Miranda, but also through the more unintended exposure of Browning's own historically determined limits, limits that continue to renew themselves in our own time and that may make any border-crossing gesture seem limited when viewed from the future. The poem does not provide a blueprint for cosmopolitanism, but rather a warning of its complexity, one that takes us back, in some ways, to Clough's suspicion of the communication technologies and transportation networks that were to inaugurate a new age of global unity and understanding. *Red Cotton Night-Cap Country*, in fact, has its own postal moment, when Browning surveys the Channel and remembers a mail-packet that had gone down in a storm: "thirty paces off, this natural blue / Broods o'er a bag of secrets, all unbroached, / Beneath the bosom of the placid deep, / Since the Post Director sealed them safe" (90–93). Crossing borders, this image reminds us, is an endeavor fraught with the danger of loss and misreading. Browning may have promised too much in vowing to lay open the bag of secrets that is France, but the true measure of his poem's value may lie in that very same effort to exceed its grasp. Browning strives for a way of traveling and of inscribing travel that would overcome travel's essential contradiction: the wish to inhabit a foreign culture and yet not to abandon one's own. *Red Cotton Night-Cap Country* thereby pays tribute to the border itself as a defining metaphor of modernity, when dwelling at borders seems both increasingly inevitable and desirable, an empowering state but one fraught with anxiety.

5

Bodies in Translation

Swinburne's *Poems and Ballads*
and the Fleshly School of Cosmopolitanism

BY JUST ABOUT any definition apart from extended residence or travel abroad, Swinburne probably ranks as the most recognizably cosmopolitan Victorian poet. Throughout his career, even up to the last volume of poetry published in his lifetime, *A Channel Passage* (1904), he consistently sought to cross boundaries of European culture and poetics. In addition, with *Songs before Sunrise* (1871), he assumed Barrett Browning's mantle as the British poet-laureate of Italian nationhood and republican ideals. But it was the cultural eruption known simply as *Poems and Ballads* (1866) that earned Swinburne a lasting reputation for a more dangerous if not directly political kind of cosmopolitanism, one that helped to inspire later channel-crossing aesthetes and Decadents such as Arthur Symons and Oscar Wilde. As one of those early critics had written in the *London Review* shortly before Moxon decided to withdraw *Poems and Ballads* from publication, Swinburne had apparently "familiarized himself with the worst circles of Parisian life, and drenched himself in the worst creations of Parisian literature," to the point that he could "see scarcely anything in the world, or beyond it, but lust, bitterness, and despair." Perhaps Swinburne *was* French, he suspected.[1]

A more balanced critical insight into the unique nature of Swinburne's cross-channel poetics comes from the poet himself, although in a poem that might appear to suffer from its own aversion to Anglo-French hybridity. In the spring of 1882, Swinburne lent his name to the same petition that Browning had, a petition aimed at stopping a proposed tunnel connecting England to France. Swinburne, however, took the added measure of writing a sonnet for the occasion, published later that year in *Tristram of Lyonesse and Other Poems*.[2] While full of admiration for France, "The Channel Tunnel" mostly dwells on the kind of *mésalliance* that would result from a "suppression of the sea" between the two countries. Indeed, the poem seems addressed to two suitors contemplating a marriage for the wrong reasons:

> Not for less love, all glorious France, to thee,
> > "Sweet enemy" called in days long since at end,
> > Now found and hailed of England sweeter friend,
> Bright sister of our freedom now, being free;
> Not for less love or faith in friendship we
> > Whose love burnt ever toward thee reprehend
> > The vile vain greed whose pursy dreams portend
> Between our shores suppression of the sea.
> Not by dull toil of blind mechanic art
> Shall these be linked for no man's force to part
> > Nor length of years and changes to divide,
> But union only of trust and loving heart
> > And perfect faith in freedom strong to abide
> > And spirit at one with spirit on either side.[3]

As does so much of Swinburne's work in verse and prose, "The Channel Tunnel" asks, in effect, what it means to be joined to France, always ground-zero for British cosmopolitanism. With the despised Louis Napoleon having been deposed some ten years earlier and now fading into history, France, Swinburne claims, can rank itself among free nations such as England. His unqualified characterization of England as "free," however, is about all the poem shares with the patriotic fervor one might expect from the Tunnel's opponents, many of whom were driven by fear of military invasion from the Continent. Swinburne's opposition is based more on distrust of commercialism and its oversimplified vision of international brotherhood via free trade: one imagines Barrett Browning would have nodded approvingly as Swinburne decried the "vile vain greed" and "pursy dreams" of the tunnel's promoters. Like *Casa Guidi Windows*, Swinburne's poem hinges upon a tension between a materialistic empire of free trade and a more cultural, secular-spiritual fellowship, one spearheaded by poets.

What made Swinburne's engagement with France so threatening earlier in his career—an obsession with the "body" of France, so to speak—at first glance seems to hold no place in this more platonic "union only of trust and loving heart." A closer look, however, reveals that "The Channel Tunnel" does not restrict itself to an "intellectual and spiritual" conception of Europe alone. Swinburne hints that this spiritual union could be a prelude to a more intimate kind of consummation: as he had always insisted, his poetry was never about celebrating the body at the expense of the spirit but about exploring where the two intersected.[4] In this regard, the poem mirrors the complexity and unpredictability that have historically characterized Anglo-French relations and thus reinforces Swinburne's case for resisting the "normalization" of borders that would come with the tunnel. If the poem is not patently "fleshly" in the manner of *Poems and Ballads,* it does share that volume's characteristic blurring of boundaries, twisting and turning desire beyond its more readily recognized guises: France is friend, sister, and lover in the same fourteen lines. To draw on a metaphor from Swinburne's *Notes on Poems and Reviews,* "The Channel Tunnel" offers not a sterile kind of political hermaphrodite—lovers uniting at the expense of their own unique selves—but rather equal partners who retain a productive, creative antagonism that nourishes the other: "perfection once attained on all sides is a thing thenceforward barren of use or fruit; whereas the divided beauty of separate woman and man—a thing inferior and imperfect—can serve all turns of life." England and France must remain separate bodies, separate sexes even, although which culture is the more masculine or feminine to Swinburne is seldom made clear.[5]

Inhabiting the same cross-European, turbulent in-between space as the more obviously daring *Poems and Ballads,* "The Channel Tunnel" neatly captures the dynamics of Swinburne's career-long engagement with France and his broader attempts to open English poetics to European sources and experimental trends. Despite the claims of his critics—and even some of his champions—Swinburne's poetry was never about building a secret tunnel to France that would expose England to cultural invasion. Nor was it about a more modest "assimilation" or "importation" of France, Italy, and some of the less-wholesome aspects of ancient Greek and Roman literature—all efforts that his detractors tended to link together as symptoms of the same misguided, denationalized looking outward. The dominating impulse in Swinburne, as I suggest in the title of this chapter, is translation—not in the idealized sense of a closure of difference—but a translation that, in Lawrence Venuti's terms, resists "suppressing the linguistic and cultural differences of the foreign text, assimilating it to dominant values in the target-language culture, making it recognizable and therefore seemingly untranslated."[6] *Poems and Ballads* foregrounds and confronts difference as the necessary condition to establishing the common ground of translation between England and France or ancient Greece and the present. Thus John Morley, who wrote another of the early attacks on *Poems and Ballads,* may have been more astute than he realized when he charged that "there is an enormous difference between an attempt to revivify among us the grand old pagan conceptions of Joy, and an attempt to glorify all the bestial delights that the subtleness of Greek depravity was able to contrive." He added later, "It was too rashly said, when *Atalanta in Calydon* appeared, that Mr. Swinburne had drunk deep at the springs of Greek poetry, and had profoundly conceived and assimilated the divine spirit of Greek art."[7] This is indeed precisely the kind of assimilation Swinburne resists, what Venuti calls the "ethnocentric reduction of the foreign text to target-language cultural values."[8] Whether strolling the same Parisian back streets as Baudelaire, or parading the open secret of ancient Greek sexuality, Swinburne had crossed an unofficial boundary between civilization and "depravity," between England and the rest of Europe. Swinburne's was a cosmopolitanism of repulsion—bodily, sexual, "unnatural" to many of his contemporaries, and, as I will argue, absolutely true in a larger sense to the complex attractions between inhabitants of different cultures.

Poems and Ballads travels widely across Europe in its sources, forms, and settings. This geographical reach is complemented by a historical one that goes back to the Bible and pays special attention, as we will see, to intersections of medieval and classical Europe. Nor does *Poems and Ballads* lose sight of the present, with odes "To Victor Hugo" and "A Song in Time of Revolution. 1860." European culture emerges from the volume as something always in flux and in debate with itself, something continuously adapting and readapting—continuously translating.[9] Swinburne recognizes in turn that poetry, as a literary form, demands similar acts of translation. Varied and intricate plays on diction, meter, and structure reinforce the idea that the discourse of poetry, even to a native speaker, is itself a foreign language, requiring the reader to translate and interpret on multiple levels.[10] The cosmopolitan prosody of *Poems and Ballads* thus constitutes one more significant "in between" space inhabited by the poem.

In keeping with the overall aims of this book, however, I am less interested in how Swinburne adapts specific non-British authors or forms than in how *Poems and Ballads* comments critically upon the challenge of cosmopolitanism even as it performs multiple forms of cross-cultural intermingling. Overall, there are three kinds of translation at work in *Poems and Ballads:*

1) the actual translations or "imitations" of works by Théophile Gautier, for instance, or, with more license, Sappho; 2) reverse translations—Swinburne's invented medieval French sources for "Laus Veneris" and "The Leper," which he "quotes" to either introduce or conclude the poems; and 3) more broadly, the kinds of cultural and sectarian clashes—translations, mistranslations, failures to translate at all—that Swinburne depicts, again, in "Laus Veneris," but also compellingly in the "Hymn to Proserpine" and "St. Dorothy." This last category forms my primary focus. Swinburne's critics were correct that there was something uniquely subversive about his kind of translation, something beyond "fleshliness." My analysis of Swinburne begins, in fact, by revisiting the claims of his most notorious critic, Robert Buchanan, whose efforts to equate fleshliness with foreignness, hysterical as they are at times, effectively highlight what made Swinburne so daring. He was doing much more than polluting poetry with emanations from "Holywell St.," as Buchanan put it— hiding behind verse to deliver a message that, in a more liberal society, could have been delivered just as successfully in prose. It is all about the poem in Swinburne, but not in the same way that is invoked by the aestheticist motto "art for art's sake." He was redefining the literary space as one of complex translation, one that instigated productive clashes between national identities along with other kinds of cultural "givens."[11]

I follow my discussion of Buchanan by looking first at how questions of sexual desire, translation, and identity converge in "A Ballad of Life," "Anactoria" and "The Leper." These poems drive home the idea that erotic desire between individuals—the ultimate destabilization and reassessment of personal identity—has the power to compel them into other often frustrated acts of communication and translation. "Laus Veneris," "Hymn to Proserpine," and "St. Dorothy" add a third element to this equation of desire and communication by dramatizing how the body becomes a meeting ground over which competing cultures enter into creative dialogue—that productive impasse of translation Venuti alludes to. Cosmopolitanism, in turn, is an act of reading and interpretation defined by longing but also by uncertainty and conflict, a much more compelling, much less *prosaic* exchange than conversation alone.

Swinburne, *The Fleshly School of Poetry,* and the Cultural Dynamics of Translation

The Fleshly School of Poetry and Other Phenomena of the Day (1872) indelibly linked Robert Buchanan's name with Pre-Raphaelite and aesthetic poetry, and while Dante Gabriel Rossetti is his primary target in the volume—an expanded version of an earlier piece he wrote for the *Contemporary Review*—it still offers perhaps the most extensive contemporary critique of Swinburne. Buchanan helped to amplify Swinburne's cultural impact even as he solidified objections many already had to him, including, as we have seen, Robert Browning, who echoes Buchanan's language closely in complaints about Swinburne and Rossetti.[12] Notwithstanding this impact, however, one might question the need to revisit Buchanan at all, who is about as dead, surely, as a critical dead horse can get. While it is true that Swinburne hardly needs to be defended from Buchanan at this point in literary history, to understand the unique nature of Swinburne's cosmopolitanism, I think it is important to return to the question of just what made it so troubling to Buchanan, who otherwise was willing to reaffirm that England must not isolate itself from continental influences. If anything, as Gavin Budge has argued recently, *The Fleshly School* is worthy of more serious critical attention for the way it intervened in a lively contemporary debate about the relationship between morality and physical health: Buchanan was not simply recycling moralistic pieties but drawing on his grounding in Scottish Common Sense philosophy, which "regard[ed] as radically impoverished a life lived without transcendent intuitions of something beyond the material world."[13] This impoverishment also had political implications for Buchanan. To him, Swinburne was a gifted poet who had deliberately chosen to alienate himself from the sympathies of his readers, thereby abnegating the poet's duty to champion democratic reform. Tellingly, Buchanan had little problem with the few openly political poems in *Poems and Ballads* and took *Songs before Sunrise* as evidence that Swinburne was moving in a more promising direction.[14] The charge of elitism, in fact, would be repeated by one of Swinburne's most articulate champions, William Michael Rossetti. As I discuss at the end of this section, these charges in some ways get to the heart of Swinburne's cosmopolitanism, an ideal, one would assume, that demands just the kind of broad, egalitarian reach Buchanan calls for. The confrontation with Buchanan, then, goes beyond the question of obscenity and encompasses larger issues of translation and national identity—of determining what British poetry properly owed to European influences and what kind of cultural and ideological work it should perform at home.

The history of English poetry for Buchanan *is*, in fact, the history of its engagement with Europe. *The Fleshly School* opens with a capsule overview of English poetry since the Middle Ages that traces its triumphs and failures to the way it negotiated Italian and French influences, with Chaucer emerging as his hero of English poetic cosmopolitanism:

Chaucer and his contemporaries were, as all readers know, under deep obligations to the poets and romancists of medieval Italy; and it is a most significant token of Chaucer's pre-eminent originality that, while Gower and the rest had only been inspired to imitate what was bad in the great models, he, on the contrary, merely derived inspiration and solace from their music, assimilated what was noble in it, and carefully prepared a breezier and healthier poetic form of his own. What is grandest and best in Chaucer is Chaucer's exclusively. (8–9)

From here, Buchanan delivers a kind of literary weather report, contrasting the vigorous, clear atmosphere of England with a creeping miasma from Europe. Ideally, cosmopolitanism should not disrupt native culture but provide "inspiration and solace" from abroad: its negative opposite simply embraces all that is new and enticing without resisting what is fundamentally non-English. After Chaucer, according to Buchanan, English poetry fell into a long period of decline as the Italian miasma, "sucking up all that was most unwholesome from the soil of France" (10), settled over England. Riding this cloud were a class of cheap imitators of "what was absurd and unnatural in Dante" that in turn fostered a new "falsetto school" of English poetry, whose symptoms were inauthenticity, effeminacy, and a general obsession with the sounds and surfaces of poetry rather than its meaning and depth. The English poetic body would not recover fully, in fact, until Wordsworth and other Romantic poets who were more firmly grounded in the traditions and landscape of England emerged to redomesticate poetry.

Setting the stage for his attack on Swinburne, Buchanan remarks that English poetry might have continued to regain its health but for a "fresh importation of the obnoxious matter from France. The Scrofulous School of Literature had been distinguishing itself for many a long year in Paris, but it reached its final and most tremendous development in Charles Baudelaire" (15–16). With this possible nod to Browning's depraved, scrofulous French novel-reading monk in "The Soliloquy of the Spanish Cloister," Buchanan segues into the next section of *The Fleshly School,* an extended examination of Swinburne's chief French enabler. Like a modern-day John Gower, Swinburne could never "free himself from the style of the copyist," whether in Baudelaire's presence or among more ancient influences, a charge Buchanan first made in an earlier attack on *Poems and Ballads.*[15] Buchanan highly over-dramatizes Swinburne's debt to Baudelaire, as many have noted, but his primary aim is to deny Baudelaire any legitimate access to British poetic culture. Buchanan plays up a patently "French" orientation to Baudelaire's poetry that restricts its ability to speak to English concerns and tastes: he communicates only with those already favorably predisposed toward the Continent, like Swinburne. Buchanan likewise *deliteralizes* Baudelaire, in some sense, cutting off lines from their contexts and redisplaying them as evidence of his perversity rather than as poetry.

Buchanan's overview of Baudelaire mostly amounts to announcing what is objectionable in a passage and then leaving it to the reader to make the fuller translation. "It is quite impossible for me, without long quotation, to fully represent the unpleasantness of Baudelaire" (24), he writes, implying that there was no way to engage Baudelaire without "copying" him so that one could clearly recognize the Otherness of his verse. Buchanan's use of italics for more damning key words further highlights the sense of difference. Detecting, for instance, the "Swinburnian female" in much of Baudelaire's *Les Fleurs du Mal* (1857), Buchanan, in a comically effective if unfair way, notes that

> She "bites," of course:—
>> "Pour exercer les dents à ce jeu singulier,
>> Il se faut chaque jour un cœur au râtelier!"
>
> She has "cold eyelids that shut like a jewel":—
>> "Tes yeux, où rien ne se révèle
>>> De doux ni d'amer,
>> Sont *deux bijoux froids*!"
>
> She is cold and "sterile":—
>> "La froide majesté de la femme stérile!"
>
> She is, necessarily, like "a snake":—
>> . . . "un serpent qui danse," &c, &c. (23–24)[16]

Buchanan's efforts to "translate" Baudelaire for his readers here reveal something of the damage that can be done by disingenuous attempts at cross-cultural dialogue—damage caused not by actual "mistranslation" of specific phrases, but by his implication that the reader can *know* Baudelaire through the samples he quarantines here. Even the most accurate of translations, as David Simpson cautions, involve loss, "a making over into English of something foreign, something that must inevitably be familiarized and robbed of some of the challenge of the potentially alternative values therein offered."[17] In Buchanan's case, that loss is perhaps best captured by the ampersands at the end of the passage, which serve to stereotype the rest of Baudelaire as so much more sensual indulgence. Even the way Buchanan frames the text on the page—indented, confined within his translations—imprisons Baudelaire and robs him of any transformative potential. *Les Fleurs du Mal* is made *familiarly* strange, a British idea of France that can only repel, not challenge or enlighten, the reader. There could be no productive dialogue with this aspect of French culture, Buchanan implies; it was simply foreign. All one needs to do to understand Baudelaire (and Swinburne) is to be offended by them. To continue to explore, to grant them the status of poetry or literature is to misread them in Buchanan's eyes.

By denying Swinburne's originality in dealing with his French and Greek models, Buchanan could also deny the legitimacy of the encounter between cultures Swinburne crafted. In this regard, Buchanan resembles some of Swinburne's other most vocal detractors. Alfred Austin, for instance, insisted that Swinburne's eroticized flirtations with ancient Greece underscored his tendency toward "sheer and mere imitation—imitation of the very best kind, no doubt, but still nothing more."[18] For Swinburne's accusers, there was no middle space where the foreign and English could converse with each other, as the *London Review* also hopefully concluded in an unsigned review of *Poems and Ballads:* "This kind of writing is so alien to the spirit of our country that it can obtain no root in the national soil. Men may wonder at it for a time; they will cast it out and forget it in the end."[19] Buchanan likewise advised readers to take comfort in knowing "that our contemporary blasphemy, as well as so much of our contemporary bestiality, is no home-product, but an importation transplanted from the French Scrofulous School, and conveyed . . . at second hand" (28). Translation as practiced by these critics amounts to cultural border control, what Venuti calls the "violence of translation . . . the reconstitution of the foreign text in accordance with values, beliefs and representations that pre-exist in the target language."[20] Buchanan indeed performs a kind of violence on Baudelaire, dismembering his text, like Swinburne's, into so many lips, eyelids, necks,"&c."

In decrying the kind of "domestic translation" one sees at work with Buchanan, Venuti arrives at an alternative very close to Swinburne, I would argue, "a theory and practice of translation that resists dominant target-language cultural values so as to signify the linguistic and cultural difference of the foreign text."[21] Translation in this sense also calls to mind Gloria Anzaldúa's *mestiza* or border subject, someone whose very identity constitutes "a struggle of flesh, a struggle of borders, an inner war."[22] What mattered for Swinburne was this very clash, the continuous sense of disruption and uneasiness that defines the reading experience of *Poems and Ballads.* Cosmopolitanism brings cultures together not with the aim of assimilation but rather in order to question assumptions about what is 'natural' and 'national' in the first place.

A comparison between Buchanan's comments on Baudelaire's "Femmes Damnées" and Swinburne's defense of the poem in *Under the Microscope* highlights how the divide between unnatural/natural, and, relatedly, queer/heterosexual could hinge upon the broader issue of cultural translation. Like Swinburne's "Anactoria," which, again, Buchanan suggests, is simply "copied" from its French counterpart, Baudelaire dwells upon the "Sapphic passion," the term itself employing a kind cultural distancing from England, "the vilest act conceivable in human debauchery . . . the theme and the treatment [of which] are too loathsome for description" (22). In taking up the defense of "Femmes Damnées," however, Swinburne attempts to reveal something of the allusive richness of the poem—an essential dimension of its literary quality easily lost when the poem is reproduced piecemeal with an eye only to its offensiveness:

> [T]hat side of their passion which would render them amenable to the notice of the nearest station is not what is kept before us throughout that condemned poem; it is an infinite perverse refinement, an infinite reverse aspiration, "the end of which things is death;" and from the barren places of unsexed desire the tragic lyrist points them at last along their downward way to the land of sleepless winds and scouring storms, where the shadows of things perverted shall toss and turn for ever in a Dantesque cycle and agony of changeless change; a lyric close of bitter tempest and deep wide music of lost souls.[23]

Swinburne subtly reminds the reader that the venerable Dante was not afraid to deal with sexual transgression, and that Baudelaire, rather than being a sick aberration in the tradition of European poetry, was in truth returning to long-standing concerns and questions. We should recall, of course, that Dante condemns same-sex desire in *The Inferno* and that Swinburne's own remarks here do nothing explicit to challenge judgment against the "Sapphic passion."[24] But what Swinburne does do is recall some of the sympathy that Dante feels for Paolo and Francesca in the Second Circle of hell, where they are swept around by strong winds. Swinburne also alludes to the pelting cold rains endured by Sodomites in the Seventh Circle. While he makes no direct defense of lesbianism, Baudelaire, as Swinburne reveals, upends easy judgments. "Femmes Damnées" causes the reader to resee what for Buchanan was simply a crime, an "obtrusion of unnatural passion" into poetry (22).[25] Swinburne emphasizes that to restrict poetry to what is "natural," to close off discussion of Baudelaire based on the subject of the poem, is simply to contain poetry and ultimately the mind of the reader. The way to get the reader to begin to question what is natural—or national for that matter—is to affront, to upend—but in a specifically *literary* way. Poetry takes what would otherwise be simply a matter for the "station" and reframes it for the reader, inviting a productive interrogation of borders. Poetry holds the potential to open up dialogue between diverse authors—Baudelaire, Dante, even Buchanan—and between literary periods.

This kind of literary cosmopolitanism nonetheless leaves itself open to charges of elitist isolationism—the concern that Swinburne's readers, rather than broadening their horizons along with him, would retreat in the face of an onslaught that simply overwhelmed them with its allusive richness and unsettling choice of subject. For William Michael Rossetti, the "specially artistic or literary turn of his genius" prevented a broader, perhaps more politically significant engagement between author and reader: although sympathetic with democratic politics, Swinburne "is radically indifferent, and indeed hostile, to what most persons care for; and he poetizes, for the greater part, from a point of view which they will neither adopt nor understand."[26] The charge is not unfair: Rossetti does not misread Swinburne here, although he does underestimate the transformative potential of poetic *miscommunication,* of challenging the reader's instincts. If, as Rossetti indicates, *Poems and Ballads* is marked by the failure to connect, a "defect in sympathy—this want of a bond to unite him with his fellow-men such as they are," it still invites readers to engage the wider world on a new level, to make them *more than* they were.[27] To say that the "literary"—the poem's complex allusions, its interweaving of the cultural matter of Europe's past—stands in the way of poetry's impact misses its ability to activate the imagination. In some sense, Swinburne was working toward the same democratic ends as Percy Bysshe Shelley in *A Defence of Poetry,* although by different means. Shelley famously remarks, "The great instrument of moral good is the imagination; and poetry administers to the effect by acting upon the cause. Poetry enlarges the circumference of the imagination by replenishing it with thoughts of ever new delight, which have the power of attracting and assimilating to their own nature all other thoughts."[28] The key word for Swinburne here, however, is no longer *nature* but *poetry.* Folding the body and sexuality into poetic discourse, Swinburne began to reach the reader on a more visceral level—engaging the intellect in ways that invited resistance and fashioning a more complex kind of empathy that shaded into bodily desire. I am thinking in part here of what Hazard Adams calls the "offense of poetry" in his study of the various attacks and apologies the form has inspired over the centuries, an offense contingent not on choice of subject but on poetic discourse itself: "The ethical [work of poetry] arises in presentation, demanding imaginative involvement, a challenge to pass into the particularity of events, other minds, sympathetic identification, or active repulsion."[29]

Poems and Ballads couples cosmopolitanism with feelings of guilt, surprise, and uncertainty: it takes full advantage of the anxiety that comes with being *lost* in translation. Like "Femmes Damnées," *Poems and Ballads* underscores the risks of cosmopolitanism, the fear that one will reemerge altered, contaminated, and unrecognizable following cross-cultural contact. For Swinburne, as far as cosmopolitanism was concerned, a ready recognition of oneself or one's values in the poem was the *problem,* not the solution. The reader's experience of the volume mirrors that of many of the speakers and protagonists in *Poems and Ballads:* interpretation registers uncomfortably, uncertainly along the body, but neither are these poems ever simply pornographic or rigidly doctrinaire or moralistic. Swinburne's is very much a mediated, poeticized experience of the body: a complex interplay of textuality, sexuality, and translation that will always tempt some readers simply to turn away in frustration or seek refuge in the dismissive certainty of Buchanan or Austin. Turning now to *Poems and Ballads,* I wish to examine those modes of translation more closely.

Love or Confusion?
Translating Desire in *Poems and Ballads*

Many of the dramatic lyrics in *Poems and Ballads* feature speakers seeking affirmation of long-held sympathies—cultural warriors of a sort determined to reinstitute borders even as they crumble around them. As one might expect, the poem that opens the volume, "A Ballad of Life," serves as a template for the kind of border-crossing that typifies the rest of the volume. Addressed to Lucrezia Borgia, the subject of Swinburne's later unfinished prose "Chronicle," the poem introduces Swinburne's practice of mining European cultural history in search of the same disturbing sorts of attractions he discovered in Baudelaire, he who had "chosen to dwell mainly upon sad and strange things—the weariness of pain and the bitterness of pleasure—the perverse happiness and wayward sorrows of exceptional people."[30] Swinburne inhabits a poetic time zone that is clearly not the present but not obsessively historicized either: he speaks in the voice of a court poet of Borgia, although she is not mentioned by name and revealed as the addressee of the poem until close to the end. The poem's national and cultural identity is even more difficult to pinpoint. Borgia had been the subject of recent works by Alexandre Dumas and Victor Hugo, and, in fact, Swinburne modeled the poem in part after D. G. Rossetti's rendition in *The Early Italian Poets* (1861)—thus, in effect, retranslating another translation. This Anglo-Italian, cross-European space is formally represented through Swinburne's adaptation of the *canzone,* a verse type distinguished by a particularly complex and interwoven rhyme scheme that Swinburne observes closely (*abbaccdeed,* concluding with a sonnet envoi). The form was pioneered by Petrarch but rarely used in English and works to redouble the complex patternings and crossovers of the poem's expression of powerfully unsettled desire.

In many ways, what "A Ballad of Life" does is simply confuse the question of love, introducing the sorts of conflicting emotions that will surface again in other poems of problematic desire in the volume such as "The Leper" and "Felice." Borgia becomes the twin symbol of art and desire in the poem as Swinburne enumerates the seven strings of her cithern: "the first string charity, / The second tenderness, / The rest were pleasure, sorrow, sleep, and sin, / And loving-kindness, that is pity's kin / And is most pitiless" (16–20).[31] Continuing in this numerological vein, the poem complicates the equation still further, introducing three men with her who embody Lust, Shame, and "Fear, that is akin to Death; / He is Shame's friend, and always as Shame saith / Fear answers him again" (38–40). In this manner, the poem juxtaposes different iconic representations of emotion in order to establish their kinship, stressing the intersections between art, lust, and the body: "Then Fear said: I am Pity that was dead. / And Shame said: I am Sorrow comforted. / And Lust said: I am Love" (48–50). Swinburne, perhaps, invites more questions than he answers with these overlapping identities, but this, in fact, is the poem's aim.

What actual communication exists in "A Ballad of Life" comes more from bodily gestures than verbal expression. Mouths and lips proliferate, as early critics dutifully noted, but one seldom hears voices in *Poems and Ballads* and lovers rarely speak directly to each other. Swinburne, for instance, stresses the bodily nature of Borgia's voice: "Thereat her hands began a luteplaying / And her sweet mouth a song in a strange tongue" (51–52). The passage spotlights Borgia's hands rather than the music of the cithern, just as it draws our attention to her mouth rather than the song that emerges, which is in a strange "tongue" to begin with. "A Ballad of Life" invites one to look for meaning not simply in words and language but in their sensual effects on the reader. Borgia's song "transfigureth / All sin and sorrow and death, / Making them fair as her own eyelids be, / Or lips wherein my whole soul's life abides" (62–65). *Transfigure* has specific religious connotations which Swinburne no doubt intends to invoke here. The transfiguration of Christ on the mountain is one of the few moments in the Bible before the crucifixion when his divinity is visibly encoded on his body, when the word becomes flesh in a new and sensational way. Jesus "was transfigured before them: and his face did shine as the sun, and his raiment was white as the light" (Matthew 17:2). Interpretation, essentially, becomes an act of transfiguration, a discursive process involving mind, body, and word. In the poem's envoi, it is finally *Poems and Ballads* itself that emerges out of this tangled web of desire, that which will "transfigureth": "Borgia, thy gold hair's colour burns in me, / Thy mouth makes beat my blood in feverish rhymes" (76–77). Poetry fuses body and spirit as the poem ends in a kind of ecstasy of synesthesia: "And kiss thee with soft laughter on thine eyes, / Ballad, and on thy mouth" (84–85). The poem revels in its ability to transfigure, to blur boundaries of form and challenge established patterns of communication and understanding.[32]

Authentic, pure love can never be "liberated" or expressed freely in *Poems and Ballads* : love can only be translated or continuously re-presented. What is natural to love are these complications that seem to pervert or hinder its expression, and a good portion of *Poems and Ballads* consists of poems that probe these situations of problematized love. Especially in "Anactoria," where Swinburne presumably would be at his most fleshly, he dwells instead on the frustrations of desire. Sappho's will to control the object of her desire, and be controlled *by* her, inspires feelings of guilt that overwhelm the poem and consume all other aspects of life, including her poetry: "My life is bitter with thy love; thine eyes / Blind me, thy tresses burn me, the sharp sighs / Divide my flesh and spirit with soft sound" (1–3). Notably, the first explicit statement of lesbianism in the poem could apply just as easily to any heterosexual lover's wish to possess the beloved for herself: "I charge thee keep thy lips from hers or his, / Sweetest, till theirs be sweeter than my kiss" (19–20). Like Baudelaire's "Femmes Damnées," the poem works to *naturalize* the *unnatural,* even more so, perhaps, since Sappho's desire for Anactoria is not damned and seems categorically no different, other than in its intensity, from the other forms of problematic desire presented in *Poems and Ballads.* Hence also the poem's remarkable ability to translate across different sexual orientations: Thaïs Morgan and Richard Dellamora have both commented that the poem is as much about sex between men as sex between women, providing a space where, as Dellamora puts it, Swinburne could explore "poetic fantasies of male-male genital activity."[33] I would add that Swinburne here draws on the ancient Greek setting not just to authorize same-sex desire but to reemphasize that Greek sexuality, in all of its variegations and orientations, embodied a recognition that desire could be neither disciplined (made heteronormative) nor liberated (released from inhibitions). As with the incestuous desire revealed in "Phaedra," another Greek poem in the volume that critics bemoaned for its "bestial delights," all love, by its very nature, is "cast out of the bound of love" (74). It is transgressive and oversteps boundaries of self and morality. In "Anactoria," Swinburne recognizes that there is no way of imagining love that does not involve a kind of reciprocal trespassing, even a killing of the desired, which accounts for the sado-masochistic quality of many of its sexual images. The longing to merge with the object of desire engenders a strange mix of empathy and assault, an irresistible longing to trust oneself to another with all of the risks that involves: "O that I / Durst crush thee out of life with love, and die, / Die of thy pain and my delight, and be / Mixed with thy blood and molten into thee!" (129–32).

In her despair, Sappho calls on the gods to help her sort through the complications of desire, a move repeated across the various cultures and historical time periods that make up *Poems and Ballads*. Each time, the plea seems to fall on deaf ears: "Him would I reach, him smite, him desecrate, / Pierce the cold lips of God with human breath, / And mix his immortality with death. / Why hath he made us?" (182–85). Ironically, perhaps, the god she imagines seems remarkably close to the pale Galilean of the "Hymn to Proserpine," a god of death and indifference to human erotic emotion, a creator who sets forces in motion that the individual cannot negotiate according to the ideals of divine justice.[34] Sappho wishes to remove the borders between god and man, mortal and immortal, lover and self, but finally remains defined by these very borders. And love, like human existence, remains indeterminate, caught between, on the one hand, an intense will for life that fulfills itself in the expression of desire and, on the other, the self-destruction that also awaits one in the end. The gods are born out of a wish to end this frustrating uncertainty, and as Swinburne makes clear in other poems, attempts to employ religion to smooth out love's rough edges seldom prevail (with one notable exception, as we will see). By and large, religion, like extreme forms of nationalism, mostly embodies the will *not* to have to translate.

"Anactoria" concludes with a kind of fantasy of poetic transcendence that substitutes itself in some ways for the fulfillment of the poem's divine longing. Sappho hopes that her poem can negotiate the web of desire and power that her attraction gives birth to and that compelled her bitter, anguished prayer. Poetry itself comes the closest to transcending the boundaries of time and nature:

I Sappho shall be one with all these things,
With all high things for ever; and my face
Seen once, my songs once heard in a strange place,
Cleave to men's lives, and waste the days thereof
With gladness and much sadness and long love. (276–80)

This is a strong statement of poetry's cosmopolitan potential—that it can communicate across borders and "cleave to men's lives." At the same time, Sappho resists turning poetry into an idealized universal discourse: poetry starts the process of conversation, promising not to erase the difference between self and other but only to articulate the longing they have for each other in all of its sadness and gladness.[35] Poetry is merely that which best mediates desire. Thus even Sappho, "the very greatest poet that ever lived," according to Swinburne, bequeathed to posterity a love freighted with complications, "mutilated fragments fallen within our reach from the broken altar of her sacrifice of song."[36] These fragments, for Swinburne, compelled in him his strongest, perhaps most creative effort at translation and poetic archaeology.[37]

"The Leper" would offer another complex take on how love inevitably invites feelings of apprehension, violation, and guilt. Although not explicitly about crossing national borders, the poem was perhaps the most distant from England culturally and to Swinburne's critics recalled the worst transgressions of French decadence. Buchanan more than likely had "The Leper" in mind when he charged that Swinburne "attempted to surpass Baudelaire, and to excel even that frightful artist in the representation of abnormal types of diseased lust and lustful disease" (20). This may indeed be the most uncomfortably bodily poem in *Poems and Ballads,* if not for the necrophilia and leprosy, then for the speaker's fetishization of his patroness's feet and hair. Disease, love, and art cross paths here as they had in Baudelaire, for whom "the loathsomest bodily putrescence and decay," Swinburne said, could be turned to "some noble use."[38] The body in turmoil, at the limits of the natural, becomes the ultimate site of aesthetic investigation. "The Leper" too would come into contact with foreign, diseased bodies, underscoring the complex attraction between self and other, and freighting cosmopolitanism with feelings of violation and sickness.

"The Leper" opens with the deceptively simple declaration, "Nothing is better, I well think, / Than love; the hidden well-water / Is not so delicate to drink: / this was well seen of me and her" (1–4). The repetition of "well" immediately gets the reader's attention and seems strangely uncreative, even inattentive for a poet of Swinburne's craftsmanship. Buchanan, in fact, singled out these lines in an attempt to refute those who had praised Swinburne's "careful choice of diction" (80), and he is right to suggest that the repetition of "well" betrays a mind unsure of itself: the mind in question, however, is not Swinburne's but the speaker of the poem's. Similarly, the poem's quatrains of short, tetrameter lines make the rhymes more pronounced and add to the impression that we are dealing with a speaker prone to oversimplifying what it is frustratingly complex. The poem leaves us nonetheless with a hopelessly qualified and confusing vision of who loves whom and the kind of consummation the speaker of the poem is after. It is unclear, for instance, whether he's motivated by love or by a longing to pay his liege-lady back for the "scorn" she had shown him in his earlier role as "poor scribe" and liaison to her lovers (9–10). The speaker clearly takes some satisfaction in the reversal of power that has come with her demise, but he also notes sympathetically how her former lovers now have no use for her. As a leper, she is the ultimate outcast: "And they spat out and cursed at her / And cast her forth for a base thing" (51–52). He cares for her affectionately, nurturing her with his own "water and poor bread" (70), but also clearly lusts after her: "Her hair, half grey half ruined gold / Thrills me and burns me in kissing it" (103–4).

The speaker's love and longing for companionship for her thus cannot be uncoupled from what might be baser motives, and that, in some sense, is Swinburne's point: untainted, uncomplicated love is not love at all.[39] The "wells" and the uncertainty in the poem keep coming back: "I know not / If all were done well, all well said, / No word or tender deed forgot" (94–96). Right through to the end, death, decay, and disease adhere to love as the speaker continues to question whether or not he failed. "I am grown blind with all these things" (137), he says, and, like so many of the other lost lovers in *Poems and Ballads,* he asks, "Will not God do right?" (140). The poem ends in doubt and second-guessing, the speaker wondering, "It may be all my love went wrong— / A scribe's work writ awry and blurred" (129–30). Hers, like his, is a "body broken up with love" (62), a line that also serves well as a metaphor for cosmopolitanism overall in Swinburne. He presents us once more not with sexual gratification as liberation but as something that is disorienting and threatens one with contamination. Love is unhealthy, perhaps, and seldom makes all things "well," but it wouldn't be worth much else otherwise. Similarly, a cosmopolitanism that remains at the level of Buchanan's disembodied intellect fails to cross boundaries and threatens to leave the most rigid and uncompromising of cultural assumptions undisturbed.

Making the issue of translating desire across specific national or religious boundaries more explicit, Swinburne adds an endnote to the poem in invented, archaic French that traces its source to a 1505 *Grandes Chroniques de France*. The note reads in part,

> Mesme dist-on que ce meschant homme et mauldict clerc se remémourant de la grande beauté passée et gaustée de ceste femme se délectoyt maintesfois à la baiser sur sa bouche orde et lépreuse et l'accoller doulcement de ses mains amoureuses. Aussy est-il mort de ceste mesme maladie abhominable. Cecy advint près Fontainebellant en Gastinois.

> [People even say that this wicked man and cursed clerk, remembering this woman's former great beauty, [now] ravaged, often delighted in kissing her foul and leprous mouth and in caressing her gently with his loving hands. Therefore, he died of this same abominable disease. This happened near Fontainbellant in Gastenois.][40]

The French "source" thus continues the awkward juxtaposition of devotion and lust in the poem and opts not to differentiate between the two, revealing only that "Et quand ouyt le roy Philippe ceste adventure moult en estoyt esmerveillé. (And when King Phillip heard the story he marveled greatly)." The endnote serves less to explain or interpret the poem than simply to highlight the unresolved conflicts it contains. More broadly, the French note begs the question of who is translating whom, and just where Swinburne is trying to locate the poem culturally and historically.

This is a trick of sorts that *Poems and Ballads* would repeat in its rendition of the Tannhäuser myth, itself an unusual combination of German folklore and Mediterranean sensualism. "Laus Veneris" adds yet another element of trans-European cultural migration to the poem with an epigraph citing a 1530 *Livre des grandes merveilles d'amour, escript en latin et en françoys par Maistre Antoine Gaget*. Even more so than "The Leper," "Laus Veneris" dwells simultaneously in multiple cultures and historical moments: the poem is set in the early middle ages while its 1530 "translator" is someone who, like the reader, must make sense of a tale that travels between pagan and Christian sensibilities, between the North and South of Europe. This introduction, like the "Leper" endnote, underscores the difficulty of translating love in a way that synthesizes its differences. Venus and Tannhäuser "là vescut tristement en grand amour (lived sadly there in great love)." The poem figures cross-cultural and interreligious clash in terms of physical longing and desire, as Swinburne's Tännhauser engages himself in a heroic act of diplomacy between cultural extremes. His efforts fail, ultimately, but he paves the way for the poem's 1530 Renaissance translator, in a sense, by attempting to negotiate Europe's dual pagan and Christian cultural heritage.[41]

Swinburne's French introduction to the poem immediately confronts the reader with overlapping, somewhat confusing borders. The poem then continues in this vein, foregrounding the knight's efforts to sort between body and soul. The opening line—"Asleep or waking is it?"—begins in indecision and proceeds to weigh the relative benefits of Christianity and paganism as embodied in Christ and Venus. Although pulled in different directions, he touches on similarities that lie concealed by Christian dogma. Venus and Mary become sisters of a sort:

> Lo, this is she that was the world's delight;
> The old grey years were parcels of her might;
>   The strewings of the ways wherein she trod
> Were the twain seasons of the day and night. (9–12)

The knight sees room for compromise by depicting Venus and Mary alike as bodily deities, defined by their beauty and fertility: "Nay, fair Lord Christ, lift up thine eyes and see; / Had now thy mother such a lip—like this? / Thou knowest how sweet a thing it is to me" (22–24).

Here the knight's physical and spiritual desires overlap as he imagines some sort of elusive bridge between sin and redemption. He appears to address Jesus more as a fellow human being than as a divine presence, one who, like him, had once possessed physical longings but now stubbornly refuses to acknowledge them. "Thou knowest" becomes a refrain of sorts in the poem, a persistent rhetorical question that epitomizes the one-way nature of dialogue in the poem and the knight's sense of frustrated communication: he cannot universalize and he cannot resolve. His prayer goes unanswered, and the proxy conversation he had earlier with the Pope after his pilgrimage to Rome offered little in the way of actual dialogue: "Then he spake some sweet word, / Giving me cheer; which thing availed me not" (363–64). This perfunctory exchange over, the Pope proceeds immediately to condemn Tännhauser: "Until this dry shred staff, that hath no whit / Of leaf nor bark, bear blossom and smell sweet, / Seek thou not any mercy in God's sight, / For so long shalt thou be cast out from it" (369–72). The knight then retreats to seek refuge in the Horsel of Venus.

The knight's relationship with Venus is likewise characterized by a frustrated longing to communicate. The comfort she offers him is one of total physicality and linguistic impasse; he must accept her on her own silent terms or none at all. In a kind of anti-confession, he pleads, "let thy kiss / Seal my lips hard from speaking of my sin" (322–23). Paradoxically, the knight must learn to speak a new language—one characterized by mouths that seem to do everything but talk. Swinburne thus adds a new dimension to the silence we would of course expect from the auditor in a dramatic monologue. Venus's silence becomes the dominating voice of the poem, expressed by an otherwise very forceful and ubiquitous mouth—that "eager enjoyment of the word bite," as one Swinburne critic put it—which begins to take control of the poem and of Tännhauser.[42] The dilemma the knight faces is that he must choose between the empty, sterile words of the Pope and no words at all: that is, Venus—whose contact is thrilling but also silently lacking. As Swinburne's own commentary on the poem stresses, "The tragic touch of the story is this: that the knight who has renounced Christ believes in him; the lover who has embraced Venus disbelieves in her. Vainly and in despair would he make the best of that which is the worst— vainly remonstrate with God, and argue on the side he would fain desert. Once accept or admit the least admixture of pagan worship, or of modern thought, and the whole story collapses into froth and smoke."[43] The knight nonetheless insists on finding some kind of resolution and communion of body and soul: "For till the thunder in the trumpet be, / Soul may divide from body, but not we / One from another" (417–20). The impending day of judgment renders their embrace futile, and similarly, the miraculous transformation of the Pope's staff, which would appear to celebrate the knight's erotic desire, is not something that he himself witnesses. It is mentioned in the French introduction but not referred to in the poem itself; Tannhäuser remains in doubt as to what he is actually recovering by returning to Venus. Once again, there will be no *deus ex machina* for Swinburne's frustrated lover.

"Laus Veneris" finally advocates on behalf of translation as a productive dwelling in doubt, a way out of more fixed assumptions and creeds. What is more, Swinburne reveals that the engine driving this process lies at the heart of European culture: in Arnold's clash of the "Hebraic" and "Hellenic," spirit and body. The *conflict* between the two—the middle space of translation— is where Swinburne sets up camp. Likewise, Swinburne's ideal historical moment is not classical but medieval, or more precisely, a medieval period in transition, when classical heroes and Christian saints often shared the same page—a period defined by artists such as Dante and Chaucer. Swinburne does not undercut the knight's effort to smooth over cultural conflict but does show that he lacks the aesthetic negative capability, in a sense, to dwell productively in the clash between the two. With "St. Dorothy," as we will see, Swinburne would offer an alternative vision of translation between the medieval and the classical.

In terms of cosmopolitan engagement, what "Laus Veneris" manages to achieve is perhaps best understood when it is read in comparison to the "Hymn to Proserpine." Where "Laus Veneris" has a Christian seeking dialogue between flesh and spirit, the "Hymn to Proserpine" features an unrepentant pagan who sees no possibility for such crossover. The poem dramatizes the retreat from translation, centering on a cultural paradigm shift that overlaps into religious and sexual questions. Beliefs collide rather than speak to each other in the "Hymn to Proserpine," and the tone of the poem from the very start is one of frustration and resignation: the speaker has "lived long enough" (1) and anticipates no benefits in the crossing of these religions. As he proclaims in the poem's famous anapestic lament, "Thou hast conquered, O pale Galilean; the world has grown grey from thy breath; / We have drunken of things Lethean, and fed on the fulness of death" (35–36). Historically positioned at the start of the Middle Ages, the speaker indeed exists at a time when one way of thinking will triumph while the other will go into a long period of silence. The repetition of "they say" and "men say" in the poem creates the impression of someone who merely overhears others talking rather than engaging in dialogue. The distance between the two points of view seems nontraversable.

Unlike the knight in "Laus Veneris," the speaker here sees little if any overlap in the worship of Mary and Venus. Mary has usurped the throne, and her worshipers drown out his own hymn: "Of the maiden thy mother men sing as a goddess with grace clad around; / Thou art throned where another was king; where another was queen she is crowned / Yea, once we had sight of another: but now she is queen, say these" (75–77). To the speaker, Mary and Venus present a series of either/or contrasts, each icon embodying the antithesis of the other: "For thine came weeping, a slave among slaves, and rejected; but she / Came flushed from the full-flushed wave, and imperial, her foot on the sea" (85–86). As much as these lines express Swinburne's own Hellenism, we should also be careful not to miss how overdetermined they are: the speaker overlooks a vibrant if sadomasochistic dimension to the "deathliness" of Mary, one that Swinburne toys with later in "Dolores." The tragedy of the poem is not simply that the speaker's healthy, bodily religion is crushed by the "pale Galilean" but that he finds himself, like his Christian foes, unable even to *begin* to compromise, to translate between the two. His only gain is a kind of *schadenfreude* in contemplating the inevitable demise of the new religion, which seeks to deny the reality of the body and its senses: "Yet thy kingdom shall pass, Galilean, thy dead shall go down to thee dead"

(74). Unlike "Laus Veneris," which hinges upon a revealing if ultimately frustrating clash of body and spirit and Christian and pagan—a kind of heroic struggle with translation—the "Hymn to Proserpine" captures a more determinedly anti-cosmopolitan moment, the gateway into a long period of cultural contraction. Swinburne also notably chooses not to add a later historical mediating voice here of the kind embodied in his invented source document for "Laus Veneris." Born too late for classical Europe and not late enough for its revival in the later Middle Ages and Renaissance, the speaker of the "Hymn to Proserpine" is simply left with nowhere to go and no one to turn to other than the fading image of Proserpine herself.

Poems and Ballads obviously does not seek to praise Christianity, but— less obviously—it does not seek to bury it either. Christianity's struggle with the body becomes its defining essence for Swinburne, the source of its powerful contributions to art. Swinburne draws on the Bible itself to make this point, basing his poem "Aholibah" closely on the account given of her in Ezekiel 23, which conflates artistic sensibility with movement between cultures and sexual desire. Aholibah "doted upon the Assyrians her neighbours, captains and rulers clothed most gorgeously, horsemen riding upon horses, all of them desirable young men" (Ezekiel 23:12). So attracted is she, in fact, that she has them painted on the wall of her bedchamber. Throughout Swinburne's poem, Aholibah remains a highly artistic figure, someone with a keen eye for exotic beauty: "God gave thee gracious ministers / And all their work who plait and weave: / The cunning of embroiderers / That sew the pillow to the sleeve, / and likeness of all things that live" (36–40). In the Bible, Aholibah invites Assyrian princes to her palace, where they "defiled her with their whoredom, and she was polluted with them" (23:17). Ultimately in the poem, as in Swinburne's biblical source, cosmopolitanism and art both fall under the same axe, but Swinburne denies neither the creative mastery of Aholibah and her artisans nor the immense beauty bestowed upon her by God: "In the beginning God made thee / A woman well to look upon / Thy tender body as a tree" (1–3). Swinburne and his Biblical source are both highly attuned to the subversive potential of border-crossing art as a form of cultural "pollution" and defilement. Like Aholibah, overcome by the beauty of "the Assyrians her neighbours," one either stays at home or contaminates oneself. The problem with Christianity in *Poems and Ballads,* however, is not that it seeks to impose questions of guilt and morality onto desire that in a reformed world would be free of them. Rather, the problem is that it provides no way out of the conflict except to squelch desire entirely, rendering it always perverse. By reducing border-crossing to a form of cultural and moral betrayal, religious dogma demands total allegiance, making all that is outside of it false or heretical. There is no desire to translate except on its own terms.

Swinburne, in some sense, redeems Aholibah's memory through his adaptation of the martyrdom of St. Dorothy, finding a compromise that leaves Christianity more open to the mediating potential of a sensualized aesthetic. At the same time, "St. Dorothy" stands out in *Poems and Ballads* as one of the only poems where sexual restraint and resistance are redeemed in the face of a selfish bodily overindulgence. As Swinburne joked in a letter, "I wanted to try my heathen hands at a Christian subject . . . and give a pat to the Papist interest."[44] Despite the self-mocking tone, Swinburne is attempting a curious admixture of the heathen and Christian in this poem, in some sense offering a new (mis)translation of each. Heathen and Christian will perhaps become unrecognizable from their original forms, but the offspring they produce ends up transcending the limits of both.

Like the "Hymn to Proserpine," "St. Dorothy" is set at the historical intersection of Christianity and ancient Rome, covering the fourth-century martyrdom of St. Dorothy and her conversion of the pagan prince responsible for having her martyred in the first place. But the poem is medieval in another crucial sense in which the "Hymn to Proserpine" is not. The poem's style and narrator are also medieval, with familiar echoes of the account of the martyrdom of St. Cecile in Chaucer's *Second Nun's Tale.* And, like Chaucer's *Legend of Good Women,* which also mixes classical and Christian sources, "St. Dorothy" adheres closely to the irregular pauses and mostly open couplets of Chaucer, as opposed to the more familiar heroic couplet of later English verse. Looking ahead to the Renaissance, the poem's late medieval narrator, like Chaucer, is open to cross-cultural fertilization and unapologetically drawn to the material, bodily dimension of Dorothy's appeal as much as to her religious virtue. The poem does not desexualize Dorothy despite her saintliness: she is clearly attracted to her suitor, but her desire retains a degree of power and self-assertion. Her beliefs empower her against a series of men who would reduce her to a simple object of lust. Theophilus, in fact, is first attracted to her surface beauty. She becomes a beautiful picture in his eyes, one suffused with music that overwhelms the senses:

> Now as this lord came straying in Rome town
> He saw a little lattice open down
> And after it a press of maidens' heads
> That sat upon their cold small quiet beds
> Talking, and played upon short-stringèd lutes;

And other some ground perfume out of roots
Gathered by marvellous moons in Asia;
Saffron and aloes and wild cassia,
Coloured all through and smelling of the sun;
And over all these was a certain one
Clothed softly, with sweet herbs about her hair
And bosom flowerful; her face more fair
Than sudden-singing April in soft lands. (35–47)

Theophilus's struggle to satisfy his awakening desire while not simply over-mastering Dorothy parallels the narrator's own cross-cultural, interreligious negotiation. The passage sets in motion the poem's search for translation and compromise between soul and body and between men and women. The description foreshadows Dorothy's later martyrdom, when she will prove the existence of God by delivering to Theophilus, after her death, a basket of fruit and roses—a blending of natural beauty with religious truth and understanding. Additionally, with its reference to these exotic, sensual goods imported from Asia, the passage depicts sexual desire in cross-cultural terms, thus also hinting at the narrator's own expanded cultural horizons in the wake of increased European trade with the East. Swinburne's "Chaucer" is a decidedly European poet, one ranging far beyond the breezy, chaste England to which Buchanan had confined him. Swinburne also recalls here the opening of Morris's *Earthly Paradise,* which depicts the medieval poet primarily as a trader, one eager to handle new merchandise, whether cultural or material.[45]

Pagan and Christian, lust and a more platonic, spiritual desire continue to overlap at key points in the poem. To win Dorothy, Theophilus prays to Venus that she might make her "my lady without sin" (133), and Venus in fact appears to him and promises to grant his prayer: "Thou shalt have grace as thou art thrall of mine" (147). His actual proposal to Dorothy takes the form of a rather heavy-handed command, warning her that she must become his out of a sense of religious duty and not go "[a]gainst God's ways" (154). While in effect he insists she marry him because it is the will of a goddess, Dorothy turns the tables on him, hinting that later it is indeed God's will that he marry her but on *her* terms: "I that am Christ's maid were loth / To do this thing that hath such bitter name" (172–73). Venus claims him, and Christ her, but both gods end up working together in a way not seen in either "Laus Veneris" or the "Hymn to Proserpine." He indeed becomes hers later but in a way he cannot fully conceive of as yet. At first, Theophilus is affronted by Dorothy's demand and interprets it as an attempt to mock him. He complains to Gabalus, the emperor, who has her taken prisoner and denigrated before the imperial court.

During the scene of her torture and humiliation, Swinburne draws greater attention to Dorothy as an artist figure, leaving the impression that she dies as much for a moral aesthetic that opens up both cultures as for her religious beliefs. Her self-defense is hardly a sermon at all: it is a word-picture of all that is colorful and beautiful in the world, all that is worth seeing. She speaks for instance of the "small bright herbs about the little hills, / And fruit pricked softly with birds' tender bills, / And flight of foam about green fields of sea" (263–65). She concludes with words that recall Browning's Fra Lippo Lippi, who performs a similar alliance of material and spiritual aims under the guise of art. Dorothy continues, "And all these things he gathers with his hands / And covers all their beauty with his wings; / The same, even God that governs all these things, / Hath set my feet to be upon his ways" (270–73). Dorothy is much more than a sexualized Christian martyr redeployed within a colorful Pre-Raphaelite setting. Through her, Swinburne subtly links desire for the human body with openness to spiritual awakening. The opposite—a more unadulterated voyeurism and consuming lust—is embodied in the figure of Gabalus, a kind of grotesque, unrestrained sensualist. Tellingly, Dorothy's presumptions of authority are what most infuriate Gabalus—the idea that she would seek to be anything more than the object of male desire—and he dismisses her address as being typical of "these women's jaw-teeth clattering" (285). He adds, "I pray God deliver all us men / From all such noise of women and their heat" (290–91). Gabalus exists merely to indulge his senses; the more spiritually charged, beautiful rendition of the material world she gives falls on deaf ears in his case.

Theophilus, in contrast, seems moved on two levels—both by the strength of Dorothy's faith and defiance and also by her words and their very sensuous and colorful depiction of life, a description that conjoins spiritual and bodily impulses. Forced to watch her torture and beating, he worries for her in an afterlife of the soul only, "going forth bodiless / . . . hurt with naked cold, and no man saith / If there be house or covering for death / To hide the soul that is discomforted" (360–63). In response to his concerns, she paints a portrait of heaven that surpasses her earlier depiction of the beauty of earth. It is one that richly appeals to the senses:

> But on the other side is good and green
> And hath soft flower of tender-coloured hair
> Grown on his head, and a red mouth as fair

As may be kissed with lips; thereto his face
Is as God's face, and in a perfect place
Full of all sun and colour. (368–73)

The "him" she describes in these lines is death given new life, death redeemed by the body and material world. Fittingly, Theophilus asks that after death she deliver a material sign of the existence of her god, and she sends, as according to the legend of her martyrdom, gifts of flowers miraculously appearing out of season: roses and "marigolds / That have the sun to kiss their lips of love; / The flower that Venus' hair is woven of, / The colour of fair apples in the sun" (452–55). The invocation of Venus, along with the sensual personification of the flowers, again points to a "miraculous" trans-figuration. Dorothy converts body and soul, Christian and pagan in a way that allows both to reach full bloom, so to speak, unlike the offstage flower-ing of the Pope's staff in the more confrontational encounter of religions in "Laus Veneris." Taking joy in their celestial reunion, the narrator remarks, "But in his face his lady's face is sweet, / And through his lips her kissing lips are gone: / God send him peace, and joy of such an one" (474–76).

Swinburne again draws our attention to the productive mixing of the aes-thetic and religious here, a kind of Hellenized Hebraism that he associates with an ideal of late medievalism, when the discovery of classical authors was breathing new life into poetry. Again, unlike Buchanan's "Chaucer" in *The Fleshly School*, Swinburne's Chaucerian prototype is excited—quite literally, it seems—by the possibilities afforded by this vision of the world's material beauty. His narration concludes with a mix of erotic and religious desire that reaches beyond a more strictly Christian interpretation of her martyrdom: "This is the story of St. Dorothy. / I will you of your mercy pray for me / Because I wrote these sayings for your grace, / That I may one day see her in the face" (477–80). Her martyrdom is infused with a sensuality that seems out of place in a saint's life: her religious lesson cannot be divorced from her physical attractiveness, which first initiates contact with Theophilus. Like-wise, before his conversion, Theophilus is overwhelmed with his own desires, unable to truly love or connect with her. In some sense, she makes him a better consumer of art at the same time she makes him a better Christian—a "conversion" simultaneously taking place for the narrator of the poem, who uncovers a new material and spiritual aesthetic. The irony is that to experi-ence consummation, Christianity still demands the death of the artist, but what dies at the same time in "St. Dorothy" is the Christian insistence that love be divorced from physical desire and art: dogma dies too and leaves the poet to conclude with a somewhat unchaste and unchristian desire to look upon her face. Swinburne draws our attention to these historical moments when pagan and Christian achieve this odd cohabitation, when the aesthetic and literary win over against dogma and its enforcers. Featuring a Victorian poet speaking in the voice of a medieval one, "St. Dorothy" epitomizes the unique historical cross-dwelling of *Poems and Ballads*. Swinburne insists that European history—and much of the literature and art that has emerged from it—has been and continues to be defined by the conflict between body and spirit.

Conclusion: Translation, Culture, Anarchy

Despite its subversive reputation, *Poems and Ballads* might best be understood as an effort to intervene in a cultural crisis that was already underway rather than an effort to precipitate one. Arnold sought to do the same with *Culture and Anarchy*, which appeared just three years after *Poems and Ballads* and also attempted a broad remapping of European culture and England's place in it. Defined by the crossing of borders and the productive clash this engenders, Swinburne's poetry was uniquely positioned to perform the same cultural work: if anything, it showed that poetry could do more, and do it more radically, to bring England to Europe than Arnold had laid out in his various mission statements for critics and poets. Recharging Arnold's dream of a culturally receptive, cosmopolitan England, Swinburne's trans-European, trans-historical poetics at the same time reveals that crossing national boundaries could productively interrogate other cultural boundaries, including those grounded in sexuality and gender, boundaries that were not high priorities for Arnold.

Translation in Swinburne, as we have seen, was something that went well beyond an exchange of influences or even being open to other voices. It was a complex readaptation and dialogue of the kind Wolfgang Iser suggests characterizes the most influential or disruptive cultural shifts outward, when "[t]ranslatability is motivated by the need to cope with a crisis that can no longer be alleviated by the mere assimilation or appropriation of other cultures."[46] By way of example, Iser points to Carlyle's *Sartor Resartus* (1830–31) in terms that seem remarkably applicable to *Poems and Ballads*. Responding to the upheaval caused by the industrial revolution and the failure of its promise of progress, Carlyle adapted German transcendentalism in a mix of translation, travelogue, and spiritual autobiography that by and large rendered its sources unrecognizable. According to Iser, Carlyle's style of "cross-cultural discourse distinguishes itself from assimilation, incorporation, and appropriation, as it organizes an interchange between cultures in which the cultures concerned will not stay the same. A foreign culture is not just transposed onto a familiar one; instead, . . . a mutual patterning and repatterning is effected by such a discourse."[47] Donning new clothes and changing identities become the hallmarks of a cosmopolitanism that disrupts and destabilizes, whether in *Sartor Resartus* or in the career-long poetic masquerade that was Swinburne's. Thus his fondness for parody and disguise: writing as Chaucer or Sappho, adopting the mask of made-up French critics and scholars.[48] France, ultimately, or being like the French or ancient Greeks, is not the object of his cosmopolitanism. These cultural engagements all seem part of a deeper, more fundamental transformative impulse to be outside England, outside the self, and outside of familiar patterns of thinking.

It is perhaps fitting, then, to conclude with one last example of Swinburnian cultural ventriloquism, one published a year after *Poems and Ballads*. In this instance, Swinburne assumes the disguise of a French critic of Arnold to diagnose the intellectual stalemate that English poetics had reached. The "critic" questions English poetry's obsessive need to keep revisiting the Crisis of Faith:

> On perd un objet aimé, on désire le revoir, on épreuve des émotions douloureuses à songer qu'on ne le reverra point. Après? La mort, la douleur, l'oubli, la misère, voilà sans doute des choses pénibles, et que l'on voudrait éviter; il est clair que nous ferions tous notre possible pour y échaper. Cela prouve-t-il que ces choses-là n'existent pas?

> [You lose a beloved object, you long to see it again, you feel sorrowful in dreaming that you will never see it again. Afterwards? Death, grief, oblivion, distress—these are undoubtedly painful things that one would wish to avoid. Clearly, we would all do our best to escape them. Does that prove that these things do not exist?][49]

With a possible allusion to his Venerean knight caught between Christianity and paganism, Swinburne calls here for a poetics that would venture forth boldly, strengthened after the conflicts it had endured and ready to subsume them within a wider, outside perspective of itself:

> Un poëte enfermé chez lui peut être le meilleur chrétien du monde, ou bien le plus affreux païen; ce sont là des affaires de foyer où la critique n'a rien à voir; mais la poésie propre ne sera jamais ni ceci ni cela. Elle est

tout, elle n'est rien. . . . Toute émotion lui sert, celle de l'anachorète ni plus ni moins que celle du blasphémateur. Pour la morale, elle est mauvaise et bonne, chaste et libertine; pour la religion, elle est incrédule et fidèle, soumise et rebelle.

[Closeted in his house a poet can be the best Christian in the world or the wickedest pagan; those are domestic questions beside the point for critics; poetry is nether this nor that. In fact poetry is everything and nothing. It makes use of any emotion: the anchorite's is no better than the blasphemer's. For poetry, morality can be good or bad, chaste or libertine; religion can be incredulous or faithful, rebellious or submissive.][50]

It took an invented French critic to read English poetry correctly: Swinburne repeatedly insists that the self always needs to be viewed critically, with self-distancing. This is of course a highly Arnoldian impulse to begin with; Swinburne quite literally here takes up Arnold's call in "The Function of Criticism" to study at least one other language and literature intensely as a means of better understanding one's own, and "the more unlike one's own, the better" (3:284). Arnold appreciated the gesture and detected that the "French Critic" was Swinburne himself. In response to a letter from Arnold thanking him for the review, Swinburne again revealed something of his own complex cultural geography: "I must confess to you that the French critic quoted by me resides in a department of France abutting on the province of Germany where MM. Teufelsdroeckh & Sauerteig are Professors. I so often want French words for my meaning & find them easier & fuller of expression that I indulge the preference, as I write prose (I know) quicker & (I think) better in French than in English; with verse it is the other way usually."[51] Swinburne was always translating—moving between cultures, between voices, between genres—dwelling in difference. Like his French critic of Arnold, he leaves poetry seemingly everywhere at once but finally grounded in his own unique Anglo-European space.

6

Affinity versus Isolation

Cosmopolitanism and the
Racial Dynamics of Morris's Europe

UNTIL VERY RECENTLY, the name William Morris would have been unlikely to surface in discussions of cosmopolitanism or the idea of Europe, except as a by-product of his later embrace of communism. And even this commitment, it would seem, was tied to an overriding sense of English identity. As James Buzard has remarked recently of *News from Nowhere* (1890), "What else but race could underwrite the intense devotion to Britishness that Morris's utopia and his utopians exhibit?" Buzard posits that the "stay-at-home preference" of the novel's inhabitants "works serendipitously toward the preservation of what is at bottom, and for all Morris's repudiations of nationalism, a national culture grounded in race."[1] Morris's poetry would seem to fare little better, apart from the wide-ranging *Earthly Paradise,* where travelers from the North of Europe find refuge in an isolated quasi-Greek island and exchange tales with their hosts. *Sigurd the Volsung,* however, Morris's next major poem and the one that May Morris claimed "he held most highly and wished to be remembered by," would seem to return us to more firmly planted notions of racial identity.[2] As he said in the preface to an earlier prose translation of the Volsunga Saga he completed with Erikír Magnússon, "this is the Great Story of the North, which should be to all our race what the Tale of Troy was to the Greeks" (7:286). Herbert F. Tucker perhaps best captures the essential differences between these two

143

poems: where *The Earthly Paradise* endeavors to "put readers in possession of their heritage . . . as Europeans, beneficiaries alike of a Mediterranean and a Northern mythological legacy," *Sigurd the Volsung* eschews such "easy-access historicism" in favor of a "monolithic epic [that] would be as uncompromisingly, unforsakably stern as he could make it."[3] *Sigurd,* by all accounts, is remote and insular—culturally, historically, even stylistically, "a combination of pseudo-anachronism trying to escape from the realities of modern English and an inert obedience to the demands of metre," as John Goode unforgivingly described the poem's archaic diction and iambic-anapestic hexameters.[4]

Morris's place in this study, of course, implies that I see his work as forming an important stage in the development of the idea of Europe in Victorian poetry, but this significance lies neither in *The Earthly Paradise* alone nor in Morris's one major poem that followed his political conversion to socialism, *The Pilgrims of Hope* (1885–86). Rather, I want to suggest that an engaged, critical cosmopolitanism reaches its greatest depth of insight where we would least expect to find it: in the collision of kings, clans, and peoples that is *Sigurd the Volsung* and in some of the less cooperative, more racially charged encounters in *The Earthly Paradise.* In fact, Morris's apparently Teutocentric preface to the prose translation of the Volsunga Saga underscores the peculiar way that concepts of race and international fellowship could commingle in his work:

> [W]e must say again how strange it seems to us, that this Volsung Tale, which is in fact an unversified poem, should never before have been translated into English. For this is the Great Story of the North, which should be to all our race what the Tale of Troy was to the Greeks—to all our race first, and afterwards, when the change of the world has made our race nothing more than a name of what has been—a story too—then should it be to those that came after us no less than the Tale of Troy has been to us. (7:286)

At the same time Morris lends the Volsunga Saga a special racial magnetism for Anglo-Saxon readers, he is cautious to locate all such myths within the wider social context of world population shifts and the wider literary context of what we would now term "world literature." Tellingly, when asked in 1886 by the *Pall Mall Gazette* to list what he considered to be the one hundred greatest books ever written, he featured "the kind of book which Mazzini called 'Bibles;' they cannot always be measured by a literary standard, but to me are far more important than any literature. They are in no sense the work of individuals, but have grown up from the very hearts of the *people.*" The first five selections consisted of the Hebrew Bible, Homer, Hesiod, the

Icelandic Edda, and *Beowulf,* followed by the "Kalevala, Shah-nameh, [and] Mhabharata."[5] For Morris, literature must emerge first from cohesive national cultures before becoming the property of the world at large. The Tale of Troy, while not inspiring the same racial or ethnic identification as the Icelandic epic, is still a vital narrative, a key component informing European identity. By invoking Mazzini, Morris places himself in the company of other national internationalists in this study—adherents of the Herderian idea that world culture was shaped by the "hearts of the people"—cultural traditions that all have their own intrinsic value, regardless of whether that value translates across national standards of literariness.

With Morris, it is perhaps particularly important not to lose sight of what Doug Lorimer calls "the fluid and contradictory character of Victorian claims about race."[6] Morris historicizes race in ways that many of his contemporaries strongly resisted. Charles Dilke, for one, preferred in *Greater Britain* (1869) to take comfort in the belief "that race distinctions will long continue; that miscegenation will go but little way toward blending races; that the dearer are, on the whole, likely to destroy the cheaper people, and that Saxondom will rise triumphant from the doubtful struggle."[7] In contrast, Morris argues that literature will outlast race and continue to enrich the lives of readers. His primary goal is not to use art to restore and resolidify race: in some sense, race's only real importance is through its association with art. Morris's preference for the term "Gothic"—as much an artistic signifier as a racial one—over "Teutonic" is revealing in this respect. Morris is at pains not to over-stress any affinity contemporary "Englishness" might share with the Icelandic sagas and Eddic poems he translates and readapts: he strives just as hard to remind the reader of their distance—in part through those same infelicities of diction and meter that Goode disparaged. In Simon Dentith's analysis, Morris's prosody constitutes a "radical break" with Tennyson and other contemporaries who emphasized historical continuity with a poetic voice and style that stayed "within the predominant tradition in English poetry as it was available in the nineteenth century."[8] Tucker as well stresses how Morris, "surely the least progressivist Marxist on record, was never tempted by the dream of cumulative cultural *translatio* that entranced his generation" and the forms of epic they produced.[9] For Morris, poetry inhabits its own unique time zone, which gets to why he felt compelled at all to "versify" what was already essentially poetic—a question I return to below.

Morris's ethical default setting, to put it one way, was one of tolerance and self-criticism: celebrations of English racial or national superiority always seemed to alarm him. As he argued later in "Our Country Right or Wrong," patriotic rhetoric typically serves to cloak the imposition of economic or political power at the expense of the disenfranchised: "it prates of the interests of our country, while it is laying the trail of events which will ruin the fortunes, and break the hearts of its citizens: it scolds at wise men and honest men for a policy of isolation, while itself it would have nothing to do with foreign nations except for their ruin and ours."[10] Likewise, the neutral tone in which Morris delivers his observation about racial dissolution in reference to the Volsunga Saga betrays little of the angst surrounding the "extinction discourse" of some later Victorian commentators on race.[11] At the same time, Morris resists making global racial assimilation the crowning achievement of world progress, a position Arnold adopts in *On the Study of Celtic Literature* that enables him to cope with the loss of Welsh as a living language: "the swallowing up of separate provincial nationalities, is a consummation to which the natural course of things irresistibly tends; it is a necessity of what is called modern civilisation."[12]

Morris's wider perspective is evident even in that most persistent of his racial or cultural distinctions, between the North and South of Europe. Morris, of course, was an early devotee of Ruskin's commentary on "The Nature of Gothic" in *The Stones of Venice* (1851–53), where he contrasts two Europes, one rugged and organic in its approach to the arts and architecture, the other more rigidly precise. When the Kelmscott Press reprinted "The Nature of Gothic" in 1892, Morris's preface called it "one of the very few necessary and inevitable utterances of the century." Ruskin "seemed to point out a new road on which the world should travel."[13] That road clearly led north: Morris did not travel often in Europe, but he did make two important trips to Iceland in 1871 and 1873 at a time when British visitors there were still few. Morris also kept journals of his trips that were published in 1911 as part of the *Collected Works*. Nonetheless, there is little indication in Morris of the need to judge the South as morally and politically deficient vis-à-vis the North. Morris stops well short of the Teutonic one-upmanship displayed, for instance, by Matthew Arnold's father Thomas or by Charles Kingsley in his attack on Browning noted in chapter 1—ideas that Kingsley developed in a series of lectures later published under the title *The Roman and the Teuton*.[14] Morris's goal is more to expand the map of Europe—to include those places on the margins, such as Iceland and Scandinavia—and to reveal how they have always informed the cultural identity of Europe. His Northernness is less a repudiation of the South than a recontextualization of it.[15] The interest he shares with Swinburne in the medieval, Gothic encounter with classical Greece and Rome is indicative of this attitude as well. Morris sees this crossover not as a travesty but as something that deserved to be understood on its own terms—and on a grander, more epic scale than Swinburne's.[16]

As with Swinburne, however, Europe emerges from Morris's work not as a series of separate, inviolate cultures but as regions in continuous negotiation, exchange, and retranslation. His major poems and translations of the North and South—*The Life and Death of Jason* (1867), *The Odyssey* (1887), *The Earthly Paradise, Sigurd the Volsung*—all promote the kinship of sea-oriented traveling cultures in Europe. Morris seems just as consumed by the journeys *between* places and races as the clashes that occur when travelers arrive. These are very much mobile communities defined by their proximity to coasts and united in ways that go beyond nationality, as the geographer Barry Cunliffe insists in *Facing the Ocean: The Atlantic and Its Peoples* (2001): "the peoples of the long Atlantic façade of Europe have shared common beliefs and values over thousands of years, conditioned largely by their unique habitat on the edge of the continent facing the ocean. They lived in a resource-rich zone, in many ways remote from neighbours by land yet easily linked to others by sea."[17] In this grouping, Cunliffe includes most of the same regions Morris traverses—England, Iceland, and the northern and western coasts of France. *Sigurd* especially, as I will discuss, foregrounds the geographical contingencies of the racial and political clashes it explores. Thus well before *News from Nowhere,* Morris was looking for innovative ways to integrate social and environmental contexts in his work.

Ideologically, Morris's poetry can be difficult to characterize, seeming neither culturally conservative nor progressive in the manner of later works, although it does champion an early form of internationalism in the person of Sigurd. Poetry itself, in some sense, fills the gap of clear political aims or ambitions for racial recovery in Morris. What Morris aims for is a poetry of the "science of origins," as Arnold called the new ethnography in another passage from *On the Study of Celtic Literature:*

> Science has and will long have to be a divider and a separatist, breaking arbitrary and fanciful connections, and dissipating dreams of a premature and impossible unity. Still, science,—true science,—recognises in the bottom of her soul a law of ultimate fusion, of conciliation. To reach this, but to reach it legitimately, she tends. She draws, for instance, towards the same idea which fills her elder and diviner sister, poetry,—the idea of the substantial unity of man; though she draws towards it by roads of her own. But continually she is showing us affinity where we imagined there was isolation. (3:330)

Like the forays onto foreign coasts that constitute much of the movement between nations in *The Earthly Paradise* and *Sigurd the Volsung,* Morris shuttles between these modes of affinity and isolation. Morris's poetry attempts to negotiate between a limiting, defining sense of race and the understanding that coming together as a region—Europe—and beyond that, humanity—were equally desirable consummations. The poems test and critique racial affinities, acknowledging their power, but also set them adrift to collide and negotiate with each other. For Morris and Arnold, poetry must be the wide, interdisciplinary discourse that fostered understanding between cultures.

Where, then, does cosmopolitanism assert itself in Morris? Where do his protagonists escape isolation and reach toward affinity? It takes visionary, transcendent figures who in many ways disrupt the normal course of cultural relations in the poems: cosmopolitanism takes wing primarily in the lives and actions of border-crossing, fellowship-seeking heroes such as Kiartan, in "The Lovers of Gudrun" and, to an even greater degree, Sigurd. When they are successful, the fog of tribal and national allegiances lifts to reveal an idealized medieval Europe of free trade, where goods, ideas, and people flow with ease, governed by the laws of guest and host. It is an ideal, however, that tends to vanish as quickly as it appears in Morris. Those factors that stand in the way of cosmopolitanism are never fully reduced: the ties of family and clan, and the violence often necessary to assert them, ultimately overwhelm the Europe of these poems. However, rather than straining against the original sagas and stamping his own political longings on them, Morris remains true to the struggles of these cultures to preserve their identities even as they seek entry into a world that demands engagement of some kind, a world defined by travel. Cosmopolitanism in Morris is always under threat and tempered by this historical reality. Like Clough, Morris pushes hard on the concept before he can claim it as his own.

Turning first to *The Earthly Paradise,* I want to look closely at how notions of cultural migration manifest themselves in the Prologue and in the poem's major Northern tale, "The Lovers of Gudrun," a precursor in many ways to *Sigurd the Volsung* and the idea of Europe that emerges there. If, as Angela Flury suggests, "to be outside of one's national boundaries among others is, in fact, to become European," then *The Earthly Paradise* attempts to understand the challenges that adhere to this nomadic identity, in both intra-European and extra-European contexts.[18]

The Earthly Paradise

At the same time Morris was translating the Volsunga Saga into prose, he continued to work on his long epic *The Earthly Paradise,* published in four parts between 1868 and 1870. The poem is massive in scope, consisting of twenty-four tales—two for each month of the calendar year—and is informed throughout by notions of trans-European travel, migration, and hybridity, most pointedly in the encounter between Nordic "Wanderers" and Greek "Elders" that sets the poem in motion. The poem's cosmopolitan ambitions are thus inherent in its very design, as has been noted by several commentators on Morris including Tucker, as cited earlier, Amanda Hodgson, and Regenia Gagnier.[19] In the introduction to her recent scholarly edition of *The Earthly Paradise,* Florence Boos draws similar attention to how the poem's celebration of storytelling embodies cosmopolitan ideals of fellowship, "as tellers of tales from several cultures and chronological periods listen to other tellers of other tales, and contemporary and future hearers share emotions of empathetic recognition."[20] In my own analysis, I want to elucidate some of the other ways in which the poem dramatizes ideals of European cooperation and exchange while stressing what can be learned from the poem's emphasis on *clashes* between cultures, both in the Prologue and in "The Lovers of Gudrun."

Before the Prologue gets underway in earnest, however, *The Earthly Paradise* invokes a different, more optimistic kind of travel and exchange that serves as an ideal to which the rest of the poem aims. The opening lines take the form of a command challenging the modern reader's historical and ecological frame of reference:

> Forget six centuries overhung with smoke,
> Forget the snorting steam and piston stroke,
> Forget the spreading of the hideous town;
> Think, rather, of the packhorse on the down,
> And dream of London, small, and white, and clean,
> The clear Thames bordered by its gardens green. (1–6)[21]

As he would later in *News from Nowhere,* Morris invites the reader to imagine a landscape freed from the engine of industrialism but not devoid of commerce either. Among the goods traded in the port of London are "pointed jars that Greek hands toiled to fill / And treasured scanty spice from some far sea, / Florence gold cloth, and Ypres napery, / And cloth of Bruges, and hogsheads of Guienne" (10–13). Each good embodies some unique and vital connection to its source, together forming the image of a preindustrial Europe of sustainable free trade, one that will resurface in *Sigurd.* Presiding over it all, whose "pen / Moves over bills of lading," is Geoffrey Chaucer in his less familiar role of customs officer (14–15). Morris's tribute to his poetic forbear resonates in several ways: the image of the worldly poet, like Morris himself comfortable in the realms of business and art, reinforces the sense of a natural, almost organic Anglo-European cross-cultural fertilization.

In the way the poem sets up each tale, Morris stresses some of the more complex ways that cultures "trade" knowledge of each other through storytelling: after hearing the tale "The Writing on the Image," the listeners "praised the tale, and for a while they talked / Of other tales of treasure-seekers balked, / And shame and loss for men insatiate stored, / Nitocris' tomb, the Niblungs' fatal hoard" (340–43). The Wanderers themselves represent something of a cross-section of Northern European travelers and expatriates, including the "Breton squire" Nicholas (135), who "much lore of many lands" knew and first proposes their journey (139), and a "Swabian priest," Laurence, skilled in medicine and alchemy (153). The Wanderers also often note the source of their tales in countries they either visited or traded with. The Norwegian teller of "The Proud King" reveals "it happed to me, / Long years agone, to cross the narrow sea / that 'twixt us Drontheimers and England lies" (1.344.5–7), where "many tales we heard, some false, some true, / Of the ill deeds our fathers used to do / Within that land" (15–17). In this case, as he recalls the invasions of England by his ancestors, the teller underscores how these stories can serve as a form of diplomatic recovery going forward in the wake of invasion and war. In some sense, Morris warns against his own perhaps premature celebration of Chaucer's Europe of free trade and the Wanderers' investment in finding an even more fanciful "earthly paradise." In another such reminder, after crossing paths with Edward III of England off the coast of France, Nicholas reveals that his life has always been characterized by the turmoil and unrest of intra-European conflicts: "Thy foes, my Lord, drove out my kin and me, / Ere yet thine armed hand was upon the sea" (519–20). His earliest memory consists of being chased into exile by French royal armies: the "arrow-flight now seems / the first thing rising clear from feeble dreams" (571–72). Indeed, following this opening, Chaucer's happy port of entry recedes, and the poem segues into the precarious experiences of the Wanderers themselves, for whom peaceful and cooperative encounters are much more elusive.

The Wanderers never find their paradise, but they do arrive finally at a sort of Atlantis, "a nameless city in a distant sea" (17) populated by highly accommodating, sympathetic hosts, not without a sense of cultural kinship to the Wanderers, as the Elder of the City proclaims to them: you are "[n]o barbarous folk, as these our peasants say, / But learned in memories of a long-past day, / Speaking, some few at least, the ancient tongue / That through the lapse of ages still has clung / To us, the seed of the Ionian race" (75–79).[22]

If not actually Greek, then, the islanders identify themselves as cultural for-bears of Mediterranean European culture. The leader of the Wanderers, Rolf, reveals that as a child he dwelt with his father, a kind of knight-errant, at Byzantium, the medieval ideal of cosmopolis. The Elders invite him to tell the story of their wanderings, which, along with some of the tales in the body of the poem, begin to reveal a certain nomadic kinship between European cultures north and south. Although the Elders do not travel, several of the stories they tell capture the prevalence of sea-travel in the Greek world. Fol-lowing the conclusion of "The Lovers of Gudrun," for instance, one of the Elders introduces the next tale, "The Golden Apples," which recounts Her-cules's dealings with the sea-god Nereus and his theft of the apples from the daughters of Hesperus, by stating, "My masters! If about the troublous sea / Ye needs must hear, hearken a tale once told / By kin of ours in the dim days of old" (24–26). The longest of the Greek sea-based tales, "The Doom of King Acrisius," features the island-hopping Perseus, who with the gift of flight ranges across the entire known Greek world, from the western edge of the Atlantic, to Africa, to the distant north where he slays Medusa: "He had passed o'er the Danube and the Rhine, / and heard the faint sound of the northern sea; / But ever northward flew untiringly, / Till Thule lay beneath his feet at last" (964–67).

The Wanderers' own story, however, is the most expansive and dramatic of the traveling tales in *The Earthly Paradise,* ranging widely across Europe but dwelling more outside its borders in a half-real, half-invented landscape to the West. Here the protagonists hope to find the paradise of the poem's title but instead encounter a bewildering mix of hospitality and hostility, as if Morris aims to use them to test a broad range of different historical encoun-ters and negotiations. In preparing for the poem, Morris drew on Scandina-vian descriptions of the New World centering on the exploits of Leif Erikson, along with accounts of Spanish colonization in Central America, including William Prescott's *Conquest of Mexico* (1843) and Washington Irving's biog-raphy of Christopher Columbus (1828). What might at first seem like a rather odd textual assortment enables the poem to occupy a unique border-land between past and present, travel writing and fantasy, and Europe and its Others. In some ways, the Wanderers' contact there seems a more hopeful, less imperialistic revision of history. As Rolf notes at one point, "Certes, we might have gathered wealth untold / Amongst them, if thereto had turned our thought. / But none the glittering evil valued aught" (1240–42). With this admission, Morris in fact rewrites an earlier, ballad version of the Pro-logue where, as Boos puts it, the Wanderers assume the character of "mer-cenary adventurers—disloyal to each other, heedless of the consequences of their actions, and brutal to the native peoples they encounter."[23] This racial antagonism is conveyed in the language of the early draft as well: the most violent of the peoples they clash with is a strangely displaced tribe of "Black men such as our people bring / With ivory and spices rare, / When southward they go sea-roving, / Or like the Greek kings' eunuchs are."[24] The later version avoids such racial descriptors; one encounters the term "folk" much more often than race. Morris's use of the term "forest people" to describe one group they encounter indicates the shift as well to more geographic signifiers. The final impression the Prologue leaves is of a journey historically familiar enough to be recognizable as emblematic of the general European contact with the Americas, yet critically reimagined by Morris: in some respects their encounter is more cooperative and peaceful, but it is still subject to conflicts and misunderstandings by both the Wanderers and those they come across.[25] Morris probes the demands that travel places on both peoples. For the Wanderers, their journey is a process, a test of how to engage others: is their travel motivated by exchange, the desire for fellowship, or by the need to possess and occupy? In some sense, they will not know until they arrive.

The New World of the Prologue is a highly complex, unique kind of contact zone, one that frustrates the Wanderers' desire to read "paradise" onto the various locations they discover. Morris sets the stage for these potential misreadings when he notes the Wanderers' dependence for navigation upon Nicholas's knowledge of the "lore of many lands." As Rolf explains,

> since I knew
> Nought but old tales, nor aught of false and true
> Midst these, for all of one kind seemed to be
> The Vineland voyage o'er the unknown sea
> And Swegdir's search for Godhomme, when he found
> The entrance to a new world underground;
> But Nicholas o'er many books had pored,
> And this and that thing in his mind had stored,
> And idle tales from the true report he knew. (333–41)

Based on this knowledge, Nicholas advises that, once reaching the West, they steer south of Greenland where they "shall find / Spice-trees set wavering by the western wind, / And gentle folk who know no guile at least" (363–65). Eventually, however, we discover that Nicholas's knowledge has little more to offer in the way of fact than Rolf's legends of Vineland: Morris reminds us that these are stories written *on* the New World, imported from the West. Overall, their journey traverses an elusive, uncertain geography, and they end up continuously revising their destinations and assumptions about them.

Their first impression of the world beyond Europe is literally one of impenetrability: a "thick, black wood" (944) confronts them, and after failing to cut their way through it, they return to their ships and set out again to find a more accommodating destination. So begins the Prologue's alternating pattern of sites characterized by strife and confusion followed by oases vaguely resembling the earthly paradise they seek but always leaving something wanting. Morris in many ways brilliantly underscores the confusion of motives and reactions of his travelers, who are never sure how to judge or how to engage the new races they find. The first people they encounter greet them warmly, even as gods: "sure of all the folk I ever saw / These were the gentlest" (1203–4), Rolf says. These natives create a sense of comfort and even familiarity: "though brown indeed through dint of that hot sun," Rolf surmises, they "[w]ere comely and well knit, as any one / I saw in Greece, and fit for deeds of war, / Though as I said of all men gentlest far" (1227–30). Rolf's comparison to the fitness of his Ionian hosts reveals a kind of tolerance but also his understanding that he and his listeners must inevitably interpret this new landscape through European racial and cultural norms. Ten of these brown warriors join up with the Wanderers, and other scenes of such cooperation follow, but with a sense of ambivalence on Rolf's part. At another landing, after first falling victim to a surprise attack that kills their navigator Nicholas, they meet again with a more peaceful people, "most untaught and wild, / Nigh void of arts, but harmless, good, and mild, / Nor fearing us" (1473–75). The Wanderers "built them huts, as well as we could, for we / Who dwell in Norway have great mastery / In woodwright's craft" (1499–501). The poem leaves open the question of whether these "forest people" are good because they are peaceful or because they are passive and allow themselves to be improved upon. What to take from these people, and what to give them, poses something of a problem for the Wanderers and causes some of them to revise the aims of their quest.

Rolf reflects this uncertainty in several ways, as he expresses the limits of his engagement with the "forest people": "They learned our tongue, and we too somewhat learned / Of words of theirs; but day by day we yearned / To cross those mountains" (1505–7). He is willing to go a certain distance to understand and bond with them, but their overriding quest and mission—the promise that beyond the hills lies the earthly paradise—compels them onward, although not without some debate. Rolf in fact berates those who refuse to join him and "think it well / With this unclad and barbarous folk to dwell" (1551–52). Anticipating the modern reader's potential discomfort with Rolf's remarks here, Boos suggests in an annotation that "Rolf and the others move on because they are impelled by their quest, not for reasons of racist contempt" (119–20n)—contempt of the kind she suggests is evident, by way of comparison, in Tennyson's "Locksley Hall" (1842). If the poem is free of the unabashed Eurocentrism of Tennyson's speaker—and Morris's attempts to tone down the racial language of the first draft of "The Wanderers" would also support this—the passage remains emblematic of the sense of cultural proprietorship in Western colonial encounters. At the same time, Morris reveals his own struggle over how to present native American peoples, not just from his own point of view, but from the late-medieval perspective of the Wanderers he is attempting to recreate.

Morris's larger point seems to be, simply, that the Wanderers don't know what they are getting themselves into, and there is a good deal of debate among them about how to proceed and engage the people they encounter. In what might be a form of poetic justice for his eagerness to read his own desires onto a landscape resistant to them, Rolf's journey over the mountain brings them up against "folk the worst of all we came to know; / Scarce like to men, yea, worse than most of beasts, / For of men slain they made their impious feasts" (1614–16). Their fighting with them represents some of the most brutal in the poem. The Wanderers kill their wounded prisoners, and Rolf recognizes that "[s]o with the failing of our hoped delight / We grew to be like devils" (1632–33). After some weeks Rolf and his men return to those they had left behind, some of whom, in a possible allusion to Tennyson, have taken "brown wives" (1664). By now, however, Rolf has gained new-found respect for those "grown too wise / Upon this earth to seek for paradise" (1591–92). There remains throughout the poem a conflict between the benefits of staying put, or negotiating with this new world on its own terms, and an equally powerful wanderlust that brings Europe into contact and conflict with others. Even later, when Rolf and his men find themselves happily ensconced in an idealized Aztec city of gold, "We longed to be by some unknown far shore; / Once more our life seemed trivial, poor, and vain, / Till we our lost fool's paradise might gain" (2056–58).

The Wanderers' final stop in the West comprises Morris's most sophisticated commentary on the confused, often contradictory nature of European encounters abroad and what they reveal about European identity overall. While still living in the gold city, a "young man strange within the place" (2127) convinces Rolf that, if he will follow him to a different island, they will finally achieve their goal of immortality. They make the journey, but, once there, find they have been tricked. They are greeted as gods, but in a sort of contemptuous, self-serving way that the young man explains:

> O ye, who sought to find
> Unending life against the law of kind,

Within this land, fear ye not now too much,
For no man's hand your bodies here shall touch,
But rather with all reverence folk shall tend
Your daily lives, until at last they end
By slow decay: and ye shall pardon us
The trap whereby beings made so glorious
As ye are made, we drew unto this place.
Rest ye content then! for although your race
Comes from the Gods, yet are ye conquered here,
As we would conquer them, if we knew where
They dwell. . . . (2459–71)

It is an altogether bizarre episode: stripped of their armor, the Wanderers must sit imprisoned as they behold the "many mummeries that they wrought / About the altar" in a rite of worship as torture (2505–6). The incident also recalls a moment from earlier in the poem, when, as the Wanders contemplate what the New World has in store for them, they remember a warning from a Genoese trader: "for mayhap men dwell here / Who worship dreadful gods, and sacrifice / Poor travellers to them in such horrid wise" (858–60). In effect, the Wanderers become those gods *and* their sacrificial victims, overtaken, in some sense, by the narrative that they projected onto the New World. Eventually the Wanderers are freed—not by their own efforts—but as a result of a rebellious attack on the city. The specific motives of the attackers, or why the Wanderers' captors thought possessing them would somehow prevent the attack, are not made clear—and what to conclude from the encounter overall, with its many layers of irony, is also ambiguous. Postcolonial theorization of the self-defeating nature of the colonial gaze, "as anxious as it is assertive," according to Homi K. Bhabha, provides one way of interpreting this scene.[26] Joining Frantz Fanon with Jacques Lacan, Bhabha continues, "In the objectification of the scopic drive there is always the threatened return of the look; in the identification of the Imaginary relation there is always the alienating other (or mirror) which crucially returns its image to the subject."[27] Morris similarly captures the schizophrenic, self-contradictory nature of Western views of civilizations in the New World. The Wanderers, in essence, are made captive by the same motives that propelled their own quest: they encounter a people seeking divine favor that will preserve their wealth and comfort in an earthly paradise. They become the captive audience to a parody of their own pretensions to immortality and the status of gods.

Does Morris suggest, then, that the better alternative for the Wanderers was simply to have stayed at home? *The Earthly Paradise* does not appear to advocate this either: somewhat ironically, perhaps, it was only through their travel that the Wanderers were able to question and revise their impression of that unknown world. In addition, for all of the misunderstanding overshadowing the Wanderers' travels, Morris points as well to a future of conversation, if only briefly. As Rolf describes the process, "Those forest folk with ours their lot had cast" begin the process of translation: "when all our tongue at last they knew / They told us tales, too long to tell as now" (1732, 34–35). One could argue here, from a more critical perspective, that the forest people nonetheless remain silenced, accompanying the Wanderers but not really saying or doing anything of consequence. While their untold stories remain a blank space in the poem, to his credit, Morris acknowledges that he does not really know (or can faithfully render) the stories of the forest people. Elsewhere, however, as we have seen, he stresses the importance of learning these stories, absorbing the "Bibles," as he put it in the *Pall Mall Gazette* letter, that undergird world literature. What the Prologue to *The Earthly Paradise* presents is a kind of fellowship in the making—a dialogue that has begun but with the translation still ongoing, and this is where Morris's own social goals as a poet come into play. Fictional narratives of travel, poetic or otherwise, grow out of real world encounters: the dialogue that *The Earthly Paradise* consists of in its entirety, and that we participate in as readers, represents one way to break free from internecine conflicts.

Morris's own creative engagement with the North of Europe could also be seen as part of that ongoing dialogue—the need to bring to the fore neglected stories, in this case from the outlands of Europe. His major effort to set the dialogue in motion in *The Earthly Paradise* is "The Lovers of Gudrun," the longest tale in the volume and the one he regarded most highly.[28] "The Lovers of Gudrun" anticipates the direction Morris would soon take with *Sigurd the Volsung* by offering a more concentrated investigation of a culture defined by travel, one also at a historical crossroads in its relations with the rest of Europe. Like "The Wanderers," it foregrounds the question of what compels people to travel and what can be achieved, not merely lost, when cultures make contact.

By the time Morris began the poem, he was already deep in his study and translation of Icelandic literature. He had experimented with doing a prose translation of the Laxdaela Saga from which the Gudrun story derives, but later abandoned it, thinking his efforts would be better directed toward composing his own poetic re-vision of the material. As he explained in a letter:

> The saga itself is full of interesting incident, but has no pretensions to artistic unity, being indeed what it calls itself, a chronicle of the dwellers in Lax-

dale: it is disjointed even for that withal, and in some important places very bald, much more so than in any of the good translated sagas: with that too were coarseness both of manners and character that seemed alien to other parts of the characters therein, and wh[ich] I thought I had a right to soften or disregard: All these things, to my mind, joining with the magnificent story made it the better subject for a poem as one could fairly say that that story had never been properly told.[29]

Phrases such as "coarseness of manner" and "I had a right to soften" are red flags for readers anticipating a quintessentially "Victorian" mistranslation of Morris's source, and it remains something of a commonplace among critics to lament the way he apparently sentimentalized the story or infused it with elements of his own troubled marriage. Morris did concede that Gudrun's role in the original saga was minor and more one-dimensional, "much more the stock 'stirring woman' of the north than I thought fit to make her."[30] Morris also expounded more fully on the thoughts and motives of the other members of the love triangle in the poem, Kiartan and his brother-in-arms Bodli. By updating the characters' emotional and psychological dimensions for a modern audience, so the argument goes, Morris thus diminished the spare, dignified tone that he admired of Icelandic literature in general.[31] At the same time, Morris's poem lost some of its purchase on the "science of origins," teaching us less about the culture that conceived the Laxdaela Saga. I want to argue, however, that these changes, especially as concern Gudrun, who comes to embody the larger cultural struggle between home and abroad, work to reinforce the poem's exploration of the competing demands of situated versus traveling identities. Morris, in fact, would perform a similar makeover on Gudrun's namesake in Book IV of *Sigurd,* who relives the dilemma faced by the homebound Laxdaela-Gudrun but would take bolder action in the political sphere.

Just as he promises, Morris provides greater narrative unity in his rendition of the saga, but he does not lose the sense of a tale historically and geographically grounded in the transformations of Icelandic and Scandinavian culture. "Herdholt my tale names for the stead" (1), it begins, identifying the location in western Iceland where the families of Gudrun and Kiartan reside. The plot shifts between Iceland and Norway—where King Tryggivson, at his seat in Drontheim, had begun the process of Christianizing the region around A.D. 1000. In several ways, Morris draws attention to how much Icelandic culture is defined, on the one hand, by isolation, being "[c]ooped up in this cold corner of the world" (1003), and, on the other, by necessary and frequent contacts with the outside world. Morris, for instance, reminds us that the wood used to construct King Olaf's homestead has been "brought / Over the sea" from Norway (406–7). Christianity was another cultural import Iceland struggled with at this time. The historical Thangbrand, the same "German bishop" (1542) who converts Tryggivson, later travels to Iceland to evangelize there but is forced to flee. The tale thus features a culture already well defined by the nomadic movements that sustain it but also pose unique challenges to its identity.

Kiartan, who pledges himself to Gudrun shortly before setting out abroad, is the character most defined by travel. The poem notes his gifts as a swimmer (522) and his related longing to be on the sea in order to establish his true identity: "I yet must think of roving" (1021), he tells Gudrun at one point, summing up his identity as the quest-oriented male. The poem, however, does not restrict this longing to him. Gudrun offers to accompany Kiartan overseas, a scene Morris develops much more fully than the original saga does. Morris chooses to underscore Gudrun's longing to take control of her fate:

> Things have there been more strange,
> Than that we three should sit above the oars,
> The while on even keel 'twixt the low shores
> Our long-ship breasts the Thames flood, or the Seine.
> Methinks in biding here is little gain. (998–1002)

Sensing that Kiartan gives serious attention to this possibility, another difference from the saga, Gudrun attempts to persuade him further: "let the rough salt sea / Deal with me as it will, so thou be near! / Let me share glory with thee" (1128–30).[32] Gudrun has already lost another husband at sea and senses she is about to lose another, and we see her frustration at not being able to infiltrate the male culture of travel in the poem. With Kiartan unable to say yes or no, Gudrun finally answers for him, "I know my heart, thou knowest it not; farewell" (1152). This becomes a crucial failure to connect in the poem, one that overshadows Kiartan's happy prediction to Bodli of the potential fruits of their voyage, which could take them as far as Byzantium:

> He fell to talk of all that they should do
> In the fair countries that they journeyed to.
> Not Norway only, or the western lands,
> In time to come, he said, might know their hands,
> But fairer places, folk of greater fame,

Where 'neath the shadow of the Roman name
Sat the Greek king, gold-clad, with bloodless sword. (1230–36)

Kiartan here speaks as much to the lost potential in his relationship with Gudrun, the voyage together never undertaken. Tellingly, Bodli barely listens to him, his mind still wandering back to Gudrun. Kiartan nonetheless undergoes a significant transformation once abroad, as he endeavors to find ways to bridge the distance between Norway and Iceland and between Christian and pagan Europe.

Kiartan must face this challenge the moment he arrives in Norway, where, for King Tryggivson, "nothing else . . . was good / But that all folk should bow before the Rood" (1280–81). Historically, the kingdom's acceptance of Christianity represents an important stage in Scandinavia's integration with the traditions of continental Europe, and Morris does much to show what was at stake in the conversion. Kiartan strongly repudiates the new faith at first: "I left Iceland for another thing / Than to curse all the dead men of my race" (1375–76), capturing the threat posed by the new religion to native culture. Morris also stresses the political motives on the King's part, subtly conveyed at one point through the image of his enormous church, which "cast its shadow down / Upon the low roofs of the goodly town" (1324–25). Kiartan instinctively resists the not-so-subtle ways King Tryggivson tends to mix hospitality with threats. Tryggivson invites them to his hall only to insist on their conversion, and Kiartan must struggle with the question of whether to defend his honor through violence: "It seems the master of this new-found lore / Said to his men once: Think ye that I bring / Peace upon earth? nay, but a sword. O king, / Behold the sword ready to meet thy sword!" (1455–58). The lines represent an unlikely familiarity with the Bible on Kiartan's part and reveal less about him than they do Morris's medieval narrator. Speaking from the perspective of a fourteenth-century Christian European, the narrator struggles to balance his admiration of the pagan heroes of the tale with the spiritual investment in Christianity that he and the other Wanderers share—betrayed on occasion by lines such as, "Fair goes the ship that beareth out Christ's truth / Mingled of hope, of sorrow, and of ruth" (1796–97). The cultural border-crossing of the poem thus operates on two textual and historical levels.

At the hands of Morris and his medieval spokesman, Kiartan's struggle between the two directions is amplified more than in the original saga, where he breaks down rather suddenly after hearing a Christmas sermon.[33] In the poem, after an uneasy feast together, Kiartan returns to the king the following day and describes a more pitched mental struggle between the two traditions:

> He looked upon the king a little while,
> Then slowly sank his sword, and, taking it
> By the sharp point, to where the king did sit
> He made his way, and said: Nay, thou hast won;
> Do thou for me what no man yet has done,
> And take my sword, and leave me weaponless:
> And if thy Christ is one who e'en can bless
> An earthly man, or heed him aught at all,
> On me too let his love and blessing fall;
> But if no Christ, nor Odin help, why, then
> Still at the worst are we the sons of men,
> And will we, will we not, yet we must hope,
> And after unknown happiness must grope,
> Since the known fails us, as the elders say. (1621–34)

Even as he says of the new religion, "all these things are but words" (1636), Kiartan seems to be turning into a Christ figure himself, echoing another passage from the Bible as he brings the "Son of Man" down to a human level. Kiartan appears more willing to be transformed by the new religion on its merits, unlike Tryggivson, who sees it primarily as a means to greater power. In turn, a kind of role reversal takes place, with Kiartan's speech converting *him*—if not to the dogma of Christianity than at least to its message of peace and brotherhood. Tryggivson tells him to keep his sword and "[d]eem of my land and house e'en as thy home" (1639). The remainder of Kiartan's stay is marked by peace and gestures of fellowship, even though technically Kiartan is held in ransom pending Iceland's conversion, while Bodli is allowed to return to Iceland: "Great love there grew 'twixt Kiartan and the king / From that time forth, and many a noble thing / Was planned betwixt them" (1652–54).

What these plans lead to is a Kiartan increasingly set off from those around him, such as Bodli, who has always seemed the more reluctant traveler. Kiartan's vision and leadership continue to evolve, however, while everyone else's remains stagnant. His attention to the king's daughter Ingioborg, for example, seems less a betrayal of Gudrun than an act of kindness and fellowship. Ingioborg senses this, and is remarkably forgiving of his decision to return to Iceland, when one considers the vows of vengeance that usually follow broken engagements in the sagas. She makes a telling gesture of hospitality to him and Gudrun: "Fain were I she should hate me not. Behold, / Here is a coif, well wrought of silk and gold / By folk of Micklegarth, who had no thought / Of thee or me, and thence by merchants brought / who perchance loved nought" (2248–52). The reference to Micklegarth, the Norse settlement near Constantinople, is also significant, invoking the idealized cultural crossroads that Rolf had mentioned in the Wanderer's prologue.

Upon his return to Iceland, however, Kiartan discovers the consequences of not taking Gudrun with him and the difficulties that can overwhelm the return of the native: "well-known things, did seem / But pictures now or figures in a dream" (2382–83). Kiartan is unable to transcend the family rivalries that have continued to fester in his absence: Bodli has married Gudrun after convincing her that Kiartan no longer wished to return to her. Kiartan in turn also marries someone else, but the tension between clans goes on unabated. The gift of the coif is stolen amidst a series of other insults and retaliations between clans, all pointing toward the general breakdown of hospitality that had peaked in Drontheim. Completing his transition into a sacrificial Christ figure, Kiartan is finally ambushed and killed by Bodli at Gudrun's behest. The lost promise of Kiartan's and Gudrun's never realized marriage and journey together haunts the poem right up until the end and is captured in Gudrun's famous line, when called upon to look back at her life, "I did the worst to him I loved the most" (4903).

Left behind in her cold corner of the world, Gudrun's emotions have nowhere to go and turn inward. In the end, as much as Kiartan, she epitomizes the struggles between affinity and isolation that define Iceland. In the closing scene of the tale, Morris offers one final glance into the limitations gender imposes on her. The son to whom she speaks her final assessment of Kiartan enjoys the freedom to range abroad, making it to Byzantium as a member of the Scandinavian bodyguard that attended the emperor. If he lacks the messianic overtones of Kiartan, he does recover something of his wider vision: "A travelled man and mighty, gay of weed, / Doer belike of many a desperate deed / Within the huge wall of the Grecian king" (4844–46).[34] The contrast between maternal and filial identities here could not be clearer: Bodli (her son's name) goes where she might have. Longing to reach outward, she is charged instead with preserving and fostering domestic identity. In the end, her character serves as a microcosm of the larger ebb and flow of the culture she embodies. In Morris's next major poem of the North, Kiartan, the noble traveler figure sacrificed to family quarrels and ambitions, will reappear as Sigurd. Gudrun, the woman of restricted movements and ambitions, will also reappear, as Morris asks again how these seafaring cultures will engage the world around them.

Sigurd the Volsung

Sigurd the Volsung is much more than a longer, bloodier version of "The Lovers of Gudrun": the poem's settings, peoples, and history all change in significant ways. On all of these fronts, the poem is a good deal less specific. Where the Volsungs reside is never made clear, except that it must be somewhere near the shore since it is easiest to reach the kingdom of Siggeir the Goth to the south by sea. J. M. S. Tompkins theorizes that "Morris's conception of the story of Sigurd as a developing myth, valid for his own age and those to come, probably accounts for his snapping the twisted and eroded links which still hold the *Volsungasaga* to the history and topography of the North."[35] Of the racial makeup of the poem, Tompkins observes, "All his characters, except Atli and his Easterners, are Goths, and worship Odin the Goth. His only place-name is Lymdale."[36] Indeed, there are few if any appeals to what might be called Anglo-Norse ethnic or genetic pride in the poem, apart from the fact that Sigmund is taller than his foreign adversary Siggeir whom, as Tompkins notes, is racially akin to him anyway (4).[37]

This racial and topographical indeterminacy is even stronger than Tompkins implies. Morris consistently opts to stress culture more by compass heading than race: in Book 4, Atli is never the Hun, but the "Eastland" lord, who rules by the "inner sea" (254). Other geographical allusions include references to Atli's "[w]hite steeds from the Eastland horse-plain" (247) and how the sun sets differently relative to the horizon there, "hold[ing] dusky night aloof" (257). In turn, the poem's cultural collisions have the feel of inevitable movements or migrations across the face of the earth: the quest for power and wealth seems almost an afterthought. Along similar lines, Morris drops the family connection between Brynhild and Atli, so that he is no longer drawn to engage the Niblungs out of the need to avenge her death. Gudrun, as Atli's envoy describes her, is "the glory of the Westland" (247): only later does Atli find out about the treasure horde the Niblungs have acquired from Fafnir via Sigurd. Peoples are defined by their proximity to each other and the topography of the lands they inhabit. One is east, west, south, north; or resides in the outlands or on the sea-rim; or, if not as fortunate, in the "waste places of the earth" with the shape-changing serpent Fafnir (61). It's also worth recalling that the poem, unlike the prose translation, makes no claim in a preface or prologue to inspire readers along racial lines.

These changes all contribute to what might be called Morris's "geographical vision," one that organizes, in a sense, his aesthetic and ethnographic aims, and points to something more innovative than the kind of dehistoricizing Tomkins describes. In Morris's time, geography, as an organized field of study, was first coming into being and was more closely tied to exploration. Even more so than today, geography was a highly interdisciplinary field, as Helena Michie and Ronald R. Thomas explain: "the tools and discourse of geography were being appropriated by a host of other disciplines—for example, biology, anthropology, ethnology, physics, and literary and travel writing—and the influence of geography expanded well beyond the confines of the profession of geography itself."[38] Morris had a broad understanding of the cultural and natural forces that shape human societies—one of "the most interdisciplinary figures in all of western culture," as David Latham has described him. All of these interests—in work, travel, translation, race, politics—in some ways come together under Morris's geographical vision.[39] What Morris is up to might best be equated with the subfield of "human geography," as it became known in the twentieth century, which concerns itself with how human beings adapt to the topographical and meteorological conditions of their environment.[40] Morris's geographic rendition of the poetry of the "science of origins" thus places culture, nation, and race within a new intellectual frame of reference. War and other struggles between peoples do not form part of a social-Darwinian contest to see which race is the more fit. Morris instead foregrounds how cultures come to terms with the challenges, threats, and opportunities posed to them by their environment and the peoples that come in contact with them. These encounters can trigger intense and bloody defenses of tribal honor, but the poem also seeks some way out of this cycle through more cooperative negotiations spearheaded by Sigurd.

Viewed from this geographical angle, Morris's objection to Richard Wagner's rendition of the Volsunga Saga, made before he had decided to "versify" it himself, is all the more revealing. Morris appears to have disliked opera to begin with, but he seems equally concerned about German colonization of the story. Two years before he began work on *Sigurd the Volsung,* he complained, "I look upon it as nothing short of desecration to bring such a tremendous and world-wide subject under the gaslights of an opera: the most rococo and degraded of all forms of art—the idea of a sandy-haired German tenor tweedledeeing over the unspeakable woes of Sigurd, which even the simplest words are not typical enough to express!"[41] First, by accusing Wagner of co-opting a "world-wide" subject for German nationalist ends, Morris fashions a space for his own somewhat denationalized version later.[42] The reference to opera as a "rococo" form also resonates along national lines, betraying his fear of an Italianate, spectacle-oriented treatment of the saga; Wagner becomes a kind of unholy German-Italian hybrid in Morris's eyes. It was therefore important to return the saga to its most unadorned, authentic state, and he saw poetry as the vehicle for this endeavor. It is ironic, perhaps, to claim that an English poetic translation would be more "world-wide" than a German operatic one, but what this points to is how Morris has all along defined poetry as the genre of a more objective science of origins. Only through the more historically grounded, ideologically less determined medium of Morris's poetry could the saga retain its "world-wide" relevance and argue on behalf of those same cosmopolitan values.

Book 1 of the poem sets the stage for Sigurd's later arrival by focusing on the generation previous to him. The lives of his grandfather Volsung, father Sigmund, and step-brother Sinfiotli are all largely defined by insults to tribal honor and the reprisals that must inevitably follow them. If anything, Book 1 displays the failure of cosmopolitanism and diplomacy amid a world of disorder that Sigurd must later set to rights. Book 1 also raises the question of whether a tradition-bound, largely self-contained community such as the Volsungs can fruitfully engage a more complex, threatening modern world and still survive. This challenge appears in the shape of King Siggeir of Gothland, who sends an envoy asking for the hand of Volsung's daughter Signy. They feel vaguely insulted by Siggeir's offer to make them, essentially, *his* ally: "Now he deems thy friendship goodly, and thine help in the battle good, / And for these will he give his friendship and his battle-aid again" (2). Although Siggeir's kingdom is wealthier and militarily more powerful, the Volsungs still recall with pride "how they fared with the Goths o'er ocean and acre and wood, / Till all the north was theirs, and the utmost southern lands" (2). They accept the proposal, but it is almost immediately overshadowed by feelings of hurt pride between the kingdoms, exacerbated in many ways by the arrival of the "one-eyed and seeming ancient" Odin at the marriage celebration. Odin thrusts a sword into the Branstock at the center of Volsung's hall, precipitating a contest of national prowess in which each of the Goth guests fails to retrieve the sword before Sigmund finally succeeds. Siggeir grumbles, "They have trained me here / As a mock for their woodland bondsmen; and yet they shall buy it dear" (7). When Siggeir asks for the sword as a gift, offering in return "a store-house" filled with "iron, and huge-wrought amber, that the southern men love sore," Sigmund refuses: "when the purple-selling men / Come buying thine iron and amber, dost thou sell thine honour then?" (8–9). The exchange underscores the clash of values embodied in the two cultures: one more expansive, defined by wealth cultivated through trade and conquest, the other content more to stay within its boundaries and traditions.

It soon appears that the Volsungs might have been better off had they remained at home and refused Siggeir's initial offer of intermarriage between the kingdoms. The poem also makes clear, however, that there is no alternative to this engagement. Cultures will collide, especially those defined so much by their proximity to the sea. Volsung himself recognizes this and will not refuse Siggeir's offer to "come to the house of the Goth-kings as honoured guests and dear," even though he knows he has grounds for concern. Volsung "speedily" replies to him, "'No king of the earth might scorn / Such noble bidding, Siggeir: and surely will I come / To look upon thy glory and the Goths' abundant home'" (9). Later Signy and the other Volsung women warn them not to go, but Volsung reveals the dilemma his sense of honor leaves him in: "shall a king hear murder when a king's mouth blessing saith?" (12). These are the values he clings to and that have defined an orderly Europe of hospitality and exchange. Unable to heed Signy's final warning to "turn back from the murderous shore" (13), Volsung and his sons are ambushed upon their arrival in the land of the Goths. The poem thus foregrounds the question of what, or who, might emerge to restore the values Volsung dies upholding, or enable them to travel and readapt to a world inhabited by the likes of Siggeir.

Sigmund is only the partial answer, since he must first lend himself to an existence defined by survival, war, and vengeance for his father's killing. After the ambush, all are wiped out except for Sigmund and nine of his brothers, who have been taken prisoner and chained to trees in a remote forest where a she-wolf appears nightly to devour them in succession. Sigmund alone survives when he "too grew woolfish" and bites into her before freeing himself and strangling her (21). Morris seems eager to play upon these clashes between civilized and barbaric behavior and, similarly, between human and animal that characterize the sagas and ancient epic in general (one thinks of *Gilgamesh,* for instance, or *The Odyssey*). Morris retains another scene from the saga when Sigmund, with his son Sinfiotli, go on a kind of killing spree after donning wolf-skins: "and they howled out wolfish things, / Like the grey dogs of the forest; though somewhat the hearts of kings / Abode in their bodies of beasts" (32). Sinfiotli, in fact, points to another taboo Morris links with animalism—incest—since he is conceived when Signy appears to Sigmund in disguise. Signy cites the demands of family honor to justify her incestuous sin: "my child and thine he is, / Begot in that house of the Dwarf-kind for no other end than this; / The son of Volsung's daughter, the son of Volsung's son. / Look, look! might another helper this deed with thee have done?" (41). Signy here links her actions to the barbarous, prehuman race of dwarves, highlighting the sort of regression embodied in her deed and in the fierce, ruthless Sinfiotli. Later, Sinfiotli kills Signy's children—his own half-brothers—when they storm Siggeir's castle: "Sinfiotli taketh them up / And breaketh each tender body as a drunkard breaketh a cup" (36). He personifies the last, violent gasp of the all-for-the-clan mentality that gave him birth. Sigmund too must grow wolfish at times to survive and win vengeance, but he remains more sober and humane in contrast. Signy calls upon him first to slay her children, and he replies, "Nay this shall be far from me / To slay thy children sackless" (36). The incidents serve as a reminder of the strong demand that acting on behalf of blood ties places on human morality and human communities at large. Family and national pride, displayed in excess by both Siggeir and the Volsungs, feed upon themselves even if in retaliation: indeed, incest and cannibalism become twin taboos in the poem. They are stark violations of the body—of oneself and one's fellow humans— an unhealthy turning *inward* that is about as anti-cosmopolitan, presumably, as one can get. Signy, in fact, commits suicide after revealing the incest to Sigmund. Later, foes taunt Sinfiotli as the one who "slay[s] his brothers" (44), ironic for someone whose very existence is for the vindication of family honor. It is fitting, then, after they return to the Volsung kingdom, that Sinfiotli's stepmother Broghild poisons him in retaliation for murdering her son Gudrod. Vengeance on behalf of family and clan is associated with a kind of inevitable, necessary animalism if it is to be successful, but it is also clearly a dead end in the poem, one indeed characterized primarily by murder and suicide.

The killing over bonds of kinship finally overwhelms Sigmund as well. Its demands have always dictated the battles he engages in and his movements back and forth across borders. Following the death of Siggeir, he at last departs from "the strangers's shore" (43), but only to see his kingdom come apart later in the conflict between Broghild and Sinfiotli. With strong echoes of Tennyson's "Ulysses," he declares, "'I would cross this water, for my life hast lost its light, / And mayhap there be deeds for a king to be found on the further shore'" (48). He travels to an unspecified island kingdom to wed another queen, the mother of Sigurd, the hero and leader who will begin to break the cycle of vengeance killing. In the end, Sigmund lives and dies as a kind of transitional figure, caught between the animalistic Sinfiolti and the more hopeful future embodied in Sigurd. Caught between civilization and the forest, wolf and man, he also seems caught between home and abroad, longing to travel but impeded by the demands of family honor. Fittingly, his last battle and his death occur by the sea, "on the edge of a stranger-land" (58), the realm of Hiordis's scorned suitor Lyngi. Book 1 leaves open the question of whether cultures can travel, engage others, and still remain internally cohesive. These are the priorities Morris puts to the test in Books 2 and 3 of the poem and that he embodies in Sigurd.

The circumstances surrounding Sigurd's birth and upbringing differ remarkably from Sinfiotli's. As Book 2 opens, "Peace lay on the land of the Helper and the house of Elf his son" (61), where Hiordis is taken after the battle by the sea: "There no great store had the franklin, and enough the hireling had; / And a child might go unguarded the length and breadth of the land" (61). The land of the Helper seems a model community distinguished by fellowship and cooperation among its inhabitants, values Sigurd puts into practice later among the Niblungs. As is prophesied of him in his childhood,

> Men heard the name and knew it, and they caught it up in the air,
> And it went abroad by the windows and the doors of the feast-hall fair;
> It went through street and market; o'er meadow and acre it went,
> And over the wind-stirred forest and the dearth of the sea-beat bent,
> And over the sea-flood's welter, till the folk of the fishers heard,
> And the hearts of the isle-abiders on the sun-scorched rocks were stirred.
>   (66)

Despite his ultimate goal to use Sigurd to steal the Reingold from his half-brother Fafnir, Sigurd's tutor, the dwarf Regin, offers his pupil a remarkably well-rounded education, one not without attention to languages and the arts:[43]

>   he learns him many things;
> Yea, all save the craft of battle, that men learned the sons of kings:
> The smithying sword and war-coat; the carving runes aright;
> The tongues of many countries, and soft speech for men's delight;
> The dealing with harp-strings, and the winding ways of song. (68)

Sigurd's destiny is to travel, but not without some reluctance to abandon the home that has treated him so well—a dilemma that will be repeated later with Brynhild and the Niblungs, who pull him in opposing directions. Only through Regin's pleading, which Sigurd knows is mostly self-serving, is he able to leave: "thou, a deedless man, too much thou eggest me: / And these folk are good and trusty, and the land is lovely and sweet" (73).

Considering the case for going, Sigurd says to himself, "I dwell in a land that is ruled by none of my blood" (72). It stands out as the only time in the poem when Sigurd expresses anything that amounts to family or racial identification—and it comes at a time when he's somewhat disingenuously searching for reasons to abandon the foster-land of the Helper. Thus rather than emphasizing Sigurd's Volsungian allegiances, the reference foreshadows that Sigurd's ideal state is to be unaffiliated—a kind of free-agent bestowing on others what he has gained from the Elf-kingdom. Sigurd also overlooks his family in another more literal way that distinguishes Morris's poem from the original saga: he forgets that he has to avenge the death of his father at Lygni's hands, a mission he undertakes in Morris's prose translation before going after Fafnir but which Morris drops from his itinerary in the poem (*Collected Works* 7:324–27). Morris is careful not to cast Sigurd in the same clan-focused, vengeance-fueled mold as his step-brother Sinfiotli or even his more civil father. The omission, if not "true" to Morris's source material, does help to lend unity of purpose to his more highly evolved rendition of Sigurd.

Vengeance and the promise of riches are never enough to motivate Morris's hero. Even with Regin, it is not until Sigurd inadvertently tastes of Fafnir's heart and undergoes an animalistic reversion that he is able to kill him: "wise in the ways of the beast-kind as the Dwarfs of old he grew; / And he knitted his brows and hearkened, and wrath in his heart arose; / For he felt beset of evil in a world of many foes" (115). Sigurd, however, soon forgets this taste of anti-social feeling, and the rest of his deeds in the poem reaffirm the commitment to the wider ideals of friendship and egalitarianism he first exhibited in the land of the Helper. After taking the treasure that had been guarded by Fafnir, "somewhat south he turneth; for he would not be alone, / But longs for the dwellings of man-folk, and the kingly people's speech" (119). After first meeting and rescuing Brynhild, Sigurd briefly visits among her people, where he is welcomed in a way typical of the spontaneous hospitality that he seems to invite everywhere: "Hail, thou that ridest hither from the North and the desert lands! / Now thy face is turned to our hall-door and thereby must be thy way" (141). His hosts "are all unsatiate of gazing on his face / For his like have they never looked on for goodliness and grace" (143). Sigurd's arrival among the Niblungs evokes similar feelings of awe, although this time he will stay and forge an alliance. Sigurd announces to them what amounts to a justice-driven interventionist foreign policy:

> For peace I bear unto thee, and to all kings of the earth,
> Who bear the sword aright, and are crowned with the crown of worth;
> But unpeace to the lords of evil, and the battle and the death;
> And the edge of the sword to the traitor, and the flame to the slanderous
>   breath:
> And I would that the loving were loved, and I would that the weary should
>   sleep,
> And that man should hearken to man, and that he that soweth should reap.
> Now wide in the world would I fare, to seek the dwellings of Kings.
>   (154–55)

Duty to others rather than personal glory fuels his quest narrative. He touches as well on what will become a recurring theme of communication and cooperation between others under his leadership—the different peoples he encounters all begin to "hearken" to each other.

Sigurd's status among the Niblungs is best described by King Giuki: "thou, our guest and our stranger, thou goest to the war, / And who knows but thine hand may carry the hope of all the earth" (159). Giuki recognizes that Sigurd is not merely a vassal or mercenary who has joined up with them out of convenience: as an outsider with a higher purpose, there are limits to what he will do on their behalf. Being a guest *and* stranger, Sigurd is not kin, but he is still something more than a visitor. True to his promise, Sigurd accomplishes much more than merely going to war and raking in the spoils. He and the Niblung sons range across the north of Europe, "to the sea . . . and the battle-laden oak" (160), and the continent seems transformed in their wake. The Niblung women "sing of the prison's rending and the tyrant laid alow, / And the golden thieves' abasement, and the stilling of the churl" (161). Rather than creating enemies in the lands they invade, Sigurd and his men forge allies and open up lines of communication and trade. They sing too "in the streets of the foemen of the war-delivered land; / And they tell how the ships of the merchants come free and go at their will" (161). The contrast to the original saga, as rendered in Morris's prose translation, is noteworthy. While certainly heroic, the Saga-Sigurd is still part of the same warrior culture where conquest and treasure-seeking require no justification beyond being that they're just what great kings do: "His sport and pleasure it was to give aid to his own folk, and to prove himself in mighty matters, to take wealth from his unfriends, and give the same to his friends" (7:342). Morris's poetic Sigurd is much more careful about the friends he chooses and the quests they undertake, which are never about self-aggrandizement or profiteering: he is redistributing wealth more than anything else.[44] In *Sigurd* the poem, the peaceful, medieval Europe of free trade seen at the beginning of *The Earthly Paradise* reemerges:

> So fares the tale of Sigurd through all kingdoms of the earth,
> And the tale is told of his doings by the utmost ocean's girth;
> And fair feast the merchants deem it to warp their sea-beat ships
> High up the Niblung River, that their sons may hear his lips
> Shed fair words o'er their ladings and the opened southland bales;
> Then they get them aback to their countries, and tell how all men's tales
> Are nought, and vain and empty in setting forth his grace,
> And the unmatched words of his wisdom, and the glory of his face.

Came the wise men too from the outlands, and the lords of singers' fame.
(162–63)

Morris attributes a free flow of goods, ideas, and the arts to Sigurd's leadership that is global in its reach. In many ways, this passage records Sigurd's and the poem's high-water mark, the complete disappearance of tyranny and tribal infighting: "And no foe and no betrayer, and no envier now hath he" (162). The next section of the poem is entitled, "Of the cup of evil drink that Grimhild the Wise-wife gave to Sigurd," and it marks the resurgence of family allegiances and ambitions in *Sigurd the Volsung.*

The central role of the "stirring woman" Grimhild in Sigurd's downfall and the end of the poem's outward-looking ethos begs the question of whether women merely impede cosmopolitanism in Morris's adaptations of Icelandic sagas. Do women have any role to play—other than as diplomatic barter—in peaceful negotiations between kingdoms? Women in Morris do embody stronger feelings toward kin and homeland, as we have already seen with Signy, and often seem to be in the position of pleading with the men in the poem *not* to leave home. In turn, their most important investment in Sigurd's global village, it would seem, is the preservation of domestic peace: it is women, primarily, who sing in the streets when Sigurd brings tyrants low. Even this, however, points to women's greater investment in preserving and strengthening the home front. Denied the journey themselves, their attention is fixed inward, as with Gudrun in "The Lovers of Gudrun." The same pattern repeats itself in *Sigurd* with Grimhild and with Brynhild too. Only the *Sigurd*-Gudrun strikes out in a different direction, as we will see. As concerns gender relations and empowerment in the poem, the ideal state seems to be premarital—Gudrun and Kiartan imagining their journey together, Brynhild and Sigurd surveying the continent before their commitment to each other: "So they climb the burg of Hindfell, and hand in hand they fare, / Till all about and above them is nought but the sunlit air, / And there close they cling together rejoicing in their mirth; / For far away beneath them lie the kingdoms of the earth" (129). Like Sigurd, Brynhild is a traveler who has "ridden the sea-realm and the regions of the land, / And dwelt in the measureless mountains and the forge of stormy days" (126). She assumes a more passive, inward role only upon her marriage to Gunnar, which also means abandoning her own "high-built tower," where Sigurd at first assumes a great king must dwell (144). Only upon marriage, then, do the women start stirring or, more accurately, interfering. And in some sense, by interfering, they are simply performing the role assigned to them in these intensely patriarchal societies: the promotion and preservation of the nation.

In many ways, this promotion is what Grimhild of the poison cup has undertaken, but with extreme methods. Gudrun falls in love with Sigurd of her own accord, but Grimhild recognizes that there is more than her daughter's happiness to be gained by securing this match. Grimhild's drink causes Sigurd to forget his promise of betrothal to Brynhild, and it also represents the first stage in restricting his movements politically by removing the main reason for his eventual departure from their kingdom. Grimhild aims to transform Sigurd from an unaffiliated, free-lance knight-errant into a mercenary fighting on behalf of the Niblungs. And with Brynhild no longer betrothed as well, Grimhild sets up a plan that will win her for her son Gunnar and thereby extend the Niblungs' influence over Lymdale. These goals all float just beneath the surface of the congratulations she offers Sigurd when he agrees to marry Gudrun:

> But uplift thine heart and be merry, for new kin hast thou gotten today;
> Thy father is Giuki the King, and Grimhild thy mother is made,
> And thy brethren are Gunnar and Hogni and Guttorm the unafraid.
> Rejoice for a kingly kindred, and a hope undreamed before!
> For the folk shall be wax in the fire that withstandeth the Niblung war;
> The waste shall bloom as a garden in the Niblung glory and trust,
> And the wrack of the Niblung people shall burn the world to dust:
> Our peace shall still the world, our joy shall replenish the earth;
> And of thee it cometh, O Sigurd, the gold and the garland of worth!
>   (166–67)

Becoming "new kin" carries duties at odds with the aims Sigurd had fashioned for himself as "guest and stranger." Grimhild stresses rewards of gold and glory that have never held much motivation for Sigurd, and she transforms his wars of peaceful intervention into quasi-imperialist ventures. Her words craftily interweave the language of peace and conquest: they shall "still" the world—subdue it, in effect—and impose their "joy" on others.

Against the backdrop of Grimhild's co-opting of Sigurd, the scene shortly after, when he blends his blood with his new brothers in the bosom of the earth, takes on more sinister tones: "Then each an arm-vein openeth, and their blended blood falls down / On Earth the fruitful Mother where they rent her turfy gown: / And then, when the blood of the Volsungs hath run with the Niblung blood, / They kneel with their hands upon it and swear the brotherhood" (182). Morris turns the scene into a macabre spectacle, a violation of the earth that overcompensates for the lack of genuine fellowship between the men. No longer true to his political visions, much less his eventual reunion with Brynhild, Sigurd seems only an empty shell of what he once was: "the smile is departed from him, and the laugh of Sigurd the young, / And of few words now is he waxen, and his songs are seldom sung" (182). As in the saga, Sigurd does literally become someone else—Gunnar—whom he disguises himself as in a complicated effort to entice Brynhild into marrying Gunnar. She agrees to his request, but with the understanding that Sigurd is still true to her in his heart. Later, however, when Gudrun boasts to Brynhild that Sigurd has given her Brynhild's ring, she turns on Sigurd and impels her new husband Gunnar toward vengeance, framing it in terms of the preservation of his family honor: "I look upon thee. . . . I know thy race and thy name, / Yet meseems the deed thou sparest, to amend thine evil and shame" (225). Now begins a cycle of "honor" killings that will consume the Niblungs for the remainder of the poem, or as Gunnar describes it, "the war without hope or honour, and the strife without reward" (225). Gunnar himself is unable to carry out the deed, and once more it falls to Grimhild, who now sees Sigurd as a threat to the family, to prepare a potion that facilitates his murder. She gives it to the only one of her sons who did not participate in the blood-brother ritual. With "the heart of the ravening wood-wolf and the hunger-blinded beast" (227), Guttrom is able to overcome the bond he nonetheless feels for Sigurd and kill him as he lies in bed. Guttrom "knows not friend nor kindred" (228), recalling Sinfiotli's wild, debased killing of his half-brothers. As word of Sigurd's death spreads, Morris stresses what the community and wider world has lost due to this internal familial struggle: "many there were of the Earl-folk that wept for Sigurd's sake; / And they wept for their little children, and they wept for those unborn" (232). Gudrun flees when she realizes what has happened, remarking, simply, "my kin hath slain my lord" (231), capturing how the ties of kinship and guest have been overturned, never to be fully restored for her.

Book 4 of the poem, "Gudrun," in many ways returns us to the clashes and false overtures of diplomacy between powerful families and kingdoms that characterize Book 1. The impending demise of the Niblungs again underscores what has been lost with Sigurd, although Gudrun remains true to his cosmopolitan vision in a profound if dark way, as we will see. For the Niblungs, a new threat emerges out of the East, "a King of the outlands . . . Atli was his name" (245), based, as in the saga, on Attila the Hun: "Great are his gains in the world, and few men may his might withstand, / But he weigheth sore on his people and cumbers the hope of his land" (255). When he comes asking for Gudrun to be his wife, the Niblungs agree with the hope that he can be appeased and that a pointless conflict can be avoided. As Gunnar states, "What then . . . shall we thrust by Atli's word?

/ Shall we strive, while the world is mocking, with the might of the East-land sword, / While the wise are mocking to see it, how the great devour the great?" (249). As in Book 1, however, following the marriage, a diplomatic invitation that disguises other motives leads to a bloody ambush. The Niblungs travel to Atli's "land far-off and grey" (272) only to be betrayed: "where is the ransom that shall buy your departure again?" (277). Morris thus sets the stage for a clash of East and West, another contest of family and tribal honor, and the battle that ensues makes Book 1 seem peaceful by comparison. But history does not simply repeat itself. The central role of Gudrun in Book 4 alters the course that this encounter takes. Through her strategy, neither side will win: "In this house, in the house of a stranger shall be the tale and the end" (254).

Morris makes several crucial changes to Gudrun from her counterpart in the original saga, changes that critics have generally not noted to his credit. The first concerns the effects of the potion Grimhild gives her so that she will forget about Sigurd's murder and thus accede to her family's request to marry Atli. Instead of forgetting Sigurd entirely and willingly joining up with the alliance they have planned for her, "many a thing she forgat, / But never the day of her sorrow, and of how o'er Sigurd she sat" (252). As a result, what motivates her actions later becomes more ambiguous. If she remains determined to wreak vengeance on her brothers, why then does she kill Atli as well? As Henry Hewlett complained in a July 1877 review in *Fraser's Magazine,* "Gudrun . . . is consistently delineated by the Saga-man as . . . dominated, after the manner of her race, by the superiority of her congenital ties to those created by marriage. Mr. Morris less truthfully depicts her as of a more modern type; gentle by nature and mastered by a noble passion."[45] Noting her "gentle" attachment to her first husband, Hewlett in some ways anticipates modern feminist criticism of Gudrun. Whereas in the original Gudrun has forgotten Sigurd and actively sides with her brothers—even taking up arms and joining in the battle—Morris's Gudrun becomes "a strange, passive creature," as Heather O'Donoghue describes her, choosing to watch silently over the battle while the hem of her gown becomes drenched in blood.[46] Echoing some of the criticism leveled at the "Lovers of Gudrun," O'Donoghue charges Morris with crafting "an atmospheric family drama" out of his source material, "smoothing away its rough edges and elaborating its emotional currents."[47] What both of these complaints overlook, however, are the ways Gudrun *is* exercising a will of her own, covertly defying Grimhild's overriding family pride, rather forcefully stated as she presents Gudrun with the demand she accept Atli: "By me and my womb I command thee that thou worship the Niblung name" (252). Gudrun agrees to the marriage, but with a bitter undertone that betrays her awareness of how she is being manipulated: "Bear me back to the Burg of the Niblungs, and the house of my fathers of old, / That the men of King Atli may take me with the tokens and treasure of gold" (253). She has become political barter being passed along with the hope of preserving the Niblung kingdom. Once she is in the East, however, she encourages Atli to invite her Niblung brothers there, but not with the object of freeing herself and warning them of Atli's designs on their kingdom, as in the saga. She plays upon the personal and national pride of each side, goading Atli by asking, "Have I wedded the king of the Eastlands, the master of numberless swords, / Or a serving-man of the Niblungs, a thrall of the Westland lords?" (257). This kind of reverse-nostos on her part—longing not for return home to family and kindred but to lead them away to destruction—did not make sense to Hewlett except as a noble if excitable devotion to the institution of marriage. Morris does more, however, than rerender her a "gentle" passive creature in line with Hewlett's "modern" and O'Donoghue's Victorian woman. Rather, Morris compels the reader to reweigh the "congenital" motive entirely, challenging notions of the determining power of race and home, which have been especially powerful in women up to this point in the poem. In more senses than one, Gudrun is "the white and silent woman above the slaughter set" (282).

In a grim way Gudrun reassumes Sigurd's unallied presence in the poem, choosing to play both sides against each other. The more noble position, of course, is to take neither side, but it is an option that her status as a woman does not leave her. She is either a wife or a sister and daughter, as she explains to Atli: "I have neither brethren nor kindred, and I am become thy wife / To help thine heart to its craving" (256). She turns on Atli as well, but there is nothing in the poem to suggest that she has second-guessed herself and now demands atonement for the loss of her brothers. Her motivation seems more to extinguish the kingly pride and will to power over others that Atli boasts of after subduing the Niblungs: "For this day the Eastland people such great dominion win, / That a world to their will new-fashioned 'neath their glory shall begin" (301). The hitherto mostly silent Gudrun now begins to speak, and knowing the plans she has in store for Atli and his men—to set fire to the hall while they sleep off their drunken celebration—her words to him become an ironic commentary on his political ambitions, likening his deeds more to a kind of cannibalistic feast: "Thou hast swallowed the might of the Niblungs, and their glory lieth in thee: / Live long, and cherish thy wealth, that the world may wonder and see!" (302). Morris here alludes to the original saga, where Gudrun murders the children she begat with Atli and feeds them to him: "thou hast lost thy sons, and their heads are become beakers on the board here, and thou thyself hast drunken the blood of them blended with wine; and their hearts I took and roasted them on a spit, and thou hast eaten thereof (7:390). And while Morris's more "gentle" Gudrun refrains from this act of revenge, she makes a more subtle point about how Atli has always been feasting upon others—first his own oppressed people, now the Niblungs. She remains, until the end, the "Stranger-Queen" (303), alienated from family and her later husband alike, repudiating the cycle of conquest and national pride. If she cannot play the role of peacemaker or diplomat, she can at least pass stern judgment on the motives of the participants in this conflict.

Through her actions, the memory of what Sigurd stood for returns at the end of the poem. Before setting fire to the hall, she sees his image: "I woke and looked on Sigurd, and he rose on the world and shone! / And we twain in the world together! and I dwelt with Sigurd alone" (304). Her thoughts may seem selfish, given the slaughter she has just witnessed, but they are also self-assertive: Sigurd returns for Gudrun, alone, without the family and social contexts that have dictated most of her existence. Gunnar's final words, spoken from the snake-pit in which Atli casts him, recall Sigurd as well and speak accurately to his impact: "Sigurd, child of the Volsungs, the best sprung forth from the best: / He rode from the North and the mountains and became my summer guest, / My friend and my brother sworn." Recalling his just leadership and worldwide appeal, Gunnar adds, "The praise of the world he was, the hope of the biders in wrong, / The help of the lowly people, the hammer of the strong" (291).

The last word and reflection on Sigurd belongs to Morris, as narrator, who concludes that he "dwelt upon Earth for a season, and shone in all men's sight" (306), suggesting a transcendent, idealized figure caught in a world beset by indifferent cycles of birth and death, the rhythms of nature and human geography, where there's always another threat out of the south or east. Affinity and isolation seem the natural, inevitable poles of human existence and of the players, both individual and collective, in Morris's poetry. The overriding sense of Sigurd's loss also helps explain Morris's decision to end Gudrun's story with her leap into the sea: in the original, the winds carry her to a new land where she will again marry and give birth to Swanhild, who becomes the next point of focus in the saga (7:392). Morris, however, writes, "the sea-waves over her swept, / And their will is her will henceforward; and who knoweth the deeps of the sea, / And the wealth of the bed of Gudrun, and the day that yet shall be?" (306). She too is subsumed, overtaken by the forces of the earth, which like Odin seem to come and go in the poem with no more apparent purpose than to keep the drama going.

Indeed, one does sense an almost Hardyan Immanent Will at work in the poem, a kind of naturalistic pessimism where human actions play an at best uncertain role. As Brynhild tells Sigurd, "Know thou, most mighty of men, that the Norns shall order all, / And yet without thine helping shall no whit of their will befall" (126).

The poem thus ends on a solemn note, as it only could given Morris's source material and his determination to be true to the aims of the poetry of origins. Morris veers away from the kind of historical allegory one sees, for instance, in Arnold's only Nordic poem, *Balder Dead* (1855), which fore-shadows the return of the Christ-like Balder with the progress of modern civilization: "From the bright Ocean at our feet an earth / More fresh, more verdant than the last, with fruits / Self-springing, and a seed of man pre-served, / Who then shall live in peace, as now in war" (528–31). In contrast, when the risen Balder makes an appearance in Morris's poetry, as in "Iceland First Seen," it's almost as if Morris is not sure what to do with him: "Ah! when thy Balder comes back and we gather the gains he hath won, / Shall we not linger a little to talk of thy sweetness of old, / Yea, turn back awhile to thy travail whence the Gods stood aloof to behold?" (9:126). Defined by this backward glance, Morris's poetry reveals something of what he would later call a "sympathy with history"—a vague expression, perhaps, but one that captures the diminished, ambivalent ideology of his poetry of the North— his refusal to overinvest in race even as he insists on its crucial relevance to European culture and identity.[48] Sigurd's promise ends with the deaths of Sigurd and Gudrun. It would be up to Morris's generation to invent its own cosmopolitan future, and for Morris, that future would of course take on an increasingly revolutionary cast of appearance.

It was a future that he initially saw poetry playing little part in. Judging his verse against the higher stakes of this later commitment to communism, Morris continues in the letter quoted above, "Poetry goes with the hand-arts I think, and like them has now become unreal: the arts have got to die, what is left of them, before they can be born again."[49] Only when armed with the more directive ideological blueprint of socialism would Morris himself be "born again" and attempt another long poem, although one that would still fall short of the epic length or ambitions of *Sigurd*.[50] With *The Pilgrims of Hope,* published serially in the *Commonweal* from 1885 to 1886, Morris would return to questions of European identity and fellowship. The poem paints, in some ways, a more satisfying vision of Europe in the beginning stages of a revolution he hoped would unite all classes and nationalities. In a section entitled "A Glimpse of the Coming Day," the poem's protagonist, Richard, travels abroad for the first time to take part in the Paris Commune:

"Never yet had I crossed the sea / Or looked on another people than the folk that fostered me" (24:400). The differences that had divided folk from folk disappear, however, under the "red and solemn" flag of communism: "when we came unto Paris and were out in the sun and the street, / It was strange to see the faces that our wondering eyes did meet; / Such joy and peace and pleasure! That folk were glad we knew, / But knew not the why and the wherefore" (24:401–2). On this more modest poetic scale, Morris was able to reaffirm the hope that appeared to have died with Sigurd—that affinity would be Europe's and humanity's ultimate destination. As he would succinctly put it later in *A Dream of John Ball* (1887–88), "fellowship is heaven, and lack of fellowship is hell" (16:230). The dreams and hopes of Morris's later works, of course, would not be borne out in the twentieth century, as the internecine conflicts that had plagued Europe though much of its history returned on a more modern, mechanized, and horrific scale. Not long before the outbreak of that violence, however, one more Victorian poet would try his hand at staging a cosmopolitan future for the continent. Thomas Hardy, the "last Victorian," as he became known, would have the last word.

7

Europe in Perspective

The Dynasts

STEPHEN DEDALUS, in James Joyce's *A Portrait of the Artist as a Young Man* (1916), attempts to give order and shape to the locations of his identity with the following diagram:[1]

Stephen Dedalus
Class of Elements
Clongowes Wood College
Sallins
County Kildare
Ireland
Europe
The World
The Universe

One could easily draw something similar for Thomas Hardy:

Thomas Hardy
Wessex
England
Europe
The World
The Universe

Like most spatial analogies, the latter one is helpful but also perhaps a little reductive. Where is London, one could ask? Or Oxford? Or should it be Christminster? Stephen's list also seems oversimplified and deceptively symmetrical in ways that he would not fully understand until much later in the novel, if at all: Jason Howard Mezey notes the telling absence of Great Britain from his topography, for instance.[2] Additionally, one could argue that the structure of both lists misleadingly casts identity as an autonomous growth outward and misses the give-and-take among its different elements. Perhaps the classic Stoic model of cosmopolitanism would be more accurate, which places the individual at the center of a series of concentric circles of collective identity expanding outward. It might be more accurate still simply to write, or continuously rewrite, each of these signifiers on top of each other—a palimpsest of the kind familiar from more postmodern accounts of identity.

My larger point, and in many ways the point of this entire study, is that staging cosmopolitanism is a problem of perspective: sorting between competing identities and understanding when to assert and when to check different affiliations. The same endeavor motivates many of the contemporary theorists I have summoned to provide insight into parallel Victorian efforts. In the manner of Kwame Anthony Appiah's "rooted cosmopolitanism" or "cosmopolitan patriotism," *The Dynasts* explores what it means to be firmly rooted while also floating freely above the locations of identity.[3] The poem, in turn, highlights the conflict that can ensue between these perspectives. At its core, the Immanent Will, the mysterious energy that impels all action in the poem, is simply the logical outgrowth of Hardy's effort to spatially imagine the kind of interchange between self and outside world that has always confronted cosmopolitan philosophy. Hardy's force is *immanent*—within oneself but also paradoxically imposed from outside. Discovering where this Will begins and ends—getting a handle on it, essentially—is the task he confronts in *The Dynasts,* with all of its complex staging of history and sight for the benefit of his "mental spectator" (4.8), the reader.[4] Throughout *The Dynasts,* Hardy dramatizes, questions, and reevaluates the different notions of history and identity that came to him via the locations of his life. What *The Dynasts* is about, finally, is the struggle for perspective. It looks toward the future even in a world where "*old Laws operate yet; and phase and phase / Of men's dynastic and imperial moils / Shape on accustomed lines*" (I. Fore Scene. 76–78).

In the preface, Hardy attempted to explain how these potentially contradictory aims could work together: how *The Dynasts* could function as a patriotic poem—one about England at war, no less—and still be cosmopolitan. He would develop the full significance of England's role in this wider

European conflict while also looking beyond England in ways that his novel of the same historical period, *The Trumpet-Major,* had neglected:

> When . . . *The Trumpet-Major* was printed, more than twenty years ago, I found myself in the tantalizing position of having touched the fringe of a vast international tragedy without being able, through limits of plan, knowledge, and opportunity, to enter further into its events; a restriction that prevailed for many years. But the slight regard paid to English influence and action throughout the struggle by so many Continental writers who had dealt with Napoleon's career, seemed always to leave room for a new handling of the theme which should re-embody the features of this influence in their true proportion. (4:5–6)

Hardy probes what the war signifies to him as an English citizen and as a resident of "Wessex"—which, as in the novels, becomes an actual place name and the home to minor characters already familiar to readers. Old Granfer Cantle of *The Return of the Native* (1878), for instance, becomes Private Cantle of the "Bang up Locals." In fact, Hardy states that the poem would not exist at all were it not for "three accidents of locality" (4:5), locations that would in turn inform his own artistic priorities. The first of these was the near proximity of King George III's "watering-place" (Budmouth in *The Return of the Native*); the second, the lingering traces along the coast of defenses made in preparation for a possible invasion; and the third, the fact that this same region was the birthplace of "Nelson's flag-captain at Trafalgar," Hardy's namesake and distant relation Thomas Hardy. Part I, Act 4, for example, begins at the first of these locations, a "room in the red-brick royal residence known as Gloucester Lodge" (4:93). Hardy even adds a footnote for the reader-as-traveler, one of several that show his concern for highlighting the trace remnants of history still dimly visible on the landscape: "This weather-beaten old building, though now an hotel, is but little altered" (4:414). The aptness of King George's residence becoming a hotel was probably not lost on Hardy: in some sense, he invites his reader to tour the places of the poem with something akin to his own nostalgia and longing to revisit the signs and stories that reverberated through his childhood. Like *Childe Harold's Pilgrimage* and *Red Cotton Night-Cap Country* before it, *The Dynasts* is part poem, part tour guide, intended to coach the reader on how to experience historical places on a satisfying personal level but also as a means toward a more engaged global citizenship.

Just as Barrett Browning sought for the best perspective on Europe—be it as an expatriate observing events from her balcony in Florence or in the more mobile persona of Aurora Leigh—Hardy endeavors to craft a poetic form wide enough to encompass multiple affinities, points of view, and historical moments. In this chapter, I divide my analysis of these perspectives into three varied but codependent scales of vision in *The Dynasts*. I begin by looking at the larger design of the poem—its distanced, telescopic points of view and the wider perspective on history and national identity provided by its free-ranging spirit commentators. The second section probes the efforts of the poem's human participants to access something akin to this wider cosmopolitan vision—first Napoleon and then the soldiers themselves, whose experience Hardy dramatically revises in comparison to *The Trumpet-Major*. The third section explores the transformation of the Immanent Will into a force that could bridge all of these perspectives—above and below, past and future, national and international. The chapter concludes by considering the poem's afterlife during the First World War, which demanded reassessment not only of Hardy's cosmopolitan vision, as he himself recognized, but of the hopes and expectations of an entire era.

Cosmopolitanism from Above: Staging Perspective in *The Dynasts*

The philosophical and spiritual superstructure Hardy devised for *The Dynasts* was the end result of some two decades of reflection. One could argue even that the Wessex novels themselves—*The Trumpet-Major,* as we will see, but not it alone—formed another testing ground for concepts of space, travel, and Anglo-European identity that Hardy would revisit in *The Dynasts*. Hardy had a long-abiding interest in what might be called the collapsing space of modernity: the closer but uncertain interchanges between rural and urban, periphery and metropole, and England and the wider world that defined the Victorian era.[5] In *The Return of the Native,* these forces reach a kind of stalemate in Clym Yeobright, who arrives home from the Continent with an expanded mind but still longing for the rooted sense of identity he associates with Egdon Heath: "His imagination would then people the spot with its ancient inhabitants: forgotten Celtic tribes trod their tracks about him, and he could almost live among them."[6] His exposure to advanced European ideas leaves him with an earnest if flawed moral complexity that Hardy clearly sympathizes with: "Yeobright loved his kind. He had a conviction that the want of most men was knowledge of a sort which brings wisdom rather than affluence. He wished to raise the class at the expense of individuals rather than individuals at the expense of class."[7] As a result, Clym is

someone at odds with himself, divided between tradition and modernity—
a division in turn written on his physiognomy: "In Clym Yeobright's face
could be dimly seen the typical countenance of the future."[8] For the world
of Wessex, as in Clym's case, contact with Europe mostly seems to pose problems, as if Hardy doesn't quite know how to integrate Europe satisfactorily
into the vision of the novels. Europe saps Clym's apparently more healthy
Englishness, and later novels, most pointedly *The Woodlanders* (1887), continue to perpetuate a kind of anti-European bias and resistance toward travel
outside of the regions of one's birth. One scene in particular from that novel
encapsulates this point. Demanding that a logging train headed by Giles
Winterborne give way, Mrs. Charmond's coach driver blurts out, "you are
only going to some trumpery little village or other in the neighbourhood;
while we are going straight to Italy."[9] With echoes of another Hardy anti-
heroine fixated on the continent, Eustacia Vye, the circumstances of Charmond's demise imply a sort of poetic justice for her disloyalty to Wessex:
she is murdered abroad by a foreigner living abroad, the shady "Italianized-
American" who appears only once in the novel.[10] England was going global,
speeding up in ways that the novels register uncomfortably, even bitterly at
times. In the opening pages of *Jude the Obscure* (1895), Hardy off-handedly
mentions "a certain obliterator of historic records who had run down from
London and back in a day" to replace the church at Marygreen. This nameless, rootless architect erects "a tall new building of modern Gothic design,
unfamiliar to English eyes."[11]

As an alternative vision, *The Dynasts* does not simply "sell out" Wessex by
embracing globalization. What it does do, essentially, is *reposition* the deep
sensitivity to native attachments and communities on display in the novels.
The Dynasts remaps the world of the novels as a wider web of such locations
and attempts to imagine the future as something more than the gateway to
humanity's physical and spiritual decline, "the beginning of the coming universal wish not to live" that plagues *Jude the Obscure* (a disease, not surprisingly, with roots outside of England).[12] In *The Dynasts*, Hardy reaches after
a more affirmative global existence. Not coincidentally, the poem's planning
and publication took place during the same historical interval covered by
Stephen Kern in *The Culture of Time and Space: 1880–1918* (1983; rev.
2003). Writing about the failures of diplomacy that preceded World War I,
Kern describes what sounds a lot like the crises underpinning *The Dynasts*:
"Individuals behave in distinctive ways when they feel cut off from the flow
of time, excessively attached to the past, isolated in the present, without a
future, or rushing toward one. Nations also demonstrate distinctive attitudes toward time."[13] To uncover the "distinctive new modes of thinking

about and experiencing time and space" brought about by nineteenth-century advances in science and technology, Kern draws almost exclusively on modernist literature and art, with cubism being the most notable example.[14] Hardy's notebooks, however, reveal his own ambition to paint a new, revolutionary kind of literary landscape, one that would encompass these spatial and temporal shifts in perception. The first reference to what would become *The Dynasts* dates back to 1874, when he wrote, "Let Europe be the stage & have scenes continually shifting."[15] In 1875, after visiting with survivors of Waterloo at Chelsea Hospital, Hardy conceived of an epic poem along classical lines: "Mem: A Ballad of The Hundred Days. Then another of Moscow. Others of earlier campaigns—forming altogether an Iliad of Europe from 1789 to 1815."[16]

As the poem continued to evolve in his mind, Hardy began to envision something that would indeed travel across the breadth of Europe but in increasingly unconventional ways. He wanted to represent life as it is perceived by individuals on the ground but also to probe more deeply into the reality of their experience from other vantage points in space and time. *The Life of Thomas Hardy* quotes some undated notes where Hardy reflects, with oddly specific numbers, "Now these 3 (or 3000) whirling through space at the rate of 40 miles a second—(God's view)" (449). *The Dynasts* would ultimately deploy something like this advanced, space-age literary technology, although Hardy would also keep the poem grounded in the past in crucial ways, as we will see. In the same series of notes, he recalls what seem like the words of actual soldiers but recasts them within the wider cosmic vision of his planned poem and its governing force, the Immanent Will: "The intelligence of this collective personality Humanity is pervasive, ubiquitous, like that of God. Hence e.g. on the one hand we could hear the roar of the cannon, discern the rush of the battalions, on the other hear the voice of a man protesting, etc." (*Life* 449). The last stage of the poem's conception reveals Hardy turning away from a narrative epic or collection of ballads to a verse-drama with a celestial, mobile point of view. In 1886, Hardy noted, "The human race to be shown as one great network or tissue, which quivers in every part when one point is shaken, like a spider's web if touched. Abstract realisms to be in the form of Spirits, Spectral figures, &c" (*Life* 183). And in 1891, he wrote, "A Bird's-Eye View of Europe at the beginning of the nineteenth century" (*Life* 245). Hardy's challenge was to look at something utterly familiar to readers but from a new point of view.

After all of this planning, what kind of poem did *The Dynasts* become? On the practical level of readability, Hardy may have attempted too much: in a recent reassessment of the poem, Keith Wilson perhaps best captures its accomplishment and limitations: "*The Dynasts,* for all its quirkiness and at times derivativeness, its sometimes laboured blank verse . . . its dutiful progress through Napoleon's campaigns to the inevitable end . . . is indeed one of the great works of modern English literature, albeit one honoured more in the invocation than in the reading."[17] Others have not been as kind as Wilson. Comparing *The Dynasts* unfavorably to Hardy's novels, Sheila Berger writes, "Rather than being pulled into the process of making meaning, the reader is pummeled with repetitive sight, movement, and narrative into a position of disinterested passivity."[18] Many of the poem's initial readers found the poem's unusual form bewildering as well: *The Dynasts,* one could argue, dwells in a kind of no-man's-land of genre, mixing passages of verse, prose dialogue, stage direction, and what Hardy called "dumb shows"—narrative descriptions of a setting or event, such as the action of a battle. Anticipating Berger, at least one Edwardian critic lamented that Hardy had abandoned the form of the novel for a strange "drama of nations" where "[t]he real characters . . . prove to be, not Napoleon, Nelson, Pitt, and the rest, but England, France, Austria and Russia, or even, it may be, Europe." The critic in turn singled out for highest praise the Wessex portions of *The Dynasts,* where "we have life, a warm life and a quaint humour of phrase that recall the Thomas Hardy of 'Far from the Madding Crowd' and 'Under the Greenwood Tree.'"[19]

These are criticisms with which, perhaps, all readers of the poem could identify on some level. It is telling that Hardy himself could not settle on what the actual form of the poem was—an "epic-drama"—until the 1909 release of the first one-volume edition. He may have been prompted to settle on this label by A. B. Walkley, the drama critic for the *Times Literary Supplement,* who attacked the poem for being unstageable and poorly conceived: "Obviously it is not possible for the ordinary theatre. It 'thinks in continents' and deals in whole fleets and armies . . . it is on too vast a scale for the ordinary stage."[20] Hardy took the unusual step of replying publicly to Walkley, perhaps sensing that his criticism got to the heart of what he was attempting. The poem manipulates space and time in ways that could not be rendered on stage but were nonetheless vital to its meaning. "I believe that anyone who should sit down and consider at leisure how to present such a wide subject within reasonable compass would decide that this was, broadly speaking, the only way."[21] This was a "wide" subject geographically, historically, and temporally, an altogether unique experiment in generic border crossing that sought to trace its protagonists' roles within larger currents of national and even cosmic identity.

Hardy's experiments with form and perspective culminated in a peculiar hybrid of ancient and modern that would make the poem tough going for many readers and perhaps equally tough to locate in literary historical terms. In its formal features and in its representation of history, *The Dynasts* looks backward and forward in a number of senses. The poem's experimentation with perspective would seem to place *The Dynasts* on the cusp of modernism, but it is typically left out of studies that attempt to claim Hardy's poetry on the movement's behalf.[22] Others have suggested that the poem anticipates the quintessential modern form of the cinema: "*The Dynasts* is neither a poem, nor a play, nor a story," as John Wain says, "It is a shooting script."[23] Isobel Armstrong takes the parallel a step further, linking it to her concept of the double poem: "It is as if Hardy carries the virtuosity of the dramatic monologue from drama to cinema by superimposing a number of limited and everchanging perspectives on one another."[24] Although there is no evidence Hardy himself saw the parallel, he did liken it in the Preface to some Victorian prototypes of the cinema, including the panorama and magic lantern (4:7). But, again, it seems, *The Dynasts* falls short of being modernist or even fully "modern" in the broader sense of the term: it is difficult to imagine *The Dynasts* becoming a successful film without ruthless excision, whether of the spirit Overworld, which would turn it into a straight war film, or of its historical breadth and human actors, which would perhaps make for an interesting fusion of science fiction and ancient Greek drama but would also no doubt amplify the difficulties Berger attributes to reading the poem.[25] These problems with *The Dynasts: A Film,* however, simply point to why it makes a better poem, why it could be *only* a poem—or an epic drama. Hardy was deliberately trying to be ancient and modern at the same time, planting one foot in history and another in the future, just as he was writing a vaguely nationalistic poem with cosmopolitan sympathies. The past was who he was, what Europe was, not something that could be evaded. Hardy wanted to dwell on the past as a way of identifying laws of metaphysics still undergirding individual and collective identities, laws that were finally revealing themselves from modern perspectives. Hardy was attempting something like what would become cubism or avant-garde cinema in the hands of a later generation of artists. Unlike these other inventions, however, *The Dynasts* would be an experiment in perspective and genre that could not be repeated—huge, ambitious, totally encompassing—something that could have come only out of the nineteenth century.

Hardy's own detailed description of the poem's "supernatural spectators" reveals that he understood he was undertaking something new and old with the spirit apparatus in the poem. He describes them as "certain impersonated abstractions, or Intelligences, called Spirits" (4:6), which he compared to the chorus of ancient Greek drama. Hardy insisted, however, "In point of literary form, the scheme of contrasted Choruses and other conventions of this external feature was shaped with a single view to the modern expression of a modern outlook, and in frank divergence from classical and other dramatic precedent which ruled the ancient voicings of ancient themes" (4:7). What gives this apparatus its "modern outlook," I would suggest, and a tentative foothold in what would become "modernism," is precisely the way Hardy destabilizes the judgments of this Overworld. Its speakers are mere shadows of the divine, and they are often just as confused as the human players on the ground. As a group, the Spirits from a sort of intellectual bric-a-brac, embodying the mental tools that history up through the nineteenth century had handed down to make sense of human events: "Their doctrines are but tentative, and are advanced with little eye to a clear metaphysic, or systematized philosophy warranted to lift 'the burthen of the mystery' of this unintelligible world" (4:6). In other words, the spirit apparatus of the poem does not embody one clear world or religious view but all of the different orientations toward God that Hardy entertained over the course of his literary career: a divine essence that is occasionally sympathetic but more often coldly rational and ironic. For example, the Spirit of the Pities and its chorus, which holds the most in common with ancient Greek choruses, was "impressionable and inconsistent in its views," according to Hardy, "which sway hither and thither as wrought on by events." The Spirit of the Years "approximates to the passionless Insight of the Ages" (4:7). These Spirits exchange views with "Spirits Sinister and Ironic" and a fourth "Spirit of Rumour," who underscores humankind's and the Spirits' own inability to see the working of the Will. The Spirit of the Years best captures the overall power and limitations of the supernatural spectators in the poem:

> *The ruling was that we should witness things*
> *And not dispute them. To the drama, then.*
> *Emprizes over-Channel are the key*
> *To this land's stir and ferment.—Thither we.* (I.1.1.95–98)

The Spirits are gifted with the speed to shift rapidly from one geographic location to the next, developing insights which the reader shares. In the end, however, they remain *spectators:* they have the power to expose the Will but not direct it in any way. Hardy thus contains our understanding at the same time he sets it free. The Spirits' variety of perspectives embody changes in notions of place, time, and speed that had taken place up to the beginning of the twentieth century and that could provide a new if still limited outlook on history and culture. Hence as well the peculiar diction and tone of the Spirits, who sound at once archaic or Blakean in the manner of *Europe: A Prophecy* (1794) but who also inhabit a world contemporary with H. G.

Wells, one in which life exists on other planets and "*systems of the suns go sweeping on / With all their many-mortaled planet train / In mathematic roll unceasingly*" (I.1.6.7–9).

Ultimately, as readers of *The Dynasts*, we see earth from above and below, and we are made familiar with the limitations of human vision while being invited to look beyond it. Such is the dual nature of the poem's rooted cosmopolitanism, a perspective perhaps best captured in the poem's opening stage direction, one that, as we have seen, Hardy had been contemplating for a long time before he started to write the poem:

> The nether sky opens, and Europe is disclosed as a prone and emaciated figure, the Alps shaping like a backbone, and the branching mountain-chains like ribs, the peninsular plateau of Spain forming a head. Broad and lengthy lowlands stretch from the north of France across Russia like a grey-green garment hemmed by the Ural mountains and the glistening Arctic Ocean.
>
> The point of view then sinks downwards through space, and draws near to the surface of the perturbed countries, where the peoples, distressed by events which they did not cause, are seen writhing, crawling, heaving, and vibrating in their various cities and nationalities. (4:20)

The poem periodically returns us to this distanced view and the universal perspective it casts on human events. At the same time, Hardy wishes to dwell near the surface, where "old laws operate yet," understanding the energy that agitates individual soldiers within their own limited points of view, limitations we all share within our various local, national, and continental spaces. The poem dwells on the failure of a true cosmopolitan idea to emerge in the Napoleonic Era—showing why the world was not ready for it, in some sense, as its human actors struggle to see beyond themselves. Napoleon himself, in fact, the principal human actor in Hardy's poem, best captures these competing impulses as someone who manipulates national pride at the same time he gestures uncertainly toward a cosmopolitan future.

Cosmopolitanism on the Ground: The Struggle for a Wider Human Perspective in *The Dynasts*

The Dynasts is in many ways a critical reevaluation of Napoleon's efforts to spearhead the nineteenth century's first movement toward pan-Europeanism. In his memoirs, which Hardy consulted for the poem, Napoleon portrays

himself as "the natural mediator between the old and the new order," someone who had hoped to initiate a new "European confederacy" (association
européene), one with "the same principles, the same system, every where—a
European code; a European court of appeal." In the future, Europe "would
soon have formed, in reality, but one and the same people, and every one,
who travelled, would have every where found himself in one common country."[26] To liberate Europe, Napoleon invites the inhabitants of other nations
to look beyond national allegiances, and for a brief moment this did become
the Continent's future. Napoleon, however, fails to appreciate the power of
the national identities he has violated and how, in the wake of his own shift
toward authoritarianism, ideals of pan-European progress would begin to
sound hollow.

Hardy combines these tactical oversights on Napoleon's part with certain
flaws of character to convey an overall impression of someone ahead of his
times, so to speak, but not ahead of himself—someone quick to abandon
high ideals in favor of personal dynastic ambition. As the Spirit of the Pities
remarks, Napoleon

> *Professed at first to flout antiquity,*
> *Scorn limp conventions, smile at mouldy thrones,*
> *And level dynasts down to journeymen!—*
> *Yet he, advancing swiftly on that track*
> *Whereby his active soul, fair Freedom's child,*
> *Makes strange decline, now labours to achieve*
> *The thing it overthrew.* (I.1.6.33–39)

Hardy adds a further dimension to this image of Napoleon as self-betrayer:
he is not simply a tyrant or megalomaniac but someone whose concepts of
government and international relations seem profoundly oversimplified, even
outmoded. Despite brief moments of cosmopolitan vision, he lacks the willingness to commit himself in that direction. His obsession with England, for
instance, seems underpinned by a belief that by choosing to influence world
affairs through trade and finance, England is underhandedly avoiding the
full-blown military showdown that Napoleon deems natural between rival
states. In attempting to win Tsar Alexander as an ally and a supporter of his
"continental system" that would boycott English goods in Europe, Napoleon
labels England

> That country which enchains the trade of towns
> With such bold reach as to monopolize,

Among the rest, the whole of Petersburg's—
Ay!—through her purse, friend, as the lender there!—
Shutting that purse, she may incite to—what?
Muscovy's fall, its ruler's murdering. (II.1.8.38–43)

England's naval power frustrates Napoleon, but more important, the country's grip on world markets—the linchpin of the emerging Victorian free-trade empire—hinders his ability to influence other states. Through military conquest and forming alliances, Napoleon hopes to overcome England's commercial power. Throughout this scene, he has been appealing to a camaraderie he and Alexander share as absolute rulers: "By treating personally we speed affairs / More in an hour than they [ministers] in blundering months" (II.1.8.23–24). International relations, however, have become more complicated, and power gained via laissez-faire capitalism and free trade, as Hardy knows from historical hindsight, will play a more decisive role in determining the status nations hold in relation to each other. Nations that control commerce, and need global stability to do so, would soon begin to co-opt Napoleon's own rhetoric of European brotherhood. Napoleon's geopolitical vision boils down to a simple military power play between countries: "I want nothing on this Continent: / The English only are my enemies" (I.4.5.32–33).

Napoleon remains deeply concerned that history portray him as a noble and progressive figure, but Hardy again reveals his tendencies toward oversimplification: he is too quick to justify his more expedient decisions as being forced upon him by fate. Napoleon correctly acknowledges the difficulty of challenging the old order of Europe, but misses how he might have resisted those forces:

> I came too late in time
> To assume the prophet or the demi-god,
> A part past playing now. My only course
> To make good showance to posterity
> Was to implant my line upon the throne.
> And how shape that, if now extinction nears?
> Great men are meteors that consume themselves
> To light the earth. This is my burnt-out hour. (III.7.9.44–51)

At first, Napoleon's somewhat fatalistic interpretation of himself might seem to accord well with the forces of history at work in Hardy's poem: the Immanent Will would indeed seem to undermine the "great men" theory of history and deny individual attempts to intervene in its course—to disrupt the powerful will of nations. Napoleon, however, misreads his failure: if anything, he is born not too late but too soon. He does not challenge himself to use the power he *does* have to redirect history and thus is incorrect to imply that his only recourse was to become a "dynast" himself. As the Spirits emphasize, Napoleon is one "*of the few in Europe who discern / The working of the Will*" (II.1.8.208–9), who has the ability to stand back from events and see larger forces at work. Rather than use this knowledge to effect some kind of progress, as Hardy implies he might, Napoleon chooses to turn away from knowledge of the Will and to act according to established patterns. Holding onto power has become his main concern: he will gild the dome of the Invalides, he cynically observes,

> To give them something
> To think about. They'll take to it like children,
> And argue in the cafés right and left
> On its artistic points.—So they'll forget
> The woes of Moscow. (III.1.12.86–90)

Napoleon reveals that he is not powerless to shape the actions of the people and that he might channel the national will of France in a progressive direction. But instead he makes conquest and expansion of borders the goals of the nation he leads. Like so many of the leaders in the poem, he has finally become a dynast—motivated by power—but with the added tragedy that he acts while recognizing that his aims are ultimately pointless.

As Napoleon himself gives in to imperial ambitions and imposes French political hegemony in Europe, he so inspires the rest of the Continent: national wills that had been briefly rechanneled begin to remobilize. Speaking of Prussia's first entry into the conflict, Hardy personifies the collective reawakening of these ancient tribal allegiances:

> *The soul of a nation distrest*
> *Is aflame,*
> *And heaving with eager unrest*
> *In its aim*
> *To assert its old prowess, and stouten its chronicled fame!* (II.1.3.75–79)

Napoleon ends up unleashing nationalist powers rather than containing them, and the Immanent Will soon reverts to its old forms. In the final assessment, it remains difficult to pinpoint just how much Hardy thinks Napoleon might have changed history and laid the groundwork for European union had he steered a less imperial course. He is chief among the "dynasts" in the poem, and more than anyone else, he personifies the contradictions at the heart of the term: on one level, a dynasty aims to implement some kind of ordered, benevolent progress for the future. On a more basic level, however, dynasties simply perpetuate the old order. At the very least, it is clear that Hardy feels Napoleon embodies a moment of lost opportunity—undone by himself and a world still grounded in the dynastic ambitions that dictate political action. Hardy's Napoleon, perhaps, is less a historical "intermediary" than someone who stranded himself at the crossroads of history.

If *The Dynasts* remains mostly unforgiving of Napoleon, England by no means represents a democratic oasis in a world of dynastic ambition. Napoleon, at least, recognizes the need for change while England stands resolute against modernity or anything resembling a postnational idea of Europe.[27] By portraying England's leaders in this way, Hardy again broadens our perspective and prevents settled identification with one nationality. In the afterglow of Trafalgar, Pitt's famous remark that "England has saved herself, by her exertions: / She will, I trust, save Europe by her example!" (I.5.5.75–76) has a double-edged meaning, for at this point in history, aristocratic England sets an ambiguous example at best. King George, for instance, calls Napoleon "[t]his wicked bombardier of dynasties / That rule by right Divine" (I.4.1.98–99). England's ultimate goal, according to one minister, is that "[t]he independence of the Continent / May be assured, and all the rumpled flags / Of famous dynasties so foully mauled, / Extend their honoured hues as heretofore" (I.1.5.10–13). Hardy also takes pains to reveal the propagandistic uses of Nelson's victory even as he celebrates it in other respects. Granted, the battle of Trafalgar receives due reverence in the poem, rendered complete with Nelson's instructions to the surgeon to attend to those wounded who can be saved and his famous dying words, "Kiss me, Hardy" (I.5.4.144). But in the next scene, Hardy shows how easily such acts of individual heroism can be manipulated for suspect political ends. Nelson's glorified death helps to ensure the commitment of the people in a larger dynastic struggle that is not really theirs. At a rally outside the Guildhall in London, a citizen proclaims, "They say he's to be tombed in marble, at Paul's or Westminster. We shall see him if he lays in state. It will make a patriotic spectacle for a fine day" (I.5.5.5–7). The myth of Nelson is undercut in a more macabre way by another citizen who repeats the rumor that the crew of the *Victory* drank the rum in which his body was preserved. Viewing Nelson from these different perspectives serves to forestall Hardy's own flights of nostalgia. Hardy, recall, felt a dim personal connection to Nelson via his forbear and namesake Captain Thomas Hardy. *The Dynasts* also invites us to consider the plight of Nelson's foe at Trafalgar, Admiral Pierre Villeneuve, by devoting a scene to the unjust circumstances that led to his suicide. These multiple perspectives, and the commentary of the Spirits, form complementary parts of Hardy's comprehensive critique of deceptively stable, nationalistic interpretations of events.

The poem explores historical events from multiple social levels as well as multiple national ones, reminding one of the similar shift in focus often attributed to the novel following the Napoleonic Wars. As Georg Lukács argues in *The Historical Novel,* "It was the French Revolution, the revolutionary wars and the rise and fall of Napoleon, which for the first time made history a *mass experience,* and moreover on a European scale."[28] For Hardy, however, the epic verse drama would be the genre that most fully encompassed these changes, the one that could best convey this sense of people moving *en masse.* At the same time, Hardy's cosmopolitan perspective does not lose sight of the more minor participants in history—how people, especially individual soldiers, operate within and against these collective forces. To illustrate the kind of change in perspective history undergoes in the poem, one needs only to turn to Hardy's novel of the period, *The Trumpet-Major,* which performs, to some extent, the kind of ideological work Lukács attributes to the historical novel: aligning the interests of all classes of society under the banner of national identity, an identity that before had been more exclusively the property of the aristocracy.

Hardy grounds *The Trumpet-Major* in a local ethos and setting which the global reach of the war, and the disruption it caused to the lives of so many, never really penetrates. The war's destructive consequences come off more as awkward, somewhat perfunctory intrusions. Soldiers' deaths are reported or foreshadowed at the ends of passages that otherwise celebrate the spectacle that the conflict has given rise to on a local level. In some sense, Overcombe Mill, where soldiers gather together in moments of camaraderie and good cheer, cannot be integrated with the European stage of the war:

> Three others followed with similar remarks, to each of which Anne blushingly replied as well as she could, wishing them a prosperous voyage, easy conquest, and a speedy return.
>
> But, alas, for that! Battles and skirmishes, advances and retreats, fevers and fatigues, told hard on Anne's gallant friends in the coming time. Of the seven upon whom these wishes were bestowed, five, including the trumpet-major, were dead men within the few following years, and their bones left to moulder in the land of their campaigns.[29]

As revealed here, the trumpet-major himself is killed in the end, exiting the novel "to blow his trumpet till silenced for ever upon one of the bloody battle-fields of Spain" (377). While obviously not denying the death and destruction of war, such passages place the war in a dimly realized future that is always outside the action of the novel, like Napoleon himself—a distant, unreal ogre, his invasion a threat that will never come to fruition. *The Trumpet-Major* exists in an idealized past that has not yet passed out of "the days of high-waisted and muslin-gowned women" (59), to quote the novel's opening line, a description that also betrays its focus on middle-class, domestic identity and spaces. This is not to suggest that a text focusing on the home-front experience of war inevitably downplays war's consequences. Hardy, however, seems largely unconcerned with portraying the devastation that war could wreak on domestic life, except to note the eventual demise of some characters. In terms of war, *The Trumpet-Major* recovers a past that Hardy's audience, with memories of England's bungled efforts in the Crimea, is invited to look on with a degree of fondness: "For it was a period when romance had not so greatly faded out of military life as it has done in these days of short service, heterogeneous mixing, and transient campaigns" (376).

In *The Dynasts,* the reader travels abroad with these soldiers and learns that locally formed units are in truth destined for a particularly acute form of suffering. Hardy drives this point home in his description of the retreat under Sir John Moore from northwest Spain to Coruna, the low point of British efforts to expel French forces from the Iberian Peninsula. We observe the retreat from the cellar of an abandoned farmhouse where a number of soldiers have hidden themselves. Hardy recreates the impressions of soldiers clinging somewhat tragically to notions of home as they try to make sense of hectic and unfamiliar surroundings. Hardy's description of the interior stresses the intoxicated, half-blind despair of the deserters:

> In the gloom of the cellar are heaps of damp straw, in which ragged fig-
> ures are lying half-buried, many of the men in the uniform of English line-
> regiments, and the women and children in clouts of all descriptions, some
> being nearly naked. At the back of the cellar is revealed, through a burst
> door, an inner vault, where are discernible some wooden-hooped wine-
> casks; in one sticks a gimlet, and the broaching-cork of another has been
> driven in. The wine runs into pitchers, washing-basins, shards, chamber-
> vessels, and other extemporized receptacles. Most of the inmates are drunk;
> some to insensibility. (4:266)

War gives rise to a kind of perverse cultural exchange in the scene: soldiers and refugees are thrown together indiscriminately, joined in desperation, but still ultimately alienated and isolated from one another. Eyeing the confusion outside, which includes the destruction of wounded animals and the execution of deserters, one of the cellar inmates remarks,

> Would that I wer at home in England again, where there's old-fashioned tipple, and a proper God A'mighty instead of this eternal 'Ooman and baby;—ay, at home a-leaning against old Bristol Bridge, and no questions asked, and the winter sun slanting friendly over Baldwin Street as 'a used to do! 'Tis my very belief, though I have lost all sure reckoning, that if I wer there, and in good health, 'twould be New Year's day about now. What it is over here I don't know. Ay, to-night we should be a-setting in the tap of the "Adam and Eve"—lifting up the tune of "The Light of the Moon." (II.3.1.51–60)

In *The Dynasts,* Hardy takes those scenes only dimly foreshadowed in *The Trumpet-Major* and reveals just how isolated, just how unprepared an intensely local upbringing leaves one for contact with other nationalities. Literally, the soldiers have become *disoriented:* England, it seems, occupies another corner of the universe entirely, with a different god. Time and space likewise seem to operate according to different laws. Hardy, in fact, subtly reminds us here that uniform time keeping and time-zones were inventions that followed later in the nineteenth century, just as earlier in the poem, he underscored such changes by placing one scene at "Rainbarrows' Beacon," one of the pre-electric telegraphs along England's shore that would be lit up in case of invasion—thus spreading the word "quickly" inland. For Hardy, then, the kind of space-time compression that later technological advances helped more visibly to perpetuate had already been set in motion during the Napoleonic period, and his poem records the efforts of the people of the time to cope with these changes.

As the soldiers lie lost in this limbo, the action of the war continues outside as a drama in itself that can be only passively observed. Napoleon himself suddenly appears, leading one deserter to exclaim, "Yes, I could pick him off now!" (II.3.2.9–10). But we sense there is no real possibility of this—obviously, because Napoleon does not die here—but also because he seems to walk on a different stage entirely. The deserters, in contrast, are powerless, displaced spectators of the war, with no real role to play as events, propelled by the Immanent Will, proceed along on a preordained course.

One senses an intense empathy for the soldiers on Hardy's part as the Spirit of the Pities remarks,

> On earth below
> Are men—unnatured and mechanic-drawn—
> Mixt nationalities in row and row,
> Wheeling them to and fro
> In moves dissociate from their souls' demand,
> For dynasts' ends that few even understand! (II.6.4.8–13)

Overall, the spirit commentary lends the conflict an air of tragic inevitability, making it part of a regrettable ongoing historical cycle, rather than, as in *The Trumpet-Major,* an event locked in an idealized past, when war was more palatable. When juxtaposed with the prose passages above encompassing the soldiers' points of view, the Pities' remarks underscore again how Hardy's unique admixture of genres, of poetry and prose, takes us places the novel alone could not—not even Tolstoy's great rendering of the same epoch. Its other achievements aside, of which Hardy was well aware, *War and Peace* (1869) could not perform the same refractive, multi-faceted layering of perspective as Hardy's epic-drama. That does not make *The Dynasts* a better work of art, necessarily, but it does remind us that the novel did not render the long poem obsolete either, as much as it may have marginalized its cultural viability in other ways.

A 1920 production of *The Dynasts* by the Oxford University Dramatic Society testifies in another way to the poem's remarkable ability to translate across multiple forms. Their rendition of the retreat to Coruna appears to have struck an especially profound chord in audience and performers alike, many of whom had only just returned from the battlefields of the Great War.[30] Alienated and hunkered down in a dim cellar—a kind of trench—the players may indeed have felt as if they were reenacting what had only recently passed. The scenes of displacement over which the Spirits brood emphasize the need to envision new ways of international connection, a travel that transforms without destroying in the process. By expanding our view of history and individuals to encompass stages on the scale of identity beyond Wessex, Hardy makes it difficult to see life the same way again. As one review of the Oxford production noted, *The Dynasts,* "like all great works of art, makes us think greatly, not of ourselves, but of mankind, nor only of England but also of the enemies of England."[31]

Cosmopolitanism from the Ground Up:
Toward a Postnational Immanent Will

Overlooking the retreat to Coruna described in the previous section, the Spirit Ironic remarks, "*Quaint poesy, and real romance of war!*" (II.3.1.73), to which the Spirit of the Pities rejoins, "*Mock on, Shade, if thou wilt! But others find / Poesy ever lurk where pit-pats poor mankind!*" (74–75). Their exchange typifies in many ways the ongoing conflict among the poem's different spirit commentators. More emotionally invested in the drama going on beneath them, the Pities come to represent values of empathy and hope that persist in the face of the tragic events recorded in the poem. The Pities are the only Spirits who seem willing to challenge the blind engine of the Immanent Will, voicing the human will for a God who takes moral, spiritual charge over its agents. At another point, the Pities cry, "*Something within me aches to pray / To some Great Heart, to take away / This evil day, this evil day!*" (II.6.5.96–98). Implicit in the Pities' description is the desire that a "soul" emerge to overpower the mechanical forces of the dynasts who merely execute the Will. Hardy's Ironic spirit replies, "*where do Its compassions sit? / Yea, where abides the Heart of It? / Is it where sky-fires flame and flit, / Or solar craters spew and spit, / Or ultra-stellar night-webs knit?*" (II.5.6.100–104). The Ironic Spirit reminds the Pities here of the essentially material nature of the universe—filled with movement and energy but missing any kind of spiritual essence or purpose (apart from themselves, that is, and they can only watch). The dynasts of the poem are motivated by this same understanding. As the term implies, they are concerned with maintaining power over the material world and regard individuals as *subjects* only, means to power rather than spiritual beings or souls. The poem remains stuck at this philosophical impasse. The Heart that the Pities seek must have some sort of location—it must be grounded somewhere—but the universe, as the Spirits Ironic describe it, seems merely to hold infinite stores of matter for the Will and its dynastic agents to act upon. To paraphrase Tennyson, there appears to be no far-off, divine spiritual event to which the whole creation of *The Dynasts* moves.

The way out of this impasse, however, is for humanity to reinvent a god of compassion and lovingkindness, to advance intellectually and ethically to the point that this benevolent impulse resides *immanently* within us, as the Will already does. Love thus becomes a powerful collectivizing force in the poem, although its presence is mostly overshadowed by the tragedy of war. The Pities nonetheless never miss an opportunity to emphasize the enduring human capacity for compassionate fellow feeling, even in what is for Hardy the premature, corruptible form of religion. Early on in the poem, as the

Spirits overlook Napoleon's coronation as emperor, the Spirit of the Pities asks, "*What is the creed that these rites disclose?*" to which the Spirit of the Years replies,

> *A local cult, called Christianity,*
> *Which the wild dramas of the wheeling spheres*
> *Include, with divers others such, in dim*
> *Pathetical and brief parentheses,*
> *Beyond whose span, uninfluenced, unconcerned,*
> *The systems of the suns go sweeping on*
> *With all their many-mortaled planet train*
> *In mathematic roll unceasingly.* (I.1.6.2–9)

From one angle, this is Hardy's proclamation of Christianity's cosmological demise in the face of nineteenth-century discoveries in science and of its decreasing relevance in other spheres of intellectual life. As noted earlier, the Spirits' astronomical vantage point recalls the "big picture" of H. G. Wells and other late Victorian pioneers of science fiction. In the *War of the Worlds* (1900), for instance, Wells's representative Anglican clergyman is utterly bewildered by this post-Darwinian race of Martian beings with "intellects vast and cool and unsympathetic."[32] But in another sense, Hardy is less dismissive than Wells and casts Christianity as one of many attempts by sentient beings throughout the universe to understand its workings—to assert some kind of authority over its blind Will. Through the Pities, Hardy also repudiates the idea of a universe governed by survival of the fittest alone and the corollary notion that war was a necessary political exercise in determining who should reside at the top.[33] The Pities' reply to the Spirit of the Years contains this crucial revelation about Christianity: "*I did not recognize it here, forsooth; / Though in its early, lovingkindly days / Of gracious purpose it was much to me*" (I.1.6.10–12). When juxtaposed with the possibility of the Immanent Will becoming conscious of itself, the Pities' observation represents a radical affirmation of mankind's ability to recover itself, to craft new forms of fellowship that grow out of the same need that led to the invention of God. This impulse should not be cast as a rejection of atheism *per se* on Hardy's part, but he does acknowledge that a space remains for some kind of spiritual, loving force to become the essence of humanity. It is a force, however, that requires human activation.

Consider again another of the poem's X-ray moments when Hardy lifts the veil on the Will's hidden workings within the body. Human beings, in essence, become "will tissues":

[A] preternatural clearness possesses the atmosphere of the battle-field, in which the scene becomes anatomized and the living masses of humanity transparent. The controlling Immanent Will appears therein, as a brain-like network of currents and ejections, twitching, interpenetrating, entangling, and thrusting hither and thither the human forms. (4.160)

At this juncture of *The Dynasts,* as we have seen, the Will brings people together only ironically, in a kind of belligerent anti-cosmopolitanism: they congregate merely to practice killing each other. Nonetheless, the exposure of the will-web implies that human beings are hardwired, so to speak, to act collectively and could, conceivably, serve some entity beyond the nation. Hardy expressed as much in his preliminary notes for what would become *The Dynasts:* "We—the people—Humanity, a collective personality—(Thus 'we' could be engaged in the battle of Hohenlinden, say, and in the battle of Waterloo)—dwell with genial humour on 'our' getting into a rage for we know not what" (*Life* 449). As with the Immanent Will itself, this connection is already present within human beings—it infiltrates and connects both armies—even if they cannot recognize it among their various local and national subdivisions. Seeing the connection (and acting purposefully on it, unlike Napoleon) is the key to breaking free of the same destructive cycles of history. What the poem finally offers is not the possibility of God in the traditional sense but human beings taking control of their own fate, of the realignment of humanity with the most powerful forces of the universe. In this way, *The Dynasts* embodies a mixture of spiritual and political ambitions not all that different from the ones that motivated Barrett Browning's "Italy and the World." As the Spirit of the Pities surmises, "*must not Its heart awake, / Promptly tending / To Its Mending / In a genial germing purpose, and for loving-kindness' sake?*" (III. After Scene.96–99).

In geopolitical terms, the evolution of the Immanent Will mirrors a kind of all-encompassing, border-crossing sympathy. One must see the forces that move nations and avoid becoming swept up by them; one must gain, essentially, the perspective that the Spirits hold. The full expression of the poem's last words, which up to now I have quoted only in part, makes this mandate clear:

> But—a stirring thrills the air
> Like to sounds of joyance there
> That the rages
> Of the ages
> Shall be canceled, and deliverance offered from the darts that were,

Consciousness the Will informing, till It fashion all things fair!
(III. After Scene.105–10)

The Immanent Will's becoming aware of itself is essentially *our* becoming aware of it: individuals and nations are encouraged to act with a wider awareness of their interconnectedness. Such a realization, as Herbert F. Tucker suggests, would enable humankind to transcend the more passive, ethically restricted role of the Spirits: "we are enjoined to practice a form of participant-observation that becomes possible only by acknowledging our entanglement within the larger fabric of history of which even Hardy's immense cinematic canvas is but a small portion."[34] That cinematic lens, whether embodied in Hardy's stage directions or in the commentary of the Spirits, sees and reveals hidden connections to readers with vantage points, for instance, that stress the relative nearness of London and Paris when viewed from space: "A view now nocturnal, now diurnal, from on high over the Straits of Dover, and stretching from city to city. By night Paris and London seem each as a little swarm of lights surrounded by a halo; by day as a confused glitter of white and grey" (4.197). Hardy seems to deliberately invoke the religious connotations of "halo" in this instance: there is indeed something magical or holy about masses of humanity living together peacefully and cooperatively. The light of day may expose this vision as a trick of perspective, perhaps, but the poem's aim is to get readers to look to the future as much as to the reality of the present.

At the point in history covered by *The Dynasts*, however, the opportunities to dramatize such coming together are rare and mostly form brief counterpoints to the destruction of the war. While war uproots and displaces, it connects as well. Alliances of people come about either to invade nations or to fend off invasion, as when, before Leipzig, "Nationalities from the uttermost parts of Asia here meet those from the Atlantic edge of Europe for the first and last time" (5.80). The fiercest moments of conflict can also lead to poignant scenes of connection, even between enemies. During a momentary truce in the battle of Talavera, the Spirit of the Pities comments,

What do I see but thirsty, throbbing bands
From these inimic hosts defiling down
In homely need towards the prattling stream
That parts their enmities, and drinking there!
They get to grasping hands across the rill,
Sealing their sameness as earth's sojourners.—What more could plead the

> *wryness of the times*
> *Than such unstudied piteous pantomimes!* (II.4.5.1–8)

It was just this realization of sameness—and the threat it might pose to the proper business of war—that made the Christmas Day truce of 1914, when some soldiers left their posts to momentarily share greetings with the enemy, the last of its kind. Hand-shaking among enemy combatants stands out precisely because of the potential it reveals for a very different kind of exchange between nations, underscoring a latent tendency in humankind that might begin to flourish under different social circumstances, in a post-dynastic world.

Coda:
World War I and *The Dynasts*

The Dynasts finally invokes the Victorian faith in progress and a cosmopolitan future, as do all of the poets studied here to varying degrees of confidence: Hardy affirms poetry's place in envisioning new forms of social, political, and spiritual cohesion. However, just as the Great War became a historical referendum on Victorian optimism, so too would it pass judgment on *The Dynasts*. Hardy later claimed that he would not have ended the poem so optimistically had he known that "so mad and brutal a war" sat waiting just over the historical horizon. The war "destroyed all Hardy's belief in the gradual ennoblement of man" (*Life* 398). To say as much was to admit that this most committed of pessimists had let his guard down in *The Dynasts,* choosing to side with an uncertain future rather than the more hardened realism voiced by the Spirit of the Years. Hardy would return to form, in a sense, with the world-weary cynicism of "Channel Firing" (1914), where a spiritually and morally bankrupt Europe gears itself up for the next great conflict, "all nations striving strong to make / Red war yet redder" (13–14).[35]

If the war made the optimistic ending to *The Dynasts* seem premature, it did not necessarily invalidate it. To some extent, current events were now dramatizing the same fluctuation between ancient and modern and national and international that characterized the poem. Another comment Hardy made around the same time reveals a reaction to the war more akin to that of Pities in *The Dynasts:*

> It was seldom he had felt so heavy at heart as in seeing his old view of the gradual bettering of human nature . . . completely shattered by the events

of 1914 and onwards. War, he had supposed, had grown too coldly scientific to kindle again for long all the ardent romance which had characterized it down to Napoleonic times, when the most intense battles were over in a day, and the most exciting tactics and strategy led to the death of comparatively few combatants. (*Life* 395)

From this perspective, the war ultimately affirmed the mix of pessimism and optimism that was *The Dynasts*. Likewise, the struggle for a just peace that followed the conflict, along with efforts to forge a new political framework for internationalism—what would become the League of Nations—would underscore the difficulties Hardy faced when he attempted to craft his own cosmopolitan future in a poem where "old laws" were still in full force. Was any such effort to prove hopelessly naive or doomed to collapse under the weight of its own contradictions? Would human history be forever at the mercy of the blindly destructive Immanent Will? An actual participant in the 1919 Paris Peace Conference, John Maynard Keynes, made perhaps the most famous critical reflection on the poem's implications for these questions:

> The proceedings of Paris all had this air of extraordinary importance and unimportance at the same time. The decisions seemed charged with consequences to the future of human society; yet the air whispered that the word was not flesh, that it was futile, insignificant, of no effect, dissociated from events; and one felt most strongly the impression, described by Tolstoy in *War and Peace* or by Hardy in *The Dynasts*, of events marching on to their fated conclusion uninfluenced and unaffected by the cerebrations of Statesmen in Council.[36]

Keynes was witnessing firsthand just how difficult it was to grasp the forces that moved nations and just how untenable the optimistic conclusion to *The Dynasts* might be. The hope that the ambitions of leaders and nations could somehow be controlled and predicted by diplomats and treaties seemed vain. Indeed, Keynes' thoughts run against the grain of the times, when there was a new sense of optimism regarding the possibilities for world cooperation. The goal of the League of Nations, like that of Hardy's self-aware Immanent Will, was to check nationalistic excess through implementation of an impartial global vision. It was an idea, we know now, that proved premature in a Europe still fully engaged in colonial enterprises and by no means depleted of nationalistic rhetoric. Cosmopolitanism was an ideal that yet had a long way to go.

202 • CHAPTER 7

Hardy's final words on *The Dynasts* are worth recalling as we attempt to assess this poem's ultimate statement about war, nationalism, and cosmopolitanism—what it achieves and what it misses. One month before his death in January 1928, Hardy chose to preface a proposed French translation of the poem with the following remarks:

> In reflecting on this it appeared to me that there was one very special reason why a version of this drama should be given in French. How many times, in the course of centuries, have the two countries of France and England been drawn into conflicts because of codes or irresponsible governments, when the people themselves would have preferred, quite rightly, to tend to their own business! Such was notably the case in the epoch in which this drama is located—of 1805 to 1815. I said to myself that with the passing of time the perception of that fact would lead French readers to confront the events with neither passion nor prejudice. The whole spectacle, in all truth, can now be viewed, as much in France as in England, as a singular phenomenon in which, as in all war, human reason had little part.[37]

On one level the passage is a straightforward, routine anti-war expression, but it also raises more complicated questions. First, if governments embody aggressive forces antithetical to the sentiments of most individuals, is it still possible for people to intervene to prevent these forces from burgeoning into international conflict? What does it mean for a people to "tend their own business" in a world where, of necessity, nations must act cooperatively—when the people's business is increasingly with each other, sometimes with individuals thousands of miles away? What, in sum, are the possibilities for peaceful international exchange?

One could argue that the alternatives to war and firmly entrenched national identities are only dimly realized in *The Dynasts,* positioned as it is historically at the beginning of a century that would only amplify violence on behalf of national interests. Indeed, to read *The Dynasts* is to realize how little has changed in the hundred years that have intervened since its first publication: there remains the feeling that a tenable global vision must emerge, but at the same time, there seems to be a growing need, in the face of the homogenizing tendencies of globalization, to preserve smaller cultural units grounded in common ethnicity and language. Gaining perspective on those levels of identity has, if anything, become more complex than it was for Hardy. *The Dynasts* took cosmopolitanism as far as it could travel in the early twentieth century, and it remains for us to continue to probe its possibilities—to articulate what a cosmopolitan world truly is and to understand the role of poetry and other aesthetic forms in achieving it.

8

Conclusion

"Argosies of Magic Sails":
Cosmopolitan Dreams and Challenges

THROUGHOUT MY WORK on this book, which has sought to understand how a diverse range of Victorian poets engaged, critiqued, and in many
cases transcended the frameworks of cosmopolitanism available to them in
their time, I have been reminded now and then of another, much more visible inheritance from the nineteenth century. Since their revival in Athens
in 1896, the Olympic Games have been a recurring feature of global culture, apart from the interruption of two world wars. I have been struck, for
instance, by the parallels between the opening ceremony of the Games and
Casa Guidi Windows, which bears witness to its own Parade of Nations in
the streets of Florence:

> Last, the world had sent
> The various children of her teeming flanks—
> Greeks, English, French—as if to a parliament
> Of lovers of her Italy in ranks,
> Each bearing its land's symbol reverent. (1.511–15)

Representatives from different European nations celebrate Italy but also something larger: the promise of Italy's future, the beginning of that "advance, /
Onward and upward, of all humanity" (49–50), as Barrett Browning would

describe it later in "Italy and the World." Likewise, the opening ceremony of the Olympics typically celebrates the accomplishments of the host nation before inviting athletes from around the world to march in under their own flags and then to mingle together in the center of the arena—a symbolic representation of national internationalism first devised for the Melbourne games of 1956. Spectators cheer one's nation but, it is hoped, subsume that self-interest within universal ideals of fellowship and fair play. The Olympics thus attempts to channel the spirit of nationalism into something nobler even as it puts national rivalries on display. For Pierre de Coubertin, the founder of the modern games, "Olympism" was "a religious sentiment transformed and enlarged by the internationalism and democracy that distinguish the modern age."[1]

The Dynasts and the Olympics may share an even stronger kinship. Both were conceived amidst the political tensions of the fin de siècle when Europe seemed to be gearing up for another great military conflict. By staging his own "drama of nations" within a greater, nobler philosophical framework, Hardy could redeem war, recasting it as part of the movement toward Kant's perpetual peace and universal, cosmopolitan future. *The Dynasts* likewise reflects the peculiar blend of ancient and modern that is the Olympics, which gestures back to classical times and stresses its spiritual continuity with Europe's cultural origins. Hardy dresses his poem in the language and perspectives of a quasi-ancient Greek chorus, who offer a broad philosophical and historical perspective on human events. Ultimately, *Casa Guidi Windows*, *The Dynasts*, and the Olympic games all strive to redeem patriotism and channel it toward higher ends.

So far I have managed to conduct this study, however, without paying tribute to perhaps the most famous display of cosmopolitan pageantry in all of Victorian poetry. If Alfred Tennyson's verse exists largely outside of the Anglo-European spaces of identity cultivated by the Brownings or Swinburne, he did flirt briefly and vividly in "Locksley Hall" (1842) with contemporary cosmopolitan thinking. It is only fair, in some sense, to give him his due, since all of the poets I examine here were writing against him to varying extents, or at least the Tennyson of *Idylls of the King*. Tennyson writes,

> For I dipt into the future, far as human eye could see,
> Saw the Vision of the world, and all the wonder that would be;

> Saw the heavens fill with commerce, argosies of magic sails,
> Pilots of the purple twilight, dropping down with costly bales;

Heard the heavens fill with shouting, and there rained a ghastly dew
From the nations' airy navies grappling in the central blue;

Far along the world-wide whisper of the south-wind rushing warm,
With the standards of the peoples plunging thro' the thunder-storm;

Till the war-drum throbb'd no longer, and the battle-flags were furl'd
In the Parliament of man, the Federation of the world. (119–28)[2]

In an almost psychedelic rerendering of Kant's "spirit of commerce," Tennyson, in the space of ten lines, works his way through an era of competitive free trade and global conflict before finally depositing mankind at the threshold of world cooperation and unity. Colorful and dynamic, Tennyson's effort to represent symbolically the ideals and abstractions of nineteenth-century internationalism could find a place, one imagines, in an Olympic opening ceremony even now (perhaps London in 2012?).

Tennyson's reflections on internationalism continue in the poem, but before delving more deeply into them, I wanted to cite another Victorian cosmopolitan dream that helps to put Tennyson's achievement in a wider literary context. And I do mean wide: Philip James Bailey's *Festus,* published first in 1839, revised and expanded in 1845, and again in subsequent editions up until 1889, when it reached nearly 40,000 lines, emerged out of the same apocalyptic epic tradition that gave rise to Robert Pollok's even more popular *The Course of Time.* Bailey, however, would opt for a much more inclusive final reckoning, one inconceivable under Pollok's stern Calvinism. Based loosely on *Faust,* the poem's protagonist, like Goethe's, is forlorn in love but espouses a more deeply earnest poetic sensibility. With Lucifer's assistance, he travels across time, across the globe, even across space to Venus and the Moon, before reconciling his lost loves and paving the way toward world peace—thus bypassing Tennyson's epoch of free trade entirely. In Bailey's postmillennial universe, all are saved, Lucifer too, as everyone and everything disappears within the oneness of God:

Time there hath been when only God was all:
And it shall be again. The hour is named,
When seraph, cherub, angel, saint, man, fiend,
Made pure, and unbelievably uplift
Above their present state—drawn up to God,
Like dew into the air—shall be all Heaven;

And all souls shall be in God, and shall be God,
And nothing but God, be.[3]

Thus what Herbert F. Tucker calls Bailey's "Big Hug of no-fault apocalypse," one that typifies how "the spasmodic epic replaces the . . . evangelical atonement of 1820s epic with nicer things like welcome and pardon, all in support of the unobstructed epiphany of self."[4] The poem indeed offers an intoxicating vision of poetic power: before this final heavenly consummation, dethroned kings bow before Festus in observance of what Tucker calls a "postnationalist cult of personality."[5]

It should perhaps come as no surprise, then, that Bailey's poem was on Matthew Arnold's mind in the early months of 1848 when, as we saw, events on the political stage seemed to forecast the impending arrival of Europe's cosmopolitan future. At first Arnold credited Bailey in a letter to Clough with being one of the most technically adept and "promising English verse-writers" of the day.[6] By the following spring, however, Arnold's enthusiasm had cooled. *Festus* had failed the all-important test of Europeanness:

England has fallen intellectually so far behind the continent that we cannot expect to see her assisting to carry on the intellectual work of the world from the point to which it is now arrived: for to what point it is arrived not 20 English people know: so profoundly has activity in this country extirpated reflexion. So we may expect to see English people doing things which have long been done, & re-discovering what has been discovered & used up elsewhere, like Faustism.[7]

With respect to the intellectual and spiritual confederation Arnold later called for in "The Function of Criticism," *Festus* perhaps fell into the category of being careful what you wish for. However positive-minded and ambitious Bailey's poem was, however well Bailey could hold the line poetically, the poem's intellectual appeal could not endure. *Festus* cast its vision across the cosmos and deep into the future, but in some crucial sense it never even made it across the English Channel.

Arnold's judgment of *Festus* brings me back to "Locksley Hall" and the perhaps inevitable tension that can emerge between cosmopolitan dreams and realities. What Arnold made of Tennyson's poem is not known, but we, at least, should recognize that it has something more to teach to us with respect to cosmopolitanism than Bailey, something beyond the "argosies of magic sails" in the passage already quoted.[8] Indeed, after juxtaposing that vision with the kind of world the poem imagines later, it becomes clear that

"Locksley Hall" forms a critique of the deceptive, intoxicating rhetoric of the competing global agendas available at the time. Later, in fact, the speaker rejects notions of European-led world progress for a kind of orientalist fantasy: "There methinks would be enjoyment more than in this march of mind, / In the steamship, in the railway, in the thoughts that shake mankind" (165–66). Finally overcoming his disillusionment with Amy, the English woman he imagines betrayed him, he proclaims, "I will take some savage woman, she shall rear my dusky race" (168). The speaker then quickly backs off of this alternative and reaffirms his role in Europe's march to the future—following up his sexism with one of the more forthright expressions of Eurocentrism to emerge out of the Victorian period: "Thro' the shadow of the globe we sweep into the younger day; / Better fifty years of Europe than a cycle of Cathay" (183–84).

Determining where Tennyson himself stands on these proclamations is difficult, and attempting to do so in fact diminishes the poem's rhetorical effectiveness as a dramatic monologue. John Lucas aptly describes the speaker's thoughts as "the near-hysterical strategies of a man trying to convince himself that he can make sense of himself and therefore of the world out there."[9] The unusual format of the poem, with its double-spaces between couplets, likewise suggests someone incapable of tying his thoughts together in a more sustained analysis. "I *know* my words are wild" (173), he concedes in a brief moment of self-containment. Tennyson's point, in fact, might be just how difficult it was to describe in reasoned, measured tones what motivated the Victorian encounter with the wider world, never mind the future results it would lead to. Self-absorption overlaps with fellow-feeling, universalism slips easily into Eurocentrism—a critique often made of Kant as well, whose cosmopolitan vision entails an indefinite preliminary imperial stage, with Europe, the seat of progress, always pointing the way ahead.[10] The mixed, unstable prophecies of "Locksley Hall" thus may have turned out to be more accurate than the cosmopolitan dreams of many of Tennyson's contemporaries. The road to European and finally global cosmopolitanism, if that was indeed where the world was headed, would be a confusing one with numerous digressions, one defined by conflict and competition as much as cooperation.

Such a realization, however, begs the question of whether Arnold's intellectual and spiritual confederation of Europe—along with similar, more global constructs—contains a contradiction at its very heart: can any such attempt to manifest this idea in poetry be spiritual *and* intellectual at the same time? Or, like the Olympics, is it a performance that, under closer scrutiny, always seems to undermine the cosmopolitan "religious sentiment" that

Coubertin claimed inspired them in the first place?[11] In other words, when it comes to *performing* cosmopolitanism, does the attempt to "dream big" inevitably entail the abandonment of some key intellectual anchorage and critical awareness? Poetically speaking, *Festus,* perhaps, stands most open to this charge, but we should recall that *The Dynasts* and *Aurora Leigh* also raked in high stakes as they drew to a close, predicting a better, happier future for the world. The ultimate answer to the intellectual and spiritual question may lie in the recognition that cosmopolitanism, if it is to be performed well, involves taking risks, a recognition that gets to the heart of the challenge of cosmopolitanism as recounted in this book. Cosmopolitanism demands that one look to the future—to have *faith* in that future regardless of whether some divine agency is driving it or not—while not losing sight of the political realities of the present—the need to test and refine that dream.

Tennyson meets this effort in "Locksley Hall" if only on a smaller scale than each of the poets examined in the preceding chapters, all of whom worked hard, in a sense, to test and refine the cosmopolitan, Anglo-European spaces they invented. Hardy refused to let readers rest comfortably either in nostalgia for early-nineteenth-century Britain or in the belief that the Immanent Will would become aware of itself just by itself, without human intervention. The present-day limitations of Clough's Europe were also never far from his mind, but it was still a poem that stepped tentatively toward the future in its closing envoi. Clough's was a cosmopolitanism of negation, as I have called it, but one that in other ways simply posed a greater challenge for the future, insisting we demand more out of love and more out of the political and cultural affiliations that sustain us. We should recall as well how Robert Browning brought the high-flying Miranda down to earth in *Red Cotton Night-Cap Country,* denying him his Festus-like moment of transcendence and instead reminding us that expanding cultural and spiritual horizons meant immersing oneself deeply, and often uncomfortably, within the identities and thoughts of others. Swinburne took this lesson one step further by embracing the sensations of sickness and contamination that have always adhered to the most threatening—and necessary—kinds of cultural crossovers. And Morris's *Sigurd the Volsung,* so closely tied up with notions of race, concerns itself just as fully with how to assimilate the demands of local identities within larger social and geographic environments. Finally, it was Elizabeth Barrett Browning who took the greatest risks over the course of her career in pursuit of a cosmopolitanism that would inspire readers to a higher, more responsible sense of European and global citizenship. Entry into Barrett Browning's world church, broad and open as it was, still demanded the kind of political and aesthetic toil that characterize the conclusion to *Aurora Leigh* and the deep, unflinching self-interrogation of "Mother and Poet."

Together, these poets underscore Victorian poetry's largely unrecognized potential as a form of analytical, critical cosmopolitanism. Throughout this book I have deliberately avoided using cosmopolitanism in a simple laudatory sense that positions works against each other on an idealized scale of cultural receptivity. The encounter with Europe in Victorian poetry took a different conceptual compass heading, one that wrung more out of the concept of cosmopolitanism. This more strategic effort, I think, is the essence of Arnold's intellectual and spiritual confederation of Europe, one that emerged, we should recall, out of his demand for a smarter, more objective kind of cultural criticism. His "Europe" was always as much a *state of mind*, a kind of hermeneutic, even, as an actual place.

"Europe," of course, remains a site of intense philosophical and critical inquiry, as Rodolphe Gasché underscores in *Europe, or the Infinite Task* (2009), his fine analysis of four twentieth-century philosophers' attempts to grapple with this most elusive of signifiers. As his title indicates, Europe is "a conception that is always only in the making, never closed off, and structurally open to future transformation and change."[12] If Gasché refuses to pin down more precisely just what "Europe" is and what it is working towards, it is only to capture how fluid its conceptual boundaries have necessarily become. Étienne Balibar makes a similar kind of move when he proposes the intriguing concept that Europe itself is a "border," a site of continuous exchange and renegotiation: "This is perhaps what all of Europe, and not just its 'margins,' 'marches,' or 'outskirts' must today imagine, for it has become a daily experience. Most of the areas, nations, and regions that constitute Europe had become accustomed to thinking that they had borders, more or less 'secure and organized,' but they did not think they were borders."[13] Jacques Derrida forms the capstone to Gasché's investigation, as he inevitably must, having gone farther than anyone in attempting to work critically through ideas of Europe, cosmopolitanism, hospitality, and, late in his career, religion and spirituality. Derrida recognizes that to speak of Europe at all is to engage in a dialogue with the future that is also inextricably bound with past projects undertaken on behalf of specifically Eurocentric notions of progress. "Europe takes itself to be a promontory, an advance," he writes in *The Other Heading: Reflections on Today's Europe* (1992), "the avant-garde of geography and history."[14] However, if Europe must no longer be privileged as the center of world culture, it remains the site of one of the greatest concentrations of different languages and national identities and can still be a model to the rest of the world for negotiating difference. Derrida remarks elsewhere in *The Other Heading,* "it is necessary to make ourselves the guardians of an idea of Europe, a difference of Europe, *but* of a Europe that consists precisely in not closing itself off in its own identity and in advancing itself in an exemplary way toward what it is not, toward the other heading or the heading of the other."[15]

Derrida's Europe is thus one that is carefully reconstructed in light of its volatile history and legacy of colonialism. To simply elide his notion of Europe with Arnold's has not been my goal in this book, but juxtaposing them with each other does underscore the degree to which, then and now, "Europe" could be a durable, flexible site of critical and aesthetic investigation—one that checked patriotic, self-centered excesses of various kinds. Like Arnold, the other poets I have examined here were citizens of the world's dominant power at the height of its empire-building, but they knew that that alone did not truly make them *citizens of the world.* In Europe and beyond, the cosmopolitan idea they gave voice to in their poems remains a possibility. They challenged themselves to become more open to that possibility, and they challenge *us* as well: to cultivate the same kind of intellectual openness and, not least importantly, to reevaluate Victorian poetry's capacity to engage meaningfully with the larger geopolitical forces that have shaped history and continue to shape our lives today.

Notes

Chapter 1

1. Review of *Poems before Congress, Saturday Review* 9 (31 March 1860): 402. In their introduction to a special issue commemorating the bicentenary of Barrett Browning's birth, Marjorie Stone and Beverly Taylor provide a succinct overview of critical responses to her work. See "'Confirm my voice': 'My sisters,' Poetic Audiences, and the Published Voices of EBB," *Victorian Poetry* 44, no. 4 (2006): 391–403.

2. A. [Andrew] Wilson, "English Poets in Italy: Mrs. Browning's Last Poems," *Macmillan's Magazine* 6 (May 1862): 87.

3. Barrett Browning to Arabella Barrett, February 28, 1859, in *The Letters of Elizabeth Barrett Browning to Her Sister Arabella,* ed. Scott Lewis (Waco: Wedgestone Press, 2002), 2:395.

4. Herbert F. Tucker, *Epic: Britain's Heroic Muse 1790–1910* (Oxford: Oxford University Press, 2008), 467.

5. Tucker, *Epic,* 495. *The Light of Asia* was one of the best-selling long poems of the era and could be aligned with other early formulations of what Srinivas Aravamudan calls "Guru English," a joint production of English colonialism and South Asian religions that evolved into a highly commodifiable form of "transnational religious cosmopolitanism" (*Guru English: South Asian Religion in a Cosmopolitan Language* [Princeton: Princeton University Press, 2006], 7). It is a discourse, he reveals, that historically has taken on diverse forms, from Kipling's *Kim* (1900) to the popular self-help manuals today of Deepak Chopra: "The global transmission of Hindu and Buddhist thought eventually led to the rise of the self-proclaimed ethno-religious nationalist as well as the detached and Asian-influenced cosmopolitan" (9). As a form of literary discourse, Guru English reaches its highest form, he suggests, in the works of Sri Aurobindo, especially his epic poem *Savitri: A Legend and a Symbol* (97–101).

6. Tucker, *Epic*, 12.

7. The 1850s alone, for instance, produced Kinahan Cornwallis's *Yarra Yarra; or, The Wandering Aborigine* (1858) and Thulia Susannah Henderson's *Olga; or Russia in the Tenth Century* (1855). See Tucker, *Epic*, 372–74. Other recent work on epic, including Simon Dentith's *Epic and Empire in Nineteenth-Century Britain* (Cambridge: Cambridge University Press, 2006) and Colin Graham's *Nation, Empire and Victorian Epic Poetry* (Manchester: Manchester University Press, 1998), examine epic in more specifically imperial contexts than Tucker's, but they likewise warn against overemphasizing the genre's nationalistic aims. As Graham observes, the nation "justifies and underlies imperialism, yet imperialism creates a cultural field in which (hegemonous) nationality is forced to confront the paradox of its co-existence and putative equality with other 'nations'" (2).

8. R. H. Super, ed., *The Complete Prose Works of Matthew Arnold* (Ann Arbor: University of Michigan Press, 1960–77), 3:284. All references to Arnold's prose writings are to this edition and will henceforth be noted in the text.

9. Bruce Robbins, "Introduction Part I: Actually Existing Cosmopolitanism," in *Cosmopolitics: Thinking and Feeling beyond the Nation,* ed. Pheng Cheah and Bruce Robbins (Minneapolis: University of Minnesota Press, 1998), 2–3.

10. Anthony Kwame Appiah, "Cosmopolitan Patriots," in Cheah and Robbins, 92.

11. Lauren M. E. Goodlad, "Trollopian 'Foreign Policy': Rootedness and Cosmopolitanism in the Mid-Victorian Imaginary," *PMLA* 124, no. 2 (2009): 437.

12. Lauren M. E. Goodlad and Julia M. Wright, "Victorian Internationalisms: Introduction and Keywords," *RaVoN* 48 (November 2007), Paragraph 1, http://www.erudit.org/revue/ravon/2007/v/n48.

13. Amanda Anderson, *The Powers of Distance: Cosmopolitanism and the Cultivation of Detachment* (Princeton: Princeton University Press, 2001), 21.

14. Marjorie Morgan makes a similar claim in her study of how domestic travel shaped notions of Britishness, cautioning us not to neglect the diverse kinds of contact zones through which individual Victorians encountered the wider world: "rather than privileging empire as a context, it seems more meaningful to view empire as one of many contexts in which people from Britain framed their identity" (*National Identities and Travel in Victorian Britain* [Basingstoke and New York: Palgrave, 2001], 7). By insisting on this kind of reorientation, Anderson and Morgan strike a better balance, I think, than another recent criticism of the role of empire in British cultural studies, Bernard Porter's *Absent-Minded Imperialists: Empire, Society, and Culture in Britain* (Oxford: Oxford University Press, 2004). While Porter is correct to remind us that empire was a much less visible component of education and popular culture than one might assume from the amount of attention it receives now, he brushes aside the large body of literary criticism on Victorian imperialism with the observation that "there are almost no 'good' books, poems, paintings, sculptures, musical compositions, or great buildings from the early and middle years of the nineteenth-century that have a significant imperial component to them" (134). Similarly, he omits discussion of any specific flaws in Said's *Culture and Imperialism* (1993), opting instead to repeat the claims of early critics that he reads too much into the works he studies (ix–x).

15. Mary Louise Pratt, *Imperial Eyes: Travel Writing and Transculturation* (London: Routledge, 1992), 6. In *Orientalism* (New York: Vintage, 1978), Said writes, "[t]he Orient is not only adjacent to Europe; it is also the place of Europe's greatest and richest

and oldest colonies, the source of its civilizations and languages, its cultural contestant, and one of its deepest and most recurring images of the Other. In addition, the Orient has helped to define Europe (or the West) as its contrasting image, idea, personality, experience" (1–2).

16. As Arnold remarked in "The Study of Poetry" (1880), "More and more mankind will discover that we have to turn to poetry to interpret life for us, to console us, to sustain us. Without poetry, our science will appear incomplete; and most of what now passes with us for religion and philosophy will be replaced by poetry" (9:161–62).

17. See, for instance, Tricia Lootens, "Victorian Poetry and Patriotism," in *The Cambridge Companion to Victorian Poetry*, ed. Joseph P. Bristow (Cambridge: Cambridge University Press, 2000), 225–79, and Margaret Linley, "Nationhood and Empire," in *A Companion to Victorian Poetry*, ed. Richard Cronin et al. (Oxford: Blackwell, 2002), 421–37. Matthew Reynolds's *The Realms of Verse 1830–1870: English Poetry in a Time of Nation-Building* (2001) devotes close attention to Clough and the Brownings and marks an exception to this trend, although one refracted through the prism of expatriate nationalism, which forms only one dimension of the Victorian cosmopolitical encounter with Europe. My aim, I should restress, is not to supersede these earlier investigations so much as to complement them, revealing a more complete geography of the macropolitics of Victorian poetry. Reynolds's book is perhaps second only to Isobel Armstrong's groundbreaking *Victorian Poetry: Poetry, Poetics and Politics* (1993) in helping us to reevaluate the complex ways poets sought to work in tandem with the political movements and leaders of their time.

18. See Lauren M. E. Goodlad and Julia M. Wright, eds., "Victorian Internationalisms," cited above, and Keith Hanley and Greg Kucich, eds., "Global Formations Past and Present," *Nineteenth-Century Contexts* 29, nos. 2–3 (2007). With a broader historical sweep, it should be noted, the *Nineteenth-Century Contexts* issue does include Adam Komisuruk's "Typologies of the East: Self as Vortex in Don Juan's Russian Affair" (219–36). Byron's presence indicates the central place he still holds—and held in the minds of many Victorian poets—as the figure against which their own encounters with Europe must inevitably be juxtaposed.

19. See Jan B. Gordon, "Charlotte Brontë's Alternative 'European Community,'" in *The Idea of Europe in Literature*, ed. Susanne Fendler and Ruth Wittlinger (Houndsmills: Macmillan, 1999), 3–30.

20. Similarly, James Buzard, in *Disorienting Fiction: The Authoethnographic Work of Victorian Fiction* (Princeton: Princeton University Press, 2005), features *Villette* in his discussion of modes of anti-imperial self-critique in the British novel. Lucy Snowe's "immersion in an alien realm," he argues, causes her "to begin forming an ethnographic rather than an ethnocentric conception of identity, mentality, and place" (248).

21. T. S. Eliot, *On Poetry and Poets* (New York: Faber, 1957), 19.

22. Mikhail Bakhtin, *The Dialogic Imagination: Four Essays*, ed. Michael Holquist, trans. Caryl Emerson and Michael Holquist (Austin: University of Texas Press, 1981), 287.

23. As Tucker observes and his work repeatedly demonstrates, "a great deal of what Lukács [in his 1920 *The Theory of the Novel*] and Bakhtin say about the prose fiction of the nineteenth century will also find exemplification among the period's verse epics" (15). Tucker's claim is borne out as well by previous critics who have turned Bakhtin's generic labels to Victorian poetry's advantage. See, for instance, Meg Tasker's work on

Aurora Leigh, cited in chapter 3, and her earlier "Time, Tense, and Genre: A Bakhtinian Analysis of Clough's *Bothie,*" *Victorian Poetry* 34, no. 2 (1996): 193–211.

24. Thomas Carlyle, *On Heroes, Hero-Worship, and the Heroic in History,* ed. Michael K. Goldberg (Berkeley: University of California Press, 1992), 70, 94.

25. Giving us a sense of how travel could enhance a poem's marketability, Robert Browning attempted to coax Elizabeth abroad in 1846 with the revelation that Smith and Elder had made him an offer to "print any poem about Italy, in any form." Philip Kelley and Scott Lewis, eds., *The Brownings' Correspondence* (Winfield, KS: Wedgestone Press, 1984), 13:308. Hereafter abbreviated *BC.*

26. Erik Gray, "A Bounded Field: Situating Victorian Poetry in the Literary Landscape," *Victorian Poetry* 41, no. 4 (2003): 470.

27. Joseph Bristow, "Whether 'Victorian' Poetry: A Genre and Its Period," *Victorian Poetry* 42, no. 1 (2004): 97.

28. In this respect, I join others who have sought to rescue Arnold from the extremes of the academic culture wars of the 1990s. See, for instance, Donald D. Stone's effort to engage Arnold with voices as diverse as Henry James, Nietzsche, and Foucault, in *Communications with the Future: Matthew Arnold in Dialogue* (Ann Arbor: University of Michigan, 1997). Amanda Anderson also favorably reassesses Arnold's "disinterestedness" in chapter 3 of *The Powers of Distance* (91–118). See also Herbert F. Tucker, "Arnold and the Authorization of Criticism," in *Knowing the Past: Victorian Literature and Culture,* ed. Suzy Anger (Ithaca: Cornell University Press, 2001), 100–120, and Reed Way Dasenbrock, "Why Read Multicultural Literature? An Arnoldian Perspective" *College English* 61 (1999): 691–701.

29. Iris Esther Sells, *Matthew Arnold and France: The Poet* (Cambridge: Cambridge University Press, 1935), 4–5. Sells provides a detailed account of Arnold's travels in France and of the early influence of French authors on his writing, especially George Sand and Senancour.

30. Matthew Arnold, *Arnold: The Complete Poems,* ed. Kenneth Allott (London: Longman, 1979). All references to Arnold's poetry are to this edition and will be noted in the text.

31. There are no specific references to these works in Arnold's journals or letters that I am aware of, but he did study Kant's *Critique of Pure Reason* in 1845 at Oxford and could quite possibly have become aware of other dimensions of Kant's work during this period or later. See Park Honan, *Matthew Arnold: A Life* (Cambridge: Harvard University Press, 1983), 93.

32. Immanuel Kant, *Kant: Political Writings,* ed. Hans Reiss, trans. H. B. Nisbet (Cambridge: Cambridge University Press, 1991), 51.

33. See, for instance, James Tully's cautionary assessment of Kant's influence on notions of European union today in "The Kantian Idea of Europe: Critical and Cosmopolitan Perspectives," in *The Idea of Europe: From Antiquity to the European Union,* ed. Anthony Pagden (Cambridge: Cambridge University Press, 2002), 331–58. Jürgen Habermas takes a more optimistic view of Kant's legacy in "Kant's Idea of Perpetual Peace, with the Benefit of Two Hundred Years' Hindsight," in *Perpetual Peace: Essays on Kant's Cosmopolitan Ideal,* ed. James Bohman and Matthias Lutz-Bachmann (Cambridge: MIT Press, 1997), 113–53.

34. Tully, "The Kantian Idea of Europe," 344.

35. Ruth apRoberts offers the most comprehensive assessment of Herder's influ-

ence on Arnold and concludes that he "carries out the Herderian program with his own breadth of vision, in his comparative-literature, comparative-religion mode. He combats Philistine provincialism everywhere; he will not limit culture to the English tradition, or even the European tradition." "Matthew Arnold and Herder's *Ideen*," *Nineteenth-Century Prose* 16, no. 2 (1989): 7.

36. Paul Micahel Lutzeler goes so far as to nominate Goethe "the spiritual father of European efforts toward international cooperation. While Herder stressed the insurmountable differences between the various cultures, Goethe concentrated on what they had in common" ("Goethe and Europe," *South Atlantic Review* 65:2 [2000]: 95–113, 95). Lutzeler explores other dimensions of cosmopolitan thinking in Goethe, although he may err, as I explain above, by positioning him in direct opposition to Herder.

37. Quoted in David Damrosch, *What Is World Literature?* (Princeton: Princeton University Press, 2003), 1.

38. References to Browning's poems, with the exception of *The Ring and the Book*, are to *Robert Browning: The Poems*, 2 vols., ed. John Pettigrew (New Haven: Yale University Press, 1981).

39. Matthew Arnold, *The Letters of Matthew Arnold*, 6 vols., ed. Cecil Y. Lang (Charlottesville: University of Virginia Press, 1996–2004), 1:98. Hereafter abbreviated *LMA*.

40. Cecil Y. Lang, the editor of Arnold's collected letters, could not trace a specific source for Lamartine's prophecy (1:99n7), nor could I in my own study of proclamations made by Lamartine's provisional government in the wake of the February 1848 revolution. Whether misattributed to Lamartine or not, Arnold's remarks do capture the kind of internationalist Zeitgeist that had overtaken the continent in 1848. In a diplomatic release made public to assuage fears that the French government would embark on a new Napoleonic conquest of Europe, Lamartine stressed, "by the light of its intelligence, and the spectacle of order and peace which it hopes to present to the world, the republic will exercise the only honourable proselytism of esteem and sympathy" (*History of the French Revolution of 1848* [London: George Bell, 1888], 98). The Brownings also hopefully trusted in this prediction, according to Elizabeth in a March 1848 letter: "I take up my republicanism, & am cordially glad that the experiment of the most rational & sincere of governments, a pure democracy, should be tried in Europe. Robert & I agree & thoroughly agree in politics as in other things" (*Letters to Arabella*, 1:155).

41. Two months earlier, Arnold wrote to Clough, "Do you remember your pooh-poohing the revue des deux mondes, & my expostulating that the final expression up to the present time of European opinion, without fantastic individual admixture, was *current* there: not emergent here & there in a great writer,—but the *atmosphere* of the commonplace man as well as of the Genius" (March 6, 1848; *LMA* 1: 89–90).

42. Quoted in Sandi E. Cooper, *Patriotic Pacifism: Waging War on War in Europe 1815–1914* (Oxford: Oxford University Press, 1991), 25.

43. Albert, Prince Consort of Queen Victoria of Great Britain, *The Principal Speeches and Addresses of His Royal Highness the Prince Consort* (London: Murray, 1862), 110.

44. David G. Riede, *Matthew Arnold and the Betrayal of Language* (Charlottesville: University of Virginia Press, 1988), 197.

45. Arnold visited Thun, Switzerland, in September 1848 and again the following September, when he composed the "Stanzas in Memory of the Author of 'Obermann'" along with several poems inspired by "Marguerite," whose identity Arnold's biographers have never been able to pinpoint precisely. Honan insists that the most likely candidate

is Mary Claude, a close friend of Clough and his sister Anne—someone who, like Arnold, traveled extensively and was deeply schooled in European literature (see Honan, *Matthew Arnold,* 149–50). Whether inspired by Claude or an unknown French woman, "To Marguerite—Continued" underscores the more erotic and personal attractions that intensified Arnold's longing for some kind of consummation between himself and the Continent. While staying in Paris two years earlier, Arnold developed a similar obsession with the opera singer Rachel. He would later pay tribute to her in "Rachel III" as the embodiment of a pan-European, pan-racial ideal. Essentially, Rachel had done for the stage what Heinrich Heine had for poetry: "Germany, France, Christ, Moses, Athens, Rome. / The strife, the mixture in her soul, are ours. / Her genius and her glory are her own" (12–14). Of the poets studied in this book, Swinburne goes the farthest in illuminating the complex codependence of body and spirit in initiating the desire to cross cultural borders. Clough too would probe these dueling motives in *Amours de Voyage* and *Dipsychus* (1853; publ. 1865) and may in fact have had Arnold's affair with Mary Claude in mind when he composed the former: the two principal characters of the poem are named "Claude" and "Mary." Eugene R. August explores this and other possible connections in "*Amours de Voyage* and Matthew Arnold in Love: An Inquiry," *Victorian Newsletter* 60 (1981): 15–20.

46. Riede applies this metaphor to Arnold's language in ways that again invoke the promising but distant sense of Europe conveyed by his poems: "Arnold does indeed assert the saving power of language, but in words that, ironically, are often self-referential and only enclose an empty space. Arnold is at odds with himself—he describes an inspired and almost magically full language, but he describes it with a sadly empty language (4).

47. Lord Byron (George Gordon), *The Complete Poetical Works,* ed. Jerome J. McGann (Oxford: Oxford University Press, 1980).

48. In one of the earliest references to her ambition to write a major epic-length work, Barrett wrote to Mary Russell Mitford, "I want to write a poem of a new class, in a measure—a Don Juan, without the mockery and impurity, . . under one aspect,—& having unity as a work of art,—& admitting of as much philosophical dreaming & digression (which is in fact a characteristic of the age) as I like to use" (December 30, 1844; *BC* 9:304).

49. G. K. Chesterton, *The Victorian Age in Literature* (New York: Henry Holt, 1913), 178.

50. Arnold to Arthur Hugh Clough, March 6, 1848 (*LMA* 1:90).

51. References to Barrett Browning poems other than *Casa Guidi Windows* and *Aurora Leigh* are to *The Works of Elizabeth Barrett Browning,* ed. Sandra Donaldson et al. (London: Pickering and Chatto, 2010).

52. Linda M. Lewis, *Elizabeth Barrett Browning's Spiritual Progress: Face to Face with God* (Columbia: University of Missouri Press, 1998), 115.

53. Aravamudan, *Guru English,* 19.

54. Kant, *Political Writings,* 50.

55. Swinburne, *Songs before Sunrise* (London: Chatto and Windus, 1888), 22. Swinburne wrote the volume largely at the suggestion of Mazzini himself, who chastised him, "Don't lull us to sleep with songs of egotistical love and idolatry of physical beauty: shake us, reproach, encourage, insult, brand the cowards, hail the martyrs, tell us that we have a great Duty to fulfill" (qtd. in Rikky Rooksby, *A. C. Swinburne: A Poet's Life*

[Aldershot: Ashgate, 1997], 149). *Songs before Sunrise* has been unfairly neglected by critics, as Stephanie Kuduk Weiner has argued, and she explores Swinburne's achievement in "'A Sword of a Song': Swinburne's Republican Aesthetics in *Songs before Sunrise* (*Victorian Studies* 43 [2001]: 253–78) and in *Republican Politics and English Poetry, 1789–1874* (Houndsmills: Palgrave Macmillan, 2005), 157–76, which juxtaposes *Songs before Sunrise* with contemporary republican poems by George Meredith and James Thomson. While not seeking to downplay that achievement or send *Songs before Sunrise* into renewed exile, I do think Mazzini misses the way that *Poems and Ballads* performs precisely the kind of work he describes, reproaching and insulting on behalf of a revolutionary kind of cosmopolitanism that explores the complex interplay between body and spirit, physical attraction and repulsion, and fear and desire of the Other. In chapter 5, I demonstrate why what remains Swinburne's signature work merits renewed attention as one of the most complex and dramatic interventions into Victorian debates over cross-cultural exchange.

56. Deirdre David argues compellingly that Barrett Browning's resistance to communism makes her the purveyor of an essentially patriarchal "sage discourse" in which "[w]oman's talent is made the attendant of conservative male ideals" (*Intellectual Women and Victorian Patriarchy* [Ithaca: Cornell University Press, 1987], 98). I follow a number of subsequent commentators, however, in emphasizing how Barrett Browning also challenges those ideals—in part through her resistance to patriarchal notions of women's domestic obligations, on both a personal and a national level. See, for instance, Marjorie Stone, *Elizabeth Barrett Browning* (New York: St. Martin's Press, 1995), 45–46.

57. Barrett Browning had preordained Romney's demise, in a sense, in an April 1848 letter expressing concern over the threat to the French provisional government posed by communist revolutionaries in Paris that spring: "I quite tremble to think of the wild, rampant doctrines of some of those communists, which, if carried out, would destroy the individuality of men . . . & blunt the points of all energy & genius. Monastic & conventual institutions are not, as has again & again been proved, favorable to the evolvement of great faculties—nor do they make men purer in the mass" (*Letters to Arabella*, 1:165–66).

58. Frederick L. Mulhauser, ed., *The Correspondence of Arthur Hugh Clough* (Oxford: Clarendon, 1957), 1:215.

59. Homi K. Bhabha, "Unpacking My Library . . . Again," in *The Post-Colonial Question: Common Skies, Divided Horizons,* ed. Iain Chambers and Lidia Curti (New York: Routledge, 1996), 204.

60. Aijaz Ahmad, "The Politics of Literary Postcoloniality," *Race and Class* 36, no. 3 (1995): 1–20; repr. in *Contemporary Postcolonial Theory: A Reader,* ed. Padmini Mongia (London: Arnold, 1996), 285.

61. Kwame Anthony Appiah, *Cosmopolitanism: Ethics in a World of Strangers* (New York: Norton, 2006), xv.

62. Carlyle coined the phrase "attenuated cosmopolitanism" in 1828 to describe the state of British poetry in the eighteenth century prior to the emergence of Robert Burns: "Even the English writers, most popular in Burns's time, were little distinguished for their literary patriotism, in this its best sense. A certain attenuated cosmopolitanism had, in good measure, taken place of the old insular home-feeling; literature was, as it were, without any local environment; was not nourished by the affections which spring from

a native soil." Thomas Carlyle, "Burns," in *Critical and Miscellaneous Essays* (London: Chapman and Hall, 1899), 1:286–87.

63. Charles Kingsley, "Mr and Mrs Browning," *Fraser's Magazine* 43 (1851): 175.

64. Robert J. C. Young, *Colonial Desire: Hybridity in Theory, Culture and Race* (London: Routledge, 1995), 57.

65. A. C. Swinburne, "To E. C. Stedman [A *Memoir*]," in *Major Poems and Selected Prose*, ed. Jerome McGann and Charles L. Sligh (New Haven: Yale University Press, 2004), 472.

66. Robert Buchanan, *The Fleshly School of Poetry and Other Phenomena of the Day* (1872; repr., New York: Garland, 1986), 86.

67. John Morley, Review of *Poems and Ballads* 22 (August 1866): 145–47; repr. in *Swinburne: The Critical Heritage*, ed. Clyde K. Hyder (London: Routledge & Kegan Paul, 1970), 23.

68. Quoted in Hyder, *Swinburne: The Critical Heritage*, 123.

69. Determined to make the study of race coalesce with his other ideals of tolerance, cultural openness, and European unity, Arnold sometimes leads himself into dubious claims. Among the benefits of inquiring into Europe's racial origins and tendencies, according to Arnold, would be "the strengthening of the feeling in us of Indo-Europeanism" (3:302)—a claim that begs the question of whether anyone, anywhere, has ever "felt" Indo-European. Frederic E. Faverty perhaps best captures Arnold's achievement and his limitations when it came to the study of race: "Even when his facts are wrong, or his premises unsound, or his conclusions questionable, his animating purpose is usually right. He desires not to divide races or nations, but to bring them together." *Matthew Arnold: The Ethnologist* (Evanston: Northwestern University Press, 1951), 11.

70. Arnold also applied this principle to artists themselves: "And yet just what constitutes special power and genius in a man seems often to be his blending with the basis of his national temperament, some additional gift or grace not proper to that temperament; Shakespeare's greatness is thus in his blending and openness and flexibility of spirit, not English, with the English basis" (3:358).

71. Citations of Morris's poetry, *The Earthly Paradise* excepted, refer to volume and page number in *The Collected Works of William Morris*, ed. May Morris (London: Longmans, 1910–15).

72. Tucker, for instance, sees a kind of racial retrenchment at work in Eliot's poem: "Gypsy and Jew and Christian and Moor alike find their identities and acts biologically foredoomed—and culturally policed, for good measures, within the embattled and racially polarized climate of Eliot's chosen milieu in late fifteenth-century Spain" (*Epic* 415).

73. One of Barrett Browning's earliest poems, in fact, *The Battle of Marathon* (1820), was in effect a pledge of support for Greek independence. See Simon Avery, "Audacious Beginnings: Elizabeth Barrett's Early Writings," in *Elizabeth Barrett Browning*, ed. Simon Avery and Rebecca Stott (London: Longman, 2003), 43–64, especially 54–56. Landor published numerous poems on international politics in *The Examiner* from the late 1840s until his death in 1864, including "To Kossuth" and "On Kossuth's Voyage to America." See *The Complete Works of Walter Savage Landor*, ed. Stephen Wheeler (London: Methuen, 1969), 15:54 and 60.

74. This of course does not mean that there is little to learn from British encounters with Europe's margins, which is precisely the focus of Brian Dolan's *Exploring European*

Frontiers: British Travellers in the Age of Enlightenment (Houndmills: Macmillan, 2000). As he reveals, British encounters with Russia, Eastern Europe, and Scandinavia "helped chart similarities and differences [between cultures] as perceived at the time. These in turn helped define what were considered shared, modern, European values or separate national achievements" (22).

75. In "Heinrich Heine," commenting on his subject's capacity to capture the contradictions of the German character, Arnold writes, "Is it possible to touch more delicately and happily both the weakness and strength of Germany;—pedantic, simple, enslaved, free, ridiculous, admirable Germany?" (3:123).

76. "Mr. Carlyle on the War," *The Times,* November 18, 1870: 8.

77. Robert Louis Stevenson, "Travel," in *The Collected Poems of Robert Louis Stevenson,* ed. Roger C. Lewis (Edinburgh: Edinburgh University Press, 2003), 27.

78. Tucker also notes the beginning of a "fallow period" for the production of epic in the 1890s before the genre underwent something of a resurgence in the Edwardian era (*Epic* 1).

79. Such a study could also devote greater attention than I do here to Swinburne's contemporaries Dante Gabriel and Christina Rossetti, who were, of course, themselves Anglo-European subjects and were deeply involved in translating between English and European poetic traditions.

80. Thomas Hardy, *The Life and Work of Thomas Hardy,* ed. Michael Millgate (London: Macmillan, 1984), 450. The book is Millgate's reedited version of two earlier biographies, *The Early Life of Thomas Hardy* (1928) and *The Later Years of Thomas Hardy* (1930), largely written by Hardy himself but published under the name of Hardy's second wife, Florence Emily Hardy.

81. *The Dynasts* forms Volume 4 and part of Volume 5 of *The Complete Poetical Works of Thomas Hardy,* ed. Samuel Hynes (Oxford: Oxford University Press, 1982–95). Verse passages will be noted by part, act, scene, and line number. Prose passages are cited by volume and page number.

82. Kant, *Political Writings,* 48

83. Friedrich Nietzsche, *Beyond Good and Evil,* trans. Judith Norman (Cambridge: Cambridge University Press, 2002), 148.

Chapter 2

1. Frederick L. Mulhauser, ed., *The Correspondence of Arthur Hugh Clough,* 2 vols. (Oxford: Clarendon, 1957). Additional citations of Clough's letters will be noted in the text; if the recipient or date of the letter is not clear from the context of the quotation, it is given in a note.

2. Clough to J. R. Lowell, January 20, 1858.

3. Clough in various comments on the poem warns against conflating Claude with himself, but clearly he dramatizes many of his own feelings and intellectual dilemmas through Claude. Thus, while it is important to be attuned to moments when Clough could be questioning Claude's impressions, I do not think it is necessary to qualify Claude's statements at every step. What Clough creates, in a sense, is an unreliable "unreliable narrator," a protagonist capable of satirizing himself, attuned to many of his *own* flaws and biases. Clough in this way adds another layer to the poem's trademark of

authoritative instability, a subject E. Warwick Slinn explores in his deconstructive reading of the poem in *The Discourse of Self in Victorian Poetry* (Charlottesville: University Press of Virginia, 1991). Claude, he argues, "becomes subsumed within a discourse of dynamic, shifting, and textualised process" (91). The line between author and persona, like that between language and truth, is continuously in flux.

4. From a posthumous review in *Macmillan's Magazine* (August 1862) by David Masson, qtd. in Michael Thorpe, *Clough: The Critical Heritage* (New York: Barnes and Noble, 1972), 150. With regard to the poem's literary antecedents, J. P. Phelan remarks, "Clough's employment of the epistolary form for this venture is . . . unique, but might possibly owe something to his small part in helping his friend Richard Monckton Milnes prepare the first edition of Keats's *Life, Letters, and Literary Remains* in 1848" (introduction to *Amours de Voyage*, in *Clough: Selected Poems*, 77). Clough also might have been familiar with Joseph Addison's "A Letter from Italy" (1701), which, like his poem, mixes travel with reflections on England's role in European politics: "'Tis Britain's care to watch o'er Europe's fate, / And hold in balance each contending state; / To threaten bold presumptuous kings with war, / And answer her afflicted neighbour's pray'r" (*The Poetical Works of Joseph Addison* [London: Cooke, 1796], 59). Matthew Reynolds suggests Thomas Moore's satirical *The Fudge Family in Paris* (1818) as another possible epistolary precedent (see *The Realms of Verse*, 152).

5. References to Clough's poems are to *Clough: Selected Poems*, ed. J. P. Phelan (London: Longman, 1995). Passages from *Amours de Voyage* are cited by canto and line number.

6. The poem's epistolary format has received much less attention in comparison to its other distinguishing formal feature—the hexameter. One notable exception is Matthew Reynolds, who, following Habermas, has argued that the epistolarity of *Amours de Voyage* works to emphasize Claude's inability to bridge public and private selves in meaningful ways: as a series of private letters exposed to the public, they underscore his absence from "the public field of narrative" and his failure to "achieve a sense of continuity between his own life and the processes of world history" (155). In an earlier article on Clough's divergence from Romantic period Grand Tour poetry, I commented on how the conditions of modern tourism and the post undercut any possibility of a "personal" letter in the poem: "As suggested by Claude's rapid-fire letters to Eustace, especially as he traces Mary Trevellyn's footsteps across Italy, the traveler on the continent was now more than ever a correspondent." In turn, "Trying to sound 'original' . . . becomes comically futile in *Amours de Voyage*" ("Beyond Where 'Byron Used to Ride': Locating the Victorian Travel Poet in Clough's *Amours de Voyage* and *Dipsychus*," *Philological Quarterly* 77, no. 4 [1998]: 385–86). By returning here to this subject, I hope to unpack the more pervasive ways that postal technologies inform notions of cosmopolitanism and identity in the poem.

7. The impact of the telegraph on communications and other aspects of nineteenth-century culture has been widely investigated, notably in Tom Standage's *The Victorian Internet: The Remarkable Story of the Telegraph and the Nineteenth Century's On-line Pioneers* (New York: Berkley Books, 1998) and, with greater historical depth, in Laura Otis's *Networking: Communicating with Bodies and Machines in the Nineteenth Century* (Ann Arbor: University of Michigan Press, 2001). As Otis claims, "Since the late 1840s, electronic communications networks have changed the way we see our bodies, our neighbors, and the world. For a century and a half, these networks have suggested webs, lead-

ing their users to think as though they were part of a net" (2). For all of its undeniable influence, however, the telegraph has perhaps misleadingly eclipsed postal reform in our historical understanding of Victorian communications revolutions. Even if it did not involve wires or electricity, postal reform was largely understood at the time as a *technical* innovation. In some sense, the telegraph and the penny post became twin technologies in the Victorian imagination, doing the same work of acceleration and consolidation of space. *Household Words,* for instance, in its inaugural issue, ran the first of what would become a series of approving articles on postal reform and the inner workings of the Central London Post Office. In "Valentine's Day at the Post-Office," Dickens and a companion follow the path of valentines they mailed earlier in the day: "As the visitors looked round they perceived their coloured envelopes—which were all addressed to Scotland—suddenly emerge from a chaotic heap, and lodge in the division marked 'general,' as magically as a conjurer causes any card you may choose to fly out of the whole pack" (Charles Dickens, with W. H. Willis, "Valentine's Day at the Post-Office," *Household Words,* 30 March 1850: 8). Around the same time, *Fraser's Magazine* ran a similar piece that marveled over the Central London Post Office as the epitome of modern organizational technology, an institution where "order, ingenuity, and intelligence reign." "The Post-Office" 41 (1850): 225.

8. Friedrich Nietzsche, *Human, All Too Human: A Book for Free Spirits,* trans. R. J. Hollingdale (Cambridge: Cambridge University Press, 1986), 174.

9. Barrett to Cornelius Matthews, April 28, 1843 (*BC* 7:93).

10. Howard Robinson quotes this passage as well in *The British Post Office: A History* (1948; repr., Westport, CT: Greenwood, 1970) to give an indication of the "revolution [that] had taken place" with the penny post (301).

11. Rowland Hill, *Post Office Reform: Its Importance and Practicability* (London: Charles Knight, 1837), 66–67.

12. "The Post-Office," 225–26.

13. Clough to A. P. Stanley, May 28, 1848.

14. Robinson, *The British Post Office,* 373.

15. Murray's *Handbook for Travellers in Central Italy* (London: John Murray, 1843) advises readers, "Foreign letters are despatched on Tuesday, Thursday, and Saturday." It also suggests, "Letters from England not directed to the care of a banker at Rome should be plainly and legibly directed according to the foreign usage" (250–51).

16. Clough to F. T. Palgrave, August 7, 1849; Clough to Ann Perfect Clough, May 29, 1849.

17. Bernhard Siegert, *Relays: Literature as an Epoch of the Postal System,* trans. Kevin Repp (Palo Alto: Stanford University Press, 1999), 117.

18. Ibid., 105.

19. Ibid., 9.

20. Ibid., 14. The popular uproar that ensued in 1844 after it was discovered that the Post Office had been forwarding some of Mazzini's correspondence to the Home Office for inspection also gives some sense of how highly the privacy of the mails was regarded. See Robinson, *The British Post Office,* 337–52.

21. "The Post-Office," 224.

22. David Singh Grewal, *Network Power: The Social Dynamics of Globalization* (New Haven: Yale University Press, 2008), 20.

23. Ibid., 18.

24. Thomas Babington Macaulay, *Selected Writings,* ed. John Clive and Thomas Pinney (Chicago: University of Chicago Press, 1972), 304–5. The post does not escape Macaulay's attention either, as he stresses the evolutionary progress of the Post Office as an institution since 1685 (305–7). As he notes in good statistical fashion, "It is . . . scarcely possible to doubt that the number of letters now conveyed by mail is seventy times the number which was so conveyed at the time of the accession of James the Second" (307).

25. Grewal, *Network Power,* 3.

26. Thomas Shairp to Clough, November 1849.

27. The *Handbook for Travellers in Central Italy* cites Byron far more often than any other British poet. As James Buzard argues, "The abstracting of a Byronic spirit from the political and historical contexts that figured in Byron's poetry enabled tourists to adopt Byronic gestures without any consideration of what might seem to us now the insistent political character of the verse." *The Beaten Track: European Tourism, Literature, and the Ways to "Culture" 1800–1900* (Oxford: Clarendon Press, 1993), 123.

28. Matthew Arnold to Clough, August 2, 1855 (*LMA* 1:322).

29. Erik Gray, "Clough and His Discontents: *Amours de Voyage* and the English Hexameter," *Literary Imagination: The Review of the Association of Literary Scholars and Critics* 6, no. 2 (2004): 200.

30. Shairp seems to have been particularly bothered by this feature of the poem: "Why this superabundance of oaths and other sweary words? They weaken the lines, are in bad taste and not good for yourself, if I may say so" (October 31, 1849; 1:275). In another letter sent shortly after, Shairp reiterated his complaint: "Not that I dislike your roughness, but then it should be more rock-like ruggedness not so slip-slop—not so many Well's and other monysyllables [*sic*], and not so many *oaths* above all" (November 1849; 1:277).

31. In a similar vein, Clough reassured his mother, "We are all quite safe and comfortable, with British flags hanging out of our windows, and Lord Napier, an attaché of the British Embassy at Naples, has been here and is at present I believe at Palo, a fort between this and Civita Vecchia, where the Bull-dog, H.M.S. is lying, and has arranged with Marshal Oudinot that his troops are to behave politely to us" (May 11, 1849; 1:254).

32. Clough's own experience offers further testimony on this score. Frustrated with the anti-Roman bias shown by French and British newspapers, he decided to compose his own account of the destruction left by the bombardment of 22 June. Clough concluded, sardonically, that "however skillful French generals may be in their *ménagement* of bombs, I find French journals are still more so in their *ménagement* of facts" (see Patrick Scott, ed., *Amours de Voyage,* Appendix 2 [St. Lucia: University of Queensland Press, 1974], 79–80). Clough sent the account to Palgrave, and his instructions to him are themselves telling: "do what you will with [it]. Edify a private circle or offer to an obscure corner of an obscure evening print" (July 6, 1849; qtd. in Scott 79 but not included in Mulhauser's edition of Clough's letters). Uncertain whether to regard his work as essentially private or public, Clough leaves the decision to his friend (who, apparently, did not attempt to publish it).

33. Stephanie Kuduk Weiner, *Republican Politics and English Poetry, 1789–1874,* 124.

34. John Goode, "1848 and the Strange Disease of Modern Love," in *Literature and Politics in the Nineteenth Century,* ed. John Lucas (London: Methuen, 1971), 63.

35. Ibid., 64.

36. J. P. Phelan, ed., *Clough: Selected Poems*, 111n13.

37. Raymond Williams, *The English Novel from Dickens to Lawrence* (Oxford: Oxford University Press, 1970), 16.

38. Arthur Hugh Clough, "The Beneficial and Harmful Effects of Foreign Trade," in *Selected Prose Works of Arthur Hugh Clough*, ed. Buckner B. Trawick (Tuscaloosa: University of Alabama Press, 1964), 206, 207. The essay, from Clough's 1839–40 Balliol notebook, was not published in his lifetime. Marx and Engels write, "The need of a constantly expanding market for its products chases the bourgeoisie over the whole surface of the globe. It must nestle everywhere, settle everywhere, establish connexions everywhere. The bourgeoisie has through its exploitation of the world-market given a cosmopolitan character to production and consumption in every country." They add, "In place of the old local and national seclusion and self-sufficiency, we have intercourse in every direction, universal inter-dependence of nations." *The Marx-Engels Reader*, 2nd ed., ed. Robert C. Tucker (New York: Norton, 1978), 476.

39. Clough's essay on foreign trade again anticipates the issue he would attempt to work out in *Amours de Voyage*. "Commerce has doubtless its benefits: It gives men if not so much in our times the enlarged and capacious mind free from narrow and exclusive prejudice" (207).

40. Gertrude Himmelfarb, "The Illusions of Cosmopolitanism," in *For Love of Country: Debating the Limits of Patriotism*, ed. Martha C. Nussbaum (Boston: Beacon Press, 1996), 77.

41. Clough to Edward Hawkins, February 28, 1849.

42. Arthur Hugh Clough, "Notes on the Religious Tradition," in *Selected Prose Works*, 293. Clough's essay was first published under this title in *The Poems and Prose Remains of Arthur Hugh Clough* (1869).

43. Martha C. Nussbaum, "Patriotism and Cosmopolitanism," in *For Love of Country*, 15. I am also reminded in this context of Amanda Anderson's insistence that "cosmopolitanism is a flexible term, whose forms of detachment and multiple affiliation can be variously articulated and variously motivated. In general, cosmopolitanism endorses reflective distance from one's cultural affiliations, a broad understanding of other cultures and customs, and a belief in universal humanity." "Cosmopolitanism, Universalism, and the Divided Legacies of Modernity," in Cheah and Robbins, 267.

44. Robert Micklus offers the interesting possibility that Mary and Claude are *too* devoted to themselves, "too afraid of love—and life—to experience its consummation." The poem thus ends as it should: "Mary and Claude are too temperamentally alike to make their marriage even desirable" ("A Voyage of Juxtapositions: The Dynamic World of *Amours de Voyage*," *Victorian Poetry* 18 [1980]: 411). What I am suggesting here is that their independence of mind is also what *draws* them together and makes their final separation so difficult for them to cope with. While it may never reach Werther-like proportions, their uncertain longing for each other persists to the end of the poem.

45. Clough to F. J. Child, April 16, 1858.

46. If this interpretation seems like a stretch, it is worth recalling that Clough made a similar point in *Dipsychus* with even more suggestive language: "Verses! well they are made, so let them go. / No more, if I can help. This is one way / The procreant heat and fervour of our youth / Escapes, in puff and smoke, and shapeless words / Of mere ejaculation, nothing worth" (2.2.21–25).

47. The poem's absent auditor, as Dorothy Mermin suggests, in effect allows it to be read as a "dramatic monologue or sequence of monologues" (*The Audience in the Poem: Five Victorian Poets*. New Brunswick: Rutgers University Press, 1983), 112.

48. Siegert dwells at length on this concept and offers a letter from Franz Kafka as an example of a "letter reflecting on the (im)possibility of writing letters." Kafka calls letters "an intercourse with ghosts, and not only with the ghost of the recipient but also with one's own ghost which develops between the lines of the letter one is writing" (4).

49. Alfred, Lord Tennyson, *In Memoriam, A. H. H.,* in *Tennyson's Poetry,* 2nd ed., ed. Robert W. Hill (New York: Norton, 1999), 203–91. This passage also includes one of Tennyson's more notable alterations to the poem—the decision to replace "his" with "the" in line 36 (See Hill, 263–64n7). The original conveys an even stronger sense of personal connection through the letter.

50. Armstrong's chapter on Clough from her *Victorian Poetry: Poetry, Poetics and Politics* is entitled "The Radical in Crisis: Clough." She focuses primarily on Clough's free-wheeling experimentation with language and form in *The Bothie,* calling it "a study of the upper-class radical and intellectual" (178).

51. For Baudelaire, the flâneur, like the dandy, "is the last flicker of heroism in decadent ages" ("The Painter of Modern Life," *Baudelaire: Selected Writings on Art and Artists,* trans. P. E. Charvet [Cambridge: Cambridge University Press, 1972], 421). Commenting on Baudelaire himself as an example, Chris Jenks writes that the flâneur "walks at will, freely and seemingly without purpose, but simultaneously with an inquisitive wonder and an infinite capacity to absorb the activities of the collective." "Watching Your Step: The History and Practice of the Flâneur," in *Visual Culture,* ed. Chris Jenks (New York: Routledge, 1995), 146.

52. Clough and Shairp exchanged these comments in letters written in October and November 1849.

53. The letter is of uncertain date. Mulhauser suggests August or September 1848.

54. At the beginning of *Dipsychus,* set in Venice, Clough would return to the same feeling: "The scene is different and the Place, the air / Tastes of the nearer north; the people too / Not perfect southern levity: wherefore then / Should those old verses come into my mind / I made last year at Naples[?]" (1–5).

55. Swinburne's only published comments on Clough are actually quite negative, although as Michael Thorpe suggests, they are directed more at his admirers than at his poetry, "if, indeed, he had read it" (*Clough: The Critical Heritage,* 16). In an October 1891 article on "Social Verse" for the *Forum,* Swinburne remarked, "Literary history will hardly care to remember or to register the fact that there was a bad poet named Clough, whom his friends found it useless to puff: for the public, if dull, has not quite such a skull as belongs to believers in Clough" (qtd. in Thorpe, 340).

56. Fittingly, perhaps, the poem would not see print for a number of years and only then overseas, in the *Atlantic Monthly,* where it ran in serial from February to May 1858.

57. "The millenium, as Matt says, won't come this bout," Clough had written to Tom Arnold in February 1849, summing up their opinion on developments in France. "I am myself much more inclined to be patient and make allowance for existing necessities than I was" (1:243).

58. Arnold to Clough, March 21, 1853 (*LMA* 1:258).

59. Arnold to Clough, August 2, 1855 (*LMA* 1:322).

60. Arnold, of course, attempted to pay better tribute to their long-standing and

complex relationship in his elegy on Clough, "Thyrsis" (1866), and their clashes of opinion on poetry, culture, and politics have been variously investigated by biographers and critics. Clough, for instance, strongly identified with the work of Alexander Smith, but as Charles LaPorte suggests, Arnold's condemnation of the spasmodic poet, an opinion reinforced by Clough's American friends including James Russell Lowell, may have convinced him to abandon writing poetry altogether ("Spasmodic Poetics and Clough's Apostasies" *Victorian Poetry* 42, no. 4 [2004]: 532). Other revealing recent studies of their relationship include Joseph Bristow's, "'Love, Let Us Be True to One Another': Matthew Arnold, Arthur Hugh Clough, and 'Our Aqueous Ages,'" *Literature and History* 4, no. 1 (1995): 27–49, and Joseph Phelan's, "Clough, Arnold, Béranger, and the Legacy of 1848," *SEL: Studies in English Literature, 1500–1900* 46, no. 4 (2006): 833–48.

    61. Arnold to Clough, February 12, 1853 (*LMA* 1:254).

Chapter 3

    1. Barrett Browning to Mitford, November 5–8, 1846 (*BC* 14:38). Additional citations of Barrett Browning's letters will be noted in the text; if the recipient or date of the letter is not clear from the context of the quotation, it is given in a note.

    2. Barrett Browning to Hugh Stuart Boyd, June 9, 1832.

    3. Because of the highly successful "Homes of England," Hemans still tends to be linked with a domestic, nationalist poetic agenda, but as Susan Brown argues, *Records of Woman* (1828) and *Songs of the Affections* (1830) propound "the idea of a transnational and transhistorical womanhood" ("The Victorian Poetess," in Bristow, 188). One such poem would be "Corinna at the Capitol," which, like L.E.L.'s "The Improvisatrice," exemplifies what Angela Esterhammer calls the "*cosmopolitan improvvisatore*—no longer an Italian 'curiosity,' but a widespread trope for the problematics of spontaneity, performance, and identity as they play themselves out on the international Romantic stage." "The Cosmopolitan *Improvvisatore*: Spontaneity and Performance in Romantic Poetics," *European Romantic Review* 16, no. 2 (2005): 157.

    4. Jeanne Moskal quotes the *Observer* review in her introductory note to Shelley's *Rambles* in *The Novels and Selected Works of Mary Shelley* (London: William Pickering, 1996), 8:53. Barrett Browning later loaned Shelley's book to Robert, who was critical of it for different reasons, as I discuss in the next chapter. Shelley tentatively laid out her political aims in the preface: "When I reached Italy . . . I found that I could say little of Florence and Rome, as far as regarded the cities themselves, that had not been said so often and so well before, that I was satisfied to select from my letters such portions merely as touched upon subjects that I had not found mentioned elsewhere. It was otherwise as regarded the people, especially in a political point of view; and in treating of them my scope grew more serious" (8:65). Shelley nonetheless felt compelled to reassure readers, "my book does not pretend to be a political history or dissertation" (8:70).

    5. Letter to George Barrett, February 2, 1852. Paul Landis, ed., *Letters of the Brownings to George Barrett* (Urbana: University of Illinois Press, 1958), 165.

    6. Ibid., April 18, 1860, 226.

    7. In this way, my study contributes to the ongoing critical discussion of Barrett Browning's commitment to Italian nationalism, one launched in many ways by Sandra

M. Gilbert's 1984 essay "From *Patria* to *Matria:* Elizabeth Barrett Browning's Risorgimento," in *PMLA* 99, no. 2 (1984): 194–211. More recent work includes Matthew Reynolds's chapter on Barrett Browning in *The Realms of Verse,* which I discuss in relation to *Casa Guidi Windows,* along with other recent essays on the poem. Also noteworthy is Alison Chapman's "The Expatriate Poetess: Nationhood, Poetics and Politics," in *Victorian Women Poets* (Cambridge: D. S. Brewer, 2003), ed. Alison Chapman (57–77), which examines Barrett Browning's work alongside that of other Victorian women poets in Italy, including Eliza Ogilvy and Theodosia Garrow Trollope. Chapman argues that the idea of the poetess in the nineteenth century is itself "predicated on foreignness: while Felicia Hemans and Joanna Baillie are seen as the epitome of the English poetess, her origins are given as the legendary figures of Sappho and Corinne." Later poets capitalized on this hybrid identity to adopt a more radical stance on Italy's behalf, with the poetess now "signifying her patriotism paradoxically through devotion to nations not her own" (59). As stated above, my aim here is to look more closely at how Barrett Browning comes to question even this form of exported Anglo-Italian patriotism, pursuing instead a cosmopolitanism that would be less dependent on forms of national allegiance.

8. Scott Malcomson, in "The Varieties of Cosmopolitan Experience" (Cheah and Robbins, 233–45), employs the phrase "actually existing cosmopolitanism" to denote less abstract forms of cosmopolitanism experienced by people whose way of life or economic circumstances compel them to move regularly between borders and cultures. Among such cosmopolites he includes some types of missionaries, merchants, and, above all, immigrants, who tend to show the most concern for negotiating different forms of cultural allegiance (238–39).

9. Carol A. Breckenridge et al., introduction to *Cosmopolitanism* (Durham: Duke University Press, 2002), 8–9. Shaheem Black utilizes "cosmofeminism" along similar lines in relation to Japanese author Ruth L. Ozeki, whose work "searches for ways that women might develop usable alliances across national, racial, and sexual divides to combat the spread of global problems. It is this aspiration—a particular form of transnational perception—that I call cosmofeminism." "Fertile Cosmofeminism: Ruth L. Ozeki and Transnational Reproduction," *Meridians: Feminism, Race, Transnationalism* 5, no. 1 (2004): 228.

10. For another angle on the concept of citizenship in Barrett Browning, see Richard Cronin, "*Casa Guidi Windows:* Elizabeth Barrett Browning, Italy, and the Poetry of Citizenship" (in Chapman and Stabler, 35–50), where he notes that Barrett Browning, unlike most other Victorian poets, wholeheartedly embraced the ideals of the French Revolution and sought to adapt its notions of citizenship and civic responsibility to her own work. In *Casa Guidi Windows,* for example, "citizenship is realised in an unending process of negotiation by means of which the individual defines and redefines her place within the body politic" (41). Cosmopolitanism or "world citizenship," as I explain above, represents a different kind of civic identity, one that I contend is only partially realized in *Casa Guidi Windows.*

11. Steven Vertovec and Robin Cohen, "Introduction: Conceiving Cosmopolitanism," in *Conceiving Cosmopolitanism: Theory, Context, and Practice,* ed. Steven Vertovec and Robin Cohen (Oxford: Oxford University Press, 2002), 4.

12. As even a casual review of her letters reveals, this textual encounter with Europe had been well underway long before Barrett Browning actually took up residence on the

continent. She was a skilled reader and translator of ancient and modern languages alike, with a particular admiration for contemporary French novels. Once abroad, she continued to develop expertise as a reader of German and Italian and seems to have become relatively fluent in the latter, based on descriptions in her letters. For a fuller account of her reading, the best overall source probably remains Gardner B. Taplin's biography, *The Life of Elizabeth Barrett Browning* (London: John Murray, 1957).

13. Benjamin Disraeli, Address to the National Union of Conservative and Constitutional Associations, Crystal Palace, London, June 24, 1872, in *Victorian Prose: An Anthology*, eds. Rosemary J. Mundhenk and LuAnn McCracken Fletcher (New York: Columbia University Press, 1999), 116, 119.

14. Largely ignored for much of the Barrett Browning revival of the past quarter-century, *Casa Guidi Windows* garnered significant new attention and praise from critics beginning in the 1990s. Steve Dillon and Katherine Frank's "Defenestrations of the Eye: Flow, Fire, and Sacrifice in *Casa Guidi Windows*" (*Victorian Poetry* 35, no. 4 [1997]: 471–92) was the first of a number of critical investigations into the poem's sophisticated use of visual metaphors. More recently, Esther Schor has taken up the poem's melding of artistic and political goals, suggesting that "[b]y means of an analogy between poetic making and the making of Italy, Barrett Browning shrewdly examines the complimentary roles of self-conscious intention and inspiration in the making of both nations and poems" ("The Poetics of Politics: Barrett Browning's *Casa Guidi Windows*," *Tulsa Studies in Women's Literature* 17, no. 2 [1998]: 309–10). Helen Groth, in "A Different Look—Visual Technologies and the Making of History in Elizabeth Barrett Browning's *Casa Guidi Windows*," argues that the daguerreotype "provides . . . an important discursive context for the aesthetic and political arguments" of the poem, "structurally and experientially enacting the political argument that Italy must bring past and present together to take possession of herself as a unified nation in the future" (*Textual Practice* 14, no. 1 [2000]: 33). In the latest of these sight-oriented readings of the poem, Isobel Armstrong describes it as an experimental effort to craft "a new genre of urban writing," adding that "[t]o see a political event through a window is an experience peculiar to nineteenth-century modernity: intrinsic to this modernity is that the very act of looking through the window becomes part of the political experience itself" ("*Casa Guidi Windows*: Spectacle and Politics in 1851," in Chapman and Stabler, 51).

15. Leigh Coral Harris, "From *Mythos* to *Logos*: Political Aesthetics and Liminal Poetics in Elizabeth Barrett Browning's *Casa Guidi Windows*," *Victorian Literature and Culture* 28 (2000): 117.

16. Ibid., 109.

17. It is important that my claim here not be confused with charges made by earlier critics that *Casa Guidi Windows* was politically naive and not carefully conceived. See, for example, William Irvine and Park Honan, who labeled the poem "a signal instance of the way in which the use of verse pumps Elizabeth up beyond any possibility of coherent and rational discussion" (*The Book, the Ring, and the Poet: A Biography of Robert Browning* [New York: McGraw-Hill, 1974], 253–54). Their comments, in some sense, are a reminder of how admirably Barrett Browning has been served since by her defenders, beginning with Julia Markus's 1977 introduction to the Browning Institute edition of the poem, in which she carefully refutes the charge that Barrett Browning was uninformed about political events of the day. Markus reiterates her defense in *Dared and*

Done: The Marriage of Elizabeth Barrett Browning and Robert Browning (Athens: Ohio University Press, 1995), 131–38.

18. Benedict Anderson, *Imagined Communities: Reflections on the Origin and Spread of Nationalism* (London: Verso, 1983), 19.

19. Marianne Perkins, *Nation and Word 1770–1850: Religious and Metaphysical Language in European National Consciousness* (London: Ashgate, 1999), 132.

20. Giuseppe Mazzini, *The Duties of Man* (London: Dent, 1966), 55.

21. Sydney Dobell, *The Poetical Works of Sydney Dobell*, ed. John Nichol (London: Smith, Elder, 1875), 1:185.

22. Martha Westwater quotes Mazzini's letter to Dobell in *The Spasmodic Career of Sydney Dobell* (Lanham, MD: University Press of America, 1992), 62. There is no record of Barrett Browning's opinion of the poem, although she did write to Mitford, "Have you read a poem called the *Roman,* which was praised highly in the Athenaeum, but did not seem to Robert to justify the praise in the passages extracted. . . . Have you heard anything about it or seen?" (December 13, 1850; *BC* 16:246).

23. Habermas speaks of the need "to give priority to a cosmopolitan understanding of the nation as a nation of citizens over and against an ethnocentric interpretation of the nation as a prepolitical entity." "The European Nation-state—Its Achievements and Its Limits: On the Past and Future of Sovereignty and Citizenship," in *Mapping the Nation,* ed. Gopal Balakrishnan (London: Verso, 1996), 287.

24. Maura O'Connor, *The Romance of Italy and the English Political Imagination* (New York: St. Martin's, 1998), 94.

25. Reynolds, *The Realms of Verse,* 91.

26. Simon Avery, "'Twixt Church and Palace of a Florence Street': Elizabeth Barrett Browning and Italy," in *Elizabeth Barrett Browning,* ed. Simon Avery and Rebecca Stott (London: Longman, 2003), 170.

27. Pheng Cheah, "The Cosmopolitical—Today," in Cheah and Robbins, 25.

28. As Maria Frawley notes, Victorian women travel writers typically denied being motivated by any wish to contribute to more masculinized domains of knowledge such as political philosophy or science: "If perceived as being a means to an end, particularly a published end, then it [travel] attains the status of work—and becomes problematic." *A Wider Range: Travel Writing by Women in Victorian England* (Rutherford, NJ: Fairleigh-Dickinson University Press, 1994), 52.

29. Review of *Casa Guidi Windows, Eclectic Review* (September 1851): 306.

30. Review of *Casa Guidi Windows, The Athenaeum* (June 1851): 598.

31. Aurora's mixed identity, of course, is also Barrett Browning's way of paying homage to *Corinne,* a debt reexamined more fully by Linda Lewis in *Germaine de Staël, George Sand, and the Victorian Woman Artist* (Columbia: University of Missouri Press, 2003). Staël and Sand both provided Barrett Browning with role models of women intellectuals with a broadly European outlook and influence.

32. Barrett Browning's effort to craft a novel-poem has been the focus of a good deal of critical commentary, most recently Meg Tasker's "*Aurora Leigh:* Elizabeth Barrett Browning's Novel Approach to the Woman Poet" (*Tradition and the Poetics of Self in Nineteenth-Century Women's Poetry,* ed. Barbara Garlick [Amsterdam–New York: Rodopi, 2002], 32). While one should always be cautious when deploying Bakhtin's comparison of the novel and epic, this is one case, as she reveals, where his claim that "the dialogic quality of the novel is a democratic one" bears out, especially in Barrett Browning's dramatization of Marian.

33. Alison Chapman notes an intriguing echo of this passage in Barrett Browning's later poem "A Musical Instrument": "The lily metaphor is clearly that of the water lily, but here, as in 'A Musical Instrument,' there is also a reference to the Tuscan civic emblem of the lily, although of a different genus (the iris)." This connection lends an added political significance to the latter poem, with Pan's careless destruction of lilies (see lines 1–6) being characteristic of "those poets chastised in Barrett Browning's political poetry for creating an aestheticized nation of out Italy's grief and pain." "'In Our Own Blood Drenched the Pen': Italy and Sensibility in Elizabeth Barrett Browning's *Last Poems* (1862)," *Women's Writing: The Elizabethan to the Victorian Period* 10, no. 2 (2003): 278.

34. Buzard, *The Beaten Track,* 6.

35. Marian, as Joyce Zanona carefully demonstrates, is "a new kind of muse, one who is fully integrated with the poet, a subject in her own right" ("'The Embodied Muse': Elizabeth Barrett Browning's *Aurora Leigh* and Feminist Poetics," *Tulsa Studies in Women's Literature* 8 [1989]: 243). In some sense, what I am doing here is expanding on Zanona's insight into how Marian shapes the treatment of gender and class issues in the poem. Marian and Aurora's status as displaced co-travelers creates an important point of identification between their characters; this shared identity is also what brings them together in terms of the plot, allowing for a seemingly chance encounter that, in reality, confirms the connection they had shared all along. In this way, travel functions as a bridge between two characters sharply separated by class, a bridge that facilitates the integration of poet and subject to which Zanona alludes.

36. James Clifford, "Traveling Cultures," in *Cultural Studies,* ed. Lawrence Grossberg et al. (New York: Routledge, 1992), 107.

37. Ibid., 108.

38. Review of *Aurora Leigh, Literary Gazette* (November 1856): 918.

39. Ibid., 917.

40. There is no single source for this objection, since almost every critical analysis of *Aurora Leigh* at some point attempts to untangle the complex way that the poem resolves itself. The two competing points of view are perhaps best exemplified, first, by Sandra Gilbert and Susan Gubar's *The Madwoman in the Attic: The Woman Writer and the Nineteenth-Century Literary Imagination* (New Haven: Yale University Press, 1979), which stresses how Barrett Browning, in a bow to Victorian patriarchy, undermines Aurora's authority by making Romney the instigator and voice of her revitalized poetics. At the other end of the spectrum, Herbert F. Tucker argues that Romney, in effect, disappears within Aurora's vocation as epic poet: "She herself becomes, in heralding its emergence, the dawning New Jerusalem, the city that may be *of* God and man but that *is* a woman. It is finally Aurora who 'makes all new'" ("*Aurora Leigh:* Epic Solutions to Novel Ends," in *Famous Last Words: Changes in Gender and Narrative Closure,* ed. Alison Booth [Charlottesville: University of Virginia Press, 1993], 70). Jonah Siegel adds another pillar to the argument in support of Aurora's marriage in *Haunted Museum: Longing, Travel, and the Art-Romance Tradition* (Princeton: Princeton University Press, 2005), noting that her union with Romney "may be read as a revision of the commitment to disappointment" that typifies earlier art romances such as *Corinne:* "by the end of the epic the poet will not only be recognized for her genius; she will be allowed to win the clear commitment and presence of Romney, the man she loves. Indeed, among the simple novelties of the text in the tradition is that Aurora will be allowed to *live* past the end of the story" (78).

41. Reynolds, *The Realms of Verse,* 114.

42. I explore these efforts more closely in an earlier article, "'He Shall Be a "Citizen

of the World"': Cosmopolitanism and the Education of Pen Browning," *Browning Society Notes* 32 (2007): 74–82. Despite Robert's concerns about the feminine appearance of Pen's clothes and long hair, he always supported their decision to give him a broad education in European languages and culture. Robert, in fact, once revealed to George Barrett that he hoped Pen would eventually pursue a career as a diplomat (June 17, 1870; *Letters to George Barrett,* 293). Beverly Taylor offers further insight into Pen's influence on Barrett Browning's poetry and her overall use of child figures in "Elizabeth Barrett Browning and the Politics of Childhood," *Victorian Poetry* 46, no. 4 (2008): 405–27.

43. Barrett Browning to Arabella Barrett, April 12, 1858, in *The Letters of Elizabeth Barrett Browning to Her Sister Arabella* (2:347). Editor Scott Lewis directs the reader to other letters expressing similar sentiments, including one to her sister Henrietta avowing that "we must make our boys familiar with living languages . . . an intelligent man mustn't be simply an Englishman or a Frenchman but a citizen of all countries" (qtd. in *Letters to Arabella,* 2:348n10).

44. As Barrett Browning predicted, and as noted in chapter 1, critics in England greeted the volume with hostility, earning her the label "denationalized fanatic" in the *Saturday Review. Blackwood's* added, "we regret, for her sake, that she has fallen into the error of publishing anything so ineffably bad, . . . so strangely blind, if we look upon it as a political confession of faith—or so utterly unfair to England and English feeling" ("Poetical Aberrations," *Blackwood's Edinburgh Magazine* [April 1860]: 491). These negative reviews were inspired mostly by "A Curse for a Nation," which many misinterpreted as being directed at England for not assisting Italy more vigorously. Barrett Browning later clarified in a letter to the *Athenaeum* that the poem was targeted more at the slave-holding United States. Like "The Runaway Slave at Pilgrim's Point," the poem reminds us that Barrett Browning's global vision stretched across the Atlantic as well, although I am interested here primarily in Europe as the testing ground for her cosmopolitan poetics. For more on her connection to the transatlantic anti-slavery movement, see Marjorie Stone, "Elizabeth Barrett Browning and the Garrisonians: 'The Runaway Slave at Pilgrim's Point,' the Boston Female Anti-Slavery Society, and Abolitionist Discourse in the Liberty Bell," in *Victorian Women Poets,* ed. Alison Chapman, 33–55.

45. Elizabeth Woodworth, "'I Cry Aloud in my Poet-Passion': Elizabeth Barrett Browning Claiming Political 'Place' through *Poems before Congress,*" *Browning Society Notes* 32 (2007): 42, 43. Katherine Montwieler also devotes new attention to *Poems before Congress,* focusing on its concern for "how the events that structure women's lives— courtship, motherhood, and widowhood—can structure political events." "Domestic Politics: Gender, Protest, and Elizabeth Barrett Browning's *Poems before Congress,*" *Tulsa Studies in Women's Literature* 24 (2005): 296.

46. Julia Kristeva, *Nations without Nationalism,* trans. Leon S. Roudiez (New York: Columbia University Press, 1993), 41.

47. Barrett Browning to Julia Martin, January 23, 1837.

48. Benedict Anderson, *Imagined Communities,* 140.

49. Lewis, *Elizabeth Barrett Browning's Spiritual Progress,* 13.

50. Tricia Lootens, "Victorian Poetry and Patriotism," in Bristow, 263.

51. Chapman, "In Our Own Blood," 282.

52. Julia Kristeva, *Crisis of the European Subject,* trans. Susan Fairfield (New York: Other Press, 2000), 106.

53. Barrett Browning to Arabella Barrett, June 11, 1861, in *Letters to Arabella* (2:538).

54. Bruce Robbins, *Feeling Global: Internationalism in Distress* (New York: New York University Press, 1999), 172.

Chapter 4

1. Browning to Isa Blagden, August 19, 1870, in *Dearest Isa: Robert Browning's Letters to Isabella Blagden,* ed. Edward C. McAleer (Austin: University of Texas Press, 1951), 342. Further references to Browning letters in this chapter, unless otherwise indicated, are to this source and are cited parenthetically.

2. My description of this event is based primarily on two sources: William Irvine and Park Honan, *The Book, the Ring, and the Poet: A Biography of Robert Browning,* 454–56, and Roy E. Gridley, *The Brownings and France: A Chronicle with Commentary* (London: Athlone, 1982), 257–60. One early biography, W. Hall Griffin and H. C. Minchin, *The Life of Robert Browning* (London: Methuen, 1910; revised 1938; repr., Hamden, CT: Archon Books, 1966), claims that Browning had in fact been "taken for a German spy" (243). Their source for this supposition might be Milsand's daughter, Marie Blanc-Milsand, who had written earlier that "some peasants in a neighboring village . . . mistaking the foreign accent of Browning, thought him to be a Prussian spy" (Th. Bentzon [pseud.], "A French Friend of Browning—Joseph Milsand," *Scribner's Magazine* 20 [July 1896]: 117). Perhaps because of the lack of specific details in these accounts, Irvine and Honan cast doubt on the spy story and suggest instead that it was Milsand's general concern that induced Browning's flight (456).

3. Browning to Isa Blagden, September 19, 1872, in *Dearest Isa,* 385.

4. Examples of this kind of verse abound, but the most notorious in its day might have been John Edmund Reade's *Italy* (1838), which *Fraser's Magazine* panned as a "sort of metrical history of his travels. . . . The tourist in rhyme cannot, of course, stoop so low as to say anything about the existing state of society; but a picture or a statue always acts upon him like an extra-infusion of carbonic acid gas into a bottle of beer; he fizzes for a moment internally, and then out goes the cork with a crash!" (Review of *Italy* and *The Deluge,* by John Edmund Reade, *Fraser's Magazine* 20 [1839]: 760). In a letter to Mary Russell Mitford that reveals her impressions of the *Fraser's* critique, Barrett Browning, while expressing some sympathy for Reade, noted that he seemed "a phenomenon of unconscious imitation" (August 12, 1843; *BC* 7:279) and in a later letter referred to Reade's poem sarcastically as the "Grecian column" (October 16, 1844; *BC* 9:188).

5. Robert Browning, *The Ring and the Book,* ed. Richard D. Altick (Harmondsworth: Penguin, 1967). I discuss the poem's relationship to nineteenth-century touristic practices at greater length in a separate piece, "Authenticating Italy: Poetry, Tourism, and Browning's *The Ring and the Book,*" *Journal of Anglo-Italian Studies* 8 (2006): 115–28.

6. Amanda Anderson, "Cosmopolitanism, Universalism, and the Divided Legacies of Modernity," in Cheah and Robbins, 268.

7. Gloria Anzaldúa's *Borderlands/La Frontera: The New Mestiza,* 3rd ed. (San Francisco: Aunt Lute Books, 2007), theorizes borders in a way that can be helpful for understanding Browning, despite the authors' different historical and cultural contexts. As she explains, "an Aztec word meaning torn between ways, *la mestiza* is a product of the

transfer of the cultural and spiritual values of one group to another." The border subject, culturally speaking, lives in a state of simultaneous opportunity and anxiety: "Like others having or living in more than one culture, we get multiple, often opposing messages. The coming together of two self-consistent but habitually incompatible frames of reference causes *un choque,* a cultural collision" (100). Similarly, in Browning, the most revealing moments of cross-cultural engagement tend to take the form of disruptions—moments that challenge predisposed cultural assumptions and compel the poet to reexamine his own investment in those assumptions.

8. See Claire A. Simmons, *Eyes across the Channel: French Revolutions, Party History, and British Writing, 1830–1882* (Amsterdam: Harwood Academic Publishers, 2000), 199–204. As much as a mile had been dug in each direction before work was abandoned in 1882. Browning was one of a number of prominent figures from across the political and social spectrum who signed an anti-tunnel petition prepared by James Knowles, the editor of *The Nineteenth Century,* which spearheaded opposition to the project (Simmons 204). The specific reasons that led Browning to sign are not clear, but isolationism was not necessarily the root cause of opposition. The staggering costs of the project and the potential for serious accidents were also among the concerns expressed by some. See also my comments on Swinburne's opposition in the next chapter.

9. Gridley makes the connection to naturalism, suggesting that "in choice of subject, mode of analysis, attribution of motive, and characterization, Browning had created a kind of metrical naturalistic novel" (282). Brendan Kenny's "Browning as Cultural Critic: *Red Cotton Night-Cap Country*" (*Browning Institute Studies* 6 [1978]: 137–62) stresses that Browning's aim was to produce a "radical critique of French culture" (146), and that such a critique is best delivered by an outsider, one capable of "escaping the rigidities of an alien culture because, as an artist, he was consistently involved in fighting against the rigidities of his own" (160).

10. Browning to Isa Blagden, January 19, 1872, in *Dearest Isa,* 372.

11. Since "contact zone" may more readily summon to mind the sorts of colonial encounters that form the focus of Pratt's *Imperial Eyes,* it is worth recalling that she turns to this concept precisely to avoid slipping into the generalization that all such meetings were one-sided or simply coercive. She intends the concept to encompass as well the complex patterns of "copresence, interaction, [and] interlocking understandings" that emerge among travelers and those who inhabit their destinations (7).

12. As Matthew Reynolds reminds us in *The Realms of Verse,* Browning himself once said of his relationship with Italy that "one leans out the more widely over one's neighbour's field for being effectually rooted in one's own garden" (*Browning to His American Friends: Letters between the Brownings, the Storys and James Russell Lowell 1841–1890,* ed. Gertrude Reese Hudson [New York: Barnes and Noble, 1965], 76; qtd. in Reynolds, 157). In glossing this remark, Reynolds suggests that Browning's Italian poems embody precisely this kind of distancing: "The poems are thought of, not as creations of hybrid nationality, but as images of unmitigated Italianness, which ask English readers, as they incline over Browning's pages, to lean out over their neighbor's field" (158). In the France of *Red Cotton Night-Cap Country,* if Browning still does not cultivate a kind of Anglo-French hybridity, he does, I suggest, do more than lean over from a distance. With respect to France, it might be more fitting to imagine Browning standing at the border itself—becoming a part of what he observes, even if he does not undergo complete immersion.

13. Donald S. Hair, *Robert Browning's Language* (Toronto: Toronto University Press, 1999), 257–58.

14. Milsand's piece on Browning was one of a three-part survey of contemporary English poetry, "La Poesie Anglaise depuis Byron: II—Browning" (*Revue des Deux Mondes* 11 [1851]: 661–89), with the first part devoted to Tennyson and the third to Barrett Browning. The depth of the Brownings' gratitude is captured in a January 1852 letter Elizabeth sent to Milsand, in which she expressed her hope that he would become their "friend in the good warm sense of that word; the true enduring sense of it." She added, "For my own part, long before you had been kind to me, I was bound to you as the critic who of all others, in or out of England, had approached my husband's poetry in the most philosophical spirit and with the most ardent comprehension" (*BC* 17:239; qtd. in Bentzon [Blanc-Milsand], 112). For a more extended analysis of Milsand's commentary on Browning, see Philip Drew, *The Poetry of Browning: A Critical Introduction* (London: Methuen, 1970), 375–82.

15. Bentzon [Blanc-Milsand], 117. Browning's letters seldom refer to Milsand without some expression of devotion: "no words can express the love I have for him," he wrote to Isa Blagden in March 1872, after one of Milsand's many visits to his London residence; "he is increasingly precious to me" (376). Browning also dedicated two works to Milsand: the first reissue of *Sordello,* in 1863, and *Parleyings with Certain People of Importance in the Their Day* (1887), which Browning was completing when news of Milsand's death reached him in September 1886.

16. As Browning's biographers explain, he apparently had refused an offer of marriage from Louisa, Lady Ashburton made while he visited her estate in October of 1871 (see Irvine and Honan, 444–54). For more on Browning's relationship with Thackeray, see Malcolm Hicks, "Anne Thackeray's Novels and Robert Browning's *Red Cotton Night-Cap Country,*" *Studies in Browning and His Circle* 8, no. 2 (1980): 17–45. Hicks points out that Thackeray's *The Village on the Cliff* (1867) is set in Normandy and may explain why Browning cast her as an author prone to sentimentalizing the region (25).

17. Buzard, *The Beaten Track,* 121–22.

18. On the cultural impact of the Bank Holiday Act, see Lena Lenček and Gideon Bosker, *The Beach: The History of Paradise on Earth* (New York: Viking, 1998), 109. As they note, even before the act's passage, tourism industry pioneers such as Thomas Cook had begun to make visiting the seaside more affordable for people otherwise not used to the idea of vacation (119).

19. Lenček and Bosker, *The Beach,* 95. They add, "Where these Romantic poets led—and died—others followed. It is hard to overestimate the power of their example and their grip on the imagination of their contemporaries" (103).

20. Browning to William Wetmore Story and Edith Story, August 20, 1861, in *Browning to His American Friends,* 76.

21. Brendan Kenny, in "Browning as Cultural Critic," was the first to give a definitive explanation of the importance of Milsand's presence in the poem, stressing how he complements the kind of outsider authority Browning likewise seeks to establish: "being among the first reviewers to speak out in praise of Browning's poetry, when Browning's countrymen were almost universal in their disapproval, suggests his insight into English culture to be as keen as Browning's into French" (157).

22. Browning was a member of the Cosmopolitan Club from 1863 to 1883, which counted among its regulars influential members from many walks of life, with a par-

ticular emphasis on artists and men of letters such as Browning. Anthony Trollope and Anne Thackeray's father, William Makepeace Thackeray, were also members. See Martin Garrett, *A Browning Chronology: Elizabeth Barrett and Robert Browning* (Houndmills: Macmillan, 2000), for a brief account of Browning's membership (130). What made the club "cosmopolitan" initially seems to have been its members' worldliness and interest in the arts, but as it expanded, the club's identity became more closely associated with empire, "promoting social intercourse among its members," as one account describes, "and [affording] a place of occasional resort to gentlemen from the British Colonies, or in the service of the East India Company, or to such other persons not habitually living in London (Sir Algernon West, "The Cosmopolitan Club," in *One City and Many Men* [London: Smith, Elder, 1908], 161–62). My point in citing Browning's membership, I should stress, is not to make a simple equation between his poetry and what the Cosmopolitan Club stood for, but more to emphasize the social dimensions of cosmopolitanism as an identity, one that connoted a certain cultural privilege and access to power.

23. Virginia Blain, "Period Pains: The Changing Body of Victorian Poetry," *Victorian Poetry* 42, no. 1 (2004): 76.

24. Walter M. Kendrick, "Facts and Figures: Browning's *Red Cotton Night-Cap Country*," *Victorian Poetry* 17 (1979): 347.

25. Kenny, "Browning as a Cultural Critic," 159.

26. Armstrong, *Victorian Poetry*, 126.

27. Herbert F. Tucker, "Dramatic Monologue and the Overhearing of Lyric," in *Lyric Poetry: Beyond New Criticism,* ed. Chaviva Hošek and Patricia Parker (Ithaca: Cornell University Press, 1985), 230.

28. In *The Discourse of Self in Victorian Poetry,* for instance, E. Warwick Slinn argues, "There is no separate divine truth in the poem, no dramatised position that corresponds to the position of, for example, Milton's God in *Paradise Lost,* no moment that escapes discourse. Unity, any singular truth, is deferred. A conclusive telos, towards which all events lead, is neither within nor outside the text; it is simply not available" (120).

29. Armstrong, *Victorian Poetry*, 13.

30. Vinay Dharwadker, "Introduction: Cosmopolitanism in Its Time and Place," in *Cosmopolitan Geographies: New Locations in Literature and Culture,* ed. Vinay Dharwadker (New York: Routledge, 2001), 11.

31. Robert Pinsky, "Eros against Esperanto," in Nussbaum, 87. I am indebted to Bruce Robbins for this reference, who takes up Pinsky's criticism in his essay "The Village of the Liberal Managerial Class," in Dharwadker, 15–32.

32. Robert Viscusi, "'The Englishman in Italy': Free Trade as a Principle of Aesthetics," *Browning Institute Studies* 12 (1984): 1–28; repr., in *Critical Essays on Robert Browning,* ed. Mary Ellis Gibson (New York: G. K. Hall, 1992), 263. In a more recent analysis, Ernest Fontana cautions against reading the poem as Browning's confession of his own self-indulgent pleasure in Italy. The poem, rather, "offers a subtle critique of its speaker," a sexual tourist who blithely constructs "a hedonistic and supinely available Italy" befitting his own desires. "Sexual Tourism and Browning's 'The Englishman in Italy,'" *Victorian Poetry* 36, no. 3 (1998): 302, 304.

Chapter 5

1. Review of *Poems and Ballads, London Review,* August 4, 1866: 130–31; repr. in

Swinburne: The Critical Heritage, ed. Clyde K. Hyder (London: Routledge & Kegan Paul, 1970), 35. The reviewer writes that Swinburne "speaks of having been brought up in France" (35), but Hyder notes that this is probably a misinterpretation of Swinburne's reference to France as "sweet mother-land" (91) in "To Victor Hugo." Swinburne nonetheless did have close ancestral connections to France: "we were all Catholic and Jacobite rebels and exiles," he told E. C. Stedman, in response to his request for biographical information ("To E. C. Stedman [A *Memoir*]," in *Major Poems and Selected Prose,* ed. Jerome McGann and Charles L. Sligh [New Haven: Yale University Press, 2004], 468). These expatriates included Swinburne's grandfather Sir John Edward Swinburne (1762–1860), who lived in France until his twenties before inheriting an estate in England. Hence, in "To Victor Hugo," Swinburne offers his thanks to "fair foster-mother France, that gave / Beyond the pale fleet foam / Help to my sires and home" (75–77).

2. See *Uncollected Letters of Algernon Charles Swinburne,* ed. Terry L. Meyers (London: Pickering and Chatto, 2005), 3:10n2, on Swinburne's opposition to the tunnel project. As Parliament took up the subject again in the spring of 1890, Sir Frederick Maurice wrote to Swinburne asking him to reaffirm his opposition by signing a new protest.

3. Algernon Charles Swinburne, *The Complete Works of Algernon Charles Swinburne,* ed. Edmund Gosse and Thomas J. Wise (London: Heinemann, 1925–27), 5:123.

4. *Notes on Poems and Reviews* (1866) offers Swinburne's most extensive commentary on the need for poetry to probe all dimensions of human experience: "Literature, to be worthy of men, must be large, liberal, sincere; and cannot be chaste if it be prudish. Purity and prudery cannot keep house together. Where free speech and fair play are interdicted, foul hints and evil suggestions are hatched into fetid life. And if literature indeed is not to deal with the full life of man and the whole nature of things, let it be cast aside with the rods and rattles of childhood." *Notes on Poems and Reviews,* in *Major Poems and Selected Prose,* 358.

5. Ibid., 356. "When England has again such a school of poetry . . . as France has now," he added later in *Notes,* "when all higher forms of the various arts are included within the larger limits of a stronger race; then, if such a day should ever rise or return upon us, it will be once more remembered that the office of adult art is neither puerile nor feminine, but virile" (359).

6. Lawrence Venuti, *The Scandals of Translation: Towards an Ethics of Difference* (London and New York: Routledge, 1998), 31.

7. John Morley, Review of *Poems and Ballads, The Saturday Review,* August 4, 1866, 145–47; repr. in Hyder, 23, 26.

8. Lawrence Venuti, "Translation as Cultural Politics: Regimes of Domestication in English," *Textual Practice* 7, no. 2 (1993): 210. Saclav Bercovitch also reflects insightfully on translation as a "hermeneutics of nontranscendence," one that leads potentially to an "insight [that] is problematic, provisional, and *nourished* by a frustrating sense of boundaries." The aim of translation, he writes, should be not "to harmonize 'apparent' differences . . . but on the contrary to highlight conflicting appearances, so as to explore the substantive differences they imply" ("Discovering America: A Cross-Cultural Perspective," in *The Translatability of Cultures: Figurations of the Space Between,* ed. Sanford Budick and Wolfgang Iser [Palo Alto: Stanford University Press, 1996], 150). In applying the tools of translation theory to other kinds of cultural "translations," I am in part following the lead of David Simpson, who has recently suggested that translation forms the best description for many of the kinds of cross-cultural ex-

changes taking place in the nineteenth century, especially during the Romantic period, on which he focuses. Thomas Moore's *Lalla Rookh* (1817), for instance, and other "encyclopedic epics," with their extensive historical and political endnotes, cast readers "out into an unknown world where the balance of familiar and unfamiliar, acceptable and unacceptable, has always to be discovered and can never quite be settled. Reading itself, in its rush to closure, is profitably hobbled by small print" ("The Limits of Cosmopolitanism and the Case for Translation," *European Romantic Review* 16, no. 2 [2005]: 150). *Poems and Ballads* forms a different kind of reading dynamic and translation, but it still depends upon such disruption—or reading as frustrated, interrupted desire—and configures translation "not as the fantasy of diologism but as the impasse of blocked communication" (151). Like the verse Simpson describes, Swinburne's *Poems and Ballads* also makes innovative use of notes and other framing devices, some of them written in French, that compel readers into complex acts of interpretation and translation.

9. Angela Flury speaks eloquently toward this notion of Europe as translational space, where "to be outside of one's national boundaries among others is, in fact, to become European" ("Discovering 'Europe' in the Process of Repatriation: Primo Levi's *La Tregua,*" in Fendler and Wittliner, 67–68). Flury focuses her analysis on the cultural displacements and upheavals that followed the Second World War: "The series of camps that make survival possible for Levi and others map out a European topography that creates possibilities of negotiations on a small scale." In turn, "The camp emerges as a synecdoche of Europe" (71).

10. To truly appreciate the variety and depth of Swinburne's dialogue with European poetics, there is no substitute for simply reading *Poems and Ballads* at length. Kenneth Haynes's detailed annotations for the Penguin edition, often small essays in themselves, provide invaluable insight into Swinburne's sources and allusions.

11. As Richard Sieburth suggests, what made Swinburne threatening to contemporaries was his "refusal . . . to observe the segregation of high and low, pure and impure, sacred and obscene" in his work ("Poetry and Obscenity: Baudelaire and Swinburne," *Comparative Literature* 36, no. 4 [1984]: 345). Indeed, one of the tasks Buchanan set for himself, essentially, was to recover the pornographic body from *Poems and Ballads* and display it more openly to the public. Thaïs Morgan has written several important articles exploring transgressions of sexual boundaries in Swinburne, which I cite in reference to her readings of specific poems. Overall, she sees in Swinburne a pattern of "[m]ixed metaphor, mixed genre, mixed gender . . . a threat to the language, the literature, and the social body of England." "Mixed Metaphor, Mixed Gender: Swinburne and the Victorian Critics," *Victorian Newsletter* 73 (1988): 18.

12. Buchanan corresponded with Browning on several occasions, complaining in one letter of "that conscienceless & miserable inanity, little Swinburne:—verses which brooded, with a feminine fiendishness, over the prospect of physical suffering & torture to the subject" (December 7, 1870). My source for this letter is Patrick Regan's fine website devoted to Buchanan's life and work, which includes Buchanan's letters to Browning, among other valuable materials. "Robert Williams Buchanan," http://www.robertbuchanan.co.uk (accessed November 12, 2008).

13. Gavin Budge, "The Aesthetics of Morbidity: Dante Gabriel Rossetti and Buchanan's *The Fleshly School of Poetry,*" in *Outsiders Looking In: The Rossettis Then and Now,* ed. David Clifford and Laurence Roussillon (London: Anthem, 2004), 209.

14. Robert Buchanan, *The Fleshly School of Poetry and Other Phenomena of the Day* (1871; repr., New York: Garland, 1986), 30. Hereafter cited in the text.

15. Robert Buchanan, Review of *Poems and Ballads, The Athenaeum*, August 4, 1866, 137–38; repr. in Hyder, 33.

16. Buchanan intersperses passages from three different Baudelaire poems. The first two lines, which Buchanan slightly misquotes—the original has "*tes* dents" and "*te* faut"—are from "Tu mettrais l'univers entier dans ta ruelle" (3–4). The three lines cited next, and the last line, are from "Le Serpent qui danse" (13–15, 19). "Le froide majesté . . ." appears in "Avec ses vêtements ondoyants et nacrés" (14). The exclamation points are Buchanan's addition. My source for Baudelaire's poetry is the French–English edition translated and edited by James McGowan (Oxford: Oxford University Press, 1993).

17. Simpson, "The Limits of Cosmopolitanism," 148.

18. Writing in *The Poetry of the Period* (1870), Austin adds that "Mr. Swinburne's own real genius is of anything but a classic, and, least of all a Greek turn" (qtd. in Hyder, 103). Austin takes it upon himself to stem the feminine drift he perceives in English poetry. Swinburne performs a "travesty" on his Greek sources "[b]y eliminating all that was masculine—and what a masculine epoch it was!—and intensifying and exaggerating what was not masculine by aid of his modern feminine lens" (97).

19. Quoted in Hyder, 37–38.

20. Venuti, "Translation as Cultural Politics," 209.

21. Ibid., 217.

22. Anzaldúa, *Borderlands/La Frontera: The New Mestiza,* 100.

23. A. C. Swinburne, *Under the Microscope* (1872; repr., New York: Garland, 1986), 42–43.

24. Opening up another revealing way that these poems cross borders of gender and sexuality, Thaïs Morgan argues that Baudelaire and Swinburne establish a proxy space for "male-male desire through the lesbian body" ("Male Lesbian Bodies: The Construction of Alternative Masculinities in Courbet, Baudelaire, and Swinburne," *Genders* 15 [1992]: 40). While highly transgressive for the time, "male lesbianism," Morgan cautions us, "may be seen as an attempt on the part of an all-male avant-garde to explore an enlarged range of pleasures and subjectivities without forfeiting the sociocultural privileges long accorded to a masculinity faithful to the hegemonic model for men's gender and sexuality established by hetero-patriarchy" (41). At the same time, I would caution that we not lose sight of the primary agency of the poems in bringing these identities into being: a male lesbian body is not so much appropriated as invented in a way that initiates border crossing and dialogue that otherwise would not take place. Kathy Alexis Psomiades makes a similar point in *Beauty's Body: Femininity and Representation in British Aestheticism* (Palo Alto: Stanford University Press, 1997): "Swinburne's poems often mention details of Beauty's body—eyelids, breasts, thighs, lips—but these items are seldom subjected to intense visual scrutiny or described in terms of what they look like" (59). She adds that "the sensational eroticism of *Poems and Ballads, First Series* . . . is never primarily a matter of the gaze" (70).

25. Baudelaire's poem itself performs this kind of shift in attitude. "Femmes Damnées" is actually two poems, the first ending with the descent into Hell that Swinburne describes and with the author joining in the chorus of damnation: "Make out your destiny, you poor disordered souls, / And flee the infinite you carry in yourselves" (103–4). The second "Femmes Damnées," however, rather than focusing on two specific lovers,

presents a general reflection on forbidden, hidden desires and does more to fuse the author's desire and sympathy with the condemned women. The poem closes with the lines "Poor sisters, let me pity and approve—. / For all your leaden griefs, for slakeless thirsts, / And for your hearts, great urns that ache with love!" (26–28). The poem envisions a kind of community of "disordered" love that Swinburne readapts in his own way in *Poems and Ballads*.

26. William Michael Rossetti, *Swinburne's Poems and Ballads: A Criticism* (London: John Camden Hotten, 1866); repr. in Hyder, 81.

27. Ibid., 80.

28. Percy Bysshe Shelley, "A Defence of Poetry," in *Shelley's Poetry and Prose,* ed. Donald H. Reiman and Neil Fraistat (New York: Norton, 2002), 517.

29. Hazard Adams, *The Offense of Poetry* (Seattle: University of Washington Press, 2007), 24. In words that no doubt would have pleased Swinburne—who, incidentally, is not part of Adams's study—he writes, "I argue that poetry's main value is, in fact, its offensiveness, that some of the principal or usual characteristics of poetry are in themselves offensive, and that in our time poetry should be defended *as* offensive" (3).

30. A. C. Swinburne, "Charles Baudelaire: *Les Fleurs du Mal,*" in *Major Poems and Selected Prose,* 343.

31. A. C. Swinburne, *Poems and Ballads & Atalanta in Calydon,* ed. Kenneth Haynes (London: Penguin, 2000). All references to *Poems and Ballads* are to this edition.

32. One could also draw an analogy here to the kind of "double vision" Jerome McGann attributes to Swinburne in *Swinburne: An Experiment in Criticism* (Chicago: University of Chicago Press, 1972). In the guise of "Mrs. Clara Watts-Dunton," McGann writes, "His verse is remarkably rich in boundaries—in images, poetic forms, and prosodic devices which can suggest a point of limits" (171). His poetry strives to reveal the "intimate relationships between the many worlds which border each other, because the boundary point is difficult to find and even more difficult to hold" (172). In Swinburne's landscape poems, Sarah Eron detects a similar tendency to place opposing elements in relation to each other, favoring settings in "On the Cliffs" and "Evening on the Broads" that create the "sensation of being physically in the middle of worlds and two states." "Circles and the In-Between: Shaping Time, Space, and Paradox in Swinburnian Verse," *Victorian Poetry* 44, no. 3 (2006): 295.

33. Richard Dellamora, *Masculine Desire: The Sexual Politics of Victorian Aestheticism* (Chapel Hill: University of North Carolina Press, 1990), 69. Morgan, as I discuss above in relation to her reading of "Femmes Damnées," calls Swinburne's poem "an urgent but finally problematic attempt to create a positive place for male–male desire through the analogy of lesbianism" ("Male Lesbian Bodies" 40). She remains troubled by how Swinburne, like Baudelaire, creates "transgressive female figures that carry the weight of masculine desires, values, and conflicts, while eliding questions about the cultural position of female subjects" (52).

34. Swinburne here reflects the broader "anti-Olympian topos" that Margot Louis detects in Victorian poetry at large, which tends to favor the more connected, anthropomorphic personae of mystery deities such as Dionysus and Proserpine ("Gods and Mysteries: The Revival of Paganism and the Remaking of Mythography through the Nineteenth Century," *Victorian Studies* 47 [2005]: 342). The Olympian gods and the Christian deity merge in Swinburne as centers of indifference to human suffering: "separating themselves from mortals, they also force division and separation upon us" (345).

35. In his commentary on Swinburne's medieval love poetry, Anthony Harrison notes a kind of universalist, transhistorical inclination in Swinburne as regards the complications of human desire: "Finally and most important, for Swinburne, as for his contemporaries, the age of faith was also the age of love literature, and so the poet in his medievalist works could fill out his philosophical vision that held Love—whether erotic, fraternal, or spiritual—to be the presiding albeit fatal impulse in all human lives and the power ultimately governing all activity in the world." *Swinburne's Medievalism: A Study in Victorian Love Poetry* (Baton Rouge: Louisiana State University Press, 1988), 19.

36. "Sappho," *The Saturday Review*, February 12, 1914, 228, qtd. in *Poems and Ballads*, ed. Kenneth Haynes, 332.

37. Yopie Prins makes a similar argument on behalf of the poem in *Victorian Sappho* (Princeton: Princeton University Press, 1999). In his *Notes on Poems and Reviews*, Swinburne claimed that he had "striven to cast [his] spirit into the mould of hers, to express and represent not the poem but the poet" (351). For Prins, this leads to a unique kind of poetic transference, one where "the Sapphic body emerges in Swinburne's poetry as a rhythmicized, eroticized form . . . an embodiment of the rhythm of eros itself, a scattering movement too diffuse to be contained within any single body" (112–13).

38. Swinburne, "Charles Baudelaire: *Les Fleurs du Mal*," in *Major Poems and Selected Prose*, 345.

39. This is much the same point that Swinburne makes in his commentary on the strangely passionless affair between Lancelot and Guinevere in Tennyson's *Idylls of the King*: "Wishing to make his central figure the noble and perfect symbol of an ideal man, he has removed not merely the excuse but the explanation of the fatal and tragic loves of Launcelot and Guenevere" (*Under the Microscope* 36). Swinburne adds, "Remove in either case the plea which leaves the heroine less sinned against indeed than sinning, but yet not too base for tragic compassion and interest, and there remains merely the presentation of a vulgar adultress" (37).

40. I have chosen this translation, provided by Cecil Y. Lang in his anthology *The Pre-Raphaelites and Their Circle* (Chicago: University of Chicago Press, 1975), because I think it best captures the medieval cadence and tone of Swinburne's French (521).

41. Harrison sees a more unqualified affirmation of pagan eroticism in the poem: "Tannhäuser's 'entrapment' by Venus is ultimately a mode of self-willed liberation, one that is, during the monologue, merely delayed by temporary lapses of his Venerean faith" (*Swinburne's Medievalism* 61)

42. Henry Morley, in an otherwise sympathetic review for the *Examiner*, September 22, 1866, 597–99; repr. in Hyder, 44.

43. Swinburne, *Notes on Poems and Reviews*, in *Major Poems and Selected Prose*, 355.

44. Swinburne to Pauline, Lady Trevelyan, January 19, 1861, in *The Swinburne Letters*, ed. Cecil Y. Lang (New Haven: Yale University Press, 1959–62), 1:38.

45. In a later essay, Swinburne opined that "Chaucer borrowed most from abroad, and did most to improve whatever he borrowed. I believe it would be but accurate to admit that in all his poems of serious or tragic narrative we hear a French or Italian tongue speaking with a Teutonic accent through English lips" (*The Complete Works*, 14:98; qtd. in Harrison, *Swinburne's Medievalism*, 12). The description, of course, could also be applied to Swinburne himself, who likewise sought to craft a pan-European voice that critically engaged and adapted other cultures. Note as well the contrast to Buchanan's more safely unadulterated Chaucer.

46. Wolfgang Iser, "The Emergence of a Cross-Cultural Discourse: Thomas Carlyle's *Sartor Resartus*," in *The Translatability of Cultures*, ed. Budick and Iser, 248.

47. Ibid., 262.

48. In what could have been one of the great literary hoaxes of the nineteenth century, Swinburne almost got the *Spectator* to publish his 1862 review of "Les Abîmes. Par Ernest Clouët," whose tone and style anticipated many of the attacks that would later be leveled at Swinburne himself. He is perhaps at his best when he "quotes" a sample of Clouët's unrestrained flights of decadence: "Le mal a pour moi quelque chose de mystérieux et de saint (evil holds something mysterious and holy for me)" (*New Writings by Swinburne*, ed. Cecil Y. Lang [Syracuse: Syracuse University Press, 1964], 100; my translation). I am reminded here as well of Dennis Denisoff's study of the importance of parody to the aesthetic movement overall, whether inflicted self-intentionally or by critics: "Even if they fully believed in essential configurations of human desire and attraction, parodists who turned to a sexualized discourse to undermine aestheticism and the dandy-aesthetes were also catalysts for the denaturalization of gendered and sexual norms" (*Aestheticism and Sexual Parody 1840–1940* [Cambridge: Cambridge University Press, 2001], 2). Hence, perhaps, some of the added enjoyment Swinburne seems to derive from parody, as if he were paying tribute to his critics—recognizing the vital role they were playing in drawing attention to the larger cultural stakes in debates over poetic obscenity.

49. A. C. Swinburne, "Matthew Arnold's New Poems," in *Swinburne as Critic*, ed. Clyde K. Hyder (London: Routledge and Kegan Paul, 1972), 58; Hyder's translation, 60.

50. Ibid., 59; translation, 61.

51. Swinburne to Matthew Arnold, October 9, 1867, in *Uncollected Letters*, 1:111. Arnold had written earlier to Swinburne, "I am rather proud of my discernment in having grasped and said that you were yourself the French critic; not that the French is not worthy of the best of French critics, but something in the way you brought the quotations in gave me a suspicion" (October 10, 1867; *Swinburne Letters*, 1:169).

Chapter 6

1. Buzard, *Disorienting Fiction*, 304. *News from Nowhere* is likely to remain Morris's best known work, and, as such, it will perhaps always be a struggle to decouple him from a comforting, pastoral vision of English national identity. As Michelle Weinroth reveals in her study of political efforts to co-opt Morris's legacy in the twentieth century, many activists on the left, rather than attempting to dispel this image, exploited it toward their own political ends. Morris, in effect, became a "symbolic treasure-house of Englishness" (*Reclaiming William Morris: Englishness, Sublimity, and the Rhetoric of Dissent* [Montreal: McGill-Queen's University Press, 1996], 9). Only recently has this perception begun to change, thanks in part to Regenia Gagnier's plenary lecture at the fiftieth anniversary conference of the William Morris Society in July 2005, published later under the title "Morris's Ethics, Cosmopolitanism, and Globalisation" (*Journal of William Morris Studies* 16 [2007]: 9–30). Gagnier offers an overview of Morris's career that argues for his continuing relevance toward theoretical discussions of these issues in our own time. She calls him "the great writer of pilgrims, travellers, and refugees," and

adds that "his wanderers are asking just this: what do we share, if anything, as human beings distinctly imbedded in thick but always interdependent environments?" (20). In this chapter, I apply this question more directly toward Morris's poetry, which she touches on only briefly in her wide-ranging piece. Additionally, I develop the role that race must play in any full consideration of how Morris engages cosmopolitan ideas.

2. William Morris, *The Collected Works of William Morris,* ed. May Morris (London: Longmans, 1910–15), 12:xxiii. Except for *The Earthly Paradise,* all references to Morris's works are to this edition and will be cited in the text.

3. Herbert F. Tucker, "All for the Tale: The Epic Macropoetics of Morris' *Sigurd the Volsung,*" *Victorian Poetry* 34, no. 3 (1996): 387, 388.

4. John Goode, "William Morris and the Dream of Revolution," in Lucas, 239. Fiona MacCarthy, the author of the most recent major biography of Morris, concurs: "I would not press the claims of Morris's own favourite, *Sigurd the Volsung;* it is too large, too chant-like." She advises readers unfamiliar with Morris's poetry to turn instead to his "short, spare, edgy narratives of violence and loss." *William Morris: A Life for Our Time* (New York: Knopf, 1995), ix.

5. Morris to the editor of the *Pall Mall Gazette,* February 2,1886, in *The Collected Letters of William Morris,* ed. Norman Kelvin (Princeton: Princeton University Press, 1983–96), 2:515.

6. Douglas A. Lorimer, "Race, Science and Culture: Historical Continuities and Discontinuities, 1850–1914," in *The Victorians and Race,* ed. Shearer West (Aldershot: Scolar Press, 1996), 19.

7. Charles Wentworth Dilke, *Greater Britain: A Record of Travel in English-Speaking Countries during 1866 and 1867* (New York: Harper, 1869), 545.

8. Dentith, *Epic and Empire in Nineteenth-Century Britain,* 75. Dentith argues along the same lines in an earlier essay, "*Sigurd the Volsung:* Heroic Poetry in an Unheroic Age," in *William Morris: Centenary Essays,* ed. Peter Faulkner and Peter Preston (Exeter: University of Exeter Press, 1999), 60–70. He notes, for instance, that "the heavily stressed rhythm, predominantly anapestic before the caesura in each line, goes with a diction that seeks to mark its distance dramatically from the rhythm, not only of prose, but of the more 'natural' English rhythms of the iambic line" (66). Richard Firth stipulates that Morris's prosody gestures toward two types of medievalism: one Ruskinian—committed to accurately re-presenting the unique social and artistic environment of the time—the other aesthetic or Pre-Raphaelite—interested more in "the subversively erotic elements in medieval literature and art" ("'The Worship of Courage': William Morris's *Sigurd the Volsung* and Victorian Medievalism," in *Beyond Arthurian Romances: The Reach of Victorian Medievalism,* ed. Loretta M. Holloway and Jennifer A. Palmgren [London: Palgrave Macmillan, 2005], 118). The poem's meter "proves surprisingly capable of modulation to deal with the varied materials of the story. It also serves, however, to emphasize the antiquity and strangeness of the poem's subject matter" (126).

9. Tucker, *Epic,* 513.

10. Quoted in May Morris, *William Morris: Artist, Writer, Socialist* (Oxford: Basil Blackwell, 1936), 2:53.

11. In *Dark Vanishings: Discourse on the Extinction of Primitive Races, 1800–1930* (Ithaca: Cornell University Press, 2003), Patrick Brantlinger writes, "Paradoxically one end point of extinction discourse, from the late nineteenth century on, was widespread anxiety about the degeneration or even extinction of the white race" (15). This concern

was also evident in earlier influential commentaries on race, including Robert Knox's *The Races of Men* (1850) and his French counterpart the Comte de Gobineau's *Inequality of Human Races* (1853–55). In Gobineau's view, as Robert J. C. Young explains in *Colonial Desire,* the "Aryan races are impelled by a civilizing instinct to mix their blood with the very races that will bring about their downfall" (108).

12. Arnold, *On the Study of Celtic Literature,* 3:296–97.

13. Quoted in May Morris, *William Morris: Artist, Writer, Socialist,* 1:292.

14. Kingsley, for example, writes, "To amalgamate the two races [Roman and Teuton] would have been as impossible as to amalgamate English and Hindoos. The parallel is really tolerably exact. The Goth was very English; and the over-civilized, learned, false, profligate Roman was the very counterpart of the modern Brahmin" (*The Roman and the Teuton: A Series of Lectures Delivered before the University of Cambridge* [London: Macmillan, 1864], 126). In *On the Study of Celtic Literature,* Arnold recalls, "I was taught to think of Celt as separated by an impassable gulf from Teuton; my father, in particular, was never weary of contrasting them; he insisted much oftener on the separation between us and them than on the separation between us and any other race in the world" (3:299–300). These ideas inform his father's negative view of France in *Introductory Lectures on Modern History* (1845).

15. It is also worth noting, as Amanda Hodgson explores in "The Troy Connection: Myth and History in *Sigurd the Volsung,*" that the myths of Troy and Sigurd were linked under Max Müller's influential "solar thesis," which insisted that Sigurd and Achilles showed traces of an early form of sun worship common across Europe (in Faulkner and Preston, 74).

16. Hence Morris's consciously Chaucerian *The Aeneids of Virgil,* published in 1875, a year before *Sigurd.* The fact that he was working on a translation of this Latin material in the midst of his enthusiastic work on the North warns us again not to read too much into his distinctions between North and South. He drew on classical sources as well for *The Life and Death of Jason* (1867) and, as late as 1887, published a new translation of *The Odyssey.*

17. Barry Cunliffe, *Facing the Ocean: The Atlantic and its Peoples 8000 B.C.–A.D. 1500* (Oxford: Oxford University Press, 2001), vii–viii.

18. Flury, "Discovering 'Europe,'" 67–68.

19. Following Bakhtin, Hodgson argues, "The organizing principle of *The Earthly Paradise* is profoundly dialogic—its very structure refuses epic singleness and certainty" ("'The Highest Poetry': Epic Narrative in *The Earthly Paradise* and *Idylls of the King,*" *Victorian Poetry* 34, no. 3 [1996]: 344). Gagnier calls *The Earthly Paradise* "arguably the first modern cosmopolitan poem in English," one in which Morris "learned to control his natural irascibility, extirpate anger, forgive enemies, and cultivate fellowship under inhospitable conditions" ("Morris's Ethics," 22).

20. Florence S. Boos, "Volume One: Introduction," *The Earthly Paradise* (New York: Routledge, 2002), 4.

21. William Morris, *The Earthly Paradise,* 2 vols., ed. Florence S. Boos (New York and London: Routledge, 2002). Cited in the text by line number.

22. This exchange typifies how "a warm welcome is used as a marker of a good society" for Morris, according to Marcus Waithe in *William Morris's Utopia of Strangers: Victorian Medievalism and the Ideal of Hospitality* (Cambridge: D. S. Brewer, 2006), 66.

Hospitality, he argues, is a theme that permeates Morris's writings and art and is even enshrined in the design of Red House, his home from 1859 to 1865 (34–50). Although Waithe chooses to omit the poem from his analysis, the rights due to host and guest become significant social themes as well in *Sigurd the Volsung*.

23. Boos, "Prologue: The Wanderers," *The Earthly Paradise*, 1:58.

24. William Morris, *Collected Works*, 24:103.

25. Jeffrey Skoblow stresses another significant feature of this earlier draft: "The ballad presents itself as a raw object, as if delivered from within its fourteenth-century world, rather than projected back" (*Paradise Dislocated: Morris, Politics, Art* [Charlottesville: University Press of Virginia, 1993], 113). By reframing the ballad as the imagined utterance of an "idle" singer of the nineteenth century, Morris draws more attention to his own creative intervention in the history he depicts.

26. Homi K. Bhabha, "The Other Question," *Screen* 24, no. 6 (1983): 18–36; repr. in Mongia, 40.

27. Ibid., 50.

28. In a letter to Swinburne, Morris praised "The Lovers of Gudrun" at the expense of the rest of the volume: "I am delighted to have pleased you with the Gudrun; for the rest I am rather painfully conscious myself that the book would have done me more credit if there had been nothing in it but the Gudrun, though I don't think the others quite the worst things I have done—yet they are all too long and flabby—damn it!—" (December 21, 1869; in *Collected Letters*, 1:100).

29. Morris to William Bell Scott, February 15, 1870, in *Collected Letters*, 1:109–10.

30. Ibid., 110.

31. In the same letter, Morris said of the Volsunga Saga, "it is a wonderful poem, entirely free from any affectation or quaintness, as simple and direct as the finest classical poems" (110). Of "The Lovers of Gudrun," R. C. Ellison laments that "in trying to give clearer expression to the stark tragedy he evidently felt so deeply Morris loses all that the saga had, without replacing it with anything which carries conviction. The more he strives to express feeling, the emptier and more sentimental it seems" ("The Undying Glory of Dreams: William Morris and the 'Northland of Old,'" in *Victorian Poetry*, ed. Malcolm Bradbury and David Palmer [London: Edward Arnold, 1972], 164). Andrew Wawn's recent analysis of the poem is more forgiving of how Morris transforms his source material, although he does at times adopt a biographical angle that perhaps diminishes Morris's achievement: "It is certainly tempting to look for links between Morris's domestic woes and the series of sagas about love and romance that he translated." *The Vikings and the Victorians: Inventing the Old North in Nineteenth-Century Britain* (Cambridge: D. S. Brewer, 2000), 263.

32. In the Laxdaela Saga, Gudrun says, "I want to go abroad with you this summer, and that would make up for your hasty decision [made without consulting her]; for I am not happy here in Iceland." Kiartan quickly overrules this wish: "Your brothers haven't settled down yet and your father is an old man, and they wouldn't have anyone to look after them if you leave the country. So wait for me instead for three years" (*Laxdaela Saga*, trans. Magnus Magnusson and Hermann Pálsson [Harmondsworth: Penguin, 1969], 142). In her introduction to the tale, Boos highlights this scene as an example of how Morris's Kiartan is more prone to "ambivalence and reflection" than his saga prototype (2:282).

33. The saga king is also not quite so tyrannical as he appears in Morris. Kiartan says of him, "The first time I set eyes on the king, I was so impressed by him that I realized at once that he was a man of outstanding qualities, and this has been confirmed on every occasion I have seen him since in public. But never have I been so impressed by him as I was today, and now I am sure that all our welfare depends on our believing that he whom the king proclaims is the true God" (*Laxdaela Saga,* 148).

34. In the original saga, Gudrun's son Bodli (under the variant spelling Bolli) also travels to Constantinople: "He had not been there long before he joined the Varangian Guard; we have not heard of any other Norseman entering the service of the Byzantine Emperor before Bolli Bollason did. He stayed in Constantinople for several years, and was considered exceptionally valiant in every hazard and was always in the forefront" (*Laxdaela Saga* 227–28).

35. J. M. S. Tompkins, *William Morris: An Approach to the Poetry* (London: Cecil Woolf, 1988), 237–38.

36. Ibid., 238.

37. *Sigurd the Volsung,* which I will cite by page number, appears in Volume 12 of the *Collected Works.*

38. Helena Michie and Ronald R. Thomas, introduction to *Nineteenth-Century Geographies: The Transformation of Space from the Victorian Age to the American Century* (New Brunswick: Rutgers University Press, 2003), 11.

39. In his introduction to the critical anthology *Writing on the Image: Reading William Morris* (Toronto: University of Toronto Press, 2007), Latham also captures, I think, how interdisciplinarity is itself a form of cosmopolitanism, reflective of the same commitment to the value of different modes of expression and critical inquiry in Morris: "it is the interdisciplinary nature of Morris's work that prohibits anyone from ever reaching the boundaries of Morris's literature, decorative, book design, politics, etc., 'etcetera' being a word on which I would never end an introduction for any other figure but Morris" (15–16).

40. Michie and Thomas, introduction to *Nineteenth-Century Geographies,* 9.

41. Morris to Henry Buxton Forman, November 12, 1873, in *Collected Letters,* 1:205.

42. This is another place where it is important to distinguish between Morris's enthusiasm for Icelandic sagas and the strongly pro-German sentiments of figures such as Carlyle and Kingsley. As Wawn discusses in *The Victorians and the Vikings,* the subject of how much England owed culturally and racially to Germany, as opposed to Denmark and Scandinavia, was very much open to debate, as was the overall effort to determine what "Anglo-Saxon" actually signified. George Stephens, for example, the translator of the influential *Old Northern Runic Monuments of Scandinavia and England* (1866), insisted that "German nationality is not ours; certainly *its* faults are not *our* faults. Their speech is not ours; their body, and mind, and soul, and tendencies are far from being ours, which are altogether cast in the Northern mould, in our opinion one much purer and more noble. . . . [O]ur nearest homeland is Denmark; our furthest kin-land is Germany" ("'English' or 'Anglo-Saxon,'" *Gentleman's Magazine* 36 [1852]: 475; qtd. in Wawn, 239). For those concerned about Germany's growing influence in Europe, attempts by German scholars such as the Grimm brothers to establish through linguistics that English and German were part of the same Teutonic race, separate from

Scandinavia, seemed to go hand in hand with German imperial politics (Wawn 257). Morris's negative comments on Wagner may betray something of where his own feelings stood, although *Sigurd* in some ways sidesteps this debate by avoiding racial and national monikers altogether and drawing on both the German (*Das Nibelungenlied*) and the Scandinavian (*Volsunga Saga*) sources of the poem.

43. Tompkins offers some additional insight into Regin's status as a dwarf: "They belong to a life still immersed in nature. They create and enjoy, but have no sense of good or evil, of pity or regret. They are shape-changers" (270). He adds that "Regin, the master-craftsman, moves among men, benefitting them, in their generations, by his inventions. This comes from the restlessness of his mind; his heart is cold and grim. He waits for a hero, whom he can use as his tool, to kill Fafnir and retrieve the gold" (271).

44. Morris's politicization of Sigurd is indeed dramatic and has been noted by critics going back at least to the mid-twentieth century. For Margaret Grennan in *William Morris: Medievalist and Revolutionary* (New York: King's Crown Press, 1945), Sigurd stops just short of becoming a socialist: "the concern for his own times is unmistakably present. To call that 'socialism' . . . is perhaps premature, unless we are willing to agree with Morris that men of good will have always been socialists at heart. . . . But from *Sigurd the Volsung* on, his impulse to 'straighten the crooked' became more difficult for him to deny" (44). Charlotte Oberg also sees Sigurd as a political prophet, the embodiment of a lost golden age preceding the final apocalypse or Ragnarok of Norse mythology: "his words and deeds constitute a guide for mankind in a cosmos where all is ordered by the Norns, or the forces of destiny." *A Pagan Prophet: William Morris* (Charlottesville: University Press of Virginia, 1978), 90.

45. Henry Hewlett, Review of *Sigurd the Volsung, Fraser's Magazine* 8 (July 1877): 96–112; repr. in *William Morris: The Critical Heritage*, ed. Peter Faulkner (London: Routledge and Kegan Paul, 1973), 257.

46. Heather O'Donoghue, *Old Norse and Icelandic Literature: A Short Introduction* (Oxford: Blackwell, 2004), 174.

47. Ibid., 176.

48. Morris to Georgiana Burne-Jones, August 21, 1883, in *Collected Letters,* 2A:217.

49. Ibid.

50. If *Sigurd* lacks high political ambitions, one could argue that this very lack underscores Morris's conviction that a new narrative of social and political progress was needed. Socialism, therefore, or progressivism of some kind would be the next logical step in his career. Grennan endorses this trajectory, as noted above, as does Goode, for whom *Sigurd* ends in a state of political and artistic impotence, "a sepulchre within which the lost echoes of the values of the past reverberate." Goode continues, "Socialism enables Morris to envisage its [the creative mind's] withdrawal not merely as responsive but as capable of becoming a possible social experience" ("William Morris" 246). Boos reminds us that Morris composed the poem as he underwent his first real political awakening, brought on by the "Eastern Question" and the possibility of Britain's military intervention on behalf of Turkey. While *Sigurd* never raises its head above the violence—"there is something obsessive about its Old-Norse-set-piece-arias of butchery and conflagration"—it is notable that Morris "never again wrote in this vein from 1878 to his death." "Dystopian Violence: William Morris and the Nineteenth-Century Peace Movement," *The Journal of Pre-Raphaelite Studies* 14 (2005): 29, 30.

Chapter 7

1. James Joyce, *A Portrait of the Artist as a Young Man,* ed. Seamus Deane (Harmondsworth: Penguin, 1992), 12.

2. Jason Howard Mezey, "Ireland, Europe, the World, the Universe: Political Geography in *A Portrait of the Artist as a Young Man,*" *Journal of Modern Literature* 22 (1998–99): 135. Mezey argues that Stephen does not as yet see or understand how his status as a colonial subject will shape his future artistic priorities.

3. "Rooted Cosmopolitanism" is the title of the concluding chapter to Appiah's *The Ethics of Identity* (Princeton: Princeton University Press, 2005). See especially his discussion of the overlap between nationalism and cosmopolitanism as types of imagined community (237–46). Appiah explores some of the same issues in "Cosmopolitan Patriots," his contribution to *Cosmopolitics:* "the cosmopolitan patriot can entertain the possibility of a world in which *everyone* is a rooted cosmopolitan, attached to a home of his or her own, with its own cultural particularities, but taking pleasure from the presence of other, different, places that are home to other, different, people" (Cheah and Robbins, 91).

4. The philosophical roots of Hardy's concept have been variously explored, including Walter F. Wright's *The Shaping of* The Dynasts (Lincoln: University of Nebraska Press, 1967), 38–55, and, more recently, G. Glen Wickens's *Thomas Hardy, Monism, and the Carnival Tradition: The One and the Many in* The Dynasts (Toronto: University of Toronto Press, 2002). J. Hillis Miller's commentary on the Immanent Will in *Thomas Hardy: Distance and Desire* (Cambridge: Harvard University Press, 1970) for me remains the clearest and most insightful description available, and I offer it here as a sort of working definition for my analysis of the Will in this chapter: "The Immanent Will . . . is a version of the inherent energy of the physical world as seen by nineteenth-century science: an unconscious power working by regular laws of matter in motion. Though what happens is ordained by no divine law-giver, the state of the universe at any one moment leads inevitably to its state at the next moment. Existence is made up of an enormous number of simultaneous energies each doing its bit to make the whole mechanism move. If a man had enough knowledge he could predict exactly what will be the state of the universe ten years from now or ten thousand. All things have been fated from all time" (14). The Immanent Will, then, contains within itself a contradiction that allows for the possibility of progress: history is fated but also predictable. The poem explores the possibilities for achieving this wider knowledge.

5. I explore this subject briefly here and later with respect to *The Trumpet-Major* in order to illustrate the broader, more European perspective Hardy assumes in *The Dynasts.* For a closer investigation into the complexities of location, geography, and regional identity in Hardy's novels, see Ralph Pite, *Hardy's Geography: Wessex and the Regional Novel* (Houndmills: Palgrave Macmillan, 2002) and Simon Gatrell, *Thomas Hardy's Vision of Wessex* (Houndmills: Palgrave Macmillan, 2003).

6. Thomas Hardy, *The Return of the Native,* ed. Tony Slade (London: Penguin, 1999), 373.

7. Ibid., 171.

8. Ibid., 167.

9. Thomas Hardy, *The Woodlanders,* ed. Dale Kramer (Oxford: Oxford University Press, 1985), 74.

10. *The Woodlanders* was published shortly before Hardy's own first extended tour of the Continent in 1887, an experience that may have convinced him, as a poet, to be less tied to Wessex and more open to the Continent as the focus of future works. During his journey he began work on a travelogue of eleven "Poems of Pilgrimage," later included with *Poems of the Past and Present* (1901). Especially in "At the Pyramid of Cestius near the Graves of Shelley and Keats" and "Lausanne: In Gibbon's Old Garden: 11–12 P.M.," Hardy, one could argue, attempts to negotiate a space for himself among other Anglo-European poets and authors.

11. Thomas Hardy, *Jude the Obscure,* ed. Patricia Ingham (Oxford: Oxford University Press, 1985), 6.

12. Ibid., 355. Little Father Time, of course, hails from Australia. As Sue Bridehead reflects after first meeting him, "It is strange, Jude, that these preternaturally old boys almost always come from new countries" (294).

13. Stephen Kern, *The Culture of Time and Space: 1880–1918* (Cambridge: Harvard University Press, 2003), 3–4.

14. Ibid., 1.

15. Thomas Hardy, *The Personal Notebooks of Thomas Hardy,* ed. Richard H. Taylor (New York: Columbia University Press, 1979), 15.

16. Thomas Hardy, *The Life and Work of Thomas Hardy,* 110. Hereafter cited in the text.

17. Keith Wilson, "'We Thank You . . . Most of All, Perhaps, for *The Dynasts*': Hardy's Epic-Drama Re-evaluated," *Thomas Hardy Journal* 22 (2006): 236. Herbert F. Tucker offers more unqualified praise of Hardy's poem and, like Isobel Armstrong, gives it pride of place as the capstone to his study of nineteenth-century poetics. Tucker calls it "one of the few masterpieces this long book has been lucky to touch on: a work commensurately vast in original conception, thorough in execution, and pervasive in contemporary relevance" (*Epic* 549). Among other recent commentaries on the poem, Trevor Johnson stresses the importance of grappling with *The Dynasts* if one is to understand the development of some of Hardy's key concepts, especially his pessimism ("Thomas Hardy Birthday Lecture 2004," *Thomas Hardy Journal* 20, no. 3 [2004]: 160–76). The poem's global perspective is taken up by James S. Whitehead, whose essay on "Hardy and Englishness" is the first to feature *The Dynasts,* rather than the Wessex novels, in arriving at a full appreciation of how Hardy understood national identity: "while reflecting Englishness in action," he notes, the poem nonetheless "is geared towards engagement with contemporary, radical European thought" (*Thomas Hardy Studies,* ed. Phillip Mallett [Houndmills: Palgrave Macmillan, 2004], 214). Whitehead stresses the importance of Hardy's reading of *War and Peace* as he conceived *The Dynasts* and his support of Tolstoy's subsequent efforts on behalf of world peace (211–14).

18. Sheila Berger, *Thomas Hardy and Visual Structures: Framing, Disruption, Process* (New York: New York University Press, 1990), 127.

19. "Mr. Thomas Hardy's Drama," review of *The Dynasts,* Part I, *Times Literary Supplement,* January 15, 1904, 11.

20. Samuel Hynes, ed., "Hardy v. Walkley: The *TLS* Letters," in *The Complete Poetical Works,* 5:388.

21. Ibid., 5:391.

22. Isobel Armstrong is one exception, arguing in *Victorian Poetry: Poetry, Poetics, and Politics* that the poem's "technique of montage, fragmentation and juxtaposition

without cupola looks forward to the poetic forms of high modernism" (488). Donald Davie's groundbreaking *Thomas Hardy and British Poetry* (London: Routledge, 1973), in contrast, mentions *The Dynasts* only in passing, calling it "ill-starred and premature" (36). Likewise, Paul Zietlow in *Moments of Vision: The Poetry of Thomas Hardy* (Cambridge: Harvard University Press, 1974) diplomatically suggests that Hardy's "achievement is most evident in his more than nine hundred brief poems" (ix). John Paul Riquelme's more recent essay, "The Modernity of Hardy's Poetry," in *The Cambridge Companion to Thomas Hardy*, ed. Dale Kramer (Cambridge: Cambridge University Press, 2000), again mostly bypasses *The Dynasts,* except to remind readers of Armstrong's "brief but important" commentary on the poem (211). That Riquelme and Armstrong deal only briefly with *The Dynasts* is itself telling, perhaps, a sign that the poem clearly bears some affinity to the aims of modernist literature but may offer little to work with for an extended study of the poem along these lines. In fact, *The Dynasts* may provide more evidence for the kind of anti-modernism Peter Howarth discovers elsewhere in Hardy's poetry in *British Poetry in the Age of Modernism* (Cambridge: Cambridge University Press, 2005). Hardy's Immanent Will and fascination with poetic forms and meter betray, he suggests, a vision at odds with the modernist insistence on individual expression and a radical break with aesthetic tradition: "It is almost irresistible to see Hardy's predetermined forms as an expression of exactly such a determining Will, which acts without regard for the conscious pain or pleasure of its subjects. No matter what shape the material world would take if left to its own devices, the form will have its way, and Hardy's insistent rhythms, the very arbitrariness of his preplanned verse skeletons, would testify to the casual, blind forces of an Immanent Will in which chance and destiny come to mean the same thing" (157). What the divergent paths taken by these critics finally reveal, I am arguing, is that the poem's engagement with "the modern," whether in general or in a specifically literary sense, is inexorably—and deliberately—ambiguous: Hardy engages in a complex effort to look backward and forward, to be ancient and modern, as reflected in the poem's philosophical underpinnings and in the commentary of its spirit Overworld.

23. John Wain, introduction to *The Dynasts,* by Thomas Hardy (New York: St. Martin's Press, 1965), x.

24. Armstrong, *Victorian Poetry,* 488.

25. This is not to say, however, that an enterprising filmmaker should not make an attempt to bring *The Dynasts* to the screen. In many ways, the technology of filmmaking is only now catching up to Hardy's poetic cinematography in *The Dynasts,* with its quick movements between landscapes and slow zooms from celestial points of view to action on the ground. Advances in computer-animated footage could also make filming Hardy's X-ray exposure of the "will web" much more feasible.

26. Emmanuel, the Count de las Cases, *Memoirs of the Life, Exile, and Conversations of the Emperor Napoleon* (London: Henry Colburn, 1836), 3:165, 166. In a subsequent conversation with Las Cases, Napoleon continued along the same lines: "Then, perhaps, by the help of the universal diffusion of knowledge, one might have thought of attempting, in the great European family, the application of the American Congress" (4:104). On Hardy's overall use of Las Cases, see Walter F. Wright, *The Shaping of* The Dynasts, 267 and 322.

27. Matthew Arnold's response to Las Cases's Napoleon is also worth noting here, since it captures some of Hardy's own efforts to represent him fairly vis-à-vis English

national interests: "The inability of the English of that time in any way to compre-
hend him, & yet their triumph over him—& the sense of this contrast in his own
mind—there lies the point of the tragedy. The number of ideas in his head which
'were not dreamed of in their philosophy,' on government and the *future of Europe,*
and yet their crushing him, really *with the best intentions*—but a total ignorance of
him—what a subject!" (Arnold to his mother, Mary Penrose Arnold, May 7, 1849, in
LMA 1:148).

28. Georg Lukács, *The Historical Novel,* trans. Hannah and Stanley Mitchell (London: Merlin Press, 1962), 23.

29. Thomas Hardy, *The Trumpet-Major and Robert His Brother,* ed. Roger Ebbatson
(Harmondsworth: Penguin, 1987), 376–77. Hereafter cited in the text.

30. According to a review of the production in the *Times Literary Supplement,* "the
retreat to Corunna . . . was magnificently done, with all the players not drilled into
their parts but drawn into them, inspiring each other to a climax. We have never seen
anything so well done by professionals, though the same scene was good enough in
London" ("'The Dynasts' at Oxford," *Times Literary Supplement,* February 19, 1920:
113). Of the production overall, the review concluded that "at Oxford *The Dynasts* was
received as it was meant, not as a flattery to England past or present, not as a song of
victory or a requiem, but as a statement of the truth about England at war. The audience, boys who had fought themselves, saw the truth and welcomed it with laughter or
silence or cheers, as was meet" (114).

31. Ibid., 113.

32. H. G. Wells, *The War of the Worlds,* ed. Martin A. Danahay (Peterborough, ON:
Broadview, 2003), 41. Comparing himself to the clergyman, Wells's narrator remarks,
"[W]e had absolutely incompatible dispositions and habits of thought and action, and
our danger and isolation only accentuated the incompatibility. At Halliford I had already come to hate his trick of helpless exclamation, his stupid rigidity of mind" (150).
Later, the clergyman finally breaks down and charges madly at one of the Martians,
shouting, "The word of the lord is upon me! . . . I must bear my witness! I go! It has
already been too long delayed" (155).

33. The Immanent Will and natural selection do nonetheless share some affinities,
the focus of much of Katherine Kearney Maynard's discussion of the poem in *Thomas
Hardy's Tragic Poetry: The Lyrics and* The Dynasts (Iowa City: University of Iowa Press,
1991): "in Hardy's mind the development of the will's consciousness is an evolutionary
operation, analogous to the natural processes Darwin describes in his researches. The
gradual development of complex life forms would reflect the operation of the will as it
achieves greater consciousness of itself" (76). She does, however, warn against simply
equating the two concepts, especially as regards the ultimate ends of both forces: "An
openness to new ideas and the refusal to accept the doctrinaire, whether religious or scientific, characterized Hardy's thought throughout his life. In Darwin's work . . . Hardy
primarily found a means to clear away the dogmatic concepts that blind human beings
to many realities of existence" (76).

34. Tucker, *Epic,* 590.

35. Thomas Hardy, "Channel Firing," in *The Complete Poetical Works,* 2:9–10.

36. John Maynard Keynes, *The Economic Consequences of the Peace* (London: Macmillan, 1919), 4–5.

37. Quoted in *The Complete Poetical Works,* 5:398–99.

Chapter 8

1. Coubertin made the remarks in a radio address entitled "The Philosophic Foundation of Modern Olympism," recorded in Geneva in August 1935. In *Olympism: Selected Writings,* ed. Norbert Müller (Lausanne: International Olympic Committee, 2000), 580.

2. Alfred, Lord Tennyson, "Locksley Hall," in *Tennyson's Poetry,* 115–21.

3. Philip James Bailey, *Festus. A Poem,* 2nd ed. (London: Pickering, 1845), 395–96. This is the edition of the poem read by Arnold and Tennyson in the 1840s when it reached its highest level of literary recognition.

4. Tucker, *Epic,* 341. See also Michael Wheeler's *Heaven, Hell, and the Victorians* (Cambridge: Cambridge University Press, 1994), 83–109, which analyzes Bailey's efforts alongside other Victorian poetic visions of apocalypse and judgment, including Pollok's *The Course of Time* and Browning's *Christmas Eve and Easter Day.*

5. Tucker, *Epic,* 345.

6. Arnold to Arthur Hugh Clough, February 24, 1848 (*LMA* 1:82).

7. Arnold to Arthur Hugh Clough, May 11, 1848 (*LMA* 1:107–8).

8. "Locksley Hall" is not a direct critique of *Festus,* it should be noted, which Tennyson did not read until it appeared in its second edition, several years after Tennyson's poem was published. Like many contemporaries in the 1840s, Tennyson admired *Festus* more generally, writing to Edward FitzGerald on November 12, 1846, "I have just got *Festus;* order it and read. You will most likely find it a great bore, but there are really *very grand* things in *Festus.*" *The Letters of Alfred Lord Tennyson,* ed. Cecil Y. Lang and Edgar F. Shannon, Jr. (Cambridge: Harvard University Press, 1981), 1:265.

9. John Lucas, *England and Englishness: Ideas of Nationhood in English Poetry 1688–1900* (Iowa City: University of Iowa Press, 1990), 176.

10. As Walter D. Mignolo remarks in "The Many Faces of Cosmo-polis: Border Thinking and Critical Cosmopolitanism," in Breckenridge et al., 157–87, "when Kant thinks in terms of 'all nations of the earth' he assumes that the entire planet eventually will be organized by the terms he has envisioned for Western Europe and will be defined by his description of national characters" (173).

11. These concerns were renewed most recently during the Beijing Summer Olympics of 2008, when many skeptics wondered whether China was opening itself to the world or whether its leaders—quick to jail dissidents and cordon off any protest—were merely cloaking their own personal and national self-interests under the guise of international friendship. Readers may also recall that on the opening day of the games, Russia invaded the neighboring republic of Georgia even as Russia's de facto premier, Vladimir Putin, sat among the foreign dignitaries invited to watch the opening ceremonies.

12. Rodolphe Gasché, *Europe, or the Infinite Task: A Study of a Philosophical Concept* (Palo Alto: Stanford University Press, 2009), 9. Gasché also reveals how competing "intellectual" and "spiritual" visions of European identity continued to evolve in complex ways into the twentieth century. See especially his juxtaposition of Edmund Husserl's commitment to Europe as the seat of a "universal rational science" with Jan Patočka's insistence that, beginning with ancient Greece, "the care of the soul" had always been the driving motivation behind European philosophical inquiry (212–13).

13. Étienne Balibar, "The Borders of Europe," trans. J Swenson, in Cheah and Robbins, 217.

14. Jacques Derrida, *The Other Heading: Reflections on Today's Europe,* trans. Pascale-Anne Brault and Michael B. Naas (Bloomington: Indiana University Press, 1992), 49.

15. Ibid., 29.

Bibliography

Adams, Hazard. *The Offense of Poetry.* Seattle and London: University of Washington Press, 2007.

Addison, Joseph. *The Poetical Works of Joseph Addison.* London: Cooke, 1796.

Ahmad, Aijaz. "The Politics of Literary Postcoloniality." *Race and Class* 36, no. 3 (1995): 1–20. Reprint in Mongia, 276–93.

Albert, Prince Consort of Queen Victoria of Great Britain. *The Principal Speeches and Addresses of His Royal Highness the Prince Consort.* London: Murray, 1862.

Anderson, Amanda. "Cosmopolitanism, Universalism, and the Divided Legacies of Modernity." In Cheah and Robbins, 265–89.

———. *The Powers of Distance: Cosmopolitanism and the Cultivation of Detachment.* Princeton: Princeton University Press, 2001.

Anderson, Benedict. *Imagined Communities: Reflections on the Origin and Spread of Nationalism.* London: Verso, 1983.

Anzaldúa, Gloria. *Borderlands/La Frontera: The New Mestiza.* 3rd ed. San Francisco: Aunt Lute Books, 2007.

Appiah, Kwame Anthony. *Cosmopolitanism: Ethics in a World of Strangers.* New York: Norton, 2006.

———. "Cosmopolitan Patriots." In Cheah and Robbins, 91–114.

———. *The Ethics of Identity.* Princeton: Princeton University Press, 2005.

apRoberts, Ruth. "Matthew Arnold and Herder's *Ideen.*" *Nineteenth-Century Prose* 16, no. 2 (1989): 1–20.

Aravamudan, Srinivas. *Guru English: South Asian Religion in a Cosmopolitan Language.* Princeton: Princeton University Press, 2006.

Armstrong, Isobel. "*Casa Guidi Windows:* Spectacle and Politics in 1851." In Chapman and Stabler, 51–69.

———. "Misrepresentation: Codes of Affect and Politics in Nineteenth-Century Women's Poetry." In *Women's Poetry, Late Romantic to Late Victorian: Gender and Genre, 1830–1900,* edited by Isobel Armstrong and Virginia Blain, 3–32. Houndsmills: Macmillan, 1999.

———. *Victorian Poetry: Poetry, Poetics and Politics.* London: Routledge, 1993.

Arnold, Matthew. *Arnold: The Complete Poems.* Edited by Kenneth Allott. London: Longman, 1979.

———. *The Complete Prose Works of Matthew Arnold.* Edited by R. H. Super. 11 vols. Ann Arbor: University of Michigan Press, 1960–77.

———. *The Letters of Matthew Arnold.* Edited by Cecil Y. Lang. 6 vols. Charlottesville: University of Virginia Press, 1996–2004.

August, Eugene R. "*Amours de Voyage* and Matthew Arnold in Love: An Inquiry." *Victorian Newsletter* 60 (1981): 15–20.

Avery, Simon and Rebecca Stott. *Elizabeth Barrett Browning.* Studies in Eighteenth and Nineteenth-Century Literature. London: Longman, 2003.

Bailey, Philip James. *Festus. A Poem.* 2nd ed. London: Pickering, 1845.

Bakhtin, M. M. *The Dialogic Imagination: Four Essays.* Edited by Michael Holquist. Translated by Caryl Emerson and Michael Holquist. Austin: University of Texas Press, 1981.

Balibar, Étienne. "The Borders of Europe." Translated by J Swenson. In Cheah and Robbins, 216–29.

Baudelaire, Charles. *The Flowers of Evil.* 1857. Translated by James McGowan. Oxford: Oxford University Press, 1993.

———. "The Painter of Modern Life." *Baudelaire: Selected Writings on Art and Artists.* Translated by P. E. Charvet, 390–435. Cambridge: Cambridge University Press, 1972.

Bentzon, Th[éodore]. [Marie Blanc-Milsand]. "A French Friend of Browning—Joseph Milsand." *Scribner's Magazine* 20 (July 1896): 108–20.

Bercovitch, Sacvan. "Discovering America: A Cross-Cultural Perspective." In Budick and Iser, 147–68.

Berger, Sheila. *Thomas Hardy and Visual Structures: Framing, Disruption, Process.* New York: New York University Press, 1990.

Bhabha, Homi K. "The Other Question." *Screen* 24.6 (1983): 18–36. Reprint in Mongia, 36–54.

———. "Unpacking My Library . . . Again." In *The Post-Colonial Question: Common Skies, Divided Horizons,* edited by Iain Chambers and Lidia Curti, 199–211. New York: Routledge, 1996.

Black, Shaheem. "Fertile Cosmofeminism: Ruth L. Ozeki and Transnational Reproduction." *Meridians: Feminism, Race, Transnationalism* 5, no. 1 (2004): 226–56.

Blain, Virginia. "Period Pains: The Changing Body of Victorian Poetry." *Victorian Poetry* 42, no. 1 (2004): 71–79.

Boos, Florence S. "Dystopian Violence: William Morris and the Nineteenth-Century Peace Movement." *The Journal of Pre-Raphaelite Studies* 14 (2005): 15–35.

———. "Volume One: Introduction." *The Earthly Paradise,* by William Morris, 3–45. New York: Routledge, 2002.

Brantlinger, Patrick. *Dark Vanishings: Discourse on the Extinction of Primitive Races, 1800–1930.* Ithaca: Cornell University Press, 2003.

Breckenridge, Carol A., Sheldon Pollock, Homi K. Bhabha, and Dipesh Chakrabarty. Introduction to *Cosmopolitanism,* edited by Carol A. Breckenridge et al., 1–14.

Breckenridge, Carol et al., eds. *Cosmopolitanism.* Durham: Duke University Press, 2002.

Bristow, Joseph. "'Love, Let Us Be True to One Another': Matthew Arnold, Arthur Hugh Clough, and 'Our Aqueous Ages.'" *Literature and History* 4, no. 1 (1995): 27–49.

———. "Whether 'Victorian' Poetry: A Genre and Its Period." *Victorian Poetry* 42, no. 1 (2004): 81–107.

———, ed. *The Cambridge Companion to Victorian Poetry.* Cambridge: Cambridge University Press, 2000.

Brown, Susan. "The Victorian Poetess." In Bristow, 180–202.

Browning, Elizabeth Barrett. *Aurora Leigh.* 1856. Edited by Margaret Reynolds. Athens: Ohio University Press, 1992.

———. *Casa Guidi Windows.* 1851. Edited by Julia Markus. New York: Browning Institute, 1977.

———. *The Letters of Elizabeth Barrett Browning to Her Sister Arabella.* Edited by Scott Lewis. 2 vols. Waco: Wedgestone Press, 2002.

———. *The Works of Elizabeth Barrett Browning.* Edited by Sandra Donaldson et al. 5 vols. London: Pickering and Chatto, 2010.

Browning, Robert. *Dearest Isa: Robert Browning's Letters to Isa Blagden.* Edited by Edward C. McAleer. Houston: University of Texas Press, 1951.

———. *The Ring and the Book.* 1868–69. Edited by Richard D. Altick. New York: Penguin, 1971.

———. *Robert Browning: The Poems.* Edited by John Pettigrew and Thomas J. Collins. 2 vols. New Haven: Yale University Press, 1981.

Buchanan, Robert. *The Fleshly School of Poetry and Other Phenomena of the Day.* London: Strahan, 1872. Reprint, New York: Garland, 1986.

Budge, Gavin. "The Aesthetics of Morbidity: Dante Gabriel Rossetti and Buchanan's *The Fleshly School of Poetry.*" In *Outsiders Looking In: The Rossettis Then and Now,* edited by David Clifford and Laurence Roussillon, 203–20. London: Anthem, 2004.

Budick, Sanford and Wolfgang Iser, eds. *The Translatability of Cultures: Figurations of the Space Between.* Palo Alto: Stanford University Press, 1996.

Buzard, James. *The Beaten Track: European Tourism, Literature, and the Ways to 'Culture,' 1800–1918.* New York: Oxford University Press, 1993.

———. *Disorienting Fiction: The Autoethnographic Work of Nineteenth-Century British Novels.* Princeton: Princeton University Press, 2005.

Byron, Lord (George Gordon). *The Complete Poetical Works.* Edited by Jerome J. McGann. Vol. 2. Oxford: Oxford University Press, 1980.

Carlyle, Thomas. "Burns." In *Critical and Miscellaneous Essays,* 1:258–318. London: Chapman and Hall, 1899.

———. *On Heroes, Hero-Worship, and the Heroic in History.* Edited by Michael K. Goldberg. Berkeley: University of California Press, 1992.

Chapman, Alison. "The Expatriate Poetess: Nationhood, Poetics and Politics." In Chapman, *Victorian Women Poets,* 57–77.

———. "'In our own blood drenched the pen': Italy and sensibility in Elizabeth Barrett Browning's *Last Poems* (1862)." *Women's Writing: The Elizabethan to the Victorian Period* 10, no. 2 (2003): 269–86.

Chapman, Alison, ed. *Victorian Women Poets.* English Association Essays and Studies 56. Cambridge: D. S. Brewer, 2003.

Chapman, Alison and Jane Stabler, eds. *Unfolding the South: Nineteenth-century British Women Writers and Artists in Italy.* Manchester: Manchester University Press, 2003.

Cheah, Pheng. "The Cosmopolitical—Today." In Cheah and Robbins, 20–41.

Cheah, Pheng and Bruce Robbins, eds. *Cosmopolitics: Thinking and Feeling beyond the Nation.* Minneapolis: University of Minnesota Press, 1998.

Chesterton, G. K. *The Victorian Age in Literature.* New York: Henry Holt, 1913.

Clifford, James. "Traveling Cultures." In *Cultural Studies,* edited by Lawrence Grossberg et al., 96–116. New York: Routledge, 1992.

Clough, Arthur Hugh. *Amours de Voyage.* 1858. Edited by Patrick Scott. St. Lucia: University of Queensland Press, 1974.

————. *Clough: Selected Poems.* Edited by J. P. Phelan. London: Longman, 1995.

————. *The Poems of Arthur Hugh Clough.* 2nd ed. Edited by F. L. Mulhauser. New York: Oxford, 1974.

————. *Selected Prose Works of Arthur Hugh Clough.* Edited by Buckner B. Trawick. Tuscaloosa: University of Alabama Press, 1964.

Cooper, Sandi E. *Patriotic Pacifism: Waging War on War in Europe, 1815–1914.* Oxford: Oxford University Press, 1991.

Coubertin, Pierre de. *Olympism: Selected Writings.* Edited by Norbert Müller. Lausanne: International Olympic Committee, 2000.

Cronin, Richard. "*Casa Guidi Windows:* Elizabeth Barrett Browning, Italy, and the Poetry of Citizenship." In Chapman and Stabler, 35–50.

Cunliffe, Barry. *Facing the Ocean: The Atlantic and its Peoples 8000 B.C.–A.D. 1500.* Oxford: Oxford University Press, 2001.

Damrosch, David. *What Is World Literature?* Princeton: Princeton University Press, 2003.

Dasenbrock, Reed Way. "Why Read Multicultural Literature? An Arnoldian Perspective." *College English* 61 (1999): 691–701.

David, Deirdre. *Intellectual Women and Victorian Patriarchy: Harriet Martineau, Elizabeth Barrett Browning, George Eliot.* Ithaca: Cornell University Press, 1987.

Davie, Donald. *Thomas Hardy and British Poetry.* London: Routledge, 1973.

Dellamora, Richard. *Masculine Desire: The Sexual Politics of Victorian Aestheticism.* Chapel Hill: University of North Carolina Press, 1990.

Denisoff, Dennis. *Aestheticism and Sexual Parody, 1840–1940.* Cambridge: Cambridge University Press, 2001.

Dentith, Simon. *Epic and Empire in Nineteenth-Century Britain.* Cambridge: Cambridge University Press, 2006.

————. "*Sigurd the Volsung:* Epic Poetry in an Unheroic Age." In Faulkner and Preston, 60–70.

Derrida, Jacques. *The Other Heading: Reflections on Today's Europe.* Translated by Pascale-Anne Brault and Michael B. Naas. Bloomington: Indiana University Press, 1992.

Dharwadker, Vinay. "Introduction: Cosmopolitanism in Its Time and Place." In Dharwadker, 1–13.

Dharwadker, Vinay, ed. *Cosmopolitan Geographies: New Locations in Literature and Culture.* New York: Routledge, 2001.

Dickens, Charles, with W. H. Willis. "Valentine's Day at the Post-Office." *Household Words,* March 30, 1850: 6–12.

Dillon, Steve and Katherine Frank. "Defenestrations of the Eye: Flow, Fire, and Sacrifice in *Casa Guidi Windows.*" *Victorian Poetry* 35, no. 4 (1997): 471–92.

Dilke, Charles Wentworth. *Greater Britain: A Record of Travel in English-Speaking Countries during 1866 and 1867.* New York: Harper, 1869.

Disraeli, Benjamin. Address to the National Union of Conservative and Constitutional Associations, Crystal Palace, London, June 24, 1872. In *Victorian Prose: An Anthology,* edited by Rosemary J. Mundhenk and LuAnn McCracken Fletcher, 115–19. New York: Columbia University Press, 1999.

Dobell, Sydney. *The Poetical Works of Sydney Dobell.* Edited by John Nichol. 2 vols. London: Smith, Elder, 1875.

Dolan, Brian. *Exploring European Frontiers: British Travellers in the Age of Enlightenment* Houndmills: Palgrave Macmillan, 2000.

Drew, Philip. *The Poetry of Browning: A Critical Introduction.* London: Methuen, 1970.

"'The Dynasts' at Oxford." *Times Literary Supplement,* February 19, 1920: 113–14.

Eliot, T. S. *On Poetry and Poets.* New York: Faber, 1957.

Ellison, R. C. "'The Undying Glory of Dreams': William Morris and the 'Northland of Old.'" In *Victorian Poetry,* edited by Malcolm Bradbury and David Palmer, 139–75. Stratford-upon-Avon Studies 15. London: Edward Arnold, 1972.

Eron, Sarah. "Circles and the In-Between: Shaping Time, Space, and Paradox in Swinburnian Verse." *Victorian Poetry* 44, no. 3 (2006): 293–309.

Esterhammer, Angela. "The Cosmopolitan *Improvvisatore:* Spontaneity and Performance in Romantic Poetics." *European Romantic Review* 16, no. 2 (2005): 153–65.

Faulkner, Peter, ed. *William Morris: The Critical Heritage.* London: Routledge and Kegan Paul, 1973.

Faulkner, Peter and Peter Preston, eds. *William Morris: Centenary Essays. Papers from the Morris Centenary Conference organized by the William Morris Society at Exeter College Oxford 30 June-3 July 1996.* Exeter: University of Exeter Press, 1999.

Faverty, Frederic E. *Matthew Arnold: The Ethnologist.* Evanston: Northwestern University Press, 1951.

Fendler, Susanne and Ruth Wittlinger. *The Idea of Europe in Literature.* Houndmills: Macmillan, 1999.

Flury, Angela. "Discovering 'Europe' in the Process of Repatriation: Primo Levi's *La Tregua.*" In Fendler and Wittlinger, 65–84.

Fontana, Ernest. "Sexual Tourism and Browning's 'The Englishman in Italy.'" *Victorian Poetry* 36, no. 3 (1998): 299–305.

Frawley, Maria H. *A Wider Range: Travel Writing by Women in Victorian England.* Rutherford, NJ: Fairleigh Dickinson University Press, 1994.

Frith, Richard. "'The Worship of Courage': William Morris's *Sigurd the Volsung* and Victorian Medievalism." In *Beyond Arthurian Romances: The Reach of Victorian Medievalism,* edited by Loretta M. Holloway and Jennifer A. Palmgren, 117–32. London: Palgrave Macmillan, 2005.

Gagnier, Regenia. "Morris's Ethics, Cosmopolitanism, and Globalisation." *Journal of William Morris Studies* 16 (2007): 9–30.

Garrett, Martin. *A Browning Chronology: Elizabeth Barrett and Robert Browning.* Houndmills: Macmillan, 2000.

Gasché, Rodolphe. *Europe, or the Infinite Task: A Study of a Philosophical Concept.* Palo Alto: Stanford University Press, 2009.

Gatrell, Simon. *Thomas Hardy's Vision of Wessex.* Houndmills: Palgrave Macmillan, 2003.

Gilbert, Sandra M. "From *Patria* to *Matria:* Elizabeth Barrett Browning's Risorgimento." *PMLA* 99, no. 2 (1984): 194–211.

Gilbert, Sandra M. and Susan Gubar. *The Madwoman in the Attic: The Woman Writer and the Nineteenth-Century Literary Imagination.* New Haven: Yale University Press, 1979.

Goode, John. "1848 and the Strange Disease of Modern Love." In Lucas, 45–76.

———. "William Morris and the Dream of Revolution." In Lucas, 221–80.

Goodlad, Lauren M. E. "Trollopian 'Foreign Policy': Rootedness and Cosmopolitanism in the Mid-Victorian Global Imaginary." *PMLA* 124, no. 2 (2009): 437–54.

——— and Julia M. Wright. "Victorian Internationalisms: Introduction and Keywords." *Romanticism and Victorianism on the Net* 48 (November 2007). http://www.erudit.org/revue/ravon/2007/v/n48.

Gordon, Jan B. "Charlotte Brontë's Alternative 'European Community.'" In Fendler and Wittlinger, 3–30.

Graham, Colin. *Nation, Empire and Victorian Epic Poetry.* Manchester: Manchester University Press, 1998.

Gray, Erik. "A Bounded Field: Situating Victorian Poetry in the Literary Landscape." *Victorian Poetry* 41, no. 4 (2003): 465–72

———. "Clough and His Discontents: *Amours de Voyage* and the English Hexameter." *Literary Imagination: The Review of the Association of Literary Scholars and Critics* 6, no. 2 (2004): 195–210.

Grennan, Margaret R. *William Morris: Medievalist and Revolutionary.* New York: King's Crown, 1945.

Grewal, David Singh. *Network Power: The Social Dynamics of Globalization.* New Haven: Yale University Press, 2008.

Gridley, Roy E. *The Brownings and France: A Chronicle with Commentary.* London: Athlone, 1982.

Griffin, W. Hall and H. C. Minchin. *The Life of Robert Browning.* London: Methuen, 1910. Reprint, Hamden, CT: Archon Books, 1966

Groth, Helen. "A Different Look—Visual Technologies and the Making of History in Elizabeth Barrett Browning's *Casa Guidi Windows.*" *Textual Practice* 14, no. 1 (2000): 31–52.

Habermas, Jürgen. "The European Nation-state—Its Achievements and Its Limits: On the Past and Future of Sovereignty and Citizenship." In *Mapping the Nation,* edited by Gopal Balakrishnan, 281–94. London: Verso, 1996.

———. "Kant's Idea of Perpetual Peace, with the Benefit of Two Hundred Years' Hindsight." In *Perpetual Peace: Essays on Kant's Cosmopolitan Ideal,* edited by James Bohman and Matthias Lutz-Bachmann, 113–53. Cambridge: MIT Press, 1997.

Hair, Donald S. *Robert Browning's Language.* Toronto: University of Toronto Press, 1999.

Handbook for Travellers in Central Italy. London: John Murray, 1843.

Hardy, Thomas. *The Collected Letters of Thomas Hardy.* Edited by Richard L. Purdy and Michael Millgate. 7 vols. Oxford: Oxford University Press, 1978–89.

———. *The Complete Poetical Works of Thomas Hardy.* Edited by Samuel Hynes. 5 vols. Oxford: Clarendon Press, 1982–95.

———. *Jude the Obscure.* 1895. Edited by Patricia Ingham. Oxford: Oxford University Press, 1985.

———. *The Life and Work of Thomas Hardy.* Edited by Michael Millgate. London: Macmillan, 1984.

———. *The Personal Notebooks of Thomas Hardy.* Edited by Richard H. Taylor. New York: Columbia University Press, 1979.

———. *The Return of the Native.* 1878. Edited by Tony Slade. London: Penguin, 1999.

———. *The Trumpet-Major and Robert His Brother.* 1880. Edited by Roger Ebbatson. Harmondsworth: Penguin, 1987.

———. *The Woodlanders.* 1887. Edited by Dale Kramer. Oxford: Oxford University Press, 1985.

Harris, Leigh Coral. "From *Mythos* to *Logos:* Political Aesthetics and Liminal Poetics in Elizabeth Barrett Browning's *Casa Guidi Windows.*" *Victorian Literature and Culture* 28 (2000): 109–31.

Harrison, Anthony H. *Swinburne's Medievalism: A Study in Victorian Love Poetry.* Baton Rouge: Louisiana State University Press, 1988.

Hicks, Malcolm. "Anne Thackeray's Novels and Robert Browning's *Red Cotton Night-Cap Country.*" *Studies in Browning and His Circle* 8, no. 2 (1980): 17–45.

Hill, Rowland. *Post Office Reform: Its Importance and Practicability.* London: Charles Knight, 1837.

Himmelfarb, Gertrude. "The Illusions of Cosmopolitanism." In Nussbaum, 72–77.

Hodgson, Amanda. "'The Highest Poetry': Epic Narrative in *The Earthly Paradise* and *Idylls of the King.*" *Victorian Poetry* 34, no. 3 (1996): 340–54.

———. "The Troy Connection: Myth and History in *Sigurd the Volsung.*" In Faulkner and Preston, 71–79.

Honan, Park. *Matthew Arnold: A Life.* Cambridge: Harvard University Press, 1983.

Howarth, Peter. *British Poetry in the Age of Modernism.* Cambridge: Cambridge University Press, 2005.

Hudson, Gertrude Reese, ed. *Browning to His American Friends: Letters between the Brownings, the Storys and James Russell Lowell, 1841–1890.* New York: Barnes and Noble, 1965.

Hyder, Clyde K., ed. *Swinburne: The Critical Heritage.* London: Routledge and Kegan Paul, 1970.

Irvine, William and Park Honan. *The Book, the Ring, and the Poet: A Biography of Robert Browning.* New York: McGraw-Hill, 1974.

Iser, Wolfgang. "The Emergence of a Cross-Cultural Discourse: Thomas Carlyle's *Sartor Resartus.*" In Budick and Iser, 245–64.

Jenks, Chris. "Watching Your Step: The History and Practice of the Flâneur." In *Visual Culture,* edited by Chris Jenks, 142–60. New York: Routledge, 1995.

Johnson, Trevor. "Thomas Hardy Birthday Lecture 2004." *Thomas Hardy Journal* 20, no. 3 (2004): 160–76.

Joyce, James. *A Portrait of the Artist as a Young Man.* 1916. Edited by Seamus Deane. Harmondsworth: Penguin, 1992.

Kant, Immanuel. *Kant: Political Writings.* Edited by Hans Reiss. Translated by H. B. Nisbet. Cambridge: Cambridge University Press, 1991.

Keirstead, Christopher M. "Authenticating Italy: Poetry, Tourism, and Browning's *The Ring and the Book.*" *Journal of Anglo-Italian Studies* 8 (2006): 115–28.

———. "Beyond 'Where Byron Used to Ride': Locating the Victorian Travel Poet in Clough's *Amours de Voyage and Dipsychus.*" *Philological Quarterly* 77, no. 4 (1998): 377–95.

———. "'He Shall Be a "Citizen of the World"': Cosmopolitanism and the Education of Pen Browning." *Browning Society Notes* 32 (2007): 74–82.

Kelley, Philip and Scott Lewis, eds. *The Brownings' Correspondence.* 17 vols. to date. Winfield, KS: Wedgestone Press, 1984.

Kendrick, Walter M. "Facts and Figures: Browning's *Red Cotton Night-Cap Country.*" *Victorian Poetry* 17, no. 4 (1979): 343–63.

Kenny, Brendan. "Browning as a Cultural Critic: *Red Cotton Night-Cap Country.*" *Browning Institute Studies* 6 (1978): 137–62.

Kern, Stephen. *The Culture of Time and Space: 1880–1918.* Cambridge: Harvard University Press, 2003.

Keynes, John Maynard. *The Economic Consequences of the Peace.* London: Macmillan, 1919.

Kingsley, Charles. "Mr. and Mrs. Browning." *Fraser's Magazine* 43 (1851): 170–82.

———. *The Roman and the Teuton: A Series of Lectures Delivered before the University of Cambridge.* London: Macmillan, 1864.

Komisurak, Adam. "Typologies of the East: Self as Vortex in Don Juan's Russian Affair." *Nineteenth-Century Contexts* 29, nos. 2–3 (2007): 219–36.

Kristeva, Julia. *Crisis of the European Subject.* Translated by Susan Fairfield. New York: Other Press, 2000.

———. *Nations without Nationalism.* Translated by Leon S. Roudiez. New York: Columbia University Press, 1993.

Kuduk, Stephanie. "'A Sword of a Song': Swinburne's Republican Aesthetics in *Songs before Sunrise.*" *Victorian Studies* 43 (2001): 253–78.

Lamartine, Alphonse de. *History of the French Revolution of 1848.* London: George Bell, 1888.

Landis, Paul, ed. *Letters of the Brownings to George Barrett.* Urbana: University of Illinois Press, 1958.

Landor, Walter Savage. *The Complete Works of Walter Savage Landor.* Edited by Stephen Wheeler. Vol. 15. London: Methuen, 1969.

Lang, Cecil Y., ed. *The Pre-Raphaelites and Their Circle.* 2nd ed. Chicago: University of Chicago Press, 1975.

Lang, Cecil Y. and Edgar F. Shannon, Jr., eds. *The Letters of Alfred Lord Tennyson.* 3 vols. Cambridge: Harvard University Press, 1981.

Langbaum, Robert. *The Poetry of Experience: The Dramatic Monologue in Modern Literary Tradition.* New York: Norton, 1957.

LaPorte, Charles. "Spasmodic Poetics and Clough's Apostasies." *Victorian Poetry* 42, no. 4 (2004): 521–36.

Las Cases, Immanuel, Comte de. *Memoirs of the Life, Exile, and Conversations of the Emperor Napoleon.* 4 vols. London: Henry Colburn, 1936.

Latham, David, ed. *Writing on the Image: Reading William Morris.* Toronto: University of Toronto Press, 2007.

Laxdaela Saga. Translated by Magnus Magnusson and Hermann Pálsson. Harmondsworth: Penguin, 1969.

Lenček, Lena and Gideon Bosker. *The Beach: The History of Paradise on Earth.* New York: Viking, 1998.

Lewis, Linda M. *Elizabeth Barrett Browning's Spiritual Progress: Face to Face with God.* Columbia: University of Missouri Press, 1998.

————. *Germaine de Staël, George Sand, and the Victorian Woman Artist.* Columbia: University of Missouri Press, 2003.

Linley, Margaret. "Nationhood and Empire." In *A Companion to Victorian Poetry,* edited by Richard Cronin et al., 421–37. Oxford: Blackwell, 2002.

Lootens, Tricia. "Victorian Poetry and Patriotism." In Bristow, 255–79.

Lorimer, Douglas A. "Race, Science and Culture: Historical Continuities and Discontinuities, 1850–1914." In *The Victorians and Race,* edited by Shearer West, 12–33. Aldershot: Scolar Press, 1996.

Louis, Margot K. "Gods and Mysteries: The Revival of Paganism and the Remaking of Mythography through the Nineteenth Century." *Victorian Studies* 47 (2005): 329–61.

————. *Swinburne and His Gods: The Roots and Growth of an Agnostic Poetry.* Montreal and Kingston: McGill-Queen's University Press, 1989.

Lucas, John. *England and Englishness: Ideas of Nationhood in English Poetry, 1688–1900.* Iowa City: University of Iowa Press, 1990.

————, ed. *Literature and Politics in the Nineteenth Century.* London: Methuen, 1971.

Lukács, Georg. *The Historical Novel.* Translated by Hannah and Stanley Mitchell. London: Merlin Press, 1962.

Lutzeler, Paul Michael. "Goethe and Europe." *South Atlantic Review* 65, no. 2 (2000): 95–113.

Macaulay, Thomas Babington. *Selected Writings.* Edited by John Clive and Thomas Pinney. Chicago: University of Chicago Press, 1972.

MacCarthy, Fiona. *William Morris: A Life for Our Time.* New York: Knopf, 1995.

Malcomson, Scott. "The Varieties of Cosmopolitan Experience." In Cheah and Robbins, 233–45.

Markus, Julia. *Dared and Done: The Marriage of Elizabeth Barrett Browning and Robert Browning.* Athens: Ohio University Press, 1995.

Marx, Karl. *The Marx-Engels Reader.* 2nd ed. Edited by Robert C. Tucker. New York: Norton, 1978.

Maynard, Katherine Kearney. *Thomas Hardy's Tragic Poetry: The Lyrics and* The Dynasts. Iowa City: University of Iowa Press, 1991.

Mazzini, Giuseppe. *The Duties of Man.* 1861. London: Dent, 1966.

McGann, Jerome J. *Swinburne: An Experiment in Criticism.* Chicago: University of Chicago Press, 1972.

Mermin, Dorothy. *The Audience in the Poem: Five Victorian Poets.* New Brunswick: Rutgers University Press, 1983.

Mezey, Jason Howard. "Ireland, Europe, the World, the Universe: Political Geography in *A Portrait of the Artist as a Young Man.*" *Journal of Modern Literature* 22 (1998–99): 134–45.

Michie, Helena and Ronald R. Thomas. Introduction to *Nineteenth-Century Geographies: The Transformation of Space from the Victorian Age to the American Century,* 1–20. New Brunswick: Rutgers University Press, 2003.

Micklus, Robert. "A Voyage of Juxtapositions: The Dynamic World of *Amours de Voyage.*" *Victorian Poetry* 18, no. 4 (1980): 407–14.

Mignolo, Walter D. "The Many Faces of Cosmo-polis: Border Thinking and Critical Cosmopolitanism." In Breckenridge et al., 157–87.

Miller, J. Hillis. *Thomas Hardy: Distance and Desire.* Cambridge: Harvard University Press, 1970.

Milsand, Joseph. "La Poesie Anglaise depuis Byron: II—Browning." *Revue des Deux Mondes* 11 (1851): 661–89.

Mongia, Padmini, ed. *Contemporary Postcolonial Theory: A Reader.* London: Arnold, 1996.

Montwieler, Katherine. "Domestic Politics: Gender, Protest, and Elizabeth Barrett Browning's *Poems before Congress.*" *Tulsa Studies in Women's Literature* 24 (2005): 291–318.

Morgan, Marjorie. *National Identities and Travel in Victorian Britain.* Basingstoke and New York: Palgrave, 2001.

Morgan, Thaïs. "Male Lesbian Bodies: The Construction of Alternative Masculinities in Courbet, Baudelaire, and Swinburne." *Genders* 15 (1992): 37–57.

———. "Mixed Metaphor, Mixed Gender: Swinburne and the Victorian Critics." *Victorian Newsletter* 73 (1988): 16–19.

Morris, May. *William Morris: Artist, Writer, Socialist.* 2 vols. Oxford: Basil Blackwell, 1936.

Morris, William. *The Collected Letters of William Morris.* Edited by Norman Kelvin. 4 vols. Princeton: Princeton University Press, 1983–96.

———. *The Collected Works of William Morris.* Edited by May Morris. 24 vols. London: Longmans, 1910–15.

———. *The Earthly Paradise.* 1868–70. Edited by Florence S. Boos. 2 vols. New York and London: Routledge, 2002.

Moskal, Jeanne. "Introductory Note: *Rambles in Germany and Italy.*" In Shelley, 8:49–57.

"Mr. Thomas Hardy's Drama." Review of *The Dynasts*, Part I, *Times Literary Supplement,* January 15, 1904: 11–12.

Mulhauser, Frederick L., ed. *The Correspondence of Arthur Hugh Clough.* 2 vols. Oxford: Oxford University Press, 1957.

Nietzsche, Friedrich. *Beyond Good and Evil.* 1887. Translated by Judith Norman. Cambridge: Cambridge University Press, 2002.

———. *Human, All Too Human: A Book for Free Spirits.* 1878–80. Translated by R. J. Hollingdale. Cambridge: Cambridge University Press, 1986.

Nussbaum, Martha C., with respondents. *For Love of Country: Debating the Limits of Patriotism.* Boston: Beacon, 1996.

———. "Patriotism and Cosmopolitanism." In Nussbaum, 3–17.

Oberg, Charlotte H. *A Pagan Prophet: William Morris.* Charlottesville: University Press of Virginia, 1978.

O'Connor, Maura. *The Romance of Italy and the English Political Imagination.* New York: St. Martin's Press, 1998.

O'Donoghue, Heather. *Old Norse and Icelandic Literature: A Short Introduction.* Oxford: Blackwell, 2004.

Otis, Laura. *Networking: Communicating with Bodies and Machines in the Nineteenth Century.* Ann Arbor: University of Michigan Press, 2001.

Perkins, Marianne. *Nation and Word, 1770–1850: Religious and Metaphysical Language in European National Consciousness.* London: Ashgate, 1999.

Phelan, Joseph. "Clough, Arnold, Béranger, and the Legacy of 1848." *SEL: Studies in English Literature, 1500–1900* 46, no. 4 (2006): 833–48.

Pinsky, Robert. "Eros against Esperanto." In Nussbaum, 85–90.

Pite, Ralph. *Hardy's Geography: Wessex and the Regional Novel.* Houndmills: Palgrave Macmillan, 2002.

"Poetical Aberrations." *Blackwood's Edinburgh Magazine* (April 1860): 491.

Porter, Bernard. *The Absent-Minded Imperialists: Empire, Society, and Culture in Britain.* Oxford: Oxford University Press, 2004.

"The Post-Office." *Fraser's Magazine* 41 (1850): 224–32.

Pratt, Mary Louise. *Imperial Eyes: Travel Writing and Transculturation.* London: Routledge, 1992.

Prins, Yopie. *Victorian Sappho.* Princeton: Princeton University Press, 1999.

Psomiades, Kathy Alexis. *Beauty's Body: Femininity and Representation in British Aestheticism.* Palo Alto: Stanford University Press, 1997.

Regan, Patrick. "Robert Williams Buchanan." http://www.robertbuchanan.co.uk (accessed November 12, 2008).

Review of *Aurora Leigh,* by Elizabeth Barrett Browning. *Literary Gazette,* November 22, 1856: 917–18.

Review of *Casa Guidi Windows,* by Elizabeth Barrett Browning, *Athenaeum,* June 7, 1851: 597–98.

Review of *Casa Guidi Windows,* by Elizabeth Barrett Browning, *Eclectic Review* (September 1851): 306–17.

Review of *Italy* and *The Deluge,* by John Edmund Reade. *Fraser's Magazine* 20 (1839): 758–62.

Review of *Poems before Congress,* by Elizabeth Barrett Browning, *Saturday Review,* March 31, 1860: 402–4.

Reynolds, Matthew. *The Realms of Verse, 1830–1870: English Poetry in a Time of Nation-Building.* Oxford: Oxford University Press, 2001.

Riede, David G. *Matthew Arnold and the Betrayal of Language.* Charlottesville: University Press of Virginia, 1988.

Riquelme, John Paul. "The Modernity of Hardy's Poetry." In *The Cambridge Companion to Thomas Hardy,* edited by Dale Kramer, 204–23. Cambridge: Cambridge University Press, 2000.

Ritchie, Anne (Thackeray). *Records of Tennyson, Ruskin, Browning.* 1892. Port Washington, NY: Kennikat Press, 1969.

Robbins, Bruce. "Comparative Cosmopolitanisms." In Cheah and Robbins, 246–64.

———. *Feeling Global: Internationalism in Distress.* New York: New York University Press, 1999.

———. "The Village of the Liberal Managerial Class." In Dharwadker, 15–32.

Robinson, Howard. *The British Post Office: A History.* Princeton: Princeton University Press, 1948. Reprint, Westport, CT: Greenwood, 1970.

Rooksby, Rikky. *A. C. Swinburne: A Poet's Life.* Aldershot: Ashgate, 1997.

Said, Edward. *Culture and Imperialism.* New York: Vintage, 1993.

———. *Orientalism.* New York: Vintage, 1978.

Schor, Esther. "The Poetics of Politics: Barrett Browning's *Casa Guidi Windows.*" *Tulsa Studies in Women's Literature* 17, no. 2 (1998): 305–24.

Sells, Iris Esther. *Matthew Arnold and France: The Poet.* Cambridge: Cambridge University Press, 1935.

Shelley, Mary. *The Novels and Selected Works of Mary Shelley.* Edited by Jeanne Moskal. Vol. 8. London: William Pickering, 1996.

Shelley, Percy Bysshe. "A Defence of Poetry." In *Shelley's Poetry and Prose,* edited by Donald H. Reiman and Neil Fraistat, 508–35. New York: Norton, 2002.

Sieburth, Richard. "Poetry and Obscenity: Baudelaire and Swinburne." *Comparative Literature* 36, no. 4 (1984): 343–53.

Siegel, Jonah. *Haunted Museum: Longing, Travel, and the Art-Romance Tradition.* Princeton: Princeton University Press, 2005.

Siegert, Bernhard. *Relays: Literature as an Epoch of the Postal System.* Translated by Kevin Repp. Palo Alto: Stanford University Press, 1999.

Simmons, Claire A. *Eyes across the Channel: French Revolutions, Party History, and British Writing, 1830–1882.* Amsterdam: Harwood Academic Publishers, 2000.

Simpson, David. "The Limits of Cosmopolitanism and the Case for Translation." *European Romantic Review* 16, no. 2 (2005): 141–52.

Skoblow, Jeffrey. *Paradise Dislocated: Morris, Politics, Art.* Charlottesville: University of Virginia Press, 1993.

Slinn, E. Warwick. *The Discourse of Self in Victorian Poetry.* Charlottesville: Universirty Press of Virginia, 1991.

Standage, Tom. *The Victorian Internet: The Remarkable Story of the Telegraph and the Nineteenth Century's On-line Pioneers.* New York: Berkeley Books, 1998.

Stephens, George. "'English' or 'Anglo-Saxon.'" *Gentleman's Magazine* 36 (1852): 323–27; 472–76.

Stevenson, Robert Louis. *The Collected Poems of Robert Louis Stevenson.* Edited by Roger C. Lewis. Edinburgh: Edinburgh University Press, 2003.

Stone, Donald D. *Communications with the Future: Matthew Arnold in Dialogue.* Ann Arbor: University of Michigan Press, 1997.

Stone, Marjorie. *Elizabeth Barrett Browning.* New York: St. Martin's Press, 1995.

———. "Elizabeth Barrett Browning and the Garrisonians: 'The Runaway Slave at Pilgrim's Point,' the Boston Female Anti-Slavery Society, and Abolitionist Discourse in the Liberty Bell." In Chapman, *Victorian Women Poets,* 33–55.

——— and Beverly Taylor. "'Confirm my voice': 'My sisters,' Poetic Audiences, and the Published Voices of EBB." *Victorian Poetry* 44, no. 4 (2006): 391–403.

Swinburne, Algernon Charles. *The Complete Works of Algernon Charles Swinburne.* Edited by Edmund Gosse and Thomas J. Wise. 20 vols. London: Heinemann, 1925–27.

———. *Major Poems and Selected Prose.* Edited by Jerome McGann and Charles L. Sligh. New Haven: Yale University Press, 2004.

———. *New Writings by Swinburne.* Edited by Cecil Y. Lang. Syracuse: Syracuse University Press, 1964.

———. *Poems and Ballads & Atalanta in Calydon.* Edited by Kenneth Haynes. London: Penguin, 2000.

———. *Songs before Sunrise.* 1870. London: Chatto and Windus, 1888.

———. *Swinburne as Critic.* Edited by Clyde K. Hyder. London: Routledge and Kegan Paul, 1972.

———. *The Swinburne Letters.* Edited by Cecil Y. Lang. 6 vols. New Haven: Yale University Press, 1959–62.

———. *Uncollected Letters of Algernon Charles Swinburne.* Edited by Terry L. Meyers. 3 vols. London: Pickering and Chatto, 2005.

———. *Under the Microscope.* London: D. White, 1872. Reprint, New York: Garland, 1986.

Taplin, Gardner B. *The Life of Elizabeth Barrett Browning.* London: John Murray, 1957.

Tasker, Meg. "*Aurora Leigh:* Elizabeth Barrett Browning's Novel Approach to the Woman Poet." In *Tradition and the Poetics of Self in Nineteenth-Century Women's Poetry,* edited by Barbara Garlick, 23–41. Amsterdam: Rodopi, 2002.

———. "Time, Tense, and Genre: A Bakhtinian Analysis of Clough's *Bothie.*" *Victorian Poetry* 34, no. 2 (1996): 193–211.

Taylor, Beverly. "Elizabeth Barrett Browning and the Politics of Childhood." *Victorian Poetry* 46, no. 4 (2008): 405–27.

Tennyson, Alfred, Lord. *Tennyson's Poetry.* Edited by Robert W. Hill. New York: Norton, 1999.

Thorpe, Michael, ed. *Clough: The Critical Heritage.* New York: Barnes and Noble, 1972.

Tompkins, J. M. S. *William Morris: An Approach to the Poetry.* London: Cecil Woolf, 1988.

Tucker, Herbert F. "All for the Tale: The Epic Macropoetics of Morris' *Sigurd the Volsung.*" *Victorian Poetry* 34, no. 3 (1996): 372–94.

———. "Arnold and the Authorization of Criticism." In *Knowing the Past: Victorian Literature and Culture,* edited by Suzy Anger, 100–120. Ithaca: Cornell University Press, 2001.

———. "*Aurora Leigh:* Epic Solutions to Novel Ends." In *Famous Last Words: Changes in Gender and Narrative Closure,* edited by Alison Booth, 62–85. Charlottesville: University of Virginia Press, 1993.

———. "Dramatic Monologue and the Overhearing of Lyric." In *Lyric Poetry: Beyond New Criticism,* edited by Chaviva Hošek and Patricia Parker, 226–43. Ithaca: Cornell University Press, 1985.

———. *Epic: Britain's Heroic Muse, 1790–1910.* Oxford: Oxford University Press, 2008.

Tully, James. "The Kantian Idea of Europe: Critical and Cosmopolitan Perspectives." In *The Idea of Europe: From Antiquity to the European Union,* edited by Anthony Pagden, 331–58. Cambridge: Cambridge University Press, 2002.

Venuti, Lawrence. *The Scandals of Translation: Towards an Ethics of Difference.* London and New York: Routledge, 1998.

———. "Translation as Cultural Politics: Regimes of Domestication in English." *Textual Practice* 7, no. 2 (1993): 208–23.

Vertovec, Steven and Robin Cohen. "Introduction: Conceiving Cosmopolitanism." In *Conceiving Cosmopolitanism: Theory, Context, and Practice,* edited by Steven Vertovec and Robin Cohen, 1–22. Oxford: Oxford University Press, 2002.

Viscusi, Robert. "'The Englishman in Italy': Free Trade as a Principle of Aesthetics." *Browning Institute Studies* 12 (1984): 1–28. Reprint in *Critical Essays on Robert Browning,* edited by Mary Ellis Gibson, 243–66. New York: G. K. Hall, 1992.

Wain, John. Introduction to *The Dynasts,* by Thomas Hardy, v–xix. New York: St. Martin's Press, 1965.

Waithe, Marcus. *William Morris's Utopia of Strangers: Victorian Medievalism and the Ideal of Hospitality.* Cambridge: D. S. Brewer, 2006.

Wawn, Andrew. *The Vikings and the Victorians: Inventing the Old North in Nineteenth-Century Britain.* Cambridge: D. S. Brewer, 2000.

Weiner, Stephanie Kuduk. *Republican Politics and English Poetry, 1789–1874.* Houndmills: Palgrave Macmillan, 2005.

Weinroth, Michelle. *Reclaiming William Morris: Englishness, Sublimity, and the Rhetoric of Dissent*. Montreal: McGill-Queen's University Press, 1996.

Wells, H. G. *The War of the Worlds*. 1900. Edited by Martin A. Danahay. Peterborough, ON: Broadview Press, 2003.

West, Algernon, Sir. "The Cosmopolitan Club." In *One City and Many Men*, 155–74. London: Smith, Elder, 1908.

Westwater, Martha. *The Spasmodic Career of Sydney Dobell*. Lanham, MD: University Press of America, 1992.

Wheeler, Michael. *Heaven, Hell, and the Victorians*. Cambridge: Cambridge University Press, 1994.

Whitehead, James S. "Hardy and Englishness." In *Thomas Hardy Studies,* edited by Phillip Mallett, 203–28. Houndmills: Palgrave Macmillan, 2004.

Wickens, G. Glen. *Thomas Hardy, Monism, and the Carnival Tradition: The One and the Many in* The Dynasts. Toronto: University of Toronto Press, 2002.

Williams, Raymond. *The English Novel from Dickens to Lawrence*. Oxford: Oxford University Press, 1970.

Wilson, A[ndrew]. "English Poets in Italy: Mrs. Browning's Last Poems." *Macmillan's Magazine* 6 (1862): 79–87.

Wilson, Keith. "'We Thank You . . . Most of All, Perhaps, for *The Dynasts*': Hardy's Epic-Drama Re-evaluated." *Thomas Hardy Journal* 22 (2006): 235–54.

Woodworth, Elizabeth. "'I Cry Aloud in my Poet-Passion': Elizabeth Barrett Browning Claiming Political 'Place' through *Poems before Congress*." *Browning Society Notes* 32 (2007): 38–54.

Wright, Walter F. *The Shaping of* The Dynasts. Lincoln: University of Nebraska Press, 1967.

Young, Robert J. C. *Colonial Desire: Hybridity in Theory, Culture and Race*. New York: Routledge, 1995.

Zanona, Joyce. "'The Embodied Muse': Elizabeth Barrett Browning's *Aurora Leigh* and Feminist Poetics." *Tulsa Studies in Women's Literature* 8 (1989): 243–59.

Zietlow, Paul. *Moments of Vision: The Poetry of Thomas Hardy*. Cambridge: Harvard University Press, 1974.

Index

Adams, Hazard, 124–25, 238n29
Addison, Joseph, 220n4
aestheticism, aesthetic movement, 28–29, 33, 108, 118, 241n8
Ahmad, Aijaz, 27
Albert, Prince, 12, 16, 26, 39
Anderson, Amanda, 5–6, 7, 93, 109, 212n14, 214n28, 223n43
Anderson, Benedict, 6, 71, 85
Anglo-Europeanism. *See* cosmopolitanism; European unification
Anzaldúa, Gloria, 122, 231n7
Appiah, Kwame Anthony, 4–5, 27, 179, 246n3
apRoberts, Ruth, 214n35
Aravamudan, Srinivas, 21, 211n5
Armstrong, Isobel, 60, 110–11, 185, 213n17, 224n50, 227n14, 247n17, 247n22
Arnold, Edwin: *The Light of Asia,* 3, 211n5
Arnold, Jane (MA's sister), 15
Arnold, Matthew, 2, 5, 7, 10–23, 28, 29, 31, 34, 47, 94, 105, 107, 108, 123, 146, 148, 176, 206, 207, 209–10, 218n70, 248n27; and

Barrett Browning, 20–25; and Robert Browning, 103; and Byron, 19–20; and Clough, 22, 25, 63–64, 215n45, 224n60; and Indo-Europeanism, 218n69; influences on his ideas of Europe, 10–13; and Morris, 29–30, 146, 147; and multilingualism, 11, 13; and Swinburne, 140–42, 240n51; travels in Europe, 11, 17, 214n29, 215n45. *See also* European integration
Works: *Balder Dead,* 176; *Culture and Anarchy,* 10, 13, 23, 28, 140; "Dover Beach," 10, 17–18, 63, 99, 107; *Empedocles on Aetna,* 64; "England and the Italian Question," 22; "The Function of Criticism at the Present Time," 3, 10, 13, 15, 102, 142, 206; "Heinrich Heine," 10, 103, 219n75; "To Marguerite—Continued," 18, 216n45; "Memorial Verses," 13, 20; Preface to First Edition of *Poems,* 8, 64; "Rachel III," 216n45; "To a Republican Friend, 1848," 22; "Stanzas from

Victorian Poetry, Europe, and the
Challenge of Cosmopolitanism